SCHAUM'S OUTLINE OF

THEORY AND PROBLEMS

of

INTRODUCTION
to
PSYCHOLOGY

•

by

ARNO F. WITTIG, Ph.D.
Professor of Psychology
Ball State University

SCHAUM'S OUTLINE SERIES
McGRAW-HILL, INC.
New York   St. Louis   San Francisco   Auckland   Bogotá   Caracas
Hamburg   Lisbon   London   Madrid   Mexico   Milan   Montreal
New Delhi   Paris   San Juan   São Paulo   Singapore
Sydney   Tokyo   Toronto

07-071194-1

7 8 9 10 11 12 13 14 15 SH SH 9 8 7 6 5 4 3 2 1

Cover design by Amy E. Becker.

Library of Congress Cataloging in Publication Data

Wittig, Arno.
   Schaum's outline of theory and problems of introduction to psychology.

   (Schaum's outline series)
   Includes index.
   1. Psychology—Outlines, syllabi, etc. I. Title.
II. Title: Theory and problems of introduction to
psychology.
BF141.W56   150   77-23941
ISBN 0-07-071194-1

Preface

Psychology can be defined as the scientific study of behavior. As a scientific discipline, psychology attempts to provide understanding of how and why organisms behave as they do. Therefore, as you begin to study this subject, you should keep in mind the fact that psychology depends on the careful and objective consideration of evidence, and not on what "common sense" tells us.

This outline is an overview of the most basic principles of psychology. The outline may be used as a self-teaching tool, in conjunction with a standard textbook, or as a supplement to classroom and laboratory instruction. Each chapter begins with a concise summary of *psychological principles*, many of which are illustrated with examples. Following the discussion of theory in each chapter is a group of *solved problems*, which are used to illustrate the principles and which often contain exceptions to and refinements of the principles. Finally each chapter contains a list of *key terms*; like other disciplines, psychology has a specialized vocabulary, and familiarity with it is essential for the student who wishes to have a firm grasp of the subject matter.

The outline also contains three examinations and a final examination. By taking each examination and comparing your answers with those provided, you should be able to estimate how well you have mastered the basic principles of psychology.

ARNO F. WITTIG

Contents

Chapter 1 PSYCHOLOGY: DEFINITION AND HISTORY 1

  1.1   Definition and Purposes 1

  1.2   Areas of Behavioral Study 1

  1.3   The Background and Beginning of Psychology 2

  1.4   Early Development of Psychology 4

  1.5   The Fields of Psychology 5

Chapter 2 PSYCHOLOGICAL METHODOLOGY 15

  2.1   The Experimental Method 15

  2.2   The Hypothesis 16

  2.3   Experimental and Control Groups 16

  2.4   Independent and Dependent Variables 17

  2.5   Extraneous Variables 17

  2.6   Sampling 18

  2.7   Experimenter Bias 18

  2.8   Other Psychological Methodologies 19

Chapter 3 EVOLUTION AND GENETICS 26

  3.1   The Study of Evolution 26

  3.2   Ethology 26

  3.3   Genetics 28

  3.4   Genetic Influences 29

  3.5   The Relationship of Heredity and Environment 30

Chapter 4 DEVELOPMENTAL PSYCHOLOGY 37

  4.1   Stages of Physical Development 37

  4.2   Growth Trends 38

CONTENTS

4.3	Methods of Study	....	38
4.4	Physical (Motor) Development	....	40
4.5	Cognitive Development	....	40
4.6	Language Skills	....	41
4.7	Social Development	....	41

Chapter 5   **PHYSIOLOGICAL PSYCHOLOGY** **50**

5.1	Elements of a Neuron	....	50
5.2	Transmission of a Signal	....	50
5.3	Arrangement of the Nervous System	....	52
5.4	The Glandular Systems	....	55

Chapter 6   **SENSORY PROCESSES** **64**

6.1	The Basic Sensory Process	....	64
6.2	Detection Theory	....	65
6.3	Types of Sensory Processes	....	66

Chapter 7   **PERCEPTION** **76**

7.1	External Cues	....	76
7.2	Internal Cues	....	79
7.3	Unusual Perceptual Experiences	....	79

Chapter 8   **STATES OF CONSCIOUSNESS** **88**

8.1	Characteristics of Consciousness	....	88
8.2	Internal Influences on Consciousness	....	89
8.3	External Influences on Consciousness	....	90

Examination I **98**

Chapter 9   **MOTIVATION** **105**

9.1	The Motivation Cycle	....	105
9.2	Variables Affecting the Motivation Cycle	....	105
9.3	General Principles of Motivation	....	106
9.4	Unlearned Motives	....	107
9.5	Combination Motives	....	107
9.6	Learned Motives	....	108

CONTENTS

9.7   Conflict 109

9.8   Theories of Motivation 110

Chapter *10*   **EMOTION** **117**

10.1   General Characteristics of Emotion 117

10.2   Basic Types of Emotions 118

10.3   Expression of Emotions 119

10.4   Special Topics in Emotions 120

10.5   Theories of Emotion 121

Chapter *11*   **CLASSICAL CONDITIONING** **127**

11.1   Definition of Learning 127

11.2   Classical Conditioning 127

11.3   Extinction 128

11.4   Spontaneous Recovery 129

11.5   Stimulus Generalization 129

11.6   Differentiation (Discrimination) 130

11.7   Higher-Order Conditioning 130

11.8   Special Examples of Classical Conditioning 131

Chapter *12*   **INSTRUMENTAL CONDITIONING** **138**

12.1   Characteristics of Instrumental Conditioning 138

12.2   Comparison of Instrumental and Classical Conditioning 139

12.3   Acquisition of Instrumental Responses 139

12.4   Partial Reinforcement Effect 140

12.5   Generalization and Differentiation 142

12.6   Reinforcement Characteristics 143

12.7   Use of Instrumental Conditioning 144

Chapter *13*   **LEARNING BY MODELING** **152**

13.1   Comparison to Other Learning Forms 152

13.2   Types of Modeling 153

13.3   Factors Influencing Modeling 153

13.4   Retention 155

13.5   Reinforcement and Punishment 155

13.6   Special Concerns of Learning by Modeling 156

CONTENTS

Chapter **14** **VARIABLES AFFECTING ACQUISITION** **163**

14.1   Selection of Learning Materials 163
14.2   Characteristics of the Learner 164
14.3   The Learning Curve 164
14.4   General Factors Influencing Acquisition 165
14.5   Verbal Learning 167
14.6   Transfer of Training 168
14.7   Learning Without Awareness 169

Chapter **15** **RETENTION AND FORGETTING** **177**

15.1   Definitions 177
15.2   Different Types of Storage 177
15.3   Measures of Retention 178
15.4   The Curve of Forgetting 180
15.5   Theories of Forgetting 181
15.6   Special Issues in Retention 183

Chapter **16** **THINKING, PROBLEM-SOLVING, AND LANGUAGE DEVELOPMENT** **191**

16.1   Thinking 191
16.2   Problem-Solving 192
16.3   Language Development 195

Examination II **205**

Chapter **17** **PSYCHOLOGICAL TESTING AND MEASUREMENT** **211**

17.1   Characteristics of a Good Test 211
17.2   Types of Psychological Tests 212
17.3   Testing Concerns 214
17.4   Uses of Psychological Tests 215
17.5   Abuses of Psychological Testing 216

Chapter **18** **STATISTICS** **223**

18.1   Purposes of Statistics 223
18.2   Symbols Used in Statistics 223
18.3   Formulas Used in Statistics 223
18.4   Frequency Distributions 224

CONTENTS

18.5   Measures of Central Tendency 225

18.6   Measures of Variability (Dispersion) 226

18.7   The Normal Probability Distribution 227

18.8   Correlation 228

18.9   Sampling 230

Chapter *19*   **PERSONALITY PRINCIPLES** **238**

19.1   General Factors Influencing Personality 238

19.2   Freud's Motivational Theory of Personality 239

19.3   Other Motivational Theories of Personality 241

19.4   Type and Trait Theories of Personality 242

19.5   Learning Theories of Personality 243

19.6   Humanistic Theories of Personality 243

19.7   Research in Personality 244

Chapter *20*   **INTELLIGENCE AND CREATIVITY** **252**

20.1   Definition of Intelligence 252

20.2   Mental Age 252

20.3   Concept of Intelligence Quotient 252

20.4   Composition of Intelligence 254

20.5   Relationship of Intelligence to Other Factors 255

20.6   Creativity 257

Chapter *21*   **ABNORMAL PERSONALITY PATTERNS** **263**

21.1   Definition of Abnormal Personality Patterns 263

21.2   Explanations of Abnormal Behavior 264

21.3   Neurosis 265

21.4   Psychosomatic Disorders 266

21.5   Psychosis 266

21.6   Personality Disorders 268

21.7   Mental Retardation 268

21.8   Relationship of Abnormal Patterns to Other Factors 269

Chapter *22*   **THERAPIES** **278**

22.1   General Overview of Therapy 278

22.2   Medical Therapies 279

CONTENTS

22.3   Psychotherapy 280

22.4   Group Therapies 281

22.5   Behavior Modification 281

22.6   Therapy Effectiveness 283

Chapter **23**   **SOCIAL PSYCHOLOGY** **292**

23.1   Relationship of the Individual to the Group 292

23.2   Social Roles 293

23.3   Payoffs and Costs of Roles 294

23.4   Competition and Cooperation 294

23.5   Group Dynamics 295

Chapter **24**   **ATTITUDE FORMATION** **304**

24.1   Components of Attitudes 304

24.2   Development of Attitudes 305

24.3   Interpersonal Attraction 306

24.4   Prejudice 307

24.5   Changing Attitudes 308

24.6   Social Movements 309

Examination III 315

Final Examination 322

INDEX **335**

Chapter 1

Psychology:
Definition and History

We are all interested in how people act. Not only do we want to know what is happening, but quite frequently we want to know why. Although these questions often are answered in a rather loose or undisciplined fashion, a more rigorous body of knowledge concerning behavior has developed. This body of knowledge is called *psychology*.

1.1 DEFINITION AND PURPOSES

Psychology is *the scientific study of behavior*. As such, psychology describes behavior (the what) and tries to explain the causes of behavior (the why).

EXAMPLE 1. Why did you buy this book? What do you expect to accomplish? If you do accomplish your goals, will you be likely to buy another, similar book in a different subject matter? Psychologists try to answer questions like these to determine what it is people do and why they do it.

The description of behavior which results from psychological study is not casual or without aim. The study of behavior has as its purposes the *prediction* or *control* of behavior. Basically, *prediction* of behavior occurs when the psychologist correctly anticipates events that occur naturally, whereas *control* means the psychologist has somehow manipulated the situation and subsequently observed an expected result.

EXAMPLE 2. Teaching a child to name colors is control of behavior. Anticipating that the child can recognize the difference between blue and red (even if the child cannot name these colors) is prediction of behavior.

1.2 AREAS OF BEHAVIORAL STUDY

Humans and Animals

Behavior is defined as any observable or measurable response of a person or animal. Psychology is defined as the study of *all* behavior, including both human and animal behavior. When using human subjects for study, a psychologist must be concerned with ethical problems, the availability of subjects, the duration of the treatment, and special expenses.

Heredity and Environment

One of the questions psychology seeks to answer is whether behavior occurs as a result of inherited characteristics (*hereditary influences*) or because of some effect of learning (*environmental influences*). A controversy regarding the relative importance of these two influences has continued in psychology for a long time and remains unresolved. The general finding seems to be that both influences affect behavior—separately and as they interact. (See Chapter 3 for a more thorough discussion of this interaction.)

Conscious and Unconscious

Behavior is often the product of a *conscious* choice. Some behaviors, however, may result from motives that are below a level of awareness. Many theorists refer to these latter motives as

1

unconscious. Both conscious and unconscious motives may lead to responses, and psychology therefore studies both.

Normal and Abnormal

Psychology studies both normal and abnormal behavior. There is often great difficulty in deciding whether a behavior should be classified as normal or abnormal. The usual criterion selected is to judge behavior as abnormal if it creates a problem for the individual or for society. Obviously, the decision depends upon both the individual and the particular characteristics of the society in which the individual lives.

Age Range

Psychology studies behavior over the entire life span. Indeed, because behavior is dependent on hereditary characteristics as well as on learning, psychologists are concerned with the individual from the moment of conception until death. However, very few psychologists study the entire age range—most prefer to concentrate on a distinct span, such as early childhood, adolescence, or old age.

Theory or Applied

Finally, the breadth of psychological study is such that it includes both *theoretical* studies and the *application* of psychological principles to specific problems. Probably the majority of psychological specialities could be categorized as *applied*. (See Section 1.5.)

1.3   THE BACKGROUND AND BEGINNING OF PSYCHOLOGY

In the history of scientific endeavor, psychology is considered a relatively new discipline. While many other disciplines—such as biology, physics, and chemistry—have traditions of study dating back to ancient history, the usual date selected for the beginning of psychology is 1879. This date is chosen because in that year, *Wilhelm Wundt* (1832–1920) started the first psychology laboratory. Wundt set up the laboratory at the University of Leipzig, in Germany. Other researchers had preceded Wundt in conducting psychological investigations, but Wundt was the first to declare himself a psychologist and describe his facility as a psychological laboratory. Wundt also started the first journal for psychology and wrote an early textbook in the area of physiological psychology.

Psychology did not spring suddenly onto the scientific scene. Concern with "psychological" issues and problems extends into antiquity. Indeed, human and animal behavior has always been a concern of merchants, scientists, philosophers, and all thinking people. Some of the areas which contributed to the development of psychology as a separate discipline include philosophy, the natural sciences, medicine, and even some nonscientific and pseudoscientific areas.

Philosophy

For thousands of years, philosophers have tried to understand behavior. Indeed, many of the basic problems of psychology—such as learning, motivation, personality, perception, or physiological influences upon behavior—were first discussed by philosophers. Many departments of psychology within colleges and universities originated in departments of philosophy and only later gained independent status.

EXAMPLE 3. Psychologists are concerned with questions of how the human mind develops from birth to adulthood. Philosophers have also faced the same questions. For example, Plato, the Greek philosopher of the fourth century B.C., believed that a human was born with certain innate, or given, mental abilities and knowledge. On the other hand, John Locke, a seventeenth century English philosopher, believed that the human mind was at birth a *tabula rasa,* or "blank slate," upon which impressions were made. Neither philosophers nor psychologists have definitively concluded which, if either, of these views is true.

What made psychology separate from philosophy was a difference in approach. As philosophy of the eighteenth and nineteenth centuries began to change toward a greater emphasis on empirical values, the eventual rise of an independent psychology became possible. An attitude of scientific inquiry became the mainstay of psychology. (See Chapter 2.)

The Sciences

Much of the methodology that accompanied the introduction of scientific inquiry into behavioral areas was borrowed or adapted from other sciences. Physics, chemistry, biology, and physiology were all important as contributors to the start of psychology. The methodologies which developed are discussed in Chapter 2, but it is worthwhile to mention briefly some of the contributions that came from these sciences.

Both physics and chemistry provided not only methodology but concerns regarding sensations and perceptions. These quickly were to become part of the physiology of the time.

The biological theory of evolution gave strong support to the development of *comparative psychology,* in which the behavior of one species is compared to that of another. Biology also provided much of the information on genetics and heredity which was eventually used by psychologists considering the effects of these influences on behavior. Thus, methodology, areas for investigation, and justification for study were all taken from older scientific disciplines.

Medicine

In a somewhat indirect manner, medicine made a major contribution to the beginning of psychology. Until the early 1800s, most people exhibiting abnormal personality patterns were thought to be possessed by the devil. During the early 1800s, medical interest brought treatment for physical illnesses that were thought to cause the abnormal patterns of behavior.

By the late 1800s, the attitude had changed. These abnormal patterns were classified as *mental illnesses,* and treatment changed accordingly. This led to the development of what is now called *psychiatry* and had an important effect upon the beginnings of *clinical psychology.* The concerns of psychiatry and clinical psychology began from a medical tradition.

EXAMPLE 4. A person who wishes to become a psychiatrist must, after finishing undergraduate work, receive both a degree in medicine and subsequent specialized training. As a result, a strong orientation for psychiatrists has been what has come to be called the *medical model.* That is, the psychiatrist may treat a client as a "sick" person. But many other psychiatrists and psychologists do not accept this concept of "disease." They prefer terms such as "abnormal patterns of behavior" to describe the responses of the people they observe and treat.

Nonscientific and Pseudoscientific Influences

Some areas of psychological study arose because investigators wanted to show that commonly accepted statements about behavior were wrong. Often, these incorrect statements appeared to have some "scientific flavor"—they were labelled with sophisticated-sounding names such as physiognomy, phrenology, or typology. *Physiognomists* believed that the appearance of the face and head revealed personality characteristics. *Phrenologists* "mapped" the areas of the human skull in an attempt to label brain functions and their consequent effects on human behavior. *Typologists* tried to correlate body type with behavioral characteristics. Although all of these areas eventually were shown to be inaccurate (that is, fat people are *not* always jolly), the questions they raised did generate research that explained more about behavior. Psychological studies were often conducted as responses to nonscientific prompting.

1.4 EARLY DEVELOPMENT OF PSYCHOLOGY

Early psychology is characterized as a period of psychological *systems*. These systems were attempts to explain all of behavior by using a single set of principles. Although none continues to have major importance, all contributed significantly to present-day psychology.

Structuralism

The position developed by Wundt and later expanded by Edward Titchener (1867–1927) was called *Structuralism*. Psychology for the Structuralists was the study of the *introspective* reports of normal human adults. Trained subjects made descriptive reports of how stimuli appeared to them. These reports were supposed to allow the psychologist to interpret the structure of the mind and how it worked.

EXAMPLE 5. In a Structuralist experiment, you might be asked to report on how you sensed the weight, texture, and color of this book. You might also be asked to describe your feelings, if any, toward the book. Merely saying, "This is a psychology book," would not be sufficient as an introspective report.

As a system, Structuralism was very limited. However, the Structuralists did make important contributions to the early development of psychology (a) by testing the method of introspection, which failed because of disagreements regarding the properties of stimuli; (b) by establishing psychology as a scientific endeavor and stressing appropriate scientific methodology; and (c) by providing a starting point which was investigated by many of the later psychological systems.

Functionalism

One of the systems which developed as a reaction to Structuralism was called *Functionalism*. The Functionalists were concerned with the purposes of behavior rather than the structure of the mind. Functionalism investigated the adaptation or adjustment the subject achieved in different environments.

EXAMPLE 6. The Functionalists were not limited to the use of normal human adults as subjects for their experiments. (They did not rely on introspective reports, as did the Structuralists.) The Functionalists might, for example, investigate the ways in which very young children responded to novel problem-solving situations.

Functionalists generally adopted a broader view of psychology than did the Structuralists. This allowed them to study all age groups and a variety of subjects. Many new areas of investigation resulted, including the study of motivation and emotions, child psychology, and various areas of applied psychology.

Associationism

The Associationists were concerned particularly with the development of associations, or bonds, between stimuli and responses. Their interests included the effects of reinforcement and punishment upon such bonds, the length of practice necessary for bonds to be established, and the relationship of such bonds to the physiological properties of the subject. It was felt that such bonds provided the basis for understanding behavior.

EXAMPLE 7. Among other things, Associationists were concerned with the ways in which a child might learn to make distinctions between the parts of the human body. Through parental encouragement and reinforcement, a child might first learn the word *arm* and what it stood for. Later, the child might learn to distinguish other, more specific, parts of the arm, such as the elbow and wrist.

Behaviorism

John Watson (1878–1958) established a system for the study of behavior in which *only* the observable responses made by the subject were relevant. The system came to be known as *Behaviorism* and was characterized by an interest in the muscular movements and glandular responses of the subject. Behaviorists denied the concept of mind because a mind could not be observed.

EXAMPLE 8.   Behaviorists were interested only in observable phenomena. A strict Behaviorist would not describe a person as "happy" because happiness is a state of mind, and a mind is not observable. Instead, the Behaviorist might describe the person's smile or laugh, or some other observable response to a stimulus.

Although the system soon found much criticism, it did point out the possible futility of trying to describe nonobservable activities of the subject and helped psychology confront the ideas of stimulus control and determinism of behavior. Direct concern with the stimuli and consquent responses has become an important part of several psychological positions.

Gestalt Psychology

Gestalt psychology developed in Germany with particular interest in perceptual problems and how these could be interpreted. In general, the Gestalt psychologists pointed out that previous attempts at explaining perception (and other kinds of behavior) were simplistic because they fragmented behavior and failed to take into account the *whole* environment. The phrase frequently used to describe the Gestalt position is that "the whole of behavior is *greater than* the sum of its parts."

EXAMPLE 9.   The Gestaltists believed that other psychological systems were mistaken in their attempts to divide human behavior (including mental behavior) into discrete, or separate, functions. They believed that human behavior, and especially human mental behavior, was a creative process of synthesis that was more than the sum of its constituent parts. Gestaltists would point, for example, to a human who watched a movie—instead of seeing a series of still pictures (the separate frames of the film), the viewer would see a continuous, "moving" image.

Psychoanalysis

Sigmund Freud (1856–1939), a Viennese medical doctor, was the first person to practice *psychoanalysis*. Freud did not at first intend for psychoanalysis to become a system, but the theories he developed to support his therapeutic techniques came to be taken as such. His very extensive investigation of the development and maintenance of personality, with emphasis on such things as early childhood experiences and unconscious sources of motivation, eventually were treated as a systematic position. This, in turn, generated much inquiry intended to evaluate the principles of psychoanalysis and affected areas such as clinical psychology, counseling psychology, and developmental psychology.

EXAMPLE 10.   Freud's great contribution to psychology was his suggestion that much of human behavior arose out of motives that were unconscious—that is, motives of which a person was unaware. For example, in treating some of his patients he was able to discover *phobias* (fears) that were hidden from the patients and yet seriously influenced their behavior.

1.5   THE FIELDS OF PSYCHOLOGY

The attempt to explain all of behavior by reference to only one of the systematic positions did not work out. By itself, no single system could account for all types of behavior; and systematic theorizing thus fell into disfavor. The current trend in psychology is toward limiting areas of study to particular aspects of behavior. Theories of learning, theories of personality, and theories of development are now much more specialized than were the broad theories and claims of the psychological systems.

Today there are several hundred psychological specialties to choose from. One can, however, organize psychology as a discipline into several broad approaches to the study of behavior.

Clinical Psychology

Clinical psychology is the largest field of psychology. Approximately 30 percent of all psychologists are in the clinical area. They are concerned with the use of psychological techniques to recognize and treat behavior disorders or to conduct research into the causes of such disorders. (*Behavior disorders* are considered abnormal; that is, they create a problem for the individual or for society.)

Counseling Psychology

About 10 percent of all psychologists are involved in *counseling psychology*. They use psychological techniques to assist individuals in coping with normal personal problems. The individuals seeking such help are not classified as abnormal or mentally ill, but are seeking help with problems, such as vocational or interpersonal relationships. The counseling psychologist may use psychotherapeutic techniques, but treatment of severely abnormal problems is usually referred to a clinical psychologist or psychiatrist.

EXAMPLE 11. A college freshman may have difficulties with his first semester's studying because he cannot adjust to dormitory life, to teaching techniques that are new to him, or even to his roommates. A counseling psychologist may be called upon to help the freshman make the necessary adjustments. However, if the freshman repeatedly responds in ways that appear to be significantly out of touch with reality, a clinical psychologist or psychiatrist is likely to be called in.

Experimental Psychology

Experimental psychologists are interested in knowing about behavior even if the information obtained from their studies has no direct application. In other words, *experimental psychology* is oriented toward exploring the fundamental questions of behavior.

Experimental studies most frequently are conducted using the special approaches of the experimental method. (See Chapter 2.) Both human and animal subjects are used in the wide variety of problems that are investigated.

Physiological and Comparative Psychology

Physiological psychologists and comparative psychologists often employ experimental techniques to study problems within their areas of specialization. When they do, they can be viewed as belonging within the general field of experimental psychology. However, both are set apart by special emphasis on particular aspects of behavior and are therefore grouped separately.

Physiological psychology is the study of the physiological, or bodily, foundations of behavior. Much information in these studies is gathered purely to further the understanding of behavior, but some applications of physiological findings are important in areas such as industrial, clinical, or educational psychology.

Comparative psychology often studies bodily processes, but the primary interest is in making comparisons of the behavior of one species with that of others. A comparative psychologist may employ the experimental method or some other technique to compare the behaviors of species.

EXAMPLE 12. A comparative psychologist may test the effect of deprivation on the behavior of one species of bird and compare it to the effect of the same kind of deprivation on another species of bird. (For example, the psychologist may raise birds of both species in complete darkness and test what effect this would have on their ability to fly or gather food.)

Educational and School Psychology

Educational psychology is concerned with the use of psychological principles to increase the effectiveness of the learning experience. This frequently includes the study of learning facilities, curricula, teaching techniques, or particular student problems. A psychologist who specifically attempts to test, counsel, or guide students is referred to as a *school psychologist*, while the more general range of educational psychology encompasses school psychology and many other matters.

EXAMPLE 13. School psychologists most often work with students. Educational psychologists, on the other hand, may often work with teachers in an attempt to make them more effective in the classroom. For example, educational psychologists may suggest new teaching techniques or help to develop educational materials, such as books or audiovisual materials.

Social Psychology

Psychology pertains to the behavior of individuals; sociology studies the behavior of groups as groups. Social psychology investigates group influence upon the behavior of individuals. Many individual behaviors (for example, applauding) may be looked at as a function of membership in a group. The behavior of people in crowds, work groups, recreational groups, subcultural or cultural groups, and many other types of groups are studied by social psychologists.

Developmental Psychology

The study of an individual's behavior over an extended time span is called *developmental psychology*. Developmental psychology may concentrate on all behaviors in only part of the age span, such as childhood, adolescence, or old age. Alternately, emphasis may be on only the development of learning, or social development, or the development of physical influences on behavior.

Other Applied Psychologies

Some psychologies are theoretical—their findings do not have immediate practical applications. Other psychologies we have discussed are applied—that is, they do have direct practical applications. Modern psychology is a broad and diverse enough discipline to include many other specialties, especially in applied psychology. A sample of these applied specialties is given here:

Industrial Psychology. Industrial psychologists apply psychological principles to the solution of work-related problems. Labor, management, productivity, and hiring and firing problems often are a part of industrial psychology.

Consumer Psychology. Understanding the motivation of consumers and applying this knowledge to influence their buying habits is the prime concern of consumer psychologists. This means consumer psychologists frequently work in the areas of consumer market research.

Engineering Psychology. The engineering psychologist studies the relationships of people to machines, with the intent of improving such relationships. This may involve redesigning equipment, improving the working environment, changing the way in which people use machines, or changing the location in which the work takes place.

Community Psychology. A somewhat recent trend in psychology is the study of the effect of a community's social structure upon an individual's behavior. Community psychologists try to improve the "quality of life" for the people within the community.

Solved Problems

1.1 Upon moving into the dormitory, your new roommate asks you what will be your major. When you reply "psychology," your roommate's response is, "Gee, now I'll have to watch what I say all year long! You psychologists are always analyzing people's personality problems." Based upon the definition of psychology, explain why your roommate is in error.

The definition indicates psychology studies *all* of behavior—normal as well as abnormal, animal as well as human. Personality is included, but many other topics are investigated also. Your roommate's view of psychology is too limited.

1.2 Having been given the previous answer, your roommate says, "All of behavior? What for?" Explain the purposes of psychology.

Psychology, although far from being a complete subject matter, is trying to close gaps in knowledge about behavior in order to be able to *predict* and perhaps *control* behavior.

1.3 A psychologist presents the stimulus PS CH L GY to a subject, and the response given is "PSYCHOLOGY." Is this prediction or control of behavior?

The psychologist could probably predict the response. However, the fact that the psychologist *manipulates* the situation by presenting a stimulus makes this experiment an example of behavioral control. (The same psychologist might theorize that a person would tend to "complete" the word or sentence of a stutterer, in which case the psychologist would merely be predicting behavior.)

1.4 Some research studies involve human subjects; other studies use animals as subjects. Why?

It is generally quite easy to accept psychology as the study of human behavior, but questions often arise as to why psychologists study animals. There are basically three reasons, all of which are important: (1) Sometimes animals are studied simply because a psychologist is interested in animal behavior. Animals are important as part of the environment, and understanding their behavior may be worthwhile for that reason alone. (2) Animals are often studied because it would be improper or impossible to use humans in the research. For example, a psychologist can keep animal subjects in continued stress situations, control their breeding, and maintain them for 24 hours a day for many months while holding down to a reasonable level expenses for their housing and feeding. (3) In many cases, the behavior of animal subjects is comparable to the behavior of humans. Thus, psychologists are able to explore many problem areas with animals and predict, on the basis of the results obtained, what humans might do in comparable situations.

1.5 Describe a psychological study in which humans would not be suitable subjects and explain why animals would be used instead.

Some investigations involve techniques such as brain surgery, the isolation of subjects, or the creation of pronounced stress situations. Such conditions would be inappropriate for human subjects. Other studies manipulate breeding and may require long-term periods of confinement, care, and close observation. For example, one study separated bright rats from dull rats by testing them in a maze. The experimenters then bred bright with bright and dull with dull for seven generations. Such manipulations would be tremendously time-consuming if humans were used, and more importantly, using human subjects for such studies would be unethical.

1.6   Is heredity important in influencing behavior?

Heredity certainly influences behavior. Characteristics such as skin color, height and weight tendencies, and hair or eye color, which are all passed on from parents, may affect behavior. For example, a seven-foot-tall boy might well become a basketball player. It is not likely, however, that he would become a horse racing jockey. More importantly, hereditary influences may produce brain damage, mental retardation, colorblindness, or other characteristics that will very likely have significant effects upon the types of behavior a child will be able to engage in.

1.7   What is the relationship between hereditary and environmental influences on a person's behavior?

The influences of heredity and environment *interact*. This means the behavior observed is the result of the combined effect of hereditary background and past and current environmental experience. It is generally believed that the relative amounts of each influence cannot be separated, for example, by percentage. Each influence may affect the other to produce a result which differs from a simple summation of the two influences.

1.8   Psychology as a discipline appears to have considerable breadth. What considerations are common in describing the *general* topics covered by psychology?

Psychology is truly the study of *all* behavior over the entire age span. Psychologists study both human and animal behavior, normal and abnormal behavior, conscious and unconscious influences on behavior, and behavior from conception to death.

1.9   Did psychology start suddenly, when investigators decided to study behavior?

The date usually given for the start of psychology as an independent discipline is 1879. (See Solved Problem 1.13.) Before that date, however, there was a rich and varied background to psychology. Many of the problems studied and the techniques used in psychology were taken from disciplines such as philosophy, medicine, physics, biology, and physiology. In some cases, even nonscientific or pseudoscientific studies contributed to psychology's development.

1.10   How did philosophy contribute to the beginnings of psychology?

Philosophers have always been interested in understanding behavior, and particularly behavior that involves learning, perception, and speech. Philosophers raised many questions that psychologists attempted to answer in an objective, scientific way.

1.11   How did the natural sciences and medicine contribute to the development of psychology?

Perhaps the most important contribution of the natural sciences to psychology was the experimental method. (See Chapter 2.) In addition, various problems and theories of the natural sciences provided psychologists with subjects for investigation. From biology came a concern with heredity and its effects on an individual. From zoology came suggestions that led to the development of comparative psychology. From medicine came the idea of treatment and therapy for those showing abnormal behavior patterns.

1.12   How did *nonscientific* contributions help psychology's development?

In a number of cases, nonscientific or "quack" theories prompted psychologists to question and investigate certain types of behavior and their causes. For example, the pseudoscience phrenology was devoted to trying to "map" the brain and explain its functions by studying the bumps and indentations of the skull. Although phrenologists were shown to be wrong, their investigations suggested to psychologists that various parts of the brain had specific and discrete functions. (See Chapter 5.)

1.13   The year 1879 is usually picked as a starting date for psychology. Why?

Many "psychological" investigations were conducted before 1879, but the people doing the research did not consider themselves psychologists. In 1879, Wilhelm Wundt established the first psychology laboratory in Leipzig, Germany, and called himself a psychologist. He subsequently started a psychology journal and wrote a psychology textbook. Wundt and 1879 are traditionally chosen as the starting points for psychology because of his declaration of intent.

1.14   Why was Wundt's work important?

Three major factors made Wundt's work important. First, he did get psychology started as an independent discipline. Second, his emphasis on experimental methodology gave psychology a strong scientific footing. Third, the system of Structuralism, which he espoused, tested the method of introspection and thus provided a "target" for several other systems which followed.

1.15   How was Structuralism a "target?"

Wundt and the Structuralists after him studied the introspective reports of normal adult humans. Later psychologists felt that the Structuralist position was too limited and argued that psychology should extend into new and different areas. For example, a Structuralist's subject would not look at a box and simply call it a box. The subject would instead have to describe a rectangular object having certain sensory properties. Later changes in psychological methodology allowed any kind of answer and then studied whatever the subject said or did.

1.16   Describe the systematic positions that developed after the Structuralists.

Functionalism was the study of behavior as it was adjusted or adapted to the environment. The Functionalists were concerned with the purpose of behavior, and not with the structure of the mind. *Associationism* looked upon any given behavior as a response that was bonded to a stimulus as a result of reinforcement. *Behaviorism* studied behavior in a *completely* objective fashion. The Behaviorists were interested only in the muscular movements or glandular responses of the subject, and they denied the concept of mind. *Gestalt psychology* was a study of behavior that emphasized the interrelatedness of responses. The Gestalt psychologists did not believe, as did the Functionalists and Associationists, that a particular response could be isolated and then studied and understood. The phrase describing their position is that "the whole of behavior is greater than the sum of its parts." *Psychoanalysis* was at first developed by Freud as a method of therapy, not a body of theory. In time, however, a theory of psychoanalysis did develop. It emphasized the importance of early childhood experiences and unconscious motives in the development of a subject's personality.

1.17   How did these five positions change the original psychology which Wundt first formulated?

The field of psychological investigation was greatly broadened. Because Wundt's system depended on the introspective reports of normal adult humans, it could not cover developmental (child) psychology, learning principles, the study of abnormal behavior, and unconscious motives. Although all of these systems subsequently were to lose favor, they provided psychology with a broad base upon which to build.

1.18   What trend developed in psychology as the importance of systems diminished?

The general trend was (and continues to be) toward specialized areas of investigation. Smaller segments of behavior are studied with little or no attempt at explaining all of behavior by reference to only one system.

1.19 Has this trend toward greater specialization led to changes in psychology?

Greater specialization has meant that psychology has developed many areas of interest. These are often called the fields of psychology and include clinical psychology, physiological psychology, educational and school psychology, social psychology, developmental psychology, and many varieties of applied psychology.

1.20 Clinical and counseling psychologies sound like they might be very much alike. How do they differ?

In many respects clinical and counseling psychology *are* very much alike. Both are attempts to apply psychological principles to help people overcome problems. However, a difference does exist in that clinicians tend to deal with the more severe or perhaps abnormal problems, while counselors more often work with relatively normal problems. For example, a clinician might attempt to help a schizophrenic (see Chapter 21) regain socially acceptable behavior, while a counselor might help an individual with occupational difficulties.

1.21 How does a clinical psychologist's training differ from a psychiatrist's training?

Although the background of clinical psychology comes primarily from medicine and psychiatry, there is a difference between the two. Both often use the same methods of diagnosis and treatment, but a clinical psychologist is generally university-trained and receives a Ph.D. degree, whereas a psychiatrist is trained in medical school and obtains an M.D. degree before pursuing additional training, perhaps as a psychiatric resident.

1.22 A mother realizes that one of her children is behaving abnormally. She seeks help, and is directed to a psychoanalyst, who makes an appointment to see her and her husband. Both parents are unfamiliar with just what a psychoanalyst is and does and how a psychoanalyst differs from a psychologist or psychiatrist. They ask for an explanation. How does the psychoanalyst answer?

The psychoanalyst explains that psychiatry is a specialty of medical practice: a *psychiatrist* receives an M.D. degree and then usually pursues additional training. (A *clinical psychologist*, on the other hand, receives a Ph.D. degree, not an M.D., before entering practice.) As a subcategory, about 10 percent of all psychiatrists are also *psychoanalysts*. They have received training at psychoanalytic training institutes in the techniques developed by Sigmund Freud and have undergone psychoanalysis themselves. Although there are differences in training, psychiatrists, psychologists, and psychoanalysts all use therapeutic techniques to try to help people overcome problems.

1.23 What percentage of U.S. psychologists are employed in clinical and counseling psychology?

Research indicates that about 30 percent of U.S. psychologists are clinicians and 10 percent are counselors or guidance people. The remaining 60 percent is divided into segments of 10 percent or less for each of the remaining fields of psychology.

1.24 What makes theoretical psychology different from applied psychology?

Theoretical psychology is not necessarily directed toward findings that will have direct practical applications. The theoretical psychologist may simply want to test hypotheses and theories to judge whether or not they are tenable. On the other hand, those working in the many fields of applied psychology are interested in direct, practical applications of their findings.

1.25   How does a physiological psychologist differ from an experimental psychologist?

Physiological psychology is basically the study of the physical, or bodily, foundations of behavior. As such, much of the work of physiological psychologists is laboratory research that may provide information of either a theoretical or applied nature. Thus, a physiological psychologist may or may not be an experimental psychologist.

1.26   Is a comparative psychologist the same as a physiological psychologist?

Comparative and physiological psychology are not the same. Comparative psychology attempts to compare the behaviors of one species with the behaviors of other species. These *may* have a physical orientation, but do not have to be oriented only to physical influences. Correspondingly, physiological psychologists may work with several different species, but do not necessarily make comparisons among them.

1.27   The local Parent-Teacher organization believes that the educational effectiveness of the school system is inadequate. The organization would like to see the educational program improved, so they decide to hire a full-time psychologist. What kind of psychologist should they hire?

Because learning effectiveness is the major concern, an educational or school psychologist would be most likely to be appropriate for this school system. While both are interested in improving the learning experience, the school psychologist tends to be involved with testing, diagnosis, and counseling of particular student problems, while the educational psychologist often looks at the broader range of concerns, including research on curricula, teaching techniques, or testing methods.

1.28   Are educational and school psychologists considered applied psychologists? How many types of applied psychologies are there?

Educational and school psychologists are considered applied psychologists. Actually, almost all psychologists who are not explicitly oriented to research and theory should be considered applied psychologists. This includes clinical and counseling psychologists and many others, such as industrial, consumer, engineering, or community psychologists.

1.29   What do all these other applied psychologists do?

Just as clinical and counseling psychologists try to apply psychological principles to help overcome personal problems, other applied psychologists attempt to use psychological principles to solve practical problems. *Industrial psychologists* handle problems that develop in work situations, including productivity, labor, management, and the screening and evaluation of workers. The *engineering psychologist* is a somewhat specialized industrial psychologist who investigates the design of mechanical equipment and the relationships of people and machines. *Consumer psychologists* often work in market research to try to determine why people buy certain products. *Community psychologists* study social structure and try to improve the individual's life within the community.

1.30   Does that mean the community psychologist is a social psychologist?

Community psychology is a particular type of applied social psychology. Social psychology is the study of the group influence upon the individual's behavior. The group studied by a social psychologist may be the community *or* many other types of groups, including work groups, recreational groups, audiences, or even experimentally created groups.

1.31   What are the major concerns of a developmental psychologist?

The developmental psychologist studies behavioral changes through a time span. This may be a particular period, such as childhood, adolescence, or adulthood, or the entire life of an individual. Developmental psychologists may also have a specialized interest in learning, physical growth, social changes, or any other aspect of behavior.

1.32   It seems like psychology is very diverse. Are there more areas of study within psychology?

There are many more areas of psychology, and new areas develop quite frequently. Within the past few years, the American Psychological Association has added several new divisions, including divisions specializing in psychology and health, psychology and the environment, and the psychology of women. Psychology is still a very young discipline and should continue to expand and diversify for a long time.

Key Terms

Abnormal behavior.   Behavior which creates a problem for the individual or for society.

Applied psychology.   Any branch of psychology that applies psychological principles to the solution of practical problems.

Associationism.   A system of psychology which studied how and why bonds were established between particular stimuli and responses.

Behaviorism.   A system of psychology which studied observable stimuli and responses *only*, and which denied the concept of mind.

Clinical psychology.   The branch of psychology concerned with the theory and practice of helping people with behavioral or mental disorders.

Community psychology.   A branch of psychology which concentrates on the effect of community social structure on the individual's behavior.

Comparative psychology.   A branch of psychology which makes comparisons of behaviors of different species.

Conscious.   An activity or condition of which an individual is aware and which the individual can recognize or describe.

Consumer psychology.   A branch of psychology concerned with market research or consumers' buying habits.

Counseling psychology.   A branch of psychology which employs techniques to help clients overcome "normal" problems.

Developmental psychology.   A branch of psychology which concentrates on changes of behavior through a time span, such as childhood or adolescence.

Educational psychology.   A branch of psychology which applies psychological principles in an attempt to improve the learning experience.

Engineering psychology.   A branch of psychology which concentrates on the relationships between people and machines.

Environment.   Any external factors or conditions which may influence an organism.

Experimental psychology.   A theoretical branch of psychology, studying the basic or fundamental questions of behavior.

Functionalism.   A system of psychology which studied the purposes of behavior and the adaptation of an organism to the environment.

Gestalt psychology.   A system of psychology which adopted a wholistic approach to the study of behavior.

Heredity.   The genetic transmission of characteristics from parent to offspring.

Industrial psychology.   A branch of psychology which applies psychological principles to the solution of work-related problems.

Introspection.   A method of psychological investigation in which subjects report on their own responses to stimuli.

Physiological psychology.   A branch of psychology which studies the physiological, or bodily, foundations of behavior.

Psychiatry.   A medical specialty dealing with the diagnosis and treatment of behavioral and mental disorders.

Psychoanalysis.   A form of psychotherapy originated by Sigmund Freud; stresses the importance of early childhood experiences and unconscious motives in the development of personality.

Psychoanalyst.   A psychiatrist trained at a special institute in the techniques developed by Freud.

Psychology.   The scientific study of all behavior.

School psychology.   A branch of psychology which specializes in testing, counseling, and guiding students.

Social psychology.   A branch of psychology which studies the effects of group membership on an individual's behavior.

Structuralism.   A system of psychology which studied the adult, normal, human mind by using the method of introspection.

System of psychology.   Any particular body of theories of psychology used in the organization or interpretation of all of behavior.

Theory.   A general principle, based upon evidence or observation, suggested as an explanation for phenomena.

Unconscious.   Conditions of which the individual is unaware or barely aware, yet which seem to influence behavior.

Chapter 2

Psychological Methodology

Casual, undisciplined reports of behavior, such as gossip or rumors, occur quite frequently. Although these are descriptions of behavior, they are not acceptable to psychologists who are studying behavior. Psychologists require more reliable measures and accurate reports. This chapter describes the methods most often used by psychologists to measure and report on behavior.

2.1 THE EXPERIMENTAL METHOD

The most disciplined of the methodologies used by psychologists is the *experimental method*. Using this method, an experimenter manipulates a variable to be studied, chooses the response to be measured, and controls extraneous influences that might inappropriately affect the results of the experiment.

Information gathered in this manner is called *research information*. Properly conducted research satisfies several criteria. If these criteria are not met, the results obtained may be subject to question.

Objective

Research should be conducted so that the collection, analysis, and interpretation of behavioral information is done with maximum *objectivity*. This means that any conditions which might introduce bias or prejudice must be avoided if at all possible.

Orderly

Research should be systematic, or *orderly*. Haphazard investigation may yield results which are inappropriate for the problem being studied. Orderliness also helps an experimenter avoid needless duplication or the omission of important data. Furthermore, orderliness helps an experimenter maintain objectivity.

Repeatable

Generally, a single research result that cannot be substantiated by some similar finding may be considered suspect and not accepted widely. To overcome this, any study should be written so that a skeptical or interested investigator has sufficient information to be able to *repeat* the research and either confirm or disconfirm the reported results.

Empirical

One characteristic which helps promote repeatability is for the study to be *empirical* in nature. An empirical study employs variables that are *measurable*, avoiding concepts that may be subject to many different interpretations and that cannot be observed and recorded in an objective way.

Public

It might be fascinating to design a study which investigates ghosts' behavior, but unless the procedures and results are available *publicly* for questioning or repetition, the study is not a research study. Supposed observations that cannot be produced for public observation cannot be accepted and obviously would violate some of the criteria mentioned previously.

Meaningful Problem

This criterion summarizes the previous criteria. A *meaningful problem* is one which is public, empirical, and repeatable and which is studied in an orderly and objective manner. Research in psychology *must* investigate meaningful problems if the study of behavior hopes to progress in an understandable fashion.

2.2 THE HYPOTHESIS

A *hypothesis* is a tentative premise or proposal suggested as an explanation for a phenomenon. This proposal must be stated so that it can be tested and either confirmed *or* disconfirmed. Two forms of hypotheses, the null hypothesis and the directional hypothesis, are frequently used in psychological studies.

Null Hypothesis

The *null hypothesis* proposes that certain changes manipulated by an experimenter will *not* alter the outcome of the experiment. In other words, the results of an experiment will not be altered as the experimenter manipulates the conditions of the experiment.

EXAMPLE 1. An educational psychologist wants to test the effects of room temperature on student performance on an examination. The null hypothesis would propose that changes in room temperature would have *no* effect upon the scores obtained by the students.

Directional Hypothesis

A *directional hypothesis* proposes that a particular change in the conditions of an experiment will alter the outcome of the experiment. That is, as a condition of the experiment varies, the results will vary.

EXAMPLE 2. A directional hypothesis for the "temperature-exam" study in Example 1 might state that students tested in a room of normal temperature (68°F) will perform better than students tested in unusual temperatures (50° or 86°F). (Another directional hypothesis might propose that the students tested in the unusual temperatures would perform better.)

No matter what kind of hypothesis is formulated, the psychologist will interpret the results and draft *tentative conclusions*. In other words, the conclusions reached are considered appropriate for the moment, but the psychologist realizes that future research may reveal some other conclusion that may be more reasonable.

2.3 EXPERIMENTAL AND CONTROL GROUPS

Consider again the "temperature-exam" study. Assume that the experimenter sets out to confirm or disconfirm the null hypothesis: "Changes in temperature have no effect on the students' exam scores." To perform the experiment it would be necessary to administer the exam at least three times—once to a group who took the exam at "normal" room temperature; once to a group at the "high" temperature; and once to the group at the " low" temperature. The students who took the exam at the "normal" room temperature would be called the *control group*. The purpose of a control group is to establish a basis for comparison. The students who took the exam at either the "high" or "low" temperatures would be members of *experimental groups*. The performance of the students in the experimental groups could then be compared with the performance of students in the control group. Without the control group, the comparison of the results would be inconclusive, and the experimenter would not be able to either confirm or disconfirm the null hypothesis.

EXAMPLE 3. Suppose that the experimenter tested only two groups—the "high-temperature" and the "low-temperature" groups. Suppose also that both groups scored equally well (or equally poorly) on the examination. This would *not* confirm the null hypothesis (that changes in room temperature have no effect on student performance). Only by examining the control group's performance could the experimenter justify a tentative conclusion, either confirming or disconfirming the hypothesis.

2.4 INDEPENDENT AND DEPENDENT VARIABLES

A condition manipulated by the experimenter is called the *independent variable*. The response which is measured by the experimenter is called the *dependent variable*. Experiments in psychology attempt to either confirm or disconfirm a hypothesis that proposes a relationship between an independent variable and a dependent variable.

EXAMPLE 4. In the "temperature-exam" study, the independent variable is the temperature of the room, which is manipulated by the experimenter. The dependent variable is the performance of the students on the exam.

It is important to remember that both groups (experimental and control) differ only in the amount or level of the independent variable that they experience. Furthermore, the responses of both groups are measured in terms of the same dependent variable.

By arbitrary agreement, psychologists plot the independent variable on the *abscissa* (*x*-axis) of a graph and the dependent variable on the *ordinate* (*y*-axis) of the graph.

EXAMPLE 5. The "temperature-exam" study might be presented on a graph as in Fig. 2-1.

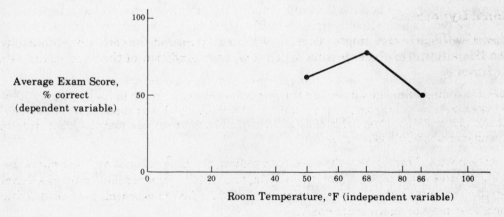

Fig. 2-1

2.5 EXTRANEOUS VARIABLES

When preparing an experiment, the psychologist must give consideration to any possible *extraneous variables*, or irrelevant variables, that might influence the results of the experiment. As much as possible, such variables should be eliminated, or at least be kept constant each time the experiment is performed. Whenever possible, the experimenter should make sure that a subject's response is the result of the effect of the independent variable, and not some extraneous variable.

EXAMPLE 6. While the subjects were taking the exam in the "temperature-exam" study, the psychologist would want to make certain that unusual interruptions (such as a janitor coming into the room) did not occur. In addition, other extraneous variables—such as the noise level, illumination, or humidity in the room—should be constant for each group that takes the examination.

2.6 SAMPLING

The number of potential subjects available for study is often very large. Consequently, a psychologist is seldom able to use the entire population. (For example, an experimenter at a large university could hardly be expected to convince every single enrolled student to take part in the "temperature-exam" study.) To select the subjects for an experiment, psychologists therefore employ *sampling* techniques. Sampling is the attempt to select a group that accurately represents the entire population. Several sampling techniques exist. The selection of a particular sampling technique depends upon the purpose of the experiment and the availability of subjects.

Random Sampling

A *random sample* exists when the group selected from the population is chosen by drawing numbers "out of a hat" or by using a table of random numbers. Every potential subject has an equal chance of being chosen. The experimenter continues to draw numbers (or names) until a large enough sample has been chosen.

Stratified Sampling

There may be subgroups within the population that should be represented in the experiment according to the composition of the population. In such cases, the experimenter may choose a *stratified sample*, in which each subgroup is represented in the experiment by the percentage it has in the total population.

Matched Sampling

An experimenter may believe that individual subjects have certain characteristics that give them distinct advantages or disadvantages in the experimental situation. If such is the case, the experimenter will make sure that each group within a sample has its "fair share" of subjects with such characteristics. This technique is called *matched sampling*.

EXAMPLE 7. The experimenter determining the groups for the "temperature-exam" study might use any one of these sampling techniques discussed above:

A *random sampling* technique would be when all the members of the population were assigned a number and groups were chosen by drawing numbers until the "low temperature," "high temperature," and "normal temperature" groups were determined.

Suppose that only sophomores and juniors were involved, and that the ratio of sophomores to juniors in the general population was 5 to 4. The experimenter might want to have the same ratio of sophomores to juniors in the sample. This would be *stratified sampling*.

Suppose the experimenter believed that each subject's IQ would play an important part in test performance. In that case, the experimenter might make sure that each group of subjects would have equal numbers of people with superior IQs, average IQs, etc. This would be *matched sampling*.

Note: In some circumstances, an experimenter cannot use one of these sampling techniques and must use whatever subjects are available. This is sometimes called *accidental sampling*.

2.7 EXPERIMENTER BIAS

Psychologists try to eliminate bias by using appropriate experimental and sampling techniques. They may, however, be unaware of unintentional biases that they have. These biases are classified under the general heading of *experimenter bias*.

EXAMPLE 8. The experimenter in the "temperature-exam" study could inadvertently indicate to the "high-temperature" or "low-temperature" subjects that they were not expected to do too well on the exam. Even a gesture or an offhand remark to the subjects might be enough to introduce such bias into the experiment. Furthermore, the very design of the experiment may indicate experimenter bias. If the "high" room temperature was 100°F (not 86°F) and the low temperature was 36°F (not 50°F) the experimenter might very well be accused of "forcing" the issue.

2.8 OTHER PSYCHOLOGICAL METHODOLOGIES

Some psychological information cannot be obtained by using the experimental method. Psychologists also use techniques such as naturalistic observation, clinical case histories, and testing and surveying as means for gathering information. These techniques may not be as precise as the experimental method is, but they do give psychologists additional ways in which to gather and analyze information.

Naturalistic Observation

Naturalistic observations are careful, unbiased examinations of events that occur in a basically unmanipulated environment. The psychologist does not control the circumstances in order to force or select a particular response from a subject. Instead, the psychologist conscientiously records whatever the subject does.

EXAMPLE 9. A psychologist who is interested in studying children at play might observe several children together in a playroom. Using a one-way mirror (or perhaps videotape equipment), the psychologist could then observe and record the children's activity without making her or his presence known. In this way, the psychologist could minimize the influence an "adult presence" might have on the children. The children could do as they wish, unless for some reason the psychologist halted their play.

Clinical Case Histories

The primary purpose of a counseling or clinical psychologist is to help people overcome their personal problems. In the course of treating someone, a counseling or clinical psychologist may make a record of problems, insights, and techniques that were important in the treatment. Such reports are called *clinical case histories*. They are often studied by other psychologists because they may expose some factor which has general significance for the understanding of behavior. Usually, the information presented for the first time in a clinical case history is subject to skeptical questioning; more controlled investigation may take place before a clinical case history is accepted by other psychologists.

EXAMPLE 10. Suppose a five-year-old girl is brought to a psychologist because of her very aggressive behavior patterns, which have alarmed her parents and teachers. The psychologist suspects that the aggressive behavior is the result of frustration brought about by a recent change in the family's attitude toward the girl. To summarize and clarify this belief, the psychologist writes a clinical case history, describing in detail the girl's aggressive behavior and her family's frustrating situation. At the conclusion of the case history, the psychologist may suggest that the problem can be lessened with appropriate alterations of the family's behavior. However, the psychologist might also want to investigate the frustration-aggression relationship in a more systematic manner. Both the case history and other records might be useful to psychologists for future reference in the treatment of people with similar problems.

Tests and Surveys

Psychologists often obtain information about behavior by asking the subjects to respond to specially designed tests, surveys, interviews, and questionnaires. All of these provide stimuli to which the subjects react. Psychologists study these reactions in an attempt to find out more about a particular subject's or group's behavior.

A test or survey technique has been designed to investigate almost every aspect of behavior, including personality, intelligence, attitudes, and aptitudes. Tests and surveys have basically two advantages: they allow for the rapid collection of information and give the psychologist the ability to compare a subject's responses with those of thousands of others who have taken the same test. (One disadvantage of tests and surveys is that a subject may purposely give misleading responses.)

EXAMPLE 11. The frustration-aggression hypothesis set forth in the case study in Example 10 might be tested for a large number of subjects, including the young girl. In one such test, a subject could be asked to respond to a picture by telling a story about it. (This is called a *projective test*; see Chapter 17.) Some subjects might be asked to tell their stories after being in a no-frustration situation (the control group). Others would be asked to tell stories following a frustration situation (the experimental group). The stories would be examined to determine whether the aggressive content of stories was more frequent following the frustrating situation.

Solved Problems

2.1   What purpose does research serve in psychology? What are the general characteristics of good research?

Research provides one of several means for gathering information about behavior. Good research should be objective, orderly, repeatable, and done in an empirical fashion. In addition, the problem studied should be meaningful, and the results obtained and the methods employed should be available for public inspection and critical review.

2.2   Give a brief explanation of what is meant by saying a research study should be objective, orderly, repeatable, empirical, public, and based upon a meaningful problem.

Objective. As much as possible, the study should avoid letting the conduct, analysis, or interpretation of the investigation be influenced by any bias or prejudice that might affect the conclusions.

Orderly. The study should progress in a systematic fashion, following procedures which will enable the researcher to obtain results appropriate to the problem under investigation.

Repeatable. The study should be reported and explained clearly enough so that another investigator, who may want to duplicate the study, would be able to do so. This allows for confirmation or questioning of the results of the reported study.

Empirical. Simply stated, *empirical* means *measurable*. If at all possible, measurement should be employed to help foster repeatability and to help avoid debate regarding what is meant by any particular finding.

Public. A study is public if its conduct and results are generally available to others. Conclusions based upon hearsay, anecdotes, or other "private" forms of communication are not given much credence in psychology.

Meaningful problem. Study of a meaningful problem is related to the previous criteria. For example, it might be interesting to investigate the behavior of angels as they dance on the head of a pin, but until someone devises a technique for identifying those angels and measuring their behavior, such a study is not meaningful. *Meaningful* in this sense implies objective, orderly, repeatable, empirical, and public.

2.3   A common procedure for investigating a psychological problem is to develop a hypothesis and then test that hypothesis. What does this mean?

A hypothesis is a proposition or prediction advanced as a possible explanation of a phenomenon. The hypothesis should be stated so that it can be either confirmed or disconfirmed.

2.4   What is the difference between a directional hypothesis and a null hypothesis?

A directional hypothesis predicts that if the conditions of an experiment are varied in some particular way, the outcome of the experiment will also vary in a particular way. The null hypothesis predicts that certain changes in the conditions of an experiment will *not* alter the outcome of the experiment. For example, a directional hypothesis might state that people who drink coffee will show faster reaction times than people who do not drink coffee. The null hypothesis would propose that the reaction times of those who had drunk coffee and those who did not drink coffee would be the same. Both kinds of hypotheses can be tested by collecting information (in this case, the reaction times of the two groups—those who drank coffee and those who did not) and comparing the results.

2.5   What does it mean to say that psychologists often reach tentative conclusions?

Psychologists know that psychology is a "young" science and that many of the principles that have been proposed so far may be superseded by future research findings. Conclusions are therefore viewed as temporary and are possibly subject to change as more information becomes available.

2.6   Explain why comparison is important in the conduct of an experiment.

Consider again the "coffee-drinking" experiment described in Problem 2.4. If only those who drank coffee had been tested for their reaction time, the experiment would not produce any meaningful results. To confirm or disconfirm the hypothesis—that drinking coffee does decrease a person's reaction time—at least two groups (including a control group) must be tested. The effects of drinking coffee could then be assessed by comparing the results from the two groups.

2.7   How many comparisons are necessary in an experiment?

The number of comparisons necessary varies with the problem being studied. A psychologist should try to design an experiment so that all the necessary comparisons can be made. In the coffee experiment, two groups would be adequate, but the addition of a third group might improve the study significantly. It is possible that some subjects might *expect* their reaction times to be quicker simply because they drink coffee. To test for this possibility, the third group would drink decaffeinated coffee without knowing that it was decaffeinated. This third group's reaction times could be compared to those of the other two groups. Note that the use of decaffeinated coffee is similar to a *placebo treatment*, which is often used by psychologists and medical doctors. (A *placebo* is a chemically inert material that has the same appearance as an active drug. It allows psychologists to test the effects of a subject's expectations in an experiment.)

2.8   Consider the "coffee-drinking" experiment described in Problem 2.7. Of the three groups, which are experimental and which is the control group?

Experimental groups usually receive "special" treatments manipulated by the experimenter. Control groups usually receive "normal" treatments; that is, they are not subject to all of or the same level of conditions manipulated by the experimenter. Two of the groups would be considered experimental groups in the "coffee-drinking" study—those drinking coffee and those drinking decaffeinated coffee. The other group, which did not drink coffee, would be considered the control group because it was the group used as the standard of comparison. It should be noted that the studies described here are relatively simple. Many psychological investigations are much more sophisticated and therefore require very elaborate treatments to establish both experimental and control conditions.

2.9   How does an experimenter, by reference to a control group and an experimental group, reach a tentative conclusion?

The confirmation or disconfirmation of a hypothesis is made by comparing the results of the experimental group(s) with those of the control group. If a significant difference exists, the tentative conclusion is that the treatment conditions affected the performance of the experimental group(s).

2.10   In an experiment, what is an *independent variable* and what is a *dependent variable*?

A condition manipulated so the effect can be investigated by the experimenter is called the independent variable. The measured responses of subjects are called dependent variables.

2.11   Identify the independent and dependent variables in the "coffee-drinking" experiment.

The condition manipulated by the experimenter was whether or not the subject drank coffee, and if so, what kind. The response measured was the reaction time of each subject. Thus, the independent variable was one of three conditions: coffee, decaffeinated coffee, and no coffee. The dependent variable was the reaction time of the subjects.

2.12   Suppose that the "coffee-drinking" experiment was run, and that the three groups responded equally well in the reaction-time test. How would the results be shown on a graph?

The independent variable would be plotted on the abscissa (x-axis). The dependent variable would be plotted on the ordinate (y-axis). Figure 2-2 illustrates how the graph would look if the average reaction time for each group was 1/2 second.

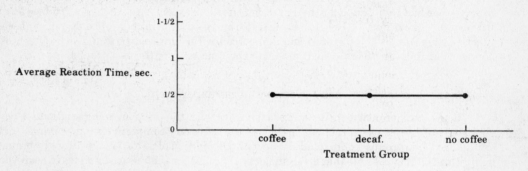

Fig. 2-2

2.13   What is an extraneous variable? Why must experimenters be concerned with extraneous variables?

Extraneous variables are conditions in an experiment that are irrelevant to the experimenter's intentions but which might affect the outcome. Experimenters must take care to eliminate or "neutralize" as much as possible the influences of extraneous variables. (Such variables might include temperature, humidity, lighting, or noises that might influence the subjects.) The experimenter tries to be certain the responses obtained in an experiment are a result of only the independent variable, rather than some outside, inappropriate variable.

2.14   What kind of extraneous variable might have to be "neutralized" in the "coffee-drinking" experiment?

Because the dependent variable was reaction time, the investigator would have to conduct the experiment in a room where no sudden or unexpected noise might produce a startle response and a "false" reaction time in one of the subjects. Furthermore, the coffee offered to the subjects at the beginning of the experiment should not be too hot, so that subjects do not burn their tongues. (Discomfort from a burn might cause a lack of attention, which would not occur for the "no-coffee" subjects and would thus affect the results.) Furthermore, the experimenter should make sure that none of the subjects drank coffee or alcohol (or took other drugs) just before the experiment.

2.15   How do experimenters avoid introducing bias when they pick subjects for an experiment?

First, an experimenter must define the population from which subjects will be drawn. (For example, the population could be all the freshmen at a university, or all enrolled students, or all women on the faculty, or all faculty members more than forty years old.) Once this population is defined, the experimenter will either use all its members as subjects or (more likely) select a *sample* of the population. The purpose of sampling is to get a manageable number of subjects who are representative of the population as a whole.

2.16   Describe these three sampling techniques: random sampling, stratified sampling, and matched sampling.

   In *random sampling*, every member of the population has an equal chance of being chosen as a subject in one of the groups in the experiment. The experimenter will select subjects from the defined population by "drawing names from a hat" or by using tables of random numbers.

   In *stratified sampling*, an experimenter identifies any significant subgroups within the population. The experimenter then makes sure that each subgroup is proportionally represented in each experimental group.

   In *matched sampling*, the experimenter identifies certain characteristics of individual subjects that may affect the experiment. The experimenter will then make sure that each group in the experiment has an equal number of subjects with such matched characteristics.

2.17   Suppose a psychologist was interested in investigating attitudes about a major social problem. The psychologist decides to compare student attitudes at College A with student attitude at College B. Describe how the psychologist would use random sampling to select the subjects for this study.

   The psychologist would decide how many subjects he or she wanted in each group. He or she would then choose that many from a roster of all the students of each college. To be certain that each student had an equal chance of being chosen, the psychologist might put all the names in a hat and then draw them until the needed number was reached. However, it is more likely that the psychologist would use a table of random numbers to select the sample from such a large population.

2.18   How would the psychologist come up with a stratified sample or a matched sample in such an experiment?

   A *stratified sample* might be used if the psychologist felt it was necessary. For example, if each college's population was made up of 35 percent freshmen, 25 percent sophomores, 20 percent juniors, and 20 percent seniors, the psychologist might want to make sure that each group accurately reflected these percentages.

   A *matched sample* might be based upon grade-point-average, age, sex, IQ, or some other characteristic that the psychologist believed was important. Each person selected from College A would be "matched" by a person with similar characteristics from College B.

2.19   When might the psychologist use an accidental sample?

   Only when psychologists find it impossible to come up with a random, stratified, or matched sample do they use an accidental sample. A psychologist who wants to gather information about attitudes may not have access to all students and may be forced to use only those students who might volunteer. This would create an accidental sample.

2.20   Do sampling techniques eliminate all bias in the groups selected?

   Sampling techniques *help* to reduce bias, but it is unlikely that they ever completely eliminate it. The groups in an experiment are selected to be as similar as possible before the experiment begins, but it is unlikely that they can ever be perfectly alike.

2.21   What is experimenter bias? How can it be reduced or eliminated?

   Unintentionally, experimenters themselves might contribute bias to an experiment, either in their design of an experiment or in the way they administer it. For example, an experimenter might have some expectations about the subjects' performance. The experimenter may inadvertently communicate these expectations to the subjects by a gesture, tone of voice, or offhand remark. To avoid such bias, some experiments are conducted so that neither the experimenter nor the subject knows which condition (experimental or control) is being tested. (In such cases, some other person sorts the subjects, and the person who actually administers the study is uninformed as to which group is being tested.) When both the experimenter *and* subject are unaware of the conditions, the study is said to have a *double-blind control*. When only the subject is unaware, the study has a *single-blind control*.

2.22   Psychologists place a lot of emphasis on information obtained from experiments conducted with appropriate methodologies and controls. What other sources of psychological information are often used to obtain information about behavior?

Three other sources of psychological information are naturalistic observation, clinical case histories, and testing and surveying.

2.23   Control in an experiment is considered very important. Why then do psychologists accept information from relatively uncontrolled naturalistic observations?

In some cases, experiments are impossible. For example, it would be unethical to experimentally create conditions which would produce severe nutritional deprivation for a young child. However, such conditions do occasionally exist. Psychologists can learn from these kinds of situations by employing careful, precise, and unbiased observation. Psychologists might be personally disgusted by the mistreatment of the child, but they would still study the situation to observe what effects these conditions had upon the child.

2.24   What are clinical case histories?

Clinical case histories are the records of treatment made by psychiatrists or by clinical or counseling psychologists. These records are a report of problems, insights, and techniques that were important to the psychologist and subject in the course of treatment.

2.25   Obviously, a clinical case history is important to a psychologist as a record of the treatment of one person. Can such a case history also have relevance to other people the psychologist may treat, and to other psychologists as well?

A clinician may gain insights in the treatment of one person that can be helpful in the treatment of others. The clinician may also observe factors important to psychologists generally. The subjectivity and uncontrolled nature of clinical observation, however, limit the usefulness of clinical case histories. Information obtained from them should be checked by using more systematic techniques, such as tests or experiments that may confirm the clinician's subjective findings or observations.

2.26   Information about behavior that cannot be observed directly is sometimes gathered by using psychological tests and surveys. What are some of the advantages and disadvantages of tests and surveys?

Psychological tests and surveys have several advantages: Because tests and surveys are standardized, they can be administered easily and their results can be interpreted rapidly. In addition, tests can be efficiently administered to very large numbers of people over long periods of time, and the responses of one person can be compared to the responses of many other people.

Psychological tests and surveys also have several disadvantages: Respondents in a test or survey may purposely falsify their answers. Furthermore, it may be difficult to determine just how valid the measures of a test are or to be sure that a certain test is appropriate to an individual's situation.

Key Terms

Abscissa.   The *x*-axis, or horizontal axis, of a graph.

Clinical case history.   Records or data from therapy situations; used to identify behaviors a. problems that need to be studied.

Control group.   In a scientific experiment, those subjects whose responses are used as a basis for compari. the experimenter compares the responses of the control group with the responses of experimental groups.

Dependent variable.   The measured response in an experiment.

Directional hypothesis.   A prediction that a specific change in the conditions of an experiment will result in a particular change in the outcome of the experiment.

Double-blind control.   An experimental situation in which both the subjects *and* those who administer the experiment are unaware of how or when the variables are manipulated.

Empirical.   Anything that is directly observable or measurable.

Experimental group.   In a scientific experiment, those subjects who respond to an independent variable that is "specially" manipulated by the experimenter; the responses of the experimental group can then be compared with the responses of the control group.

Experimental method.   A technique involving the controlled comparison of conditions to determine if the variable investigated affects the results obtained.

Extraneous variable.   A condition that may affect the outcome of an experiment but that is irrelevant to the experiment.

Hypothesis.   A tentative explanation of a relationship or a proposition that a relationship exists; an experiment should be designed so that a hypothesis can be either confirmed or disconfirmed.

Independent variable.   A condition manipulated by the experimenter; the experimenter manipulates the independent variable to determine the effect of such manipulations on the dependent variable.

Matched sampling.   A technique for selecting subjects in which an experimenter makes sure that each group in the experiment contains the same number of subjects who possess a certain characteristic that might influence the outcome.

Naturalistic observation.   The careful observation of events not manipulated by the observer.

Null hypothesis.   A prediction that a specific change in the conditions of an experiment will not result in a change in the outcome.

Objectivity.   When judgments made are free from bias or the influence of personal feeling.

Ordinate.   The *y*-axis, or vertical axis, of a graph.

Placebo.   A chemically inert material that has the same appearance as an active drug; allows psychologists to test the effects of the expectations of subjects who believe they are actually taking a drug; by analogy, the "placebo effect" is any situation in which subjects believe they are experiencing a manipulation by the experimenter when in fact they are not.

Population.   The entire group from which subjects may be chosen.

Random sampling.   A technique for selecting subjects in such a way that every potential subject in the population has an equal chance of being chosen for an experiment.

Sampling.   Selection of subjects from a population; in general, the experimenter attempts to make the sample as representative of the population as possible.

Single-blind control.   An experimental situation in which the subjects are unaware of how or when the variables are manipulated by the experimenter.

Stratified sampling.   A technique for selecting subjects in such a way that significant subgroups within the population are accurately reflected in the composition of each group in the experiment.

Subjectivity.   When judgments are affected by bias, prejudice, or personal feeling.

Chapter 3

Evolution and Genetics

Evolution refers to those changes in a species that occur very gradually over long time spans. *Genetics* is the study of the transfer of hereditary characteristics through generations. Psychologists are interested in evolution and genetics because an organism's heritage may influence its behavior significantly. Both long-term evolutionary trends and short-term genetic changes can suggest to psychologists a good deal about the causes of behavior.

3.1 THE STUDY OF EVOLUTION

Charles Darwin's *The Origin of Species*, published in 1859, was the first theoretical study of evolution. Darwin proposed that features of successive generations are modified through evolutionary processes. Darwin believed that qualities which allow an organism to adjust to the environment persist, while qualities which do not help an organism adjust to the environment eventually drop out. The major concepts of Darwin's theory are variability, adaptation, and selection.

Variability

Through several generations, it is sometimes possible to determine changes in the genetic makeup of an organism. These changes appear to enable organisms to adjust to the environment. Such changes come under the heading *variability*.

Adaptation

The label for the adjustment which the organism makes is *adaptation*. The essential aim of adaptation is for the survival of the species, although other, less dramatic functions are also served by adaptation.

Selection

Traits which seem to allow a species to adjust to the environment are generally passed on from one generation to the next. Traits which are not suitable do not generally recur in the species. The *selection* of characteristics has been summarized in the popular phrase "survival of the fittest." In his book, Darwin wrote about the *natural selection* of characteristics over long periods of time. *Forced selection* through selective breeding is also possible. (See Section 3.4.)

3.2 ETHOLOGY

A related area of investigation is *ethology*, the study of organisms in their natural habitats. Evidence gathered through naturalistic observation indicates that evolutionary processes modify both the physical and behavioral attributes of organisms.

Physical Characteristics

Evolutionary adjustments include the development of physical traits such as camouflage coloration, thick fur for warmth, and the development of a thumb that works in opposition to the other fingers of the hand. Perhaps the most dramatic example of a species' adjustment is the development of the human brain. The human brain has evolved into a structure that has tremendous capacity for sensory and motor functions, the translation of motivation and emotion, and a vast variety of learning skills.

It is particularly in their ability to learn that humans surpass all other organisms. The evolution of a highly elaborated brain, with a massive cerebral cortex, apparently enables humans to demonstrate advanced thinking, learning, and memory skills. Humans are especially distinguished from other species in their ability to depict the world symbolically by using language. (See Chapter 16.)

Behavioral Characteristics

The evolution of adaptive behavioral characteristics is sometimes easier to illustrate for lower organisms than for humans. The patterns which have developed for different organisms often are *species-specific*; that is, the behavior pattern is common to all members of a species, and only that species.

Fixed-Action Patterns (FAPs)

One frequently observed example of species-specific behavior is a *fixed action pattern* (FAP). FAPs are stereotyped sequences of movement and are found in all members of a species.

EXAMPLE 1. It has been suggested that the human facial expressions which accompany emotions are FAPs. Expressions such as smiling when happy occur at a very early age. They follow essentially the same patterns for *all* human societies and are easily identified by observation.

An FAP is usually triggered by a *releaser stimulus*, or *sign stimulus*. When the releaser stimulus is present, the response can be expected; when it is absent, the response pattern is unlikely to occur. (See, however, Example 3.)

EXAMPLE 2. Study of the male stickleback fish has shown that it will attack any fish-like model that has a red belly, but will ignore an exact replica of another stickleback that does *not* have the red belly. The red belly, which is acquired by male sticklebacks during the mating season, serves as a releaser stimulus for other male sticklebacks, which attack when they see it.

FAPs are not instincts. *Instincts* are defined as response patterns that are completely controlled by hereditary factors; FAPs, on the other hand, are also dependent on environmental factors. Instincts may be *modified* by environmental factors (a bird may use whatever material is available to build a nest) but they are not triggered by the environment.

Vacuum Activity

On occasion, FAPs appear in the absence of any observable releaser stimulus. It has been suggested that motivation level increases until the organism cannot keep from acting. This kind of FAP responding is called *vacuum activity*.

EXAMPLE 3. Researchers have experimentally deprived starlings of the opportunity to catch flies. (The presence of a fly is considered to be the releaser stimulus.) The starlings will sometimes initiate an entire fly-catching pattern even though no flies are present. The starlings are thus engaged in vacuum activity.

Displacement and Redirection

In some cases, organisms may be confronted with two sets of incompatible releaser stimuli. Often, the organism will vacillate between the two FAPs usually elicted and instead may perform an irrelevant response—one that is appropriate to neither stimulus situation. This irrelevant responding is called *displacement activity*.

EXAMPLE 4. Observation has shown that herring gulls confronted with two stimuli—one that ordinarily triggers fighting and one that ordinarily triggers fleeing—may choose to initiate nest-building. In this case, nest-building is a displacement activity because it is not appropriate to either stimulus.

Even in the presence of only one releaser stimulus, similar irrelevant responding sometimes appears. This is called *redirection*, in which a response is elicited but is inappropriate to the stimulus. Both displacement activity and redirection are somewhat comparable to the ego defense mechanism called *displacement*. (See Chapter 19.)

Habituation

FAPs are sometimes made to inappropriate stimuli. If such inappropriate stimuli are presented repeatedly, the organism eventually adjusts and no longer shows the FAP. This ability to adjust is called *habituation*.

EXAMPLE 5. A starling raised in darkness may, when it is first released in a lighted environment, chase its own shadow in an attempt to find food. Before long, however, the bird will show habituation—it will no longer pursue its shadow.

Habituation might occur for recurrent appropriate releaser stimuli, but this is unlikely to happen. The pattern probably will be rewarded and therefore be elicited again when the stimuli reappear.

Complex FAPs

Research on the migratory patterns of birds or other similar behavioral patterns indicates they are very similar to simple FAPs. However, it has been difficult to determine what releaser stimuli are involved and what specific responses comprise such complex FAPs.

3.3   GENETICS

Genetics is the study of the biological transmission of characteristics from a parent to an offspring. In higher animals, this transmission takes place when the *germ cells* (sperm from the male, egg from the female) unite during conception to form a *zygote*. The zygote is the single, original cell formed by the sperm and egg. This cell then divides again and again to form a multicellular organism.

Chromosomes

In higher organisms, all cells except germ cells contain one set of *chromosomes* inherited from each parent. For example, human body cells usually contain 46 chromosomes, arranged in 23 pairs. Human germ cells contain only 23 single chromosomes. At conception, the egg and sperm are united into the zygote, which then has the full complement of 46 chromosomes.

One particular pair of chromosomes determines the sex of the offspring. The sex-determining chromosomes are labelled X or Y. A female body cell is designated as XX; a male body cell is designated as XY. When the body forms germ cells, these chromosome pairs split. Thus, all female germ cells (eggs, or ova) carry the X designation, whereas half the male germ cells (sperm) carry the X chromosome and the other half carry the Y chromosome.

Genes

All chromosomes contain *genes*. Genes are found in a long molecule called deoxyribonucleic acid (DNA), which combines with a protein structure to become organized into chromosomes.

Genes are the basic units of hereditary transmission. They are paired, just as the chromosomes which hold them are paired. The genes hold "information" for the production of proteins; this information determines the way in which the organism will develop.

In rare cases, some kind of spontaneous or sudden change occurs in the DNA. The result of this is that the cell does not replicate itself exactly. The resultant change is called a *mutation*. Mutations are permanent and frequently produce a radical and harmful effect for human offspring.

Another instance in which the genetic code is not duplicated exactly in the offspring occurs when genes which were previously linked become unlinked or linked with a different set of genes. This is called *crossing-over*. Crossing-over alters the set of characteristics found in the offspring and, consequently, the pattern that is passed on to succeeding generations.

3.4 GENETIC INFLUENCES

Once the zygote is formed, the presence or absence of various genes determines whether or not a particular characteristic will be observed in the offspring. In some cases, a characteristic of an offspring is determined by only one or two genes. In other cases, many genes may work together to control some aspect of the offspring's development.

EXAMPLE 6. A single defective gene causes a disease called phenylketonuria (PKU), in which the body is unable to convert the protein phenylalanine into a usable form. If phenylalanine builds up to toxic levels, it attacks the cells of the central nervous system, causing mental retardation. (Research has indicated that more than 150 genes may affect brain development. Therefore, that many or more *must* function correctly if a normal brain is to develop.)

The diversity of characteristics determined by genes includes skin color, eye color, hair color, height and weight tendencies, internal organ development, and the possibilities for birth defects. In general, it is assumed that only physiological characteristics can be passed hereditarily to succeeding generations, while the parents' learned characteristics cannot be inherited.

Dominant and Recessive Genes

Each pair of genes controls specific activities of development. The members of the pair are not always alike. If the paired genes are not alike, one of the pair (the *dominant gene*) will act as a controller while the other (the *recessive gene*) does not affect the process of development. Recessive characteristics appear in an offspring only when both members of the gene pair are recessive.

EXAMPLE 7. Skin color may be either normal (which is dominant) or albino (which is recessive). The offspring will be albino only if both parents transmit that trait in the germ cells which form the zygote. It is possible that both parents could have normal skin coloring and still produce an albino child, as Fig. 3-1 shows. Although both parents show normal skin coloring, one of four conceptions could be albino (aa).

		FATHER	
		N	a
MOTHER	N	NN	Na
	a	Na	aa

N = normal skin coloring (dominant)

a = albino skin coloring (recessive)

Fig. 3-1

Birth Defects

Some birth defects, such as PKU (Example 5), result from a defective gene. Other birth defects are the result of a disruption of the pregnancy by some environmental agent, such as drugs or disease.

With advances in research, psychologists have been able to assist many couples with genetic counseling. Working with medical doctors and biologists, psychologists have been able to estimate the probabilities for difficulties before or during pregnancy. In many cases, this has helped alleviate anxiety for the couple or at least let the couple anticipate a potential problem.

Twins

Twins are of two types—*identical* and *fraternal*. Identical twins have the same hereditary pattern because they are the result of a single conception. In the process of cell division, the initial cell *cleavage* (division) may produce a complete separation, and two offspring will develop. Each identical twin has the same genetic characteristics as the other.

Fraternal twins develop from separate conceptions. Their genetic characteristics are no more alike than those of any other siblings. They are twins only because they develop and are born at about the same time.

The probability of fraternal twins (or any other siblings) having exactly the same genetic characteristics is exceedingly small. The chances of both parents exactly repeating the same combination of chromosomes are $2^{23} \times 2^{23}$, or about 1 in 70 trillion. The probability grows even slimmer if the transmission of the many genes is considered.

Selective Breeding

Recognizing that hereditary characteristics influence the offspring in a pronounced manner, it is reasonable to consider trying to mate parents in combinations which will produce favorable offspring. Such a procedure is called *selective breeding*. It has been demonstrated successfully for many different organisms, including pedigreed dogs and cattle. Humans have developed a number of social restrictions that keep them from using the same principles to breed "better" humans. However, a kind of selectivity is sometimes practiced by humans who will breed only with members of a particular race, religion, or social class. The science of "improving" the human species through selective mating, called *eugenics*, is not taken seriously by many people simply because few people are willing to say what human characteristics ought to be "encouraged" and what human characteristics ought to be "discouraged" through selective breeding.

3.5   THE RELATIONSHIP OF HEREDITY AND ENVIRONMENT

Early researchers tried to determine how hereditary or environmental events produced atypical offspring. While such research continues, a more recent trend has been to investigate how heredity and environment affect the development of offspring with ordinary characteristics.

Studies of hereditary influences on behavior have been grouped under the heading *behavioral genetics*. Disputes in behavioral genetics have arisen especially around the development of personality and intelligence in humans. While geneticists have given primary stress to the importance of hereditary influences on these aspects of behavior, other psychologists have emphasized environmental effects. This dispute, often referred to as the *nature-nurture controversy* or the *nativist-environmentalist controversy*, is not easily resolved. Attempts to attribute percentages of influence to either heredity or the environment have led to varying and often contradictory results.

Certain hereditary effects, such as the sex of the child or some birth defects, cannot be denied. However, much of the research relating hereditary variables and personality or intelligence characteristics is subject to differing interpretations. It is reasonable to conclude that both heredity and environment *interact* to influence such traits, and that trying to attribute percentages of effect to either is not meaningful.

Solved Problems

3.1 Why do psychologists study evolution?

Understanding evolution helps psychologists understand the heritage of human behavior. Humans have developed unique patterns of behavior in the same way they have developed unique configurations of physiological characteristics. These patterns of behavior are *species-specific* and are comparable to behavior patterns found for other organisms.

3.2 Who is given credit for initiating the study of evolution? What primary considerations were set forth in his theory?

Charles Darwin, an English naturalist, published *The Origin of Species* in 1859. This work was the initial statement of a theory of evolution. Darwin's primary considerations were: (a) variability—changes in genetic makeup which seem to lead to adaptation; (b) adaptation—the ability to adjust and survive within the given environment; and (c) selection—the tendency for adaptive characteristics to persist and for other characteristics to disappear.

3.3 The Darwinian theory of variability, adaptation, and selection can be summarized in a single well-known phrase. What is this phrase and what does it imply?

The phrase often used to summarize Darwin's viewpoint is "survival of the fittest." The implication is that the characteristics which best help the organism adjust to the environment are those which persevere through natural selection and appear in succeeding generations. While the most fit characteristics continue to develop, the less fit tend to disappear.

3.4 Is there evidence that a species' *behavioral* characteristics develop to help the species adapt to the environment?

Many adaptive changes, such as the development of camouflage coloration, are physiological. Other adaptive changes, however, are behavioral. Certain behaviors that are common to a species over successive generations may be modified or elaborated as a species evolves.

3.5 What feature of the evolutionary development of humans appears to be most significant in affecting behavior?

Humans, more than any other species, have developed a complex, highly integrated, and highly specialized brain. Brain activity is very important for sensory reception, motor responses, motivational conditions, thinking, learning, and memory. Compared to other organisms, humans have a greatly elaborated cerebral cortex that seems to give them great advantages in learning ability and the ability to represent the world by using symbols (most frequently language).

3.6 The study of the behaviors characteristic of a particular species is called *ethology*. How do ethologists conduct research? What are some of the general areas of study for ethologists?

Ethologists use naturalistic observation to study the behavior of organisms in their natural habitats. Areas of investigation include fixed-action patterns (FAPs), releaser (or sign) stimuli, vacuum activities, displacement activities, and redirection.

3.7 Patterns of behavior are often referred to as *species-specific*. What does this phrase mean? What are the underlying causes of species-specific behavior?

Species-specific behaviors are those behaviors which have evolved to become characteristic of a given species. They are the result of the species' heritage and the environmental conditions common to members of the species.

3.8   What is a fixed-action pattern?

A fixed-action pattern (FAP) is a set of invariant movement responses triggered by a particular stimulus. A fixed-action pattern is common to all members of a species.

3.9   What is the name given to the stimuli that trigger FAPs?

These stimuli are called releaser, or sign, stimuli. The strength of the FAP elicited appears to be a function of the releaser stimulus and the motive condition of the responding organism.

3.10   Are FAPs instincts?

FAPs are not called instincts. A response controlled exclusively by genetic influence might be called instinctive, but FAPs are modified by environmental factors. Species-specific is the preferred label.

3.11   What are vacuum activity, redirection, and displacement activities?

Vacuum activity is the initiation of FAP responding in the absence of any releaser stimulus. Usually, these are explained as evidence of the organism's need to release a high level of motivational pressure. In the absence of any releaser stimulus, the organism finally appears to *have* to respond; thus the term vacuum activity.

Sometimes, motive energy is released in a pattern not appropriate to the stimulus situation. This is called *redirection*. The motive energy is released, but aimed toward a new, different, perhaps inappropriate stimulus rather than a releaser stimulus.

Sometimes an organism is faced with two incompatible releaser stimuli. The organism in this case may respond with an FAP appropriate to neither of these stimuli. This is called *displacement activity*.

3.12   Some organisms show inappropriate FAPs to certain stimuli. What happens to such FAP responses?

If the stimulus is presented repeatedly, the organism will gradually stop responding. This particular kind of adjustment is called *habituation*. Habituation is unlikely to occur for an appropriate stimulus-response pairing if such a pairing often yields some kind of reward.

3.13   Are there behaviors which appear to be complex yet are interpreted as comparable to other, simpler FAPs?

Some behaviors, such as the information "dance" of the honeybee or the migration of birds, seem to be very similar to FAPs. However, the complexities of the stimulus situation and the responses involved have made it difficult to classify these behavior patterns as simple FAPs.

3.14   What is the study of genetics, and why are psychologists interested in it?

Genetics is a branch of biology concerned with the transfer of inherited characteristics from one generation to another. Understanding how an individual came to have certain characteristics is an aid to understanding how the individual's behavior may be affected by those characteristics.

3.15   How are characteristics transmitted from one generation to the next?

The units which are inherited are called genes. The genes are held in a long molecule (deoxyribonucleic acid, or DNA) which together with protein forms larger structures called chromosomes. The chromosomes are found in the cells of the human body and are arranged in 23 pairs.

Actual transmission of the chromosomes (which hold the genes) occurs when the male germ cell (sperm) penetrates the female germ cell (egg, or ovum). Germ cells are formed by a cell-splitting process called *meiosis*. Any one germ cell contains 23 single chromosomes. When the sperm and egg unite, a single cell (zygote) is formed. The zygote has 23 pairs of chromosomes, and contains all the genetic "information" that will direct the development of the new organism.

3.16   Is this transmission process invariant?

The actual transmission must involve the male and female germ cells. However, on rare occasions, spontaneous changes may occur in the DNA. These changes alter some aspect of the transmission code contained in the genes and produce what is called a mutation. A mutation occurs with a sudden, permanent, and often radical effect. Generally, mutations in humans produce mostly harmful effects, although the mutation of plants and some animals are considered favorable and are manipulated to breed better strains for commercial use.

3.17   What other genetic change may alter the resultant product of the conception?

When the single chromosomes of the germ cells pair in the zygote, genes that were previously linked sometimes become unlinked or linked with a different set of characteristics. This is called crossing-over, and will alter the characteristics found in the members of the following generation.

3.18   Once the zygote is formed, what characteristics of the offspring are determined?

Many characteristics are determined at the moment of conception. These include sex, skin color, eye color, height and weight tendencies, development of the nervous system, organs, and glands, and, in some cases, the physiological characteristics which will eventually appear as birth defects. In general, it can be said that physiological characteristics are established by heredity, while learned characteristics of the parent cannot be passed on by heredity.

3.19   How is the sex of human offspring determined?

One particular pair of chromosomes determines the sex of the offspring. Normal human male cells have an XY chromosome and normal human female cells have an XX chromosome. All female germ cells (eggs) have X chromosomes; male germ cells (sperm) have either an X or Y chromosome. Determination of sex is thus dependent upon the sperm cell which fertilizes the egg. A diagramatic representation appears in Fig. 3-2. Half the children are XX (female), and half the children are XY (male).

FATHER

		X	Y
MOTHER	X	XX	XY
	X	XX	XY

Fig. 3-2

3.20   Are human birth defects always the result of genetic transmission?

Birth defects may be the result of hereditarily determined characteristics *or* some environmental condition that affects the prenatal development of the child. For example, Down's Syndrome ("Mongolism") is caused by a chromosomal defect. Instead of inheriting the normal complement of 46 chromosomes, the child has 47 chromosomes, with the extra chromosome in the twenty-first pair. The result of this is mental retardation and certain physical characteristics, including a protruding tongue, stubby fingers, small ears, and eyelids with an unusual configuration.

The effects of some drugs (such as thalidomide) or diseases (such as measles) may also produce birth defects. Although chromosomally correct at conception, the child is born with a defect because of environmental influences on development during the mother's pregnancy.

3.21 Some characteristics are described as dominant and others as recessive. What does this mean, and what determines whether or not the characteristics are evident in the child?

Each chromosome contains pairs of genes. The paired genes in one chromosome may or may not be alike. In general, if the pair members are not alike, one of the pair (the dominant gene) will determine the trait which appears, while the other trait (from the recessive gene) does not appear. Recessive characteristics appear only when recessive genes from both parents are joined in the zygote.

For example, eye color is determined in this way: Suppose both parents are brown-eyed, but carry the blue, recessive, gene. (Both parents are Bb, where B = brown and b = blue.) The children of such a couple should follow the pattern shown in Fig. 3-3.

```
                    FATHER
                    B   b
            B  |  BB   Bb
MOTHER         |
            b  |  Bb   bb
```

Fig. 3-3

On the average, three of every four children would be brown-eyed, while the fourth would be blue-eyed. However, three of four could pass on the recessive characteristic to succeeding generations.

Only one child in four, the BB, would not carry the recessive gene. The characteristics which show or are measurable are called the individual's *phenotype*, while all the genes possessed by the individual constitute the individual's *genotype*.

3.22 Is it possible for two individuals to have exactly the same hereditary characteristics?

Two or more individuals may have exactly the same hereditary characteristics. Identical twins for example, result when a single zygote divides and, in the process, the resultant cells separate. Each separate cell continues to develop and becomes an individual. These individuals have identical hereditary characteristics.

The possibility that two different conceptions may result in exactly the same hereditary characteristics is exceedingly small. The chances of such an occurrence are less than 1 in 70 trillion because of the vast number of combinations of chromosomes that each parent might provide in the germ cell.

3.23 Explain the difference between identical and fraternal twins. Is it possible to have identical and nonidentical siblings born at the same time?

When a single zygote splits completely and develops as two separate individuals, identical twins are produced. Because they come from a single conception, they will carry the same hereditary pattern. Fraternal twins, on the other hand, are the result of two separate conceptions occurring at about the same time. They are independent individuals from conception on, and they may or may not be of the same sex.

Identical and nonidentical siblings may be born at the same time. For example, one highly publicized set of quintuplets appeared to consist of three identical girls, one fraternal girl, and one fraternal boy.

3.24 Suppose a couple wants advice about possible genetic problems. What kind of genetic counseling is available to them?

Biologists, medical doctors, and psychologists working together have begun to develop techniques for identifying potential genetic problems. For example, by using a technique called karyotyping, chromosomes of the prospective parents can be analyzed to determine if their germ cells might carry abnormal characteristics.

Another technique, called amniocentesis, tests fetal cells in the amniotic fluid of the pregnant woman for the presence or absence of abnormal chromosomes. Such pre- or post-conception counseling can relieve much anxiety for a couple planning to have children.

3.25 It is an established fact that the characteristics of adult organisms are very important in determining the characteristics of their offspring. What use do humans make of this knowledge?

The selective breeding of subhuman organisms has been a common procedure for many years. For example, cattle, horses, and poultry are often selectively bred. The results of such breeding provide obvious benefits: cows that produce more milk, thoroughbred horses that run faster, and chickens that lay more eggs.

Humans themselves do not practice selective breeding as such. In certain human societies, there are many people who will marry and have children only with those of their own race, religion, or social class. However, any large-scale program of selective breeding for humans would raise too many serious ethical and philosophical questions to be practicable. Furthermore, no one person can state with certainty just what human characteristics ought to be encouraged through selective breeding.

3.26 Are psychologists certain of the influence of heredity on behavioral characteristics?

The hereditary transmission of the sex of a child, hair and eye color, height and weight tendencies, and certain birth defects cannot be questioned. However, the evidence that suggests that behavioral characteristics can also be attributed to hereditary influence is much less definitive. Research may support correlations between race and intelligence, or family membership and susceptibility to abnormal personality patterns, but it is difficult to determine if these are direct cause-and-effect relationships or the result of environmental influences. Attempts to assign percentages to the relative effect of heredity versus environment have led to contradictory findings and to continued debate. In general, heredity and environment seem to interact.

3.27 The debate concerning the relative effects of heredity and environment has produced many research studies. What is the general label for such research?

Research attempting to distinguish between those characteristics due to heredity and those due to environment fall in the area called *behavioral genetics*. More popularly, they have been called "nature-nuture" investigations or "nativist-environmentalist" studies.

Key Terms

Adaptation. The evolutionary adjustment of an organism to its environment; often made as a means to improving a species' chances for survival.

Behavioral genetics. The study of the influence of heredity on behavior.

Chromosomes. Small bodies which contain genes; occur in pairs within each body cell; human body cells have 46 chromosomes, human germ cells have 23.

Crossing-over. A process in which genes that were previously linked become unlinked or linked with a different set of genes.

Displacement activity. An irrelevant response made in the presence of two simultaneous but incompatible releaser stimuli.

Dominant gene. The gene in a pair of unalike genes that acts as the controller, directing development of a certain characteristic.

Ethology. The study of organisms in their natural habitats.

Eugenics.   The science of "improving" the human species through selective breeding.

Evolution.   The theory of the selective changes in organisms that take place over long time periods.

Fixed-action pattern (FAP).   Unvarying sequences of movement, keyed by a releaser, or sign, stimulus; FAPs are species-specific.

Fraternal twins.   Two children, conceived independently as two separate zygotes, but born at approximately the same time.

Genes.   The basic "information-bearing" units of heredity; carried within chromosomes.

Genetics.   The study of the transmission of hereditary characteristics through generations.

Germ cells.   In the female, the egg; in the male, the sperm.

Habituation.   A change of behavioral pattern in which an organism ceases to respond with an FAP to an inappropriate stimulus.

Identical twins.   Two children originally conceived as one zygote, which then separates into two; the children are born independently but at approximately the same time.

Instinct.   A behavior pattern that appears in an organism regardless of environmental factors.

Mutation.   A spontaneous, sudden change in heredity pattern.

Natural selection.   The evolutionary process by which traits that aid the organism recur in future generations, while those that are unsuitable do not; often summarized by the phrase "survival of the fittest."

Recessive gene.   The gene in a pair of unalike genes that does not usually affect the process of development.

Redirection.   An organism's inappropriate responding in the presence of a single releaser stimulus.

Vacuum activity.   The appearance of an FAP when no releaser stimulus has occurred.

Zygote.   The single cell formed by the uniting of a sperm cell and an egg cell at the moment of conception.

Chapter 4

Developmental Psychology

Developmental psychology is the study of behavioral changes through a time span. A strong emphasis is usually placed on physical development, but developmental psychologists also study cognitive development and social development.

4.1 STAGES OF PHYSICAL DEVELOPMENT

Physical development, or maturation, may influence a human's behavior profoundly. Developmental psychologists therefore study both prenatal and postnatal development—from the moment of conception, when a person's hereditary patterns are set, up until death. Any one developmental psychologist may study only a part of the entire age span or a particular behavior within the time span.

Prenatal Stages of Development

The three stages of prenatal development are the germinal, embryonic, and fetal stages.

Germinal. During the first two weeks following conception, the zygote begins the process of cell division, or *mitosis*. During this time, the cells are not yet attached directly to the mother. That physical attachment occurs at about the end of the second week, and marks the beginning of the embryonic stage.

Embryonic. During the next four weeks, until approximately the end of the sixth week, the group of cells is called an *embryo*. The process of cell division and diversification continues during this period. By the completion of the embryonic stage, sufficient development has been completed so that the basic physical features of the baby-to-be can be recognized.

Fetal. The label for the baby-to-be during the remaining 32 weeks of pregnancy (assuming a full-term pregnancy of 38 weeks) is *fetus*. By the end of this period, the fetus grows to about 18 to 21 inches in length and to about 7 pounds in weight.

Postnatal Stages of Development

Postnatal development extends from the moment of birth to death, and is usually divided into five stages—infancy, early childhood, later childhood, adolescence, and adulthood. (*Note:* There often are comparable cognitive or social developments which occur at very similar times. These will be discussed later on.)

Infancy. Beginning at the moment of birth, infancy extends to about age two. During this period, there is a continued rapid growth rate and the development of motor and perceptual skills. By age two, the child's weight is approximately triple what it was at birth. The end of infancy is not marked by a particular event, but rather is designated as the point at which the child has established relative independence as a result of motor, social, and cognitive growth.

Early Childhood. The early childhood stage extends from age two until about age six. Motor, cognitive, and social development continue at a fairly rapid pace. The end of this period is marked by the fact that all *basic* skills seem well established.

EXAMPLE 1. At the end of infancy, a child can walk or run, stand or sit, and generally move about independently. During the next four years, motor development continues so that by age six, the child has the

37

capability for much more proficient movements, such as jumping, hopping, skipping, catching, balancing, or tiptoeing. While further competence can be expected to develop, basic skills are solidified fairly well by this time.

Later Childhood.   This period extends until the child reaches puberty. The time for the onset of puberty varies considerably, but typical development occurs at about age twelve or thirteen for girls, and about one-half year later for boys. Just before the actual beginning of puberty, there often is a period of very rapid physical growth called the *prepubertal growth spurt*.

Adolescence.   Adolescence extends from the onset of puberty until about age eighteen. The end of adolescence is marked by the relative completion of growth and the attainment of an adult body configuration.

Adulthood.   From the end of adolescence until death, a person is considered an adult. It should be noted that this designation usually is based upon physical characteristics; a person's social or cognitive skills may not develop at the same rate.

EXAMPLE 2.   In conversation, we often refer to a "mature" young person or an adult who "acts like a child." In these cases, the words *mature* and *child* do not refer to physical development, but to an attitude or behavioral style.

4.2   GROWTH TRENDS

Two growth trends occur almost universally in developing children—the *cephalo-caudal trend* and the *proximo-distal trend*.

Cephalo-caudal Trend

In general, the growth of the head end of the body can be expected to progress more rapidly than the growth of the lower portions of the body. This is true during both the prenatal and postnatal stages.

EXAMPLE 3.   A newborn child's head will seem disproportionately large if compared to the head of an adolescent or adult. The ratio of head size to body size is about 1 to 4 for a newborn. As the lower portions "catch up," the adult ratio is 1 to 8.

Proximo-distal Trend

In general, the growth and motor development of the central portions of the body progress more rapidly than the growth and motor development of the extremities. Again, this is true for both the prenatal and postnatal stages of development.

EXAMPLE 4.   Observation of the development of a child's arm and hand movements will show that initial attempts to reach for objects are gross movements of the entire arm. Only later does development allow independent use of the hand and fingers in a very sophisticated manner.

Individual Differences

There are general standards that seem to apply to the growth and development of all humans, but one very important point must be kept in mind: Any one person will have a unique growth pattern that may not fit exactly into the stages outlined above. This variation of growth rate (and cognitive and social development) is summarized by the term *individual differences*. Psychologists must be careful to recognize that each person's development must be treated as a unique case.

4.3   METHODS OF STUDY

The standard methods of psychological investigation described in Chapter 2 are used by developmental psychologists. In addition, developmental psychologists have come up with some specialized techniques for investigations in their field.

Longitudinal Investigations

Longitudinal investigations are studies conducted over a fairly long period of time, using the same subjects throughout. (These subjects may be used for any investigation in which age is the independent variable.)

Longitudinal investigations have certain advantages. Using them, it is possible to study the evolution of behavior within a single individual and to observe the effects of early experiences upon later behavior. Furthermore, because only one subject group is used throughout, the investigation can be sure that its hereditary patterns and experiences will be constant, and not an extraneous variable.

Longitudinal investigations also have some disadvantages. The length of time involved may lead to a fairly high expense, a fairly high subject dropout rate, or the possibility that by the time the study is completed, the problem investigated may no longer be of interest.

EXAMPLE 5. An investigator has identified two groups of children. By age five, one of these groups has had extensive exposure to educational toys. The other group has not had such experiences. Trying to determine what effects these experiences have on motor-skills capabilities, the investigator begins a two-year longitudinal study of the motor skills of both groups. Such a study would allow determination of the cumulative effects of the preschool experiences.

Cross-sectional Investigations

Cross-sectional investigations are studies that can be conducted rapidly. Using subjects in different age groupings, the investigator studies how age, the independent variable, affects behavior. These studies tend to be less expensive than longitudinal studies, but they lack the precision of experiential and hereditary control. The drop-out rate of subjects can be expected to be low.

EXAMPLE 6. Consider the longitudinal investigation of the effect of educational toys on motor development (Example 5). In a parallel cross-sectional study, the psychologist might select children at ages 3, 5, and 7 and subject them to the same tests of motor skills. The assumption is that the effects observed at any one age level would carry over to any other age level if the study could be prolonged (as in a longitudinal study). This assumption may be incorrect if any one group has a background significantly different from the others.

Retrospective Studies

Another method frequently used to collect developmental data is the *retrospective study*. Parents or other significant adults (such as teachers) are asked to recollect events from some past time concerning some individual. A retrospective study is often used because it is the only information-gathering method available. Psychologists who use this method, however, must take into account the possibility that a person's recollections or memories may be distorted or incomplete.

Developmental Scales

Developmental scales report the average, or "typical," behavior for children at different ages. The information is based upon data collected from the observation of a large number of children and can be used as a basis for comparisons.

Readiness and Critical Periods

As a special part of some investigations, developmental psychologists may try to determine when (or if) an individual is capable of learning a particular response. Two concepts have resulted from such studies, readiness and critical periods.

Readiness implies that appropriate development must have occurred before the learning can take place. Once the necessary level has been reached, the capability remains.

Critical periods also implies that appropriate development must have occurred before learning can take place, but in addition states that there is a cut-off point or time limitation which ends the period of capability or receptivity.

EXAMPLE 7. The lines in Fig. 4-1 represent the difference between readiness and critical periods.

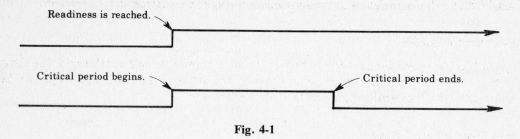

Fig. 4-1

Deprivation and Enrichment

Many children receive what can be called "normal" amounts of stimulation or opportunity. In some cases, the level may be varied considerably, and the effects of this variation may be observed.

Deprivation conditions exist when the level of stimulation or opportunity is significantly reduced. The usual result from a prolonged deprivation condition will be a level of accomplishment significantly below normal. Obviously, because of ethical considerations, this kind of condition cannot be tested experimentally on humans. (It can be observed only if it has occurred in some natural circumstance.) Research using lower organisms has helped provide information about the effects of deprivation.

Enrichment occurs when stimulation or opportunity is considerably above normal levels. In general, enrichment seems to produce beneficial results in terms of the development of motor, cognitive, or social skills.

4.4 PHYSICAL (MOTOR) DEVELOPMENT

Several different aspects of physical development are studied by psychologists. Some of these, such as height and weight and other physical characteristics, provide information which may then be correlated with behaviors. For example, what is the relationship between a subject's weight-height ratio and his or her performance on an agility test?

Psychologists also study other aspects of physical development, including the sequence of motor skills, sensory processing, and perceptual development. These may include studies relating to the progressive learning of eye-hand coordination, the development of sensory abilities, or the improvement of perceptual learning.

EXAMPLE 8. Research testing shape constancy (see Chapter 7) has shown that babies only eight weeks old are able to recognize and respond to shapes of objects to earn a reward, even when the objects are placed in new and different positions. The skill becomes more advanced as the child grows older and is eventually accompanied by the ability to label shapes correctly. This kind of sequence is very important to our understanding of the development of perceptual skills.

4.5 COGNITIVE DEVELOPMENT

Sequences of cognitive development can be identified in a manner similar to that used for physical development. Jean Piaget, a Swiss psychologist, has proposed a series of cognitive development stages which have been widely accepted.

Sensori-motor Stage

According to Piaget, the *sensori-motor stage* lasts from birth to about age two. Starting from a complete egocentrism and a failure to distinguish between self and outer reality, the child progresses to an understanding of sensations, develops perceptual skills, begins to understand cause-and-effect relationships, and creates intentional and anticipatory behaviors.

Pre-operational Stage

During the *pre-operational stage*, which lasts from about age two until seven, the child shows considerable progress in the ability to represent things by language, drawings, or symbolic play. Conceptualization and prelogical reasoning develop.

Concrete Operational Stage

From age seven until age eleven, the *concrete operational stage*, the child's thoughts are characterized by logic, the understanding of relationships, and the development of coordinated series of ideas. The child's thoughts are tied to concrete things, however, and abstract thought remains at a rudimentary level.

Formal Operational Stage

From eleven years until adulthood, during the *formal operational stage*, the child's thoughts progress to incorporate formal rules of logic. Abstract concepts become understandable, and the child can generalize from one situation to another. The child shows interest in the future and can use theories or hypotheses to propose what might happen.

EXAMPLE 9. Suppose a child is asked to describe the concept of heating the house. The child in the sensori-motor stage would only react with "It's hot," or "It's cold." A child in the preoperational stage might respond by saying, "Mom or Dad can change it with the dial." A child in the concrete operational stage might understand the relationship of the thermostat and the temperature level, but this understanding would be based upon the concrete operation of actually turning the thermostat's dial. At the formal operational level, the child could hypothesize relationships involving different kinds of thermostats or heating devices without necessarily having such objects available.

Piaget's theories stress the *sequence* of events in cognitive development. The ages are suggested as average or typical, but not necessarily binding. This emphasis on sequence tends also to underplay the *amount* of cognitive development, which is usually studied under the heading of intelligence. (See Chapter 20.)

4.6 LANGUAGE SKILLS

Development of language appears to be primarily a matter of a sequence and selective learning. All children seem to have the potential for learning any language and for some time are able to generate any required sounds. The sequence of development of language is basically the same for all languages, with reinforcement of specific modes of responding determining which particular language will be learned. (See Chapter 16 for more information on the development of language.)

4.7 SOCIAL DEVELOPMENT

Comparable to physical and cognitive skills, social characteristics have been studied in terms of sequences of development. Two aspects which appear to be important in social development are the growth of attachments and the display of independence (or detachment).

Attachment and Detachment

Attachment seems to develop in the first six months of life. Probably based upon various reward conditions, the child develops a relationship with the parents or other significant people (such as brothers and sisters).

In the second six months of the first year, the child has developed sufficient physical abilities to be able to move about in the environment. Coincident with this, the child begins to show detachment or independence. Frequently, display of such independence is first made only when a reassuring adult is nearby to reduce any potential fears.

Peer-Group Influence

A major facet of social development, which also appears to be sequential, is the attachment to or influence of *peers*, or age mates. In general, it has been found that as the child grows older, his or her values are more and more determined by what is acceptable to peers and are less influenced by the values of older persons.

Sex Roles

What is considered a "typical" or "acceptable" sex role seems to change with each succeeding generation. Some types of behavior are traditionally labelled "masculine" or "feminine," but the identification of sex roles changes constantly. Physiological differences obviously exist, but appropriate roles are in many cases determined not by physiological differences but by social influences.

EXAMPLE 10. Consider how men's hairstyles change. Both the "acceptable" length of hair and the "acceptable" amount of facial hair have varied tremendously in recent years, depending on society's whim. On the other hand, a stereotype such as "men are the warriors" has persisted largely unchallenged for a much longer period of time.

Aggression and Cooperation

The development of aggressive and cooperative characteristics seems to occur in much the same way that the development of other behaviors occurs. Opportunities to express or practice such behaviors, models to imitate, and reinforcement for responding all play a role in determining how and when these characteristics are developed.

Many of the previously mentioned variables—such as physical growth, attachment, peer-group influences, or establishment of sex roles—may contribute to the pattern which emerges. Research has paid particular attention to the possible effects of modeling (see Chapter 13) on the development of aggression.

Moral Development

Moral development often is studied as a part of social development. Learning what is considered to be right and wrong (which is obviously a function of the society in which the child is living) seems to go through a sequence comparable to the other aspects of social, cognitive, and physical development.

Three stages of moral development have been identified. In the first, the *premoral stage*, the child behaves appropriately because of fear of punishment or the chance to receive a reward, but does not recognize any higher principle. Other people's expectations of conformity are the basis for the second stage, *conventional conformity*. The third stage, *self-accepted values*, is the final stage of moral development, with appropriate behavior determined by accepted abstract principles rather than by convention or by rewards and punishment.

EXAMPLE 11. A very young child might say it was wrong to steal from a store because you might get caught and punished. In the second stage, the child might feel stealing was acceptable because "everybody" does it; if the child did believe stealing was wrong, it would be because "good" people do not do things like that. In the third stage of moral development, the child would come to the conclusion that stealing was wrong because it was contrary to the principles of honesty and fairness.

Solved Problems

4.1   What is the difference between the word "maturation" as it is used in developmental psychology and the phrase "being mature" as it is used popularly? Is *maturation* the only concern of developmental psychology?

"Maturation" in developmental psychology refers specifically to physical growth, whereas "being mature" is a colloquial phrase used to describe a person (usually a child or adolescent) who acts more like an older individual than like his or her age mates. "Being mature" is not dependent upon physical growth.

Developmental psychology includes the study of maturation processes, but is more encompassing. Studying characteristics through the entire life-span—including physical development, cognitive development, and social development—may all be part of developmental psychology.

4.2   How much of the human life-span do developmental psychologists study?

As a group, developmental psychologists are concerned with the *entire* life-span, including both prenatal and postnatal development. Any one psychologist may be interested in only a part of the life-span, or any one behavior within the life-span. In other words, the study of developmental psychology may begin at the moment of conception and continue until death.

4.3   What are the prenatal stages of development and how do they differ from one another?

Three identifiable periods of prenatal development exist. The *germinal stage* is the initial period of cell division and covers the first two weeks after conception. During this period, there is no physical attachment between the fertilized ovum and mother.

At the beginning of the third week, attachment occurs. From then until the sixth week, very rapid growth continues during what is called the *embryonic stage*. At the end of this stage, the cell development of the embryo has progressed to a point where the basic physical features of the future child are identifiable.

The period from the end of the embryonic stage until birth (usually about the thirty-eighth week if the pregnancy is full-term) is called the *fetal stage*. During this time, physical growth continues very rapidly, although not as rapidly as in the preceding stages.

4.4   What characteristics identify the "cut-off points" for postnatal development?

The postnatal period is often divided into these five major stages:

Infancy (birth to two years): Rapid motor, cognitive, and social development brings the child from being almost totally dependent to being relatively independent by the end of this period.

Early Childhood (two to six years): By the end of this period, basic motor, language, and social skills have been developed. Although these skills may grow more sophisticated, the basic patterns are established by the end of early childhood.

Later Childhood (six to twelve years): The completion of later childhood is marked by the onset of puberty. The majority of children reach puberty at about age twelve or thirteen, but variations are often found.

Adolescence (twelve to eighteen years): After puberty, physical growth continues until adult stature is reached. This usually occurs by about age eighteen. Again, noticeable variations occur in some cases.

Adulthood (eighteen years to death): Although developmental processes appear to be completed at the point of entrance into adulthood, it should be noted that physical, cognitive, or social changes may continue to occur throughout life.

4.5 How fixed are these stages of development?

While all children progress through basically the same growth pattern, the age for completion of each stage may differ considerably. The general label for such variations is *individual differences*. An extreme variation—such as reaching puberty at age seven or age seventeen—represents how much difference may exist. In addition, there is a significant difference in growth rates between females and males. In general, until adolescence, females' physical development occurs before that of males.

4.6 What two growth trends are common to all human offspring? Do these growth trends appear only before birth?

Two human growth trends are found in *both* prenatal and postnatal development. The *cephalo-caudal* trend is the tendency of the head region to develop before and more rapidly than the lower parts of the body. The *proximo–distal* trend is the tendency for the central portions of the body to develop before and more rapidly than the extremities.

4.7 Can the onset of certain stages of development and the appearance of certain growth trends be influenced by environmental variables?

Environmental variables are very important in determining the way in which a human will develop. During the prenatal stages, environmental influences such as drugs or disease may slow down development. Postnatal environmental influences—such as home setting, language exposure, nutrition and diseases—may also affect development. The stages of development and growth trends do usually appear in a set sequence, but variations in the time of their appearance are inevitable, and may be influenced by the prenatal or postnatal environment. Parents must therefore learn that their child often may not be exactly like the "average" child.

4.8 What are the differences between cross-sectional and longitudinal investigations?

The most important difference is in the time taken to complete each type of investigation. Longitudinal studies are conducted over an extended period of time, while cross-sectional studies are usually completed very rapidly. This is because longitudinal studies use the same subjects throughout the investigation (for example, the same children at ages two, four, and six), whereas cross-sectional studies use different subjects in each group (children at ages two, four, and six are all studied simultaneously).

4.9 What are the advantages and disadvantages of longitudinal and cross-sectional studies?

One major advantage of a longitudinal study is that the experimenter can study the development of a group of subjects over a period of time while controlling, or at least observing, earlier experiences that may have affected development. Additionally, the hereditary patterns of each subject remain invariant. The three disadvantages cited most frequently are: longitudinal studies take a long time to complete, are often very expensive, and frequently show a fairly high subject dropout rate because subjects may no longer be available (if, for example, a subject's family moves).

Cross-sectional studies mirror the characteristics of longitudinal studies. In general, cross-sectional studies are completed rapidly, are relatively inexpensive, and usually have a very low subject dropout rate. However, the experiential and hereditary backgrounds of the subjects in each age group may differ significantly from those of other groups. This may make it difficult for the experimenter to make accurate comparisons of the behaviors of each group.

A psychologist must weigh the values of each of these techniques and then decide which to use.

4.10   What is a retrospective study? What are some of its advantages and disadvantages?

In a retrospective study, significant adults (often parents) are asked to recall events concerning the development of an individual during some previous time. Sometimes, these recollected reports are compared with information available from other sources (such as school records or medical records). Quite frequently, the recollection of the adult is found to be inaccurate or incomplete. Often the distortions produced create a version of the past event that is more favorable than what actually occurred. These distortions are not necessarily deliberate, but may represent instead mistakes of memory.

4.11   The stages of development are usually described in terms of developmental scales. What are these scales and how are they used in research?

Developmental scales describe the "average" or "typical" behavior for children of various ages. These averages are based upon data collected from the observation of a large number of children. For example, a longitudinal study of exceptionally bright children compared their growth and performance records with those of "typical" children to determine where similarities or differences existed.

4.12   What are *readiness* and *critical periods*? Give an example of each.

Readiness and critical periods both refer to that state in which an organism is first capable of performing some behavior. (The organism is unable to perform the particular behavior until the readiness stage is reached or the critical period has begun.) *Readiness* implies that once the organism has gained the ability to learn a behavior, it will continue indefinitely to have that ability. A *critical period*, on the other hand, lasts for only a particular time period; if the organism does not learn the behavior during the critical period, it will not be able to learn it later.

Readiness can be illustrated by a child's ability to walk. A one-month-old child simply does not have sufficient motor skills or physical growth to be able to walk. However, at a later date (often about twelve months) the child reaches readiness for this behavior. In other words, the child has gained the ability to learn to walk. At *any time* thereafter, the child could actually learn to walk.

A critical period can be illustrated by imprinting, which occurs early in the life of certain organisms (for example, ducklings or chicks). Imprinting appears as a following-and-attachment response generated by moving objects in the environment. Generally, the moving object is the mother, although many other moving stimuli have been used to successfully demonstrate imprinting. If having a moving object in the environment does not occur during the critical period, imprinting becomes almost impossible. In other words, after the critical period is over, the duckling or chick loses the ability to learn the imprinting response.

4.13   The directors of a community preschool program wish to help parents, teachers, and other adult leaders to recognize those situations that encourage and those that hinder child development. To this end, they hire a developmental psychologist to speak to them. The psychologist titles her presentation "Deprivation and Enrichment." What would be the basic points of her talk?

The psychologist points out that deprivation means "doing without," and that research studies have shown that depriving children of opportunities to develop usually results in an incomplete or reduced level of accomplishment. The psychologist indicates that all children should be supported so that normal motor, cognitive, and social skills will develop. For example, the psychologist might suggest that parents not use "baby talk" when speaking to the children. ("Baby talk" would deprive the children of the chance to hear and learn from models of standard adult English.)

The talk continues with the suggestion that something more than minimal support may be very beneficial for the children. The psychologist calls this *enrichment* of the environment and informs the audience of the vast potentials which children have that may be developed if opportunities exist.

The caution is given that hereditary traits may place some limits upon just what characteristics will develop, but the benefits of enrichment are stressed. The psychologist might suggest, for example, that story-telling and conversational activities be provided in an attempt to give the children opportunities to develop their verbal skills.

4.14   How are motor development, cognitive development, and social development similar? How do they differ?

They are similar in that all show stage development and all will reveal individual differences. They differ from each other in what they emphasize. Motor development emphasizes movement and muscular control and coordination. Cognitive development is concerned with an individual's ability to mentally process information. Social development stresses the individual's attachments to and independence from other individuals. All of these developmental areas overlap and influence one another; each is labelled by its primary concern rather than by any absolute separation.

4.15   In a clinic for recreation directors who work with preschool-age children, one program features speakers who discuss the basics of motor development. What are the major topics presented?

Most important is the topic of movement abilities. The sequence of events from birth to age four or five is stressed, along with the concepts of opportunity for practice and recognition of individual differences. Stress is placed on the fact that children will have developed basic motor skills by the end of the preschool period.

Other areas of importance include the expansion of sensory processing (see Chapter 6), perceptual skills (see Chapter 7), and the relationships of motor skills to cognitive and social development.

4.16   What is an example of a typical sequence of motor-skill development?

One of the most widely studied motor skills is walking. A typical development sequence for a child's first twelve to fourteen months would be:
1. chin up
2. chest up
3. sit with support
4. sit alone
5. stand with help
6. stand holding on
7. crawl
8. walk when led
9. walk alone

This would not complete the sequence, however. Continuing development would result in the child's ability to jump, negotiate sharp turns, tiptoe, hop, skip, and go up and down stairs without difficulty. (Comparable sophistication of hand use could be illustrated.)

4.17   Do the development of sensory processes, perceptual skills, cognitive skills, and social characteristics contribute to the development of motor skills?

Yes. Motor skills are very much dependent upon information that is received. Sensory processes convert the physical energy of the environment into nerve impulses; perceptual skills interpret these sensations and make the environment understandable; cognitive skills and social characteristics allow communication, interpretation, and reinforcement of motor behavior so that movement skills may continue to become more sophisticated.

4.18 Is it possible to describe cognitive development as a series of stages?

Very careful and extensive study of cognitive processes by the Swiss psychologist Jean Piaget has led to identification of the following stages of cognitive development.

Sensori-motor (birth to two years): Child learns the difference between the self and other objects, the influence of action upon the environment, and the concept of object permanence. (See Problem 4.19.)

Pre-operational (two to seven years): Child learns the use of language, more sophisticated classification of objects, the use of numbers, and the principle of conservation. (See Problem 4.19.)

Concrete operational (seven to eleven years): Child becomes capable of logical thought and continues to develop ideas of relationships, but uses abstract terms only in relation to concrete objects.

Formal operational (eleven years and up): Child can think in abstract terms, can create and reason by hypotheses, and shows concern for the future and for ideological problems.

(*Note*: The age levels of the stages of cognitive development closely parallel the growth stages given in Problem 4.4.)

4.19 Specifically, what are the cognitive development principles of *object permanence, conservation*, and *concrete operations versus formal operations*?

Object permanence means that the child understands that something continues to exist even when it cannot be directly observed. For example, the sun is there, although blocked from view by the clouds.

Conservation refers to the child's ability to recognize that properties such as number, mass, or weight do not change simply because the materials are rearranged. For example, the amount of fluid remains the same when poured from a short, squat glass into a tall, thin glass.

Concrete operations mean that cognitive processes are intimately tied to actual objects, whereas *formal operations* can be wholly abstract. For example, the child's decisions regarding weight relationships would require the actual presence of weights in the concrete operational stage, but not in the formal operational stage.

4.20 What two characteristics are the basic indicators of social development?

The most outstanding characteristics of social development are the growth of *affiliation* (or attachment) and *independence* (or detachment) in the child. Social development seems to take two parallel courses: (1) learning to interact with others and (2) establishing self-identity. Some of the behaviors that typify these processes include attachment to and identification with parents, peer-group influence, the development of sex roles, the display of aggression, and moral development.

4.21 Attachment and detachment are obviously contradictory motives. How, then, do both develop in the same individual?

Attachment, commonly to parents, appears to develop during the first half-year of life; by the second half-year, it is strongly in evidence. Exactly what variables influence attachment is still questioned, but parental reinforcements and contact comfort are suggested as examples of favorable conditions for attachment.

Detachment, or independence, seems to begin when the child becomes capable of moving about in the environment. (This usually occurs during the second half of the first year.) At this time, the child becomes more independent while simultaneously showing strong attachment. The detachment responses (or independence) are often practiced while the parent is nearby to provide support if the child is threatened. Attachment thus complements the development of detachment.

4.22   Parents are often amazed at the values their children come to express. What would research on peer-group influence indicate about the development of values?

What the parents often do not realize is that peer-group influence becomes more and more important as a child grows older. While the parent serves as a model for young children, continued interaction with age-mates assumes greater importance in determining the older child's values. This results in adoption of values that may differ significantly from those held by the parents.

4.23   Are "traditional" sex roles an outgrowth of a child's social development?

They seem to be. Many individuals might claim to be able to describe inherently "masculine" and "feminine" characteristics, but sex roles appear to be changeable and affected by the customs of society. What is accepted as a "traditional" role by one generation is often changed by the next. Interestingly, the influence of peers and parents in the development of sex roles seems to be comparable to their influence on other behaviors.

4.24   What are the factors that seem to influence the development of cooperative and aggressive behavior?

Social reinforcement, the chance to view and imitate an appropriate model, and the opportunity to practice are all important contributors to the development of aggressive and cooperative behaviors. These behaviors may be tied to sex-role stereotypes, a particular family, or a certain cultural or subcultural environment.

Note: Much concern has been expressed regarding the possibility that many media presentations (including television, movies, and magazines) contain inappropriate models. Some research tends to support this concern.

4.25   Does moral development follow a sequence?

Much like many other behaviors, the development of moral behavior seems to follow a recognizable pattern of three stages. In the first, or *premoral*, stage, the child acts correctly because of fear of punishment or the possibility of reward, but does not understand the underlying principles. In the second stage, *conventional conformity*, the child recognizes "duty" and maintains order because that is what is expected. The third stage, *self-accepted values*, represents standards that involve conscience and principles. These stages appear to parallel cognitive development and other social developments.

Key Terms

Adolescence.   The fourth period of postnatal development, from approximately age twelve (the onset of puberty) to age eighteen.

Adulthood.   The fifth (and final) period of postnatal development; from approximately age eighteen on.

Attachment.   The relationship of a child to parents and other significant individuals; usually develops during the first six months of postnatal development.

Cephalo-caudal trend.   The tendency for the head to develop before and more quickly than the lower portions of the body.

Concrete operational stage.   According to Piaget, the third state of cognitive development; from approximately age seven to age eleven.

Critical period.   A state during which an organism is able to learn a new behavior; this state is limited in time—it has both a beginning and an end.

Cross-sectional study.　　An investigation that makes use of subjects of different age groups to determine how age, the independent variable, affects behavior.

Deprivation.　　Doing without; in developmental psychology, a significant reduction of stimulation or opportunity.

Detachment.　　The development of independent behavior; often occurs when an adult of high attachment status is nearby.

Developmental scale.　　Reports of average or typical behavior based upon data collected from large groups of individuals.

Early childhood.　　The second period of postnatal development; from approximately age two to age six.

Embryonic stage.　　The second period in prenatal development; from approximately the third week after conception until the end of the sixth week.

Enrichment.　　In developmental psychology, stimulation or opportunity considerably above normal levels.

Fetal stage.　　The third period in prenatal development, from approximately the seventh week until delivery; in a full-term pregnancy (of thirty-eight weeks), the last thirty-two weeks.

Formal operational stage.　　According to Piaget, the fourth (and final) stage of cognitive development; from approximately age eleven to age thirteen (or cognitive adulthood).

Germinal stage.　　The first period in prenatal development; from conception until approximately the end of the second week.

Infancy.　　The first period of postnatal development; from birth to approximately two years of age.

Later childhood.　　The third period of postnatal development; from approximately age six until age twelve (the onset of puberty).

Longitudinal study.　　An investigation conducted over a fairly long period of time, using the same subjects throughout; the study may be used to determine how age, the independent variable, affects behavior.

Maturation.　　In development psychology, the physical development of the body.

Mitosis.　　The process of cell division involving differentiation and the halving of chromosomes.

Peer-group influence.　　The attachment to and the effects of age mates; increasingly important as a child grows older.

Postnatal.　　After birth; the period of time from delivery until death.

Prenatal.　　Before birth; the period of time from conception to delivery.

Pre-operational stage.　　According to Piaget, the second stage of cognitive development; from approximately age two to age seven.

Proximo-distal trend.　　The tendency for the central portions of the body to develop before and more quickly than the peripheral portions.

Puberty.　　The physiological changes associated with adolescence; marked by the development of the capacity to reproduce and by the appearance of secondary sex characteristics.

Readiness.　　The state in which an organism is ready and able to learn a new behavior; once readiness is reached, the organism will always have the ability to learn the new behavior.

Retrospective study.　　An investigation involving recollected data reported by people who were significant in a person's life.

Sensori-motor stage.　　According to Piaget, the first stage of cognitive development; from birth to about age two.

Chapter 5

Physiological Psychology

Physical structure plays an important part in determining the behavior of an individual. Understanding how physical structures influence behavior entails study of the individual components of the nervous system and how these components are arranged into systems and subsystems.

5.1 ELEMENTS OF A NEURON

A *neuron* is a single cell made up of three basic elements—the *cell body* (which contains the nucleus), *dendrites*, and an *axon*. There are billions of neurons within the human body. The *neuron fibers* (dendrites and axons) are bunched together to form *nerves*, which carry signals throughout the body.

Cell Body

The cell body is the center of the neuron and serves to assimilate and make use of the nutrients that supply energy for neuron activity. Unlike the cell body of most other cells, a neuron's cell body has two different kinds of branches or extensions. These are the many dendrites and the single axon which extend from the cell body.

Dendrites

The "receiving" portion of the neuron is formed by the many dendrites. These are usually short and thin and may number more than a thousand for a single cell.

The dendrites receive (or sense) signals in the form of transmitter substances (see Section 5.2) from other nerve cells. If sufficient numbers of dendrites are excited, the signal is transmitted through the length of the cell as an impulse or wave.

Axon

Coming from the cell body, each neuron has only a single axon, although the axon may have branches at its end. The axon serves to conduct the impulse away from the cell body to its end; the axon then passes on the signal to the dendrites of the next neuron. Axons may vary in length from only several microns to several feet, depending upon the location of the particular cell.

While all of the neuron is covered by a cell membrane, many axons also are covered with a fatty substance called *myelin*. Myelinated axons will conduct impulses at a faster pace than will nonmyelinated axons.

EXAMPLE 1. An easy way to picture a myelinated axon is to think of a string of somewhat irregular beads. The axon is the "string," while the "beads" are the myelin. The signal seems to skip from gap to gap between the beads and progresses faster than a signal which flows smoothly through an unmyelinated axon.

5.2 TRANSMISSION OF A SIGNAL

Many factors are involved in signal transmission. Essentially, each signal travels the length of a cell and then crosses a gap to the next cell, where the process of transmission is repeated. Cells

50

differ in their capacity to transmit and in the type of signal transmitted, but the basic process of all transmissions is the same.

Synapse

A signal originally reaches a cell when a transmitter substance that is secreted by the axon of one cell crosses a gap between that axon and the dendrite of the next cell. This gap is called a *synapse*.

Synapses are one-way connections. Signals pass from axon to dendrite, but do not travel in the opposite direction. In most cases, the signals are received by the dendrites of the next cell, although occasionally cell bodies or axons receive messages across a synapse.

Transmitter Substance

At the end of each axon, there is a bulge or knob which holds the synaptic vesicles. As a signal reaches the end of the axon, these vesicles discharge a chemical called the *transmitter substance*, which is received by the next cell.

Graded Potential

Synapses may be either *excitatory* or *inhibitory*; that is, the transmitter substances either tend to activate or constrain the firing of the next cell. The sum of excitation and inhibition is called the *graded potential*. When the messages transmitted across the various synapses leading to the next cell surpass that cell's threshold for firing, it is activated and transmits a signal throughout its length.

EXAMPLE 2. Imagine a fountain pen full of ink. When you pull the lever on the side of the pen, ink will squirt out and be absorbed by a piece of paper. The synapse works in a similar fashion. When the transmitter chemicals are released from the axon, they cross the gap and are absorbed by the dendrites. Just as the ink cannot be released by the paper and replaced in the pen, the transmitter chemicals are not released by the dendrite and cannot return to the axon.

All-or-None Principle

If the graded potential is sufficient to cause a neuron to fire, the signal will always travel the entire length of the cell. There is no possibility that a signal can deteriorate and "die" within the length of a single cell. Thus, the firing of the cell is described by what is called the *all-or-none principle*. Each neuron fires at a fixed intensity; that is, the intensity is the same for every firing of the cell.

Resting Potential

In a resting state, the cell membrane of a neuron maintains a certain level of permeability (penetrability) such that the inside of the cell is slightly negative in electrical charge when compared to the outside. This relationship is called the *resting potential* of the neuron and exists because positive sodium ions (Na^+) are kept out of the cell by the membrane, while positive potassium ions (K^+) and negative chloride ions (Cl^-) can get in.

Action Potential

When the graded potential surpasses the neuron threshold, the signal passes through the length of the cell as an *action potential*. The action potential travels much like a wave.

The permeability of the axon membrane nearest the cell body shows a swift change, and the electrical charges reverse so that the inside of the cell becomes positive and the outside negative. This is called *depolarization*.

Although there is a rapid repolarization of the activated region, the signal does not fade. Rather, the adjoining section of the axon depolarizes. This depolarization-repolarization sequence repeats itself, conducting the impulse through the length of the axon.

EXAMPLE 3. Envision someone lighting a non-filter cigarette. If the match is held too far from the end, the cigarette will not light. Once the heat is sufficient, however, the ciagarette starts to burn. Now suppose the person places the cigarette in an ashtray and ignores it while it continues to burn. Eventually, the cigarette will burn completely.

A nerve signal operates in the same fashion. It does not fire unless the stimulus strength is sufficient; but once it is started, it goes through the entire length of the fiber. (*Note*: The axon has an advantage which the cigarette does not have—when the axon has completed its task, it can repolarize and fire again. The tobacco, on the other hand, turns to ash and cannot be reconstituted.)

Refractory Phase

The *refractory phase* is the period of time required for repolarization of the cell. Although this may be a very short period of time (less than 1/1000 second in some cases), no signal can pass through the cell during the first part of the refractory phase, called the *absolute refractory period*. The remainder of the refractory phase, called the *relative refractory period*, is the time during which the cell can be activated once again, but only if the excitation is stronger than normal.

EXAMPLE 4. Perhaps you have experienced a "personal refractory period" comparable to that of a neuron. Suppose you have devoted an immense amount of time and effort to studying for an exam. It may be that you are truly "studied out," and feel you need a recovery period. If you do not have another exam scheduled immediately, it may be possible to take a good, long rest before starting to study again. However, another important exam soon after may mean that your motivation is so high that you will take a short rest break (absolute refractory period) and then start studying again even though you are not yet fully rested (relative refractory period).

Signal Strength

The action potential is always of the same intensity for every firing of a neuron. The strength of a signal is thus dependent on factors other than the size of the action potential. Three variables appear to contribute to the identification of signal strength—the *frequency* with which any one neuron is being fired, the total *number* of neurons being fired by the signal, and the particular *route* of the neurons being fired. In general, a greater frequency of firing and a greater number being fired indicates greater intensity of signal. The route of the signal determines the particular type of stimulation that will be coded as a result of the signal.

5.3   ARRANGEMENT OF THE NERVOUS SYSTEM

The billions of neurons that make up the nervous system of the human body can be categorized into two divisions—the *central nervous system* (CNS) and the *peripheral nervous system* (PNS). Each has subdivisions that function in specialized ways.

The Central Nervous System

The central nervous system is composed of two major subdivisions, the brain and the spinal cord. These two parts are joined at the base of the brain so that there is a constant passage of signals to and from the brain and body.

The CNS is encased in protective bone, with the skull surrounding the brain and the backbone surrounding the spinal cord. Both parts receive sensory messages from the *afferent* (sensory) part of the peripheral nervous system and both can send signals to muscles and glands by connecting with the *efferent* (motor and autonomic) part of the peripheral nervous system.

In general, the spinal cord serves two major functions: (1) carrying impulses back and forth from the body to brain or brain to body; and (2) controlling many reflexes. The brain controls many more sophisticated functions, including perception, memory, voluntary movements, and many basic functions such as breathing or swallowing. (Brain signals may even modify actions which occur at the spinal-cord level.)

Structure and Function of the Brain

The brain seems to have developed three layers in an evolutionary fashion. The first two layers form what is called the "old brain." The third layer is called the "new brain." Most of the first layer now forms a *central core* for the brain and controls basic, rudimentary behaviors. The second layer contains the *limbic system* and exercises control over sequential activities and emotions. The third, most recently developed layer is the *cerebrum*. The cerebrum controls higher mental processes.

EXAMPLE 5. Picture cutting open a regular golf ball. The inner core is comparable to the central core, basic to the construction of the ball. The windings around the inner core are comparable to the limbic system, necessary to coordinate the functions of the ball and surrounding the core while lying within the cover. The cover is comparable to the cerebrum: last to be put on, dimpled as the outer layer of the cerebrum is convoluted, and essential to the function of the ball.

Central core. The central core, which was the layer of the brain that first developed, includes the *medulla, thalamus, hypothalamus,* and *cerebellum*; it has as its center the *reticular activating system*. The behaviors controlled by the central core include basic survival functions such as breathing, eating, drinking, arousal, coordination, regulation of temperature, and sexual activity. (See Fig. 5-1).

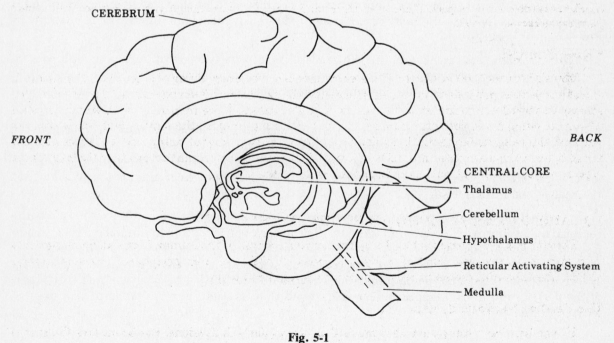

CEREBRUM

FRONT   BACK

CENTRAL CORE
Thalamus
Cerebellum
Hypothalamus
Reticular Activating System
Medulla

Fig. 5-1

Limbic system. The second layer of the brain, the limbic system, surrounds the central core. It seems to function in a coordinated fashion with the hypothalamus to program the sequences of activities necessary to satisfy the basic needs regulated by the hypothalamus. The system apparently has a regulating function for emotional behaviors also. If damaged, unusual emotional response patterns may appear.

Cerebrum. The third and most highly evolved layer of the brain, the cerebrum, is composed of two *cerebral hemispheres.* The outer layer of these hemispheres is called the *cortex.* The cerebrum is concerned with higher mental activities; complex mental skills are controlled by the cortex.

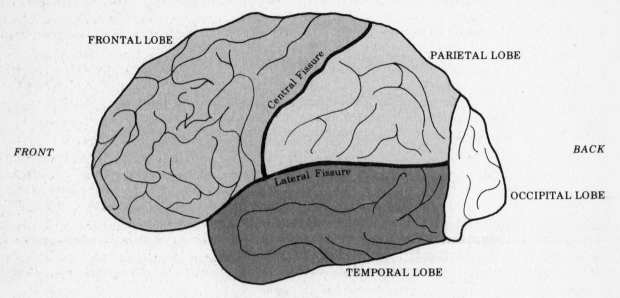

Fig. 5-2

Careful study of the cerebral hemispheres has allowed a labelling of specific areas and a "mapping" of many of their functions. (Some of the most important functions are mapped in Problem 5.19.) See Fig. 5-2.

Central fissure and lateral fissure. While all of the cortical surface of the brain is convoluted (wrinkled), two especially deep convolutions appear. The central fissure runs from the top middle of the brain toward the center side; the lateral fissure runs from the lower front of the brain toward the center side.

Cortical lobes. Each cerebral hemisphere is divided into four lobes. The *frontal lobe* is in the area from the front of the central fissure all the way to the front of the lateral fissure. The *parietal lobe* goes from the rear of the central fissure to the center back of the brain. The *occipital lobe* is the lower back portion of the brain. The *temporal lobe* is the area from the front of the occipital lobe to the rear of the lateral fissure.

Localized functions. A number of functions have been identified for different areas of the cerebral hemispheres. The *motor area* is found in the back portion of the frontal lobe cortex, just in front of the central fissure. Just to the rear of the central fissure, in the front of the parietal lobe, is the *sensory area.* *Vision* is located at the very back of the brain, in the occipital lobe. Hearing, speech understanding, and speech production are located near the lateral fissure. Much of the rest of the cortex remains unmapped, but it is believed that association and memory functions are located there.

Corpus callosum. The corpus callosum is a thick band of fibers connecting the cerebral hemispheres. These fibers serve as the pathway for signals to travel from one side of the brain to the other. These fibers may be made temporarily non-functional, by using a technique called spreading depression; they may also be permanently detached by surgical cutting. Research evidence indicates that the two halves of the brain may operate independently. In general, such studies have shown that over 90 percent of the population is left-hemisphere dominated. (*Note*: Because of a crossing-over of control, the left hemisphere controls the functions of the right side of the body.)

EXAMPLE 6. "Split-brain" research has shown that language skills usually depend upon left-hemisphere functioning. Suppose a subject has had the corpus callosum severed and is shown the word "matchbox" so that "match" is transmitted to the right hemisphere and "box" to the left hemisphere. The subject will be able to report seeing only the word "box." When asked what kind of box, the subject may guess "shoebox," or "hatbox," only getting "matchbox" by chance.

Electrical Stimulation of the Brain

Electrical stimulation of the brain (ESB) is accomplished by implanting electrodes into brain tissue and delivering mild electric shocks. This technique has been used to determine what functions appear to be affected when different areas of the brain are stimulated and has helped with the mapping of the brain. ESB also has been shown to serve as a reinforcement or aversive stimulus, depending upon the electrode placement and experimental therapeutic uses have been investigated. Much more information regarding uses of ESB remains to be gathered, but ethical problems may place limitations upon the extent of such study.

The Peripheral Nervous System

The peripheral nervous system (PNS) has two subdivisions—the *somatic system* (concerned with sensory and motor functions) and the *autonomic system* (which controls the functions of many glands and smooth-muscle organs). The somatic system, especially the sensory processes and perception, is treated thoroughly in Chapters 6 and 7.

The autonomic system is further divided into the sympathetic and parasympathetic divisions. Although there are some exceptions, these divisions usually work in an antagonistic, or opposite, manner.

Sympathetic system. To either side of the thoracic and lumbar (middle) portions of the spinal cord, there are chains of nerve fibers and cell bodies linked to both the spinal cord and to various visceral organs. These are the *sympathetic chains*. This system tends to act as a unit and is involved primarily with aroused or excited activity.

Parasympathetic system. The fibers of the parasympathetic system connect with many of the same visceral organs as the sympathetic system. These fibers originate in the cervical (top) and sacral (bottom) portions of the spinal cord. They tend to operate independently and are involved with quiet, recuperative functions.

The autonomic system is so named because many of its functions are automatic and self-regulating, continuing whether or not conscious thought is involved.

EXAMPLE 7. Antagonistic functioning within the autonomic nervous system can be illustrated by the inhibition of bladder release caused by the sympathetic system and the stimulation of bladder release caused by the parasympathetic system. Another illustration is the sympathetic system's inhibition of digestion and the parasympathetic system's facilitation of digestive processes. (*Note*: In extreme emotional situations, parasympathetic control may override sympathetic functioning, causing an involuntary discharge of the bladder.)

5.4 THE GLANDULAR SYSTEMS

The human body contains two sets of glands which are important for body functions—the *exocrine glands* and the *endocrine glands*. In general, exocrine glands secrete fluids to the outer surfaces of the body, while endocrine glands secrete *hormones*, distinctive chemicals which carry "messages" through the bloodstream to certain areas of the body.

Hormones are essential to the proper functioning of the body, helping to control growth, nervous system activity, levels of energy, moods, and reactions to stress. The nervous system controls the activity of many of the endocrine glands, but some react directly to body conditions.

Pituitary Gland

The *pituitary gland* has been designated as the body's "master gland." Connected to the hypothalamus, the pituitary gland secretes more different hormones than does any of the other endocrine glands. These hormones control numerous bodily processes, including activities such as milk production in the mammary glands, the sequence of body growth, and the actions of other endocrine glands. The pituitary gland's connection with the brain provides an important interaction between the nervous system and the endocrine system.

Other Endocrine Glands

Several other endocrine glands provide good examples of the importance of this system in the overall functioning of the body. The *adrenal glands* secrete adrenalin and noradrenalin, hormones which help the organism to prepare for emergencies and to cope with stress. The *gonads* (sex glands) secrete hormones concerned with sexual development, activity, and receptivity. The *thyroid* hormones help control the overall activity level of the body.

EXAMPLE 8. Knowledge of hormonal control has allowed medical adjustments for physiological problems. Thus, the surgical necessity to remove the thyroid gland can be compensated for by appropriate dosage of thyroxin (one of the gland's hormones) so that an appropriate activity level can be maintained.

Solved Problems

5.1   Sketch and label a simplified diagram of a neuron.

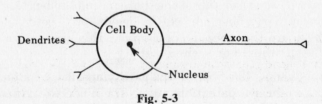

Fig. 5-3

5.2   Briefly describe the function of each of the parts of a neuron.

The dendrite is the "receiver part" of the neuron, picking up signals transmitted from other nerves or from external stimuli. The cell body, with its nucleus, has the specialized functions of absorbing and using nutrients to provide energy for the neuron activities. The axon is the "transmitter part" of the neuron, carrying impulses from the neuron to other nerves or parts of the body.

5.3   How do axons and dendrites "hook up"? Sketch a simplified diagram to illustrate your answer.

There is a gap between the axon of one neuron and the dendrite of the next. This gap is called the synapse. (See Fig. 5-4.)

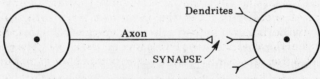

Fig. 5-4

The synaptic gap means there is not a direct physical contact between the axon and the dendrite. The signal is carried across the synaptic gap by a transmitter substance released by the axon.

5.4   If a transmitter substance is released by the axon, will the next neuron (the one across the synapse) always fire?

Synapses may be either excitatory or inhibitory; that is, the substance transmitted across the gap may either "encourage" or "discourage" the next nerve to fire. Only if the receiving neuron gets enough excitation and not too much inhibition will it fire.

5.5   Do signals ever go from the dendrite of one neuron to the axon of another?

No. The transmission of signals in the nervous system is a *one-way process*. The transmission of signals, whether they are excitatory or inhibitory, always goes from an axon to the next nerve. Usually, the transmitter substance is received by the dendrite of the next cell, but cell bodies and axons also can receive messages across a synapse.

5.6   Are a neuron and a nerve the same thing?

Neurons are individual cells comprised of dendrites, a cell body with a nucleus, and an axon. *Nerves* are bundles of neuron fibers (dendrites and axons) which transmit signals over some distance within the body. The neuron cell bodies are not part of the long nerves, but rather are grouped together in *ganglia* found near the brain, spinal cord, and some internal organs.

5.7   What is myelin and how does it affect the functioning of the nerve fibers?

Myelin is a fatty, bead-like sheath which surrounds certain nerve fibers (myelinated fibers). In general, signals travel faster and with less expenditure of energy in myelinated fibers than they do in unmyelinated fibers.

5.8   How does a signal pass through a neuron?

Whether a signal goes through a neuron or not is a function of several related properties. The input of both excitatory and inhibitory stimulation to the neuron is summated in the cell body. If the excitatory potential (called the graded potential) reaches a certain level, the axon "fires," much like a rifle, carrying the signal along its length. This signal is then transmitted to a dendrite or to a body organ.

The actual "firing" of the axon either occurs or it does not—there is no intermediate level. This is called the all-or-none principle. Before the axon fires, it is in a state called the resting potential. When it fires, an electrical charge called an action potential passes along its length.

5.9   What is the difference between a resting potential and an action potential? Can the action potential transmit different kinds of messages?

In a resting state, the cell membrane has a certain level of permeability which keeps out positively charged sodium ions (Na^+) while allowing in potassium ions (K^+) and negatively charged chloride ions (Cl^-). Thus, the inside of the cell is slightly negative compared to the outside.

When the axon is stimulated, the potential across the membrane is reduced. If this reduction in potential is great enough, a sudden change in membrane permeability occurs and the charges reverse—the outside is now slightly negative compared to the inside. This change affects the adjacent portion of the axon, and the process repeats itself along the entire length of the axon. This is the neural impulse, or action potential, which remains the same size throughout transmission.

A neuron always fires with exactly the same action potential. Thus, the signal (or "message") transmitted does not depend on the size of the action potential. Instead, the strength of the signal depends on the frequency with which a particular neuron is fired and the number of neurons firing at a particular moment. The type of message caused by the signal is determined by the pathway of the firing neurons.

5.10 The change in permeability of the membrane and the subsequent flow of ions is described by a particular term. What is this term and what does it mean?

The term describing the change in membrane permeability and the flow in ions is *depolarization*. Depolarization occurs when the graded potential reaches or surpasses the cell threshold; there is a subsequent switch of negative potential from inside to outside.

5.11 Does an axon that has become depolarized stay that way as long as there is stimulation?

The transmission of an action potential is a brief burst (or firing) which is followed by a recovery period called the refractory phase. During the refractory phase, the cell is at first temporarily inactive and cannot transmit a signal. Later, the cell can transmit a signal, but only if the graded potential is especially strong. Each transmission of a signal along an axon represents a depolarization; each refractory phase allows polarization to recur.

5.12 Are there different designations for the parts of the refractory phase? How long does the refractory phase last?

The two parts of the refractory phase are called the *absolute refractory period* (during which no signal can be transmitted) and the *relative refractory period* (during which only a strong graded potential will fire the cell). The entire refractory phase lasts only a few thousandths of a second.

5.13 The human body contains billions of neurons that make up the nervous system. What are the general designations for the different parts of the nervous system? What are the basic functions of each of these parts?

The nervous system is classified into two major divisions—the central nervous system (CNS) and the peripheral nervous system (PNS).

The CNS receives sensory messages via what is called the *afferent* nervous system. The CNS then processes or acts upon these and self-generated messages and initiates signals to be sent to all areas of the body via the nerves that comprise the *efferent system*.

The PNS conducts information from the various bodily organs to the CNS and takes the messages sent from the CNS to the organs. The PNS has two sub-divisions, the *autonomic nervous system* and the *somatic nervous system*. The autonomic nervous system is concerned primarily with control of internal body organ functions; the somatic nervous system carries messages to and from the sense receptors, muscles, and the body surface.

5.14 What are the major parts of the central nervous system? How are they alike and how do they differ?

The central nervous system has two important subdivisions—the brain and the spinal cord. They are linked continuously, so that the flow of messages remains unbroken from brain to body and from body to brain. Each is well protected by a bony structure: the spinal cord by the backbone and the brain by the skull.

The most important differences between the brain and spinal cord is the complexity of function which may occur in each. The spinal cord is capable of relaying many messages and of carrying out simple stimulus-response sequences, such as reflexes. The brain can handle much more complex functions and can modify even the simple functions which occur at the spinal-cord level.

5.15 Are there specific areas of the brain that control certain aspects of behavior?

The brain appears to have developed in layers. Evolution has progressed to the point that the brain is now viewed as having three of these layers: a first layer with a central core, which controls "primitive" behaviors; the limbic system, which is concerned with emotions and sequential activities; and the cerebrum, which is the location for higher mental processes.

5.16 What are the components of the first layer and central core? Name some examples of the "primitive" behaviors controlled there.

The central core seems to begin as an extension of the spinal cord with a structure called the medulla. Within this and several other parts of the central core is an area called the reticular activating system. Other parts of this "old brain" structure include the cerebellum, thalamus, and hypothalamus.

The kinds of behaviors controlled here include breathing, arousal or awareness, motor coordination, sleep and wakefulness, eating, drinking, temperature, and sex.

5.17 What purposes are served by the limbic system?

The limbic system appears to interact with the hypothalamus in programming the sequences of activities necessary to satisfy some of the primitive drives. For example, feeding or mating are behaviors carried out in sequences unless damage has occurred to the limbic system. Then, even slight distractions may bring interruption and an inability to complete the behavior.

In addition, the limbic system is involved in emotional responding. Damage in this area may produce unusual emotional patterns, such as inappropriate rage or complete docility even when under attack.

5.18 It was mentioned previously (Problem 5.15) that the cerebrum is the location for higher mental processes. How well have these functions been "mapped"?

The outer surface of the cerebrum, the cerebral cortex, appears to control complex mental activity. Some of these activities, such as motor control, recognition of sensations, or speech control, have been "mapped" quite accurately. Other functions, not directly related to sensori-motor processes, are less well identified. These include functions such as associations, memories, problem-solving, and sophisticated differentiations. (See Fig. 5-5.)

5.19 Sketch a "map" of the sensori-motor functions of the cerebral cortex.

(See Fig. 5-5.)

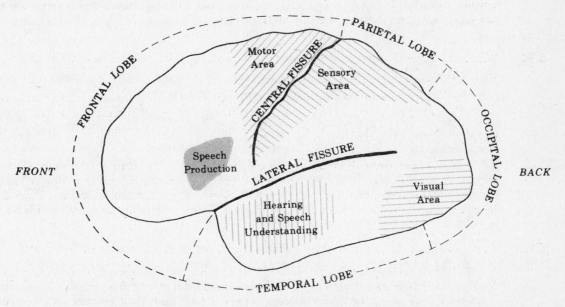

Fig. 5-5

5.20 If the remaining areas remain unmapped, how is it known that certain behaviors are controlled by them?

Research using organisms which have had damage to these areas has revealed what functions have been lost. In addition, occasional opportunities to stimulate some of the association areas with an electrical probe have shown that events of the past (memories) can be "turned on or off" by application or removal of the stimulus. However, the investigations have not revealed sufficient information as yet to allow definitive or unqualified identifications of these areas.

5.21 The corpus callosum appears to have a special function in the structure of the brain. What is this function and what happens when it is disrupted or terminated?

The corpus callosum is a broad band of fibers which connects the two cerebral hemispheres. It functions to relay messages from one side of the brain to the other. When this function is disrupted by using a technique called spreading depression or is terminated by a surgical cutting of the fibers, the two hemispheres operate independently. These "split-brain" experiments have provided information for localization of function and have illustrated that most individuals are left-hemisphere dominated.

5.22 In addition to revealing interesting demonstrations of memories, what other information has been obtained from electrical stimulation of the brain (ESB)?

The "mapping" of the brain (see Problem 5.19) has been greatly aided by the use of electrical probes. ESB also has been used as a reinforcer. Placed appropriately, ESB can be a stronger reinforcer than food or other positive reinforcers. In some experimental therapy situations, ESB has helped patients cope with certain symptoms. However, ESB may also be aversive, depending upon placement of the electrode. (*Note*: The possible uses of ESB raises a number of ethical questions, including when ESB should be used and who should make decisions regarding its use.)

5.23 The brain map seems to indicate that sensory functions are located in the cerebral hemispheres. Does this mean that the somatic nervous system does not sense stimuli?

The somatic part of the peripheral nervous system *does* receive and transmit sensory signals, but the actual registration (or interpretation) of the signal is made in the CNS. This means that seeing, hearing, touching, and other sensations are completed only when the signals have reached the sensory areas of the brain. (A thorough treatment of these sensory processes is found in Chapter 6.)

5.24 Describe the autonomic nervous system. Why is it called autonomic? What are the basic controls which the autonomic nervous system exercises?

The autonomic nervous system is part of the peripheral nervous system. Subdivided into the sympathetic and parasympathetic systems, the autonomic system controls glands and smooth-muscle organs such as the heart, blood vessels, stomach, and intestines. The sympathetic part of the system has fibers located in *chains* which are found beside the spinal cord and are connected to various visceral organs. The parasympathetic fibers originate in the cervical region (above those of the sympathetic system) and in the sacral region (below the sympathetic system). The sympathetic and parasympathetic systems are called autonomic because they tend to operate in an involuntary (or self-regulating) fashion.

5.25 How do the functions of the sympathetic and parasympathetic systems differ?

Several aspects distinguish sympathetic and parasympathetic functioning. The sympathetic system tends to act as a unit and to prepare the body for activity. The parasympathetic system generally shows separate or particular functioning and operates when the body is in a relatively quiet state. Thus, the sympathetic system is primarily oriented toward energy expenditure and action, whereas the parasympathetic system tends to conserve energy and help with body recuperation.

5.26 Does this mean that the sympathetic and parasympathetic systems do not operate at the same time?

While many of the functions of these two systems do appear to be *antagonistic* (for example, heart rate is speeded by the sympathetic system and slowed by the parasympathetic system), some functioning occurs when both systems are active at once or operate in sequence. Some of these interactions are understood. For example, the male sex act requires parasympathetic stimulation for erection and sympathetic stimulation for ejaculation. Many more interactions of the sympathetic and parasympathetic systems remain to be studied.

5.27 What system, other than the nervous system, carries messages to various parts of the body? How is this accomplished?

The autonomic nervous system acts upon the endocrine glands, stimulating the glands to produce hormones. The hormones serve as chemical communicators, circulating throughout the body via the bloodstream but affecting only particular, "key" organs. This endocrine system helps control growth, sex behavior, level of energy, reaction to stress, and even the functioning of the nervous system.

5.28 The pituitary gland has been called the "master gland" of the endocrine system. Why is that?

The pituitary gland has been called the "master gland" because it secrets the largest number of different hormones. (Many of these hormones control the hormonal output of other endocrine glands.) However, it is important to note that much of the activity of the pituitary gland and other glands in the endocrine system is monitored by the brain. Thus, there is a complex interaction between the nervous system and the endocrine system.

5.29 What are other examples of endocrine glands, and what functions do they help to control?

The adrenal glands and the thyroid gland are two very important endocrine glands. The adrenals secrete adrenalin and noradrenalin, two hormones which help the body prepare for heightened activity, such as in an emergency or in competition. The thyroid gland secretes thyroxin and other hormones. Thyroxin activates chemical reactions which help control the activity level of the body. Too little thyroxin may make an individual tired and sluggish; too much thyroxin may result in hyperactivity.

5.30 Do the endocrine and exocrine glands function in the same way?

Endocrine and exocrine glands do *not* function in the same manner. The endocrine glands secrete hormones directly into the bloodstream. The exocrine glands secrete fluids onto body surfaces or into body cavities. (Sweat glands or salivary glands are examples of exocrine glands.)

5.31 Why are psychologists interested in physiology?

Much physiological information is gathered simply to increase our knowledge about bodily functions. Often, however, practical applications of this information can help psychologists predict or control behavior. For example, understanding the endocrine system has produced data regarding the activity of the pancreas and its hormone, insulin. Diabetics have profited greatly from this by being able to regulate their bodily processes and thus gain better control over their behaviors. Furthermore, experimental testing has shown that insulin shock can be used in certain therapy situations. (Such treatment is now rarely used in therapy situations.)

Key Terms

Action potential.   The signal which passes through a neuron.

All-or-none principle.   The finding that a signal, once started, will always travel the entire length of a neuron at a fixed intensity.

Autonomic nervous system (ANS).   That part of the peripheral nervous system that controls the function of many glands and smooth-muscle organs; divided into the sympathetic and parasympathetic systems.

Axon.   The single long fiber extending from the cell body of a neuron; carries the signal to the synapse.

Cell body.   The central part of a neuron, from which extend the axon and the dendrites.

Central nervous system (CNS).   Basically, the brain and spinal cord.

Cerebrum.   The two cerebral hemispheres, controlling the more sophisticated mental processes of an individual; covered by the cortex.

Corpus callosum.   The broad band of fibers which connects the cerebral hemispheres.

Cortex.   Evolutionarily, the most recently developed portion of the brain; involved with higher mental processes.

Cortical lobes.   The four somewhat arbitrarily designated divisions of the cortex.

Dendrite.   The branched fibers which serve as the receiving portion of a neuron.

Depolarization.   The process by which the electrical charge of a neuron reverses during the passage of an action potential.

Endocrine glands.   Glands which secrete hormones directly into the bloodstream.

Exocrine glands.   Glands which secrete fluids onto the body's surface or into its cavities.

Frontal lobe.   The area of the cortex from the front of the central fissure to the front of the lateral fissure.

Graded potential.   The sum of the excitation and inhibition at a given synapse.

Hormones.   Distinctive chemicals, secreted by endocrine glands, which carry information ("instructions") to certain areas of the body.

Limbic system.   Circuits which extend from the cortex to the lower brain centers.

Myelin.   A fatty substance which covers many axons, usually surrounding the axon in a bead-like arrangement.

Nerve.   A collection of neuron fibers (axons and dendrites).

Neuron.   The basic structural unit of the nervous system, composed of a cell body, an axon, and one or more dendrites.

Occipital lobe.   The lower back portion of the cortex.

Parasympathetic system.   That part of the autonomic nervous system primarily involved with the recuperative functions of the body.

Parietal lobe.   The area of the cortex from the rear of the central fissure to the central back of the brain.

Peripheral nervous system (PNS).   Those nerves outside the central nervous system; it has two subdivisions, the somatic and autonomic systems.

Refractory phase.   The recovery period of time required by a neuron before another signal may be conducted.

Resting potential.   The nonactivated state of a neuron, in which the inside of the cell is slightly negative in potential when compared to the outside.

Reticular activating system (RAS).   The center of the oldest part of the brain, known to control basic survival functions.

Somatic system.   That part of the peripheral nervous system concerned with sensory and motor functions.

Split-brain experiments.   Research conducted when the corpus callosum has been severed, creating two entirely separate hemispheres which function independently.

Sympathetic system.   That part of the autonomic nervous system that acts primarily when the person is aroused.

Synapse.   The gap between the axon of one cell and a dendrite of the next.

Synaptic vesicles.   Openings at the end of an axon from which transmitter substances are discharged.

Temporal lobe.   The area of the cortex from in front of the occipital lobe to the rear of the lateral fissure.

Transmitter substance.   A chemical discharged from an axon's synaptic vesicles; may be either excitatory or inhibitory.

Chapter 6

Sensory Processes

Sensation is the process by which stimuli are detected, identified, and gauged. Sensation merely reveals or conveys information, while *perception* is the *interpretation* of information. (See Chapter 7 for a thorough discussion of perception.)

It is important to recognize that humans have many more sensory processes than are usually attributed to them. Many descriptions of human sensory processes detail the "basic five" senses, but it is probably more appropriate to recognize a "basic seven" and then to realize that each of these seems to have subcategories. The seven designations are vision, hearing, skin or touch, taste, smell, balance, and kinesthesis.

6.1 THE BASIC SENSORY PROCESS

No matter which sensation is being described, a certain sequence of events appears necessary for the sense to operate. First, some stimulus appropriate to that sense must be present in sufficient strength to initiate reception. The signal is picked up by a receptor (which is a nerve ending specialized for such a task) and transmitted through the sensory (or somatic) peripheral nervous system to the brain. The signal activates a particular part of the brain that records the signal as a sensation. It is not until the signal has reached the brain that sensation occurs.

Location of Receptors

Most sensory receptors are located in relatively protected positions within the body. (All but some skin receptors are at some distance from the surface of the body and are therefore difficult to damage.)

EXAMPLE 1. Receptors for vision are not on the surface of the eye, but rather at the back of the eyeball, well guarded by the eyeball itself and by surrounding tissue, bone, and hair.

Range of Reception

Each sensory process is limited in its range of reception. A human's sensory capabilities are generally quite good, although they are sometimes surpassed by other organisms' capabilities. Stimuli occurring outside an organism's range of reception are not recorded by the organism.

EXAMPLE 2. Although they are close to the range which can be sensed, ultraviolet and infrared rays cannot be seen by humans, unless some special device is used to transform the rays into the visible range. Human vision is limited to the visible spectrum. (See Section 6.3.)

Thresholds

As mentioned above, stimulation must be of sufficient strength for reception to occur. The necessary level of strength is called a *threshold*. A distinction is made between thresholds for revealing the presence or absence of a stimulus and those for detecting a change in the value of a stimulus.

Absolute Threshold. If correct detection of the presence or absence of a stimulus occurs only 50 percent of the time, the stimulus is said to be at the *absolute threshold*. (This percentage has been accepted arbitrarily.)

EXAMPLE 3. Figure 6-1 shows how the value for an absolute threshold is determined.

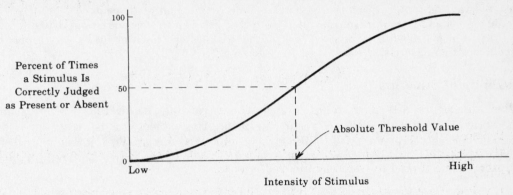

Fig. 6-1

Difference threshold. The minimum change in a stimulus value that can be detected as a change represents the *difference threshold*, often called the *just noticeable difference* (j.n.d.).

Sensory Adaptation

On occasion, stimulation is at an unusual level when compared to normal circumstances. In most of these cases, humans appear to be able to make adjustments and adopt a pattern of behavior which allows them to cope with the new level of stimulation that exists. This process of coping is called *sensory adaptation*.

EXAMPLE 4. Sensory adaptation is sometimes illustrated by a newlywed person wearing a wedding band. At first, the ring seems very noticeable and perhaps somewhat awkward. The person may twist, pull, or just "fool around" with the ring. With some experience, however, the individual usually adjusts to the "new" stimulation and no longer is aware of the ring, although the actual sensory stimulation remains the same.

Transduction

To fully understand reception of sensory stimuli, one more term must be introduced. When the stimulus (mechanical, chemical, radiant, etc.) is picked up by the receptor, its energy is changed into an action potential that then begins the sequence of events leading to the brain's registration of the sensation. This change from energy to action potential is called the *transduction* of the signal. Of course, the incoming energy level must be at least at the absolute threshold value before transduction can occur.

6.2   DETECTION THEORY

Early theories of sensory reception implied that each stimulus must have some minimum, unchanging value for its absolute threshold and some constant amount or ratio of change for its difference threshold. Later work has shown that such concepts are relatively naive. Absolute threshold values and difference thresholds may vary, depending upon a number of conditions. Three conditions have been studied extensively and appear to be most important—motivation, probability of the stimulus, and extraneous variables.

Motivation

Research in this area has suggested that certain payoffs or costs can affect a person's judgments regarding the presence or absence of a stimulus or any change of stimulus level. Evidence indicates that threshold values differ depending upon motivation, with greater or lesser sensitivity resulting.

EXAMPLE 5. Suppose that immediately following breakfast, you get into your car and set out to take some clothes to the dry cleaners. As you drove, you would be relatively unconcerned with whether or not you noticed a restaurant sign, but your response to the dry cleaner's sign would be important. If you noticed it, you could complete your chore; if you missed it, you might spend much time and energy driving around trying to find the right place. Thus, your sensitivity to the dry cleaner's signs might be very acute, while your threshold for other advertising signs might be much higher.

Probability of Stimulus

Past experience will often provide information regarding the likelihood that a stimulus will occur again in the future. With a great likelihood, the subject can be expected to detect the stimulus, whereas a very small likelihood may mean the subject will devote energies to other stimuli and miss this particular one. A threshold therefore varies with the probability of stimulus occurrence.

Extraneous Stimuli

We are often in situations where many stimuli are present. Some of these stimuli may be very important to us; others may be extraneous, or irrelevant to our goals. These irrelevant stimuli are frequently classified by the term "noise." Excesses in "noise" may raise threshold values by making it more difficult to detect the appropriate stimulus.

EXAMPLE 6. What is considered "noise" in one circumstance may not be in another. A cheering crowd may be expected and appreciated at a baseball game, but judged inappropriate and distracting by a golfer in a tournament. The golfer's ability to detect stimuli (such as the flight path of a ball or the "break" of a green) may vary with the amount of interference created by the crowd.

6.3   TYPES OF SENSORY PROCESSES

Vision

The most thoroughly researched sensory process is vision. This probably resulted because the visual apparatus is relatively accessible and because early philosophers believed vision to be the "dominant" sense.

The chain of visual reception follows the basic sensory sequence described in Section 6.1. Light energies enter the eye by passing through the cornea, pupil, and lens. There they are picked up by the visual receptors located at the back of the eyeball, in the retina. Here, these energies are transduced into action potentials and are transmitted via the occipital nerve to the visual region of the brain, where they are registered and interpreted as sights. The image is brought to the retina in an upside-down position, but transformed to an upright position by the brain.

The retina.   The *retina* is a light-sensitive surface located at the back of each eyeball. It contains two kinds of receptors, called *cones* and *rods*, which transduce the physical energy of light into action potentials.

Cones are receptors which function primarily in daylight or in highly illuminated visual circumstances. They are concentrated toward the center of the eye, particularly in the *fovea*, an area directly across from the lens where maximum visual acuity occurs. The cones provide the receptors for color vision.

Rods are receptors which function in dim light. They are found throughout the retina except in the fovea.

EXAMPLE 7. When looking at a dim star, it is sometimes easier to focus by tilting the head a little to the side. This is because cones do not operate in dim light conditions and the stimulus must be brought into focus on rod receptors, which are located more in the periphery of the retina.

The Blind Spot. One place in each retina contains no receptors at all. This is called the *blind spot*, an opening in the retina where the optic nerve exits to the brain. In general, because of the dual operation of the eyes and past visual learning experiences, the blind spot of the visual field is not readily apparent.

Color Vision. Color vision is a function of the cones. Research has shown that not all cones receive all colors. The most popular explanation of the difference among cones is the *trichromatic theory* of color vision. Essentially, the trichromatic theory says some cones are most sensitive to reds, some to greens, and a third group to blues. The color received is a result of how many of each of these receptors are activated by a given stimulus.

Properties of light. The *color* (or *hue*) of the stimulus, the *intensity* of the light source, and the *saturation* of the stimulus are all properties of light stimuli.

Color, or *hue*, is determined by the *wavelength* of the light. Humans are able to see colors ranging from reds (the longest visible wavelengths) to blues (the shortest) and any wavelengths between. This range of color vision has been named the *visible spectrum*. Stimulation by only a narrow band of these wavelengths produces a *pure spectral color*.

Intensity is the amount of physical energy produced by a light source. The viewer's reaction to this intensity is usually labelled as the *brightness* of the light.

Saturation is determined by the variety of wavelengths in a light source. A pure spectral color is said to be completely saturated. When a color is composed of light of many wavelengths, the saturation is decreased; in other words, the color becomes "washed out."

Visual dysfunctions. Several fairly common visual dysfunctions exist. Obviously, the most severe is total blindness, which often results from traumatic damage to nervous tissue. Near-sightedness, farsightedness, and astigmatism are dysfunctions in which the rays being received are not focused properly on the retina. Correction by use of glasses or contact lenses is often possible.

Colorblindness occurs when particular cones are either missing or malfunctioning. The most common colorblindness is an inability to recognize reds and greens. Much less common are inaccuracies in receiving blues or yellows, or total colorblindness, where no color reception exists. In general, colorblindness is not correctable.

EXAMPLE 8. Individuals with red-green colorblindness must rely on position and brightness cues to determine if a traffic light is red or green. (Placing the green lens above the red, as a highway system in Canada once did, would confuse the position cues for colorblind drivers, and might create a hazard.)

Hearing

Hearing (or audition) is an organism's ability to receive mechanical energy in the form of sound waves. The sound waves are generated when a source is made to vibrate, resulting in compression and expansion of adjacent molecules. The repeated compression and expansion is carried by some medium to the hearing receptors. Most frequently, the transmission medium is air molecules, although sounds can pass through other gases, liquids, and solids.

The reception and registration of sound waves follows the basic sensory sequence described in Section 6.1. The specific parts of the body involved in hearing are as follows: The *outer ear* "traps" the sound waves and funnels them to the eardrum. The *middle ear* contains three small bones, the malleus, incus, and stapes, which transfer the vibrations from the eardrum to a second membrane, called the *oval window*. The *inner ear* contains the *cochlea*, a snail-like structure filled with fluid and hair-like receptors that transduce the mechanical energy into an action potential. From the cochlea, the signals are transmitted through the *auditory nerve* to the *auditory cortex* of the brain, where the actual registration of the sound takes place.

Properties of sound waves.   The two most distinguishing characteristics of a soundwave are its *frequency* and *amplitude*. Frequency, the number of sound waves per second, determines the *pitch* a listener hears. The greater the number of waves per second, the higher the pitch. Amplitude represents the amount of energy in each wave as measured by the height of the wave. Amplitude determines the intensity of the sound—that is, how loud it will be.

Auditory localization.   In many instances, the receiver is interested not only in how the stimulus sounds, but from where the stimulus is coming. Identifying the direction of the sound source is called *auditory localization*. Basically, localization depends on the discrepancy between the time one ear receives the sound and the time the other ear receives it. When the sound source is exactly equidistant from both ears, the receiver may have to rely upon some other sensory process (for example, vision) or turn the head slightly to create a time differential in order to determine direction.

EXAMPLE 9.   To demonstrate the difficulty in determining the location of auditory stimuli that arrive at both ears simultaneously, do the following. Sit with your eyes closed and have someone sound a noise source directly in front or directly in back of you. Try to point to the location of the source. You may find you are unable to determine where the source is located unless you either open your eyes or turn you head.

Auditory dysfunctions.   The most severe auditory dysfunction is total deafness. Other hearing losses are mild dysfunctions throughout the hearing range, or partial dysfunctions in which only a segment of the range cannot be heard. Damage to the conductive mechanisms or the nerves involved may be the cause of such losses.

The Chemical Senses—Smell and Taste

Smell (olfaction) and *taste* (gustation) are sensory processes which receive stimulus energy in the form of chemical substances. Comparable to the other senses, the receptors transduce these energies into action potentials, which are relayed to specialized areas of the brain to be recorded as odors or tastes.

Smell.   The receptors for smell are hair cells located in the membranes of each nasal passage (olfactory epithelium). Human receptors are quite sensitive to certain odors but relatively insensitive to changes in the concentration of an odor.

Taste.   Taste receptors are specialized cells with hairlike endings grouped together into *taste buds*. They are found mostly in the tongue. Research has shown that taste receptors can be classified into sweet, sour, salty, or bitter, with each type most sensitive to only one of these stimuli.

Flavor.   The combination of taste and smell results in *flavor*. This is probably a result of the two types of receptors being sensitive to very similar chemical stimuli.

EXAMPLE 10.   An interesting experiment demonstrated how important odor reception is to flavor. A subject was blindfolded and had the nasal passages completely blocked. Different foods, such as an onion, a potato, and an apple were chopped into similar-sized pieces and fed to the subject one at a time. In this condition, the subject was unable to differentiate among the foods. However, once the nasal blocks were removed, the subject made rapid distinctions. (This is an easy experiment to try for yourself.)

Dysfunctions.   Unless some kind of nervous-tissue damage occurs, dysfunctions of the chemical senses are likely to be rather mild. They may occur, for example, when a person has a bad hay-fever attack or perhaps "burns" the tongue.

The Skin Senses

The skin (touch) senses provide sensory experiences from receptors found in the skin. Four varieties are identified—*heat, cold, pressure,* and *pain*. These receptors are *not* distributed evenly throughout the body. Certain areas—such as the face and hands—have many more receptors than do other areas such as the back.

The receptors consist of free nerve endings, corpuscles, and hair follicles. All appear to receive the various types of stimuli, with registration of the event occurring in the brain. The stimuli may be provided by either mechanical or radiant energy, although the latter does not create pressure stimuli.

The Kinesthetic Senses

Kinesthetic receptors are located in muscles, joints, and tendons. They provide information about the activity and position of the body. This, in turn, aids with coordination.

Which receptors are activated depends upon the direction and angle of movement. The signals from the kinesthetic receptors are registered and interpreted in the brain, just as with the other senses.

Balance

Balance (the *vestibular* sense) has receptors located in the inner ear, next to the hearing apparatus. These receptors consist of three *semicircular canals* and the *vestibular sacs*.

The semicircular canals and vestibular sacs contain hair cells that respond to changes in body orientation. Fluid in the semicircular canals moves with body rotation and generates displacement of the receptors. The hair cells of the vestibular sacs respond to the body's position or angle, such as when it is at rest.

Dysfunctions of balance may lead to vertigo or nystagmus (involuntary oscillation of the eyeballs.) These dysfunctions can frequently be overcome by relying on other sensory processes.

EXAMPLE 11. A trip to a "fun-house" can show how maintaining a vertical or upright position may sometimes be quite difficult. When visual cues make the relationship between floor and walls appear to be different from what it really is, a person may have to rely upon kinesthetic, touch, or vestibular cues. It is easy to demonstrate the complex interactions of these sensory processes by trying to stand on one foot: first with your eyes open and your head in an upright postion, then with your eyes closed and your head tilted forward.

Solved Problems

6.1   What is the difference between sensation and perception?

Sensation is simply a part of the overall perceptual processes. Using the nervous system (see Chapter 5), energies of various kinds are detected, distinguished as to kind, and interpreted for strength and difference from other stimuli. As such, the sensory processes only "report" information, whereas perception then makes inferences from or interprets the information.

6.2   What kinds of energy are detected as sensations?

The human body receives and translates energies which are detected as sights, sounds, tastes, odors, various touch sensations, information about balance, and information about body position.

6.3   The usual list of human sensations includes five sensory processes, but the preceding problem implies there are more. What are they?

The designation of five basic senses is too limited. There are at least seven sensory processes that correspond to the description in Problem 6.2. They are vision, hearing, taste, smell, skin or touch, balance, and kinesthesis. In turn, each of these sensory processes appears to have a number of separate receptors that receive particular types of energy.

6.4   Are sensations "registered" when a receptor is activated?

No. The receptor starts the chain of events which results in the sensation being "reported," but the "registration" of the sensation actually takes place in the brain. The receptors are simply specialized nerve endings that are capable of responding to the various stimuli. The entire sensory process for all sensations can be simplified as the following chain of events:

1. The stimulus is "picked up" by the receptor.

2. The nerve transduces (changes) that energy into an action potential, which is transmitted along that nerve and along succeeding nerves in the chain. (This chain is part of the sensory peripheral nervous system.)

3. The signal reaches a specialized area of the brain (part of the central nervous system) where it is recorded and interpreted as a sensation. Sensation has not occurred until the signal has reached the brain and been recorded.

6.5   Do all sensory processes work in this same manner, or are there different sequences for each type of sensation?

The sequence—stimulus, receptor, sensory peripheral nerve, and central nervous system—is essentially the same for all sensory processes. Differences exist in the types of stimuli which activate the various receptor endings, which parts of the sensory peripheral system are called into play, and which specialized areas of the cortex are activated.

6.6   Are all stimuli of a given type recorded as sensations by an organism?

No. Each sensory process is limited to stimuli within a certain range. Stimuli outside that range are not recorded. For example, humans cannot hear a "dog whistle" because its pitch is above their range of hearing.

It is important to remember, however, that stimuli out of the range of one sensory process may be within the range of another. For example, powerful low-frequency sounds cannot be heard by humans, but they can be "felt" as bodily sensations.

6.7   What is a threshold?

If the stimulus strength is sufficient to be detected, it has reached or passed the *threshold* for detection. The concept of threshold has two subdivisions: (1) *Absolute threshold*, indicating the level at which the presence or absence of a stimulus can be correctly detected 50 percent of the time. (2) *Difference threshold*, indicating the smallest change in a stimulus value that can be detected as a change. (The difference threshold of a stimulus is also referred to as the *just noticeable difference*, or j.n.d.)

6.8   What factors influence threshold values?

Early psychophysical studies tried to determine constant threshold values for many different stimuli. More recent research has shown, however, that these thresholds may change, depending upon several different factors. This latter research has been classified under the heading of *detection theory*, with three factors emerging as most important:

1. The particular motivation of the person at the time: How important is it to detect the stimulus? What will be the payoffs or costs for success or failure?

2. The probability the stimulus or stimulus change will occur: Is it a "sure thing" or very unlikely?

3. The amount of surrounding "noise": Are there many other distracting or irrelevant stimuli, or is the environment relatively free of them?

6.9   What is sensory adaptation?

Sensory adaptation occurs when sensory sensitivity changes or adjusts to the amount and type of incoming stimuli. For example, a worker who has been employed for years in a candy-making factory may no longer notice the very sweet smell of the workplace. Sensory adaptation is related to detection theory (Problem 6.8) but is distinguished from it because factors like the consistency and the amount of stimulation seem to be more important than factors like motivation, probability, or "noise."

6.10   The process of seeing is often described as being very similar to the process in which a camera is used to take a picture. Try to describe vision by relating it to how a camera works.

Basically a camera is a container with an opening (the lens) on one side and film on the opposite side. The eye has a somewhat comparable structure. The pupil of the eye serves as the opening, which can adjust to the amount of light being received. Directly behind the pupil is the lens, which focuses the stimuli being received upon the retina. The retina is similar to the film, located at the back of the eyeball and receiving the stimuli. Carrying the analogy one step further, the visual area of the brain serves as the processor, "developing" the signals transmitted from the retina and completing this visual process. (*Note*: The image projected on the retina is upside-down, but after being received, the brain converts the signal to an upright postion.)

6.11   Do the visual receptors within the retina function in the same fashion?

In this case, the answer is *yes and no*. There are two kinds of visual receptors—cones and rods. Both show adaptation to light and darkness, but the cones operate primarily in daylight vision and the rods function in dim or dark conditions. Cones provide color vision; rods give vision only for light and dark (achromatic vision).

6.12   The distribution of cones and rods is not uniform throughout the retina. How are they distributed and what effect does this have on vision?

The cones tend to be located in the center of the retina; the rods are generally located more in the periphery. The greatest concentration of cones occurs in a central area called the *fovea*, which is the point of maximum visual acuity. Thus, vision under bright illumination is best if the signal is focused toward the center of the retina. Vision in dim light is generally better if the stimulus is directed toward the periphery of the retina.

6.13   Describe how to locate the blind spot. Why does it exist?

Using the X and O below, close one eye and focus on the center of the stimulus on the opposite side. Then slowly move the page toward you. At some point, you will no longer be able to see the mark on which you are *not* focusing.

X   O

The blind spot exists because there are no receptors at that point in the retina where the optic nerve leaves the eye. The blind spot is usually not noticed because of the dual operation of the eyes and the ability of the brain to "fill in the gaps." (See Chapter 7 for an explanation of the principle of *closure*.)

6.14   Do all cones in the retina receive all colors? What causes colorblindness?

Research evidence indicates that not all the cones receive all colors. The most widely accepted theory is called the *trichromatic theory* of color vision. It states that some of the cones appear to respond best to red light, others to green, and still others to blue. What colors we see seems to depend upon how many of each of these types of cones are stimulated.

Colorblindness appears to occur when certain cones are either absent or deficient. Most commonly, colorblindness is partial—red and green are not received correctly. Blue-yellow colorblindness is exceedingly rare. Total colorblindness, with only light and dark vision existing is also quite rare.

6.15   What are the three basic properties of light?

The first basic property of light is *color* (or more properly *hue*). It is determined by the wavelength of the light. The range of wavelengths seen by humans is called the visible spectrum; the longest visible wavelengths appear as red and the shortest appear as blue. The second basic property of light is *intensity* (or brightness). Intensity is the term for the amount of physical energy produced by the light source; brightness is the term for the viewer's response to intensity. In general, more intense lights appear brighter. The third basic property of light, *saturation*, is determined by the number of light-wave components mixed with a pure spectral color; the more components mixed in, the less the light's saturation.

6.16   What dysfunctions other than colorblindness can affect visual processes?

Other visual dysfunctions include farsightedness, nearsightedness, and astigmatism. All create situations where the incoming rays do not focus properly on the retina because the cornea and lens do not bend the rays correctly. All are usually correctable by use of glasses or contact lens, which are shaped to compensate for the improper focus.

Obviously, one other visual dysfunction is total blindness. In this case, there is no vision at all. The condition is usually not correctable.

6.17   Sound stimuli reach us as waves. Describe these sound waves and the two basic properties of sound.

Sound waves are a form of mechanical energy. When a source is made to vibrate, the resultant compressions and expansions of molecules are conducted much like a chain reaction through some medium (usually air) until they reach the receptor. Sound waves have two basic properties: (1) the number of waves per second, which is the frequency of the sound and determines its pitch; and (2) the height of the wave, which is the amplitude (intensity) of the sound and determines its loudness. (*Note*: The random movement of air molecules could create sound reception. However, although the body's hearing processes are quite sensitive, sensory adaptation usually occurs and such signals are ignored.

6.18   Vision has a chain of reception involving the cornea, pupil, lens, retina, optic nerve, and brain. What is the comparable chain for hearing?

Most simply described, the chain involves the outer ear, middle ear, and inner ear. The outer ear (what is ordinarily called the "ear") traps the sound waves and funnels them into the auditory canal, where they strike the eardrum. The eardrum relays the signal into the middle ear, which consists of three small bones called the ossicles (malleus, incus, and stapes). These bones transmit the signal to a second membrane, called the oval window, which is found at the start of the cochlea, a coiled tube filled with fluid. Within the cochlea, there are tiny hair cells which are the actual sound receptors. The hair cells are found between two membranes (basilar and tectorial), which expand or contract according to the signal being received. This causes deflection of the hair cells, which in turn sends signals through the auditory nerve to the brain, where they are registered in the auditory cortex.

6.19　One of the functions of the outer ears is to trap incoming sound waves. What other function do the outer ears, working in conjunction, serve?

　　　Auditory localization, the ability to determine from where a sound has come, occurs because humans have two ears which are located some distance apart. In general, a sound which comes from any direction except directly in front or back arrives at one ear slightly before arriving at the other. Although the time differential is small, it is sufficient to allow location of the source. To locate sound sources directly in front or in back of the head, a person may have to use visual cues or turn the head to create a time differential.

6.20　Colorblindness, nearsightedness, farsightedness, and total blindness are examples of visual dysfunctions. Describe some comparable dysfunctions for hearing and some ways in which people may compensate for them.

　　　Total deafness is comparable to total blindness. It occurs in a small percentage of the population. A person who is totally deaf could communicate by using lip reading or sign language. Partial deafness in certain auditory ranges is found occasionally, and other auditory-linked problems also exist. These include problems such as aphasia, where signals are received but processed improperly, resulting in impairment of understanding, speech, or writing. Various types of hearing aids can help compensate for such dysfunctions.

6.21　Explain why smell and taste are called the "chemical senses."

　　　Smell (olfaction) and taste (gustation) are called the chemical senses because stimuli come to them in the form of chemical substances that make contact with the receptors.

6.22　Describe where the receptors for smell and taste are located.

　　　The receptors for smell are millions of hair cells located in the olfactory epithelium, the membrane found in the nasal passages. Taste receptors are specialized cells with hairlike endings. Grouped into taste buds, they are found mostly in the edges and back of the tongue, with a few in the soft palate, pharynx, and larynx. Comparable to the other senses, these receptors are well-protected and show variety in their receptivity to certain kinds of stimulation. For example, taste receptors are identified by how sensitive they are to sweet, sour, salty, or bitter stimuli.

6.23　A severe head cold can make food "taste" bland and unappetizing. Why?

　　　Generally, the word "taste" is used in too broad a sense. The reason a person with a severe head cold may find food unappetizing is that the person's smell receptors are disrupted by the head cold. It would be more appropriate to say that the *flavor* of the food has been affected because flavor is a result of the interaction of taste and smell.

6.24　The skin (touch) senses are of various types. What are these types and how are they distributed?

　　　Receptors for the skin senses appear to be sensitive to pressure, pain, heat, and cold. The distribution of these receptors is uneven, with only certain areas of the body having heavy concentrations of them. For example, the face and fingertips have numerous receptors, while the back has relatively few. It is interesting to note that the proportion of cortical tissue associated with the different skin areas of the body is comparable to the concentrations of receptors in these skin areas.

6.25　What types of stimulation are registered by the skin senses?

　　　Mechanical and radiant energy may be received by the skin senses. Mechanical energy may provide touch, hot, cold, or pain sensations, depending upon the type of stimulus. Radiant energy may be recorded as heat, cold, or pain.

6.26   How are the signals which are picked up by the touch receptors registered? Are there different kinds of receptors which are sensitive to different stimuli?

    The skin senses do have different kinds of receptors (such as nerve endings, corpuscles, and hair follicles), but these receptors apparently do not differentiate types of stimulation. The registration of touch senses occurs in a manner similar to that of all the other senses; that is, sensation occurs only when the signal reaches the brain. (*Note*: The "phantom-limb phenomenon" experienced by amputees illustrates the brain's involvement. Stimulation of an appropriate area in the brain or the nerve which would connect to the missing arm or leg is registered by the person as a sensation arising in the missing limb.)

6.27   Give an example of a kinesthetic sensation.

    If a person stands on one foot, holds the other foot behind, and wiggles the toes, he or she will realize that the toes are wiggling because of kinesthetic reception. The toes cannot be seen, heard, tasted, smelled or touched in such a position, yet the activity is recognized. Kinesthetic senses, which tell about the activity and position of muscles, joints, and tendons, are as much a basic sensory process as any of the previously mentioned five.

6.28   Explain why balance is considered a basic sensory process, yet balancing oneself may depend upon more than one sensory process.

    Balance (vestibular reception) is considered a basic sensory process because there are specific receptors particularly concerned with this single type of stimulation. These receptors are the three semicircular canals (located in the inner ear, very near the cochlea) and the vestibular sacs (located between the canals and the cochlea).

    Balancing is often a function of more than one sensory process. Just as flavor is a combination of taste and smell, balancing may depend upon vision, kinesthesis, and touch sensations as well as on strictly vestibular sensations.

6.29   Is the operation of balance receptors comparable to the operation of other sensory receptors?

    Balance is comparable to the other basic sensory processes. The semicircular canals contain fluid that moves and displaces the hair cells whenever the body moves. These, in turn, relay messages that are interpreted in the brain as body rotation. The vestibular-sac hair cells respond to the position of the resting body, with the signals being interpreted by the brain as the angle of tilt of the body.

6.30   Why does a person sometimes feel dizzy?

    Assuming the person's nervous system is normal, dizziness may result when movement of the fluid in one or more of the semicircular canals does not terminate immediately when the body stops moving. In other words, the fluid continues to "slosh around" after the body has stopped moving, and the signals sent from the hair cells are interpreted as dizziness.

6.31   How can a person's balance processes dysfunction? Can a person compensate in any way for such a dysfunction?

    Damage or disease within the inner ear may create balance problems such as vertigo or nystagmus (unusual eye movement). If the damage is limited to one side only, the other side often can assume total responsibility for balance. If both sides are affected, other sensory processes, such as vision and kinesthesis, must take over and maintain balance.

Key Terms

Absolute threshold.   The lowest level of a stimulus at which its presence or absence can be correctly detected 50 percent of the time.

Auditory localization.   Identifying the direction from which a sound was produced; often a function of the slight discrepancy between the times at which the signal reaches each ear.

Blind spot.   The area in the retina where the optic nerve exits to the brain; no vision is possible here because there are no receptors.

Cochlea.   The structure within the inner ear that transduces the mechanical energy of sound waves into signals for hearing.

Color.   The hue of a visual stimulus, determined by the wavelength of the light.

Cones.   The visual receptors which function primarily in lighted conditions; they are located toward the center of the eye and operate for color vision.

Detection theory.   A theory stressing the effects of motivation, stimulus probability, and extraneous stimuli on the decision regarding the presence or absence of a given stimulus or a change in stimulus value.

Difference threshold.   The minimum change in stimulus value that can be correctly identified as a change; also known as the just noticeable difference, or j.n.d.

Flavor.   A combination of taste and smell; the term most appropriately used when discussing food.

Fovea.   The area in the center of the retina containing only cones; the point of maximum visual acuity.

Kinesthesis.   The sensations concerned with body position and body movement.

"Noise."   In detection theory, the term used to describe any extraneous stimuli.

Perception.   Basically, the interpretation or understanding of sensory receptions.

Receptor.   A specialized nerve ending that is sensitive to a particular type of stimulus.

Retina.   That part of the eye containing the receptors for vision; located at the back of the eyeball.

Rods.   The visual receptors which function primarily in dim or dark conditions; they are located toward the periphery of the eye and operate only in a black-and-white dimension.

Semicircular canals.   Three tubes located in the inner ear; they are filled with fluid and are sensitive to changes in body and head orientation.

Sensations.   The processes which detect, judge, and identify stimuli.

Sensory adaptation.   The process of adjustment to unusual levels of stimulation.

Taste buds.   Receptors for taste; located in the pits of the tongue.

Threshold.   The level of stimulation necessary for reception to occur.

Transduction.   The change of stimulus energy into an action potential.

Trichromatic theory.   The most popular explanation of color vision, based upon the idea there are three types of cones that are sensitive respectively to red, green, and blue.

Vestibular sense.   Balance; the function of the three semicircular canals and the vestibular sacs.

Chapter 7

Perception

Perception is the process by which a person *interprets* sensory stimuli. The sensory processes merely report about the stimulus environment; perception translates these sensory messages into understandable forms.

EXAMPLE 1. Suppose you were flying in an airplane, several thousand feet above the ground, on a clear day. The cars, roads, houses, and trees below would appear doll-size or smaller (sensation), but you would realize they were normal size (perception).

Perception appears for the most part to be a function of experience. That is, it is a learned characteristic of behavior. Research evidence indicates that a subject whose perceptual experience is restricted or eliminated will be unable to develop normal perceptual reactions. Furthermore, a subject who cannot or is not permitted to interact with the stimulus environment will not show normal perceptual development. (See Problem 7.3.)

Two types of factors influence perception: *external* (stimulus) *cues* and *internal* (personal) *cues*. Both internal and external cues affect the way in which a subject will pay attention to, or attend to a stimulus. A subject must pay at least some attention to a stimulus in order for perception to occur.

7.1 EXTERNAL CUES

External cues develop from the properties of a stimulus or groups of stimuli. Interest in the effects of external stimuli on perceptual development arose during the early years of Gestalt psychology. The Gestaltists realized that stimuli provided the start for more than just sensation. They stated that the totality of a stimulus situation was more than the sum of its separate aspects.

EXAMPLE 2. Consider the following: "fiuoynacdaersiht, s'tiaelcarim!" Rearranged, these letters read: "if you can read this, it's a miracle!" However, you have to have the correct arrangement and spacing of letters to appreciate the meaning. In other words, the whole of a situation is more than its parts. The stimulus components, in and of themselves, do now always allow someone to understand or interpret the stimulus environment.

Figure-Ground Relationship

The relationship between the main or featured stimulus and any surrounding stimuli is called the *figure-ground relationship*. In general, this relationship determines how distinct the main stimulus (the figure) will be within the total context (the ground).

EXAMPLE 3. Much perceptual research is done with vision, but a figure-ground relationship can also be illustrated by listening to music. The melody represents the figure and harmony provides the ground. If one or both of these are varied, the figure-ground relationship may change.

Figure-ground relationships are called *unstable* if the figure can sometimes be perceived as the ground and the ground can sometimes be perceived as the figure. Figures may also be described as *ambiguous* if they can be "correctly" interpreted in more than one way. (See Problems 7.7 and 7.8.)

76

Intensity

Research has shown that, in general, the more intense a stimulus, the more likely a subject will pay attention to it. However, extremely high values may be painful or harmful.

EXAMPLE 4. In general, the louder a noise, the more likely it is to be heard (and thus recognized and interpreted). However, extremely loud levels may cause distortion or even damage to one's hearing. Musicians using electric amplification are frequently warned of this possibility.

Contrast

A stimulus that differs noticeably from the others surrounding it (either by virtue of quality or quantity) is more likely to be noticed than is a stimulus that is similar to the stimuli surrounding it. This is the principle of *contrast*.

EXAMPLE 5. The principle of contrast is reversed when camouflage is desired. Soldiers may wear clothing that "blends in" with the surrounding environment, and highway police may drive unmarked cars so that they will not be easily seen by speeders.

Continuity

Continuity refers to the uninterrupted "flow" of a stimulus. A subject is likely to perceive a stimulus situation as a combination of regular or continuous stimuli rather than as a combination of irregular or discontinuous stimuli.

EXAMPLE 6. In Fig. 7-1, drawing (*a*) is usually perceived as the combination of a straight line and an "accordion" line (*b*) rather than as the combination of two "sawtooth" lines (*c*).

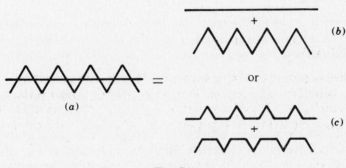

Fig. 7-1

Grouping

The placement or arrangement of stimuli can affect how we attend to and understand them. *Grouped stimuli* appear together in time or space, especially in some rhythmical pattern or arrangement. Such grouping helps the subject to apprehend the stimuli and organize them into an understandable form.

Closure

Closure is most easily defined as filling in gaps in information. A subject receives "incomplete" information, but enough so that it is possible to 'finish" the stimulus. (A person's ability to show closure depends on previous knowledge of what is appropriate, of course.)

EXAMPLE 7. Television game shows often make use of the principle of closure. Incomplete phrases, pictures, or musical themes are presented to a contestant, who must quickly complete the cue in order to win a prize.

Real and Apparent Movement

In several sensory dimensions, one of the most compelling stimulus properties is movement. Subjects are more apt to respond to moving stimuli than to those that are static. Furthermore, some stimuli that actually are static can be presented in such a way as to create *apparent movement*.

EXAMPLE 8. A movie illustrates apparent movement. A quick examination of motion-picture film reveals a series of still images. Only the rapid, coordinated presentation of these images will give the viewer the impression of movement.

Perceptual Constancies

The stimulus a person receives from any one object may change as the position or condition of the object changes. (For example, as you move away from a dinner plate on a table, the image on the retina of each of your eyes will become less and less like a circle and more like an oval.) In spite of such stimulus changes, however, a person will perceive that the object itself has not changed. (That is, the plate will still be perceived as a circular object.)

This phenomenon is called *perceptual constancy*. Research has indicated that subjects perceive size, shape, and color constancies.

EXAMPLE 9. Imagine throwing a model plane so that it moves away from you, loops, and returns toward you. The retinal image you receive is of an object that first grows smaller and then seems to increase in size. However, you perceive that the actual size of the plane remains constant throughout the flight. (This is an example of size constancy.)

Monocular Depth Cues

In visual perception, some of the most important stimulus properties provide *depth cues*. If these cues can be accurately perceived by one eye alone, they are called *monocular cues*. Examples of monocular depth cues are *interposition, perspective, texture gradient*, and *shadows*.

Interposition occurs when one object appears to "block out" part of another object in the visual field. Interposition provides information about the size, distance, and location of the various stimulus objects.

Perspective and texture gradient often operate together to provide information about three-dimensionality. Perspective is the apparent "drawing together" of parallel lines as they recede into the distance. Texture gradient is the change in the distinctiveness of the texture of the stimulus from noticeable or coarse nearby to smooth or fine in the distance. Both allow understanding of the visual field.

Shadows also offer cues that aid in the perception of three dimensions. The distance, height, and shape of an object may be made more intelligible when shadow cues are present.

Retinal Disparity

Retinal disparity refers to the fact that the visual images on the retina of the two eyes at any one moment are never exactly the same. This is called a *binocular cue*, and results from the physical separation of the two eyes in the head. (The brain is able to "blend" these two retinal images so that you see just one image, which carries information about depth and three-dimensionality.)

EXAMPLE 10. Stereoscopic viewers rely upon retinal disparity to provide the impression of three dimensions. A pair of two-dimensional pictures is viewed through special lenses. Each picture sends a slightly different image to each retina. The brain then combines these images into what appears to be a three-dimensional view.

7.2 INTERNAL CUES

Internal cues appear to be a function of a subject's cognitive processes. For example, the motivation of a subject, a subject's past experience, or the expectations of a subject at a given time may all act as internal cues.

Motivation

Perception is frequently influenced by the motivation of the subject. This may result from the subject's physiological condition or social experience. A subject may have learned to give special attention to stimuli that reinforce or satisfy the motive condition. If the subject is never motivated to perceive a certain stimulus (that is, if perception of that stimulus has not been rewarded), the subject will tend to ignore the stimulus.

EXAMPLE 11. Research studies on *perceptual defenses* have shown that some subjects may perceive "acceptable" or "safe" stimuli when in fact "unacceptable" or "dirty" stimuli have been presented to them. (For example, a person confronted with a reading selection that contains an obscenity may perceive an "innocuous" word in place of the "offensive" word. Comparable research studies on *perceptual vigilance* have shown that some subjects may perceive "unacceptable" or "dirty" stimuli even when such stimuli are not present.

Past Experience

Previous learning can make a subject anticipate the meaning of future stimulus situations. Such anticipations may be correct or incorrect.

EXAMPLE 12. Perhaps you have played the party game where one person writes a description of something and then whispers this description to a second person. This person in turn whispers to the next, and so on, until the last person receives the description and recites it aloud. The difference between the original (written) description and the final version is often striking. Part of the reason for this difference is that people may incorrectly anticipate what is being whispered to them.

Set

Set is defined as a temporary tendency (or expectancy) to respond in a certain fashion. This tendency may change as the subject is confronted with different instructions or rewards.

EXAMPLE 13. Read the following sentence: "If Frieda follows Fred frantically, Fred flees fleetingly!" How many *f*s do you count? If you counted eight, your set was accurate. If you counted only seven, you probably were caught by the first-letter set and missed the *f* in the word *if*.

7.3 UNUSUAL PERCEPTUAL EXPERIENCES

Illusions

Sometimes stimuli can be interpreted incorrectly. Some stimuli exist in a configuration that almost always leads to incorrect perception. When this occurs, the perception is described as an *illusion*.

EXAMPLE 14. The famous Mueller-Lyer illusion (Fig. 7-2) shows how stimulus cues may lead to perceptual misunderstanding. Lines *A* and *B* are exactly the same length, but *A* appears shorter than *B*.

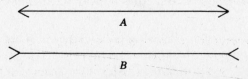

Fig. 7-2

(*Note*: Illusions are often confused in everyday speech with *hallucinations*, which are perceptions of "stimuli" that actually do not exist.)

Subliminal Perception

Several years ago, an attempt was made to create advertisements which would be presented at stimulus values just below the conscious threshold. The idea was that the person would receive the advertising message without being aware of the stimulation. Such unconscious perception is called *subliminal perception*.

Most subliminal advertising campaigns have been abandoned because of difficulties in establishing threshold values. Research has shown, however, that subliminal perception can occur.

Extremes of Sensory Load

Sensory deprivation (very little stimulation) or *sensory overload* (a great amount of stimulation) may exceed the person's "normal" capabilities for sensory adaptation. When this happens, unusual patterns of responding (such as hallucinations) may result. It seems that people are unable to continue to correctly interpret the stimulus environment if extreme sensory overload or extreme sensory deprivation is maintained over a prolonged period of time.

Extrasensory Perception (ESP)

Extrasensory perception (ESP) is said to have occurred when a correct interpretation or manipulation of the environment has taken place without any information being provided by regular sensory processes. Several varieties of ESP have been studied, including telepathy, precognition, clairvoyance, and psychokinesis.

Telepathy is the transfer of thought from one person to another without the aid of usual sensory channels. *Precognition* refers to the ability to anticipate future events. *Clairvoyance* is the ability to disclose information that could not have been received by regular sensations. *Psychokinesis* is the capacity for making objects move by using only thought processes.

Solved Problems

7.1   Describe the difference between sensation and perception and give an example of each.

Imagine riding in a boat on a wide river. Far in the distance, you can see a bridge spanning the river. If you raise your hand and hold it in front of your eyes, you will be able to completely block out any visual image of the bridge. However, at this point you still realize the bridge is much bigger than your hand and must be at least as long as the river is wide.

The "tiny" image of the bridge represents sensation, the actual stimulation being received by the receptors and transmitted to the brain. The interpretation of these signals, in which you realize that they represent a large structure, is perception.

7.2   Reception of stimulation is necessary before perception can occur. What term is used to describe this? What other general factors appear most important in influencing perception?

The reception of the stimulus means the receiver has paid *attention* to it. Perception cannot take place unless some level of attending occurs.

Other factors that seem important to perception are past experience, the characteristics of the stimulus, the characteristics of the individual, and the interaction of these factors.

7.3   How is past experience important to perception?

Previous experience is very important to perception. Research studies have repeatedly indicated that subjects must have experience with the environment to be able to correctly perceive stimuli within it. Furthermore, a subject must be able to interact with these stimuli in order to develop perceptual skills. For example, one study compared the behavior of pairs of cats that were exposed to exactly the same environment. However, one cat of each pair was permitted to be active while the other was allowed only to view the situation passively. The active cats were able to develop fairly sophisticated perceptual skills, whereas the passive cats did not.

7.4   The characteristics of a stimulus are often called external cues. Distinguish these from internal cues and explain why external cues may be very important in determining perception.

External cues are properties of the stimulus environment. Internal cues are self-generated stimuli (usually in the form of thoughts) that may be the result of previous learning, a particular set, or a motivation. External cues play an important role in determining whether or not a subject will pay attention. Moreover, the particular qualities of an external cue will affect the way in which a subject understands and interprets a stimulus.

7.5   Early in the development of psychology, one group of researchers showed particular concern with questions of perception and investigated them extensively. Who were they, what was the general statement describing their position, and how could that statement be worded in terms of sensation and perception?

The Gestalt psychologists were among the first to study perception, and the statement that summarized their position was, "the whole is greater than the sum of its parts." Reworded, their statement might read: "While each separate stimulus might be received and recognized as a sensation, the totality of stimuli and the interaction among stimuli form a perception, which is more than just the sum of sensations received."

7.6   On the back cover of many popular magazines you will find a cigarette advertisement. Suppose you are now looking at such an ad. Describe the location of the cigarette pack and name the perceptual principle that was used to determine its position.

The cigarette pack is probably located off-center and at an angle to the other features of the advertisement. The principle used in its placement is the figure-ground relationship, where the figure (or main feature) is made to "stand out" from the background by its position, angle, and other characteristics.

7.7   Distinguish between stable and unstable figure-ground relationships.

Many figure-ground relationships, such as the cigarette pack on the background, are stable. Some other figure-ground relationships, however, are unstable—one cannot be sure which part of the stimulus is the figure and which is the ground. Figure 7-3 is an example of an unstable figure-ground relationship because it can be perceived as either a dark X on a light background or a light X on a dark background.

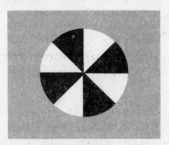

Fig. 7-3

7.8   What is an ambiguous figure? Give an example.

    An ambiguous figure is one that can be "correctly" interpreted in more than one way. Drawing
(a) in Fig. 7-4 can be perceived as representing either drawing (b) or (c). Place your hand over (c) and
compare (a) and (b). Then place your hand over (b) and compare (a) and (c). Furthermore, it is
impossible to tell whether the X in drawing (a) is on the front or the back of the box.

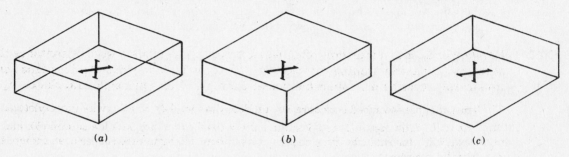

                                        (a)   (b)   (c)

                                              Fig. 7-4

7.9   Would the size of the cigarette pack in the advertisement (Problem 7.6) be important in
           determining how it was perceived?

    Probably the size would matter, at least up to a point. As the pack was made larger, a viewer
would be more likely to pay attention to it. However, if the size of the pack was very large, it might
block out the background, and the background may be important to the "message" being presented (a
cool stream, two lovers, etc.). It would thus be important to maintain some reasonable proportions
between the figure and ground.

7.10   Explain how the intensity and contrast of a stimulus can affect perception.

    In general, as the intensity of a stimulus increases, the more likely it is that a subject will pay
attention to it. Extremely intense stimuli, however, may be painful or annoying to a subject, who
may in turn *not* attend to the stimulus.

    The principle of contrast states that a subject is likely to attend to a stimulus that is noticeably
different from, or in contrast with, the stimuli surrounding it. In general, the greater the contrast,
the greater the likelihood that the stimulus will receive attention.

7.11   Sketch simple demonstrations of the effects of continuity and grouping.

    Continuity refers to the uninterrupted "flow" of a stimulus. A subject is likely to perceive a
complex stimulus as a combination of continuous stimuli rather than as a combination of discontinuous stimuli. In Fig. 7-5, drawing (a) is likely to be perceived as the combination of a line and an
arc (b) and not as the combination of two curves (c).

                        (a)   (b)   (c)

                                          Fig. 7-5

    Grouping refers to the organization of stimuli into rhythmical patterns or arrangements. It is
often easier to perceive and interpret grouped stimuli rather than ungrouped stimuli. For example, in
Fig. 7-6, the ×'s are easiest to count accurately when they are arranged in groups, as in drawing (b).

Fig. 7-6

7.12 People who talk to a stutterer often feel the need to complete a word or sentence that the stutterer is having trouble completing. What perceptual principle does this tendency illustrate? Describe a comparable visual example of this principle and sketch it.

The principle described is closure, the tendency to complete an otherwise incomplete stimulus.

The three drawings in Fig. 7-7 are usually viewed as a triangle (*a*), a square (*b*), and a circle (*c*). Closure is illustrated by them because we perceive the completed shapes even though they are not actually present.

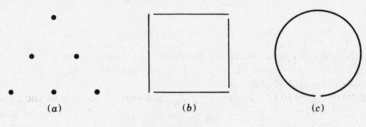

Fig. 7-7

7.13 What is apparent movement? Give some examples of it.

Apparent movement results when a static stimulus is presented in such a way as to suggest a moving stimulus. In Fig. 7-8 the lines behind the clubface give the impression of movement. Apparent movement can also be created by the rapid presentation of a succession of still images, as in a movie. This effect can also be demonstrated by quickly riffling with your thumb the upper right-hand corner of this book. As the pages flip by, the page numbers will seem to "jump" up and down or move left and right. (*Note*: Movement can also be implied by sound, such as in a stereo demonstration record where the train noise seems to move across the room, from one speaker to the other.)

Fig. 7-8

7.14 In Problem 7.1, you were asked to imagine a bridge that you could see at some distance down a river. Though you would be able to "block out" the image of the bridge with your hand, you still perceived that it was large enough to span the river. What perceptual principle would operate in such a situation?

The ability to interpret the "small" stimulus as a full-size bridge is characteristic of *size constancy*, the ability to recognize the consistent size of an object despite the varying stimulus presentations you receive. Size constancy is one of several perceptual constancies, which include shape constancy and color constancy.

7.15   Give examples of shape constancy and color constancy.

Imagine looking at a coffee cup from across a table. What is the shape of the top of the cup? You would probably answer "round." Consider, however, the stimulation you would actually receive. It would probably be an oval, not a circle. This illustrates shape constancy: although you see an oval (sensation), you report a circle (perception).

Now further imagine that the cup of coffee is on a table next to a window in a diner. Hanging in the window is a red-blue-green neon sign that changes colors every few seconds. As the sign goes through its cycles, the color reflected off the coffee cup makes it appear that the cup is changing from red to blue to green and back to red again. In spite of this, you know the cup is still white. Your ability to perceive this is an illustration of color constancy.

7.16   What are monocular depth cues? Give examples of each.

Monocular depth cues are the properties of a stimulus that permit a viewer to perceive depth even if only one eye is used. Interposition, perspective, texture gradient, and shadows are all examples of monocular depth cues.

Interposition exists when one object partially blocks vision of another. The viewer recognizes that the partially-blocked object must be behind or further away than the other object.

Perspective is the apparent "drawing together" of parallel lines as they recede into the distance. The "railroad tracks" in Fig. 7-9 illustrate this principle.

Fig. 7-9

Texture gradient is the coarseness or smoothness of the image we see. Generally, objects nearby appear coarse or distinct, but as one's view extends into the distance, the texture appears much smoother or less distinct. For example, if you are standing on a football field, the grass nearby will appear coarse—you will be able to see in it rough patches and even single blades. As you look far down the field, however, the grass will appear as a smooth, undifferentiated plane of green.

Shadows are also a help in providing cues of depth. For example, drawing (*a*) in Fig. 7-10 appears as a flat disc, whereas drawing (*b*) appears as a ball (an object with depth, or three-dimensionality).

(a)   (b)

Fig. 7-10

7.17   What is the term for vision that makes use of two eyes? Why does one have to close or cover one eye in order to experience the blind spot described in Problem 6.13?

Vision accomplished through the use of two eyes is called *binocular vision*. The two eyes do *not* receive exactly the same stimulation. This discrepancy is called *retinal disparity*. The brain coordinates the two incoming visual signals so that only one image is "seen." The blind spot illustrated in Problem 6.13 is not experienced with binocular vision because the "information" missing at one eye's blind spot is probably *sensed* by the other eye, and the brain is able to complete the stimulus image.

7.18   External cues are very important in determining attention and therefore perception. However, internal cues may also be influential. How might a perceiver's motivation affect interpretation or understanding of stimuli that are received?

A fairly common phrase summarizes the effect of motivation on perception: "You_____what you *want* to_____." Ofcourse, many sensory processes can be inserted in the blanks. People may see, hear, taste, and smell what they wish. This desire to interpret or attend to particular aspects of the stimulus environment represents the effect of motivation on perception.(See Chapter 9 for a full discussion of motivation.)

7.19   Previous learning appears to be an important internal factor in determining perceptions. Can you take the sentence in quotes from Problem 7.18 and reword it to show the effect of previous learning?

The sentence might be rephrased to read, "You_____what your past experience has taught you to expect to_____." Previous learning leads to an understanding of the stimulus environment which can carry over to future situations. (Chapters 11 to 16 discuss learning and memory in detail.)

7.20   Can a person's expectations affect the way he or she perceives the stimulus environment?

Certain types of perceptions are relatively rigid or unchanjing from one stimulus situation to to the next. Other perceptions respond to changes in the stimulus environment. For example, did you notice the two errors purposely placed in the first sentence of this paragraph? If you did not catch both the misspelled word ("unchanjing") and the incorrectly repeated word ("to to"), don't be surprised. Your past learning told you to anticipate correct English in a book such as this. Although at this point your expectations may be somewhat changed, it is likely you will lapse back into such a pattern fairly soon. The principle describing this is called *set*—the temporary tendency to perceive stimuli in a certain manner. You held one set while reading the first part of this solution, a second set right now, but probably will return to the first fairly soon.

7.21   Suppose a person looking at Fig. 7-11 says that the vertical line is longer than the horizontal line. (The lines are actually the same length.) Is this an example of an illusion or a hallucination? What is the difference between an illusion and a hallucination?

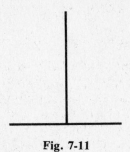

Fig. 7-11

The arrangement of the two lines creates an *illusion*, which is a misperception of a stimulus situation that really exists. A hallucination is a perception of something which does *not* exist (such as seeing an object or hearing a voice that is not really there).

7.22   What is subliminal perception?

Subliminal perception refers to situations in which a person responds to stimuli that are just below the threshold (limen) value. It is included as part of the study of perception because studies have shown that both reception and interpretation of a stimulus can occur even when a subject is not completely aware of the stimulus.

7.23   In Chapter 6, the concept of sensory adaptation to overload or deprivation was presented. What happens to perception if such conditions are maintained for a prolonged period of time?

Apparently, prolonged periods of deprivation or overload may cause a person to perceive the stimulus environment in unusual ways. These may include hallucinations or other bizarre attempts to perceive a stimulus environment that is more "normal" or "acceptable."

7.24   Why do psychologists tend to ignore extrasensory perception (ESP) as a part of psychological study?

The difficulty with studying ESP seems to result from the unreliability of the phenomena. They cannot be produced with consistency or regularity and are very difficult to study scientifically. Many ESP reports are made after the fact, and may be subject to misinterpretation because of the time lag between the event and the report. It simply seems difficult to either confirm or disconfirm most ESP research.

7.25   What types of ESP have been reported? What are the differences among them?

Four different types of ESP have been reported: *telepathy*—the transfer of thought from one person to another without the aid of speech, writing, or any other external stimuli; *precognition*—the ability to correctly predict the future; *clairvoyance*—the ability to report events not detectable by normal sensory processes; and *psychokinesis*—the ability to move objects without exerting physical force on them.

Key Terms

Apparent movement.   Static stimuli presented in such a way as to give the appearance of movement.

Attention.   The key to perception: if a subject is to perceive something, the subject must give some level of attention.

Binocular depth cues.   Cues to depth perception based upon the simultaneous functioning of two eyes.

Clairvoyance.   The disclosure of knowledge or information that could not have been received through regular sensory processes.

Closure.   In perception, the "completing" of an incomplete stimulus or piece of information.

Extrasensory perception (ESP).   Manipulation or interpretation of the environment in the absence of regular sensory processes.

Figure-ground relationship.   The interconnection of the principal stimulus and the stimuli that surround it.

Hallucination.   Perception of "stimuli" that do not exist.

Illusion.   Stimuli that exist in a configuration that creates an incorrect interpretation or understanding (misperception).

Interposition.   A monocular depth cue in which one object appears closer to the viewer because it partly blocks the view of another object.

Monocular depth cues.   Cues to depth perception that are dependent upon only one eye; perspective and interposition are examples.

Perception.   The interpretation or understanding of stimuli received as sensations.

Perceptual constancies.   Understanding the stability of an object's size, shape, color, brightness, etc., despite changing stimulus conditions.

Perspective.   A monocular depth cue in which perception of distance is based upon previous knowledge of size-distance and shape-slant relationships.

Precognition.   The correct prediction of events that have not yet occurred.

Psychokinesis.   The capacity to make objects move by using only thought processes.

Retinal disparity.   The difference between the visual images striking the retinas of the two eyes.

Sensory deprivation.   Doing without stimulation; extreme restriction of the sensory environment.

Sensory overload.   Excess stimulation; extremely high levels of a stimulus.

Set.   The temporary tendency to respond in a certain manner.

Subliminal perception.   The supposed understanding or interpretation of stimuli that occur at a level slightly below the threshold value.

Telepathy.   The transfer of thought from one person to another without the use of regular sensory channels.

Texture gradient.   The change in the appearance of texture based upon distance from the viewer; a monocular depth cue.

Chapter 8

States of Consciousness

Consciousness is the term for the internal mental experiences of which a person is aware. There may be an interaction between these mental experiences and the physiological processes of the body, but the definition of consciousness is limited to those internal characteristics that make up a person's mental experiences.

8.1 CHARACTERISTICS OF CONSCIOUSNESS

Many types of consciousness may be experienced by an individual. A few examples are thoughts or ideas, feelings, sensations and perceptions, and dreams. It appears that consciousness is a function of brain activity and that each individual may have several consciousnesses.

Differentiation of Consciousnesses

By using a device called an *electroencephalogram* (EEG), psychologists have been able to monitor and record the electrical activity in certain parts of the brain. The type of electrical activity observed may vary as the subject's state of consciousness changes, but different states of consciousness do not *necessarily* show markedly different types of electrical activity in the brain.

EXAMPLE 1. Consider your recollection of waking events as opposed to your recollection of dreams. The electrical activity of the brain is very similar for both states of consciousness, yet dreams often include illogical, dramatic, or vivid mental experiences that differ very much from mental experiences in a waking state. You may dream of flying by flapping your arms, but such a mental experience would not fit into your waking consciousness.

There are other indications of the fact that an individual has more than one consciousness. Split-brain studies (see Section 5.3) reveal that the left and right hemispheres of the brain have different conscious processes. Studies have also shown that some abnormal individuals appear to have multiple personalities, with unique conscious processes that accompany each.

EXAMPLE 2. A famous depiction of a case of multiple personality was the movie *The Three Faces of Eve*. The movie portrayed the totally separate and quite dissimilar personality patterns shown by a female client.

Limitations of Consciousness

Limitations of consciousness can be documented in at least three ways. First, if brain processes are disrupted or destroyed, conscious processes may be likewise upset or eliminated. Consciousness is a function of the brain, and therefore depends on the appropriate operation of the brain.

A second limitation is found even when all brain functioning is normal. Similar to the effect of attention on perception (see Chapter 7), consciousness is limited to the person's capacity to receive and process information. Certain behaviors such as meditation (see Section 8.2) or certain drugs such as LSD (see Section 8.3) seem to affect the limitations of consciousness, producing so-called "expansion" of consciousness. However, even these appear to have limits.

Third, environmental conditions may alter conscious processes. Interruption, conditions of fatigue, ecstasy, or sensory deprivation or overload represent examples of interferences which might place limitations upon a person's consciousness.

8.2 INTERNAL INFLUENCES ON CONSCIOUSNESS

Consciousness may be influenced by both internal states and external stimuli. Internal influences on consciousness may be the result of purposeful or non-purposeful behavior on the part of an individual.

Social Learning

Control of consciousness may be the purposeful act of an individual. Quite frequently, the decision to think or act in a certain manner is a function of the social restrictions a person has learned by past experience in a particular society.

EXAMPLE 3. Certain social standards may influence a person's consciousness and thus influence the person's behavior. For example, people who condemn a rich man for making use of tax loopholes may themselves make use of tax loopholes whenever they are able. The fact that such behavior is inconsistent may be blocked from consciousness by social learning.

Biofeedback

Biofeedback is a technique in which people can observe measurements of bodily processes that are otherwise unobservable. Individuals are then able to find ways to regulate processes such as heart rate or blood pressure, which are usually thought of as involuntary physiological responses. Quite frequently, this is accomplished by using a monitoring device that indicates the status of the otherwise "hidden" variable. As the person learns to control the bodily process, it is reflected by a change in the signal. In other words, the feedback provides information that helps the person focus conscious processes so as to manipulate the bodily activities.

EXAMPLE 4. Evidence indicates that migraine headaches may result from excessive blood flow in the brain area. To overcome this, biofeedback techniques have been used to get people to adjust their blood flow so that more blood goes to other parts of the body, thus decreasing the headache symptoms. (A monitoring device helps the person to learn conscious control of blood flow to the brain area.)

Meditation

Meditation techniques are used to try to "focus" conscious processes in a manner unlike that usually used in everyday circumstances. Two types of meditation are used frequently, concentrative meditation and opening-up meditation.

Concentrative meditation. Concentrative meditation limits conscious attention to a specific object or sound, trying to narrow attention to that direction only and to block out other stimuli from the environment. The result of concentrative meditation is supposed to be improved clarity of thought.

Opening-up meditation. Opening-up meditation tries to develop continuous attention to everything that is happeining. The technique is supposed to produce broad understanding of the total environment.

Both techniques will produce changed states of consciousness for some users. Many meditators claim profound benefits from meditation, including increased understanding of the self and the relationship of the self to the environment. Sometimes meditation is accompanied by changes in physiological processes, such as those described for biofeedback.

Sleep

Some of the most widely studied groups of conscious processes are those that occur during sleep. Extensive research has shown that several variables are quite significant in studying sleep.

Circadian rhythms. Humans appear to have a biological clock that operates in a regular, rhythmical fashion. The clock develops as a child becomes accustomed to particular environmental circumstances, resulting in daily rhythms of behaviors such as hunger, body temperature, hormonal flow, and sleeping. These rhythms usually match the 24-hour day, although research has shown that a person placed in an environment where time cues are eliminated may establish a rhythm on a shorter or longer cycle. A person whose sleep patterns are upset may require a period of adjustment (often several days to several weeks) before a new, workable sleep pattern establishes itself.

Sleep rhythms.   Sleep not only occurs at rhythmical times during the 24-hour-day, but also shows rhythmical patterns within the sleeping period. Research has identified four different stages of sleep, or depths of sleep, by recording changes in EEG frequencies and magnitudes. A person may move through this four-stage cycle several times during one night's sleep.

In general, stage 1 sleep is characterized by *alpha* brain waves (a rhythm of approximately 10 cycles per second). Stage 2 includes continued alpha activity, together with occasional *spindles* (bursts of 14-cycle-per-second activity), while in stage 3, *delta* waves (1 to 2 cycles per second) are added. Finally, stage 4 shows almost exclusive delta-wave activity.

REM sleep.   In addition to isolating four stages of sleep, psychologists have distinguished between two basic types of sleep: periods in which the sleeping subject shows rapid eye movements (*REM sleep*) and periods in which there is no rapid eye movement (*non-REM sleep*).

The average four-stage sleeping cycle lasts 80 to 90 minutes. After the first cycle is complete, each stage 1 sleeping period seems to be accompanied by REM activity. Most dreaming appears to occur during these stage 1 REM sleeping periods, while little dreaming is found in stages 2, 3, or 4.

EXAMPLE 5.   Observation of a sleeping person usually allows easy identification of the REM-sleep periods. A sleeper who is awakened during these periods will very likely report on dreams. (This is a very simple experiment to try at home, provided you can find a cooperative observer or sleeper.) Research has shown that sleepers awakened during REM sleep will report dreams about 80 percent of the time, whereas sleepers awakened from non-REM sleep will report dreams only about 15 percent of the time.

REM sleep is often called *paradoxical sleep* because the subject's heart rate, respiration rate, and EEG patterns closely resemble those observed when the subject is awake. (Other responses— such as muscle tone and reaction to external stimuli—are depressed even during REM sleep.)

Dreams.   Dreams appear to be a part of almost everyone's behavior, although some people are much more capable of recalling dreams than are others. Some research has suggested that dreams serve a recuperative function for individuals. If REM sleep is not allowed to occur for several sleeping periods in a row, irritability, anxiety, and even hallucinations may result.

Interestingly, sleepwalking and sleeptalking do not usually occur during REM sleep and do not seem to coordinate with dreams that are remembered upon awakening.

8.3   EXTERNAL INFLUENCES ON CONSCIOUSNESS

External stimuli may influence an individual's consciousness in many ways. Hypnosis, surgery, and drugs all fall within this category of external influences.

Hypnosis

Dramatic demonstrations of external control of consciousness often can be provided by hypnosis. Not all people are equally susceptible to hypnosis—5 to 10 percent of the population cannot be hypnotized at all, while a like percentage can reach very deep hypnotic trances. However, the effects of hypnosis tend to be similar for most people between these extremes. A hypnotized individual accepts the hypnotist's directions, showing increased suggestibility. The hypnotist may be able to restrict or direct the subject's attention. Furthermore, a hypnotized subject may experience a distorted perception of reality or show pronounced relaxation or alertness, depending upon the hypnotist's instructions. Very deep hypnotic states may approach a level of mystical experience.

EXAMPLE 6.   Placed in a fairly deep hypnotic state, a subject may follow the hypnotist's suggestions and talk about certain topics, experience certain motivations such as thirst, or perform somewhat unusual responses. Hypnosis is often thought of as a party or stage display; however, scientific uses include modification of pain thresholds and applications in psychotherapy.

Surgical Effects on Consciousness

Consciousness may be affected by certain types of brain surgery. The most obvious example of this is the split-brain procedure, which separates the functioning of the two hemispheres entirely by dividing the corpus callosum. (See Section 5.3.) The separated hemispheres show individualized consciousnesses and, in some cases, respond differently to the same stimulus.

It is not possible to predict all the effects that might be produced by brain surgery. Changes in emotional reactions, memory skills, or perceptual understandings have been demonstrated by testing patients before and after surgery. However, mapping of the brain is not yet complete enough for consistently accurate predictions to be made.

EXAMPLE 7.   The case of Phineas Gage is renowned in psychology as one of the first documented examples of the effects of the destruction of brain tissue upon conscious processes. Struck in a work accident by a piece of pipe that entered his eye socket and exited through the front top portion of the skull, Gage lived, but lost the brain tissue in the region of his frontal lobe. Very noticeable changes in his behavior were noted, especially in his emotional reactions to certain events. The loss of brain tissue apparently changed his way of responding, while all other variables remained relatively the same.

Psychoactive Drugs

Psychoactive drugs are those that can cause subjective, psychological changes in a person's consciousness. These include alcohol, narcotic drugs, hallucinogens, stimulants, antidepressants, sedatives, marijuana, and many more.

Frequently, psychologists try to distinguish between individuals who merely use such drugs and those who become reliant upon them. Relying upon such a drug when there is no reason to do so is described as drug *abuse*. Psychologists prefer the concepts of use and abuse rather than describing someone as an addict because a person may be a habitual user of one or more of these drugs and not be either psychologically or physiologically addicted.

Alcohol.   Alcohol, a depressant, is the most widely used of all the psychoactive drugs. When taken in sufficient quantities (which vary from one individual to the next), alcohol can depress aspects of central nervous system functioning, causing conscious reactions that are noticeably different from those produced in a nonalcoholic state.

EXAMPLE 8.   The flirtatiousness of people at a cocktail party may be the result of the depression of certain brain activity by alcohol. Continued drinking may lead to continued changes in brain activity, with the result that the previously cheerful "life-of-the-party" may become hostile, lose motor coordination, and possibly pass out.

Marijuana.   Smoking or eating marijuana may produce a psychoactive drug effect. Quite often, the marijuana "high" is a state of elation, in which the user claims an enrichment of sensory experiences.

Research into the use of marijuana has shown that the effects produced may be a function not only of the amount and characteristics of the marijuana used, but also of the expectations of the user. Motivation, past experience, and many other variables may create potential effects greater or lesser than those expected from the properties of the marijuana itself.

EXAMPLE 9.   Expectations sometimes produce remarkable effects. People have been known to get "drunk" when drinking cola or "high" when smoking oregano. The social setting, a person's beliefs, and many additional factors contribute to such behavior.

Prescription Drugs.   It is surprising to some that many prescription drugs are listed as psychoactive drugs. However, many of these drugs do produce a changed state of consciousness; in fact, this is often the effect that is sought when the drug is prescribed. Included in this category are drugs such as amphetamines, barbiturates, and many drugs, such as tranquilizers, prescribed in the course of psychiatric treatment.

The legal use of drugs has led to the development of a separate scientific discipline, called *psychopharmacology*, which investigates the psychological effect of drugs. It must be recognized that although these drugs have legal and appropriate uses, they can be abused and drug dependency may develop.

EXAMPLE 10.   One difficulty with psychiatric drugs may be that both doctor and patient may become too dependent upon their use. A doctor may prescribe them as a "cure-all," using them indiscriminately rather than carefully analyzing a patient's symptoms and considering other treatments. The patient comes to expect the drug-produced result and, in some cases, relinquishes possible self-control to the drug effect.

It should be recognized that psychological effects can also be produced by common, or nonprescriptive drugs. For example, a person could become caught up in a stimulant-sedative repetitive cycle, using caffeine or nicotine as the stimulant and "sleeping pills" as the sedative. Because tolerance levels build, more and more of each seems to become necessary.

Narcotic drugs.   Narcotic drugs are used frequently as painkillers. However, abuse of narcotic drugs such as morphine or heroin has become widespread. Initial misuse of narcotics commonly occurs for social reasons, but repeated dosages lead to a physiological dependence that continues to increase. The dependence has two aspects, the need for larger doses to prevent withdrawal symptoms (which can be quite severe) and the need for larger doses to produce the euphoric effect. Quite often, satisfaction of this need leads to illegal activities to procure the narcotic.

Hallucinogenic drugs.   Hallucinogenic (or psychedelic) drugs are so named because a major feature of their use is the production of hallucinations. These drugs, such as LSD or mescaline, are available legally only in controlled circumstances such as medical research.

One characteristic of hallucinogens is that the effect produced by their use cannot be predicted reliably. It is even difficult to predict whether the resultant mental experiences will be "favorable" or "unfavorable."

EXAMPLE 11.   Many individuals have used LSD with a positive result (particularly a feeling of increased sensory awareness), but some have experienced "bad trips," with pronounced anxiety, loss of coordination, and unpleasant hallucinations. Some claims for repeated "flashbacks" of such hallucinations have also been reported.

Reasons for Use of Psychoactive Drugs

The primary reason for using psychoactive drugs appears to be social influence from peers. Other reasons for use may involve a physical problem, such as insomnia, or a psychological need, such as relief from anxiety.

Solved Problems

8.1   A person may very well say, "My consciousness is personal." Is such a statement true, and if it is, how can psychologists investigate consciousness?

Consciousness includes mental experiences—such as thoughts, dreams, or perceptions—of which only the individual may be aware. Thus, they are personal. However, psychologists can study consciousness by soliciting verbal reports of these processes or by inferring from observable behaviors what kinds of conscious processes are going on.

8.2   Do conscious processes go on even when a person is asleep? Are there different consciousnesses which exist for one person?

Consciousness appears to be an active brain process. When the brain is functioning normally, conscious processes may occur. Because the brain functions during sleep, dreams are included in the category of conscious processes. Someone who is unconscious (as perhaps in a coma) does not appear to have comparable brain functioning.

Several consciousnesses appear to exist for any one person. Not only is there a sleeping consciousness and a waking consciousness; split-brain research, for example, indicates a left-hemisphere consciousness that is separate from the right-hemisphere consciousness. Furthermore, research in abnormal personality patterns has revealed rare cases of multiple personalities—that is, individuals with more than one distinct set of personality characteristics accompanied by independent sets of conscious processes.

8.3   Do there seem to be limitations on the kinds and intensity of consciousness a person can experience?

Three types of evidence point to limitations of consciousness. First, disruption or damage to the brain may limit consciousness. A person's consciousness thus seems to depend on the functioning of the brain. Second, even when the brain is functioning properly, a person's capacity to receive and process information is limited by learning and other previous experiences. Third, conditions in the stimulus environment, such as sensory overload or deprivation and disruptions, limit consciousness.

8.4   What kinds of disruption might affect a person's conscious processes?

Interference by some outside stimulus may be enough to disrupt a conscious process. (A person may accuse another of "interrupting my train of thought" when this happens.) Other environmental or personal conditions also may disrupt consciousness. These include such things as sensory deprivation, fatigue, or ecstasy.

8.5   A major influence creating internal control of consciousness seems to be social learning. What kinds of effects might be expected from social learning?

Most simply stated, social learning may lead to facilitation or inhibition of conscious processes. That is, learning may "encourage" or "discourage" certain kinds of mental experiences in a person's consciousness. For example, if a well-trained botanist and a well-trained geologist hiked through a forest together, it would be very likely that each would have a distinctly different consciousness of the experience.

8.6   What is biofeedback?

Biofeedback is the term popularly used to describe situations in which an individual, through observation, is able to gain control over physiological processes that are not ordinarily under voluntary control. In general, the procedure used is to create some signal that allows the individual to monitor the functions that are otherwise difficult or impossible to observe.

As the person becomes accustomed to the situation, research evidence indicates that ability to concentrate upon the feedback enables the development of control over the physiological functions. Thus, heart rate, blood flow, blood pressure, respiration rate, and EEG rhythm have been manipulated successfully by learning to concentrate consciousness in an appropriate manner.

8.7   Is meditation the same as biofeedback?

Not necessarily. Meditation may be one way in which a person can enhance the biofeedback process. However, other kinds of training, such as progressive relaxation or hypnosis, may prove effective in helping establish control associated with biofeedback.

8.8   What are the two basic types of meditation? Describe each.

Meditation techniques fall basically into two main categories: concentrative meditation and opening-up meditation. Concentrative meditation establishes a single point of focus, such as a *mantra* (a personal chant given to the learner by the meditation instructor), and restricts attention to that focus. Opening-up meditation is an attempt to pay complete attention to the complete stimulus environment. It is supposed to produce complete perception of the world at the moment, while concentrative meditation supposedly produces as its aftereffect a "clearness of thought" about the world.

8.9   Explain how "jet lag"—the fatigue and disorientation experienced by air travelers who have flown a great distance—may be the result of circadian rhythm.

Circadian rhythm is the term used to describe the "biological clock" each individual develops. Eventually, as a child grows older, a pattern is established for activities such as sleeping and bodily functions such as temperature regulation. This pattern is "fitted" to observable time cues, such as darkness and daylight.

A traveler who has crossed several time zones in a short time (as in a trans-Atlantic jet flight) will experience tiredness at the "wrong times." The circadian rhythms the traveler established in one time zone will not "fit" into the time cues of another time zone. (For example, the traveler may feel wide awake at midnight and very tired at noon.) It may take several days for a traveler's circadian rhythms to readjust to the new time zone.

8.10   Sleep often is described as occurring in stages. How are these stages identified?

The stages of sleep are identified by differences in EEG patterns, which measure brain waves. Four levels have been agreed upon, based in general upon the reduction in frequency and the increase in magnitude of the brain waves.

In addition, sleeping stages have been divided into periods accompanied by rapid eye movement (REM) and those where no rapid eye movement is observed (non-REM).

Both the depth of sleep (identified as the four stages) and the REM periods appear cyclical in nature. The sleeping cycles repeat themselves at roughly 80- to 90-minute intervals throughout a typical 8-hour night's sleep.

8.11   Is REM activity associated with one of the EEG levels? Other than eye-movement activity, what difference exists between REM and non-REM sleep?

REM activity occurs almost exclusively during stage 1 sleep. Furthermore, REM sleep differs from non-REM sleep in that most dreaming appears to occur during REM sleep. Average percentages from research reports show that waking from REM sleep yields a report of a dream about 80 percent of the time, while the percentage is about 15 percent when non-REM sleep is interrupted.

8.12   Explain why REM sleep is sometimes called paradoxical sleep.

The term *paradoxical sleep* is used to describe REM sleep because during it, several bodily functions—such as EEG, heart rate, and breathing—operate in patterns very similar to those found in a waking state. (Other bodily functions—such as response to external stimuli or muscle tone—are similar in REM sleep to those present during deep sleep.) Dreaming, the conscious activity of sleep, thus appears to occur most frequently in REM sleep.

8.13   Dreams have always been a subject of great interest for the general population. Now that psychologists have subjected dreams to careful study, what are some of the basic understandings that have developed?

One very basic principle is that almost everyone seems to dream. A second finding is that dreaming is good for a person. If REM sleep is accepted as evidence of dreaming, the difference which appears to exist between individuals is in the ability to *recall* dreams rather than in the ability to experience them. Repeated interruption of REM sleep for several days has been shown to bring about irritability, anxiety, and even hallucinations in some cases. (In this study, an experimental group was awakened repeatedly during REM sleep and showed increased anxiety and irritability. A control group that was awakened the same number of times, but during *non*-REM sleep, did not show anywhere near the symptoms of the experimental group.)

8.14   Are sleepwalking and sleeptalking a function of dreams?

Research evidence supports the idea that both sleepwalking and sleeptalking do not usually occur during REM-sleep dreaming periods, but rather during stage 2, 3, or 4 sleep. Dreams recalled the following morning usually have little or no connection with the sleepwalking or sleeptalking period.

8.15   A popular misconception is that hypnosis puts the subject in a "deep sleep." What evidence exists to contradict this belief?

The EEG measurements of a hypnotized subject are comparable to those of a waking subject rather than a sleeping subject. Furthermore, although most subjects in hypnotic states are very relaxed, it is possible to create hyperalert hypnosis, where the subject shows increased tension and recognition of stimuli.

8.16   What then are the characteristics of a hypnotic state?

Several attributes seem to mark the hypnotic state. In general, the hypnotized subject shows heightened suggestibility, develops selective attention (especially to hypnotist's voice), and is more likely to distort reality than is a person under normal conditions. Furthermore, the subject does all of this because of direction from the hypnotist rather than as a self-initiated behavior. It is possible for some subjects to reach very deep hypnotic states in which they experience mystical feelings.

8.17   If you were confronted with the task of trying to hypnotize someone, what kind of person would you select?

Not everyone is equally susceptible to hypnosis. Interestingly, your selection probably should be made on the basis of willingness to participate and the capacity the individual shows for imaginative experiences. Additionally, it appears to be important that the subject trust you (the hypnotist). Perhaps 5 to 10 percent of the population cannot be hypnotized at all, while about the same percentage can achieve deep hypnotic states. The rest of the population falls somewhere in between these two extremes.

8.18   What other external factors, besides hypnosis, can influence conscious processes?

Both drugs and surgery that affects the functioning of the brain can influence consciousness. It is important to remember, however, that the effect of either cannot always be accurately predicted.

8.19   Imagine a brain surgeon who is about to operate on a patient. The patient asks, "Will this operation affect the way I think?" What is the surgeon's answer?

The answer would have to be based upon the type of surgery being performed. As mentioned before, an operation to sever the corpus callosum will create a "split-brain" consciousness—preventing the transfer of conscious processes from one hemisphere of the brain to the other, although both sides could learn if exposed to the same stimuli. However, information about the function of many brain areas is so limited that it would be difficult to respond to the patient's question with a definitive yes or no unless one of the well-mapped areas of the brain was involved.

8.20   Are drug abuse and drug addiction the same thing?

Drug abuse is *any* misuse of a drug, and not necessarily physical or psychological addiction. For example, a person who is not an alcoholic may drink beer at a party to the point where he or she passes out. This would certainly be the abuse of a drug (alcohol), but would not necessarily be an indication of addiction.

8.21   Does the use of alcohol lead to an altered state of consciousness? What is the general affect of alcohol upon an individual?

Alcohol is a drug, and it belongs in the classification of psychoactive drugs—drugs that create subjective or psychological effects. Using alcohol may lead to an altered state of consciousness. Alcohol is a depressant and it may, if taken in sufficient quantity, depress central nervous functioning sufficiently to significantly alter conscious reactions to stimuli. (*Note*: The commonly accepted notion that alcohol stimulates an individual is incorrect. The effect produced is a *depression* of inhibitory mechanisms, thus making the individual appear to be stimulated.)

8.22   Marijuana also is classified as a psychoactive drug. Can its effect on consciousness be accurately predicted?

No. In the first place, there are many types of marijuana, and because it is illegal, "dosages" are not accurately controlled. Furthermore, the potential effect of a drug depends not only upon the quantity and quality of the drug, but on the set (or expectations) of the user. Perception, emotions, memories, sense of time, motor performance or other behaviors may be radically altered because of the person's expectations rather than the pure drug effect.

8.23   In a typical marijuana "high," what kinds of reactions can be expected?

The reported effects of marijuana most often include an enhancement of sensations accompanied by some kind of elation or euphoria. In other words, a "richness" of sensory experience occurs together with a sense of well-being. (*Note*: Some evidence indicates the drug can heighten unpleasant experiences as well as pleasant ones.)

8.24   Define *psychopharmacology*. What kinds of drugs are usually used in psychopharmacology? Why is psychopharmacology included in the study of states of consciousness?

Psychopharmacology is the study of the psychological effects of drugs. While any drug could be included in this topic, the drugs usually referred to are legal prescription drugs, including sedatives, antidepressants, and stimulants. Use of any of these drugs is likely to produce an altered state of consciousness. For example, sedatives are often prescribed to relieve insomnia, while stimulants (such as amphetamines) may be used for temporary relief from tiredness. Of course, abuse of or dependence on these drugs is possible, even when they are used legally.

8.25   Narcotic drugs have valuable medical uses, yet they have become a serious social problem. Why?

Repeated use of narcotic drugs, such as morphine or its derivative heroin, causes a person to develop a physiological dependence. The dependence creates an ever-increasing tolerance to the drug, and larger and larger doses are necessary to produce euphoria and to prevent withdrawal symptoms. While often started for social motives, the use of narcotic drugs becomes necessary to satisfy physiological needs. Nonmedical use of narcotic drugs can thus result in illegal sales and use, and those dependent on the drug may commit crimes to obtain money to buy it.

8.26   Why does a substance get classified as a psychedelic or hallucinogenic drug? How consistent are the effects of such drugs?

Certain drugs are labeled psychedelic or hallucinogenic because one of their main effects is to produce hallucinations. LSD and mescaline are examples of hallucinogenic drugs. Such drugs do not seem to have a consistent effect; that is, the resultant effects may produce "good" or "bad trips" at any given time.

8.27   What are some of the reasons why people use psychoactive drugs?

More than any other single factor, peer influence encourages or discourages the use of psychoactive drugs. Social pressure often leads to initial use, although with some drugs (such as heroin) physiological dependence may result eventually.

Other important reasons for the use of psychoactive drugs include situational circumstances, for example, the use of a stimulant to stay awake while studying for exams or the compulsive use of alcohol with meals.

Key Terms

Biofeedback.   The use of a monitoring device to reveal the status of physiological processes not otherwise easily observed.

Circadian rhythms.   Cyclical patterns of change in physiological functions such as hunger, sleep, or body temperature.

Concentrative meditation.   Meditation that limits attention to one specific object or sound.

Consciousness.   The internal mental experiences of which a person is aware.

Electroencephalogram (EEG).   A technique used to measure the electrical activity of the brain.

Hallucinogenic drugs.   Those drugs which have as a major characteristic the production of hallucinations.

Hypnosis.   A technique (or group of techniques) for inducing an altered state of consciousness that is characterized by increased suggestibility, relaxation or alertness, and possible distortion of reality.

Meditation.   Techniques used to focus or concentrate conscious processes.

Narcotic drugs.   Those drugs that can be used as painkillers, such as heroin or morphine.

Opening-up meditation.   An attempt to produce continuous attention to all aspects of the stimulus environment.

Psychoactive drugs.   Any of a number of drugs that can cause subjective or psychological effects for a person.

Psychopharmacology.   The study of the psychological effects of drugs.

Rapid-eye-movement sleep (REM).   The movement of the eyes during sleep; often the period in which dreaming occurs.

Examination I

For each of the first twenty-five questions, circle the best answer. (The correct answers appear on page 104.)

1. A psychologist who emphasizes the stimuli provoking observed responses and tends to avoid the concept of mind was most likely trained in the _____ tradition.

    (a) Psychoanalytic
    (b) Structuralist
    (c) Behaviorist
    (d) Gestaltist

2. Pseudosciences were important in the development of psychology because they _____.

    (a) accurately answered basic questions about physiology
    (b) provoked study of what is correct rather than what they suggested
    (c) were the sources of methodologies later used in experimental psychology
    (d) were particularly concerned with unconscious motives

3. A student is depressed because he has had trouble getting along with a new roommate. His grades have dropped slightly, and he wishes to talk to someone about the problem. He would most likely go to which of the following?

    (a) counseling psychologist
    (b) clinical psychologist
    (c) educational psychologist
    (d) social psychologist

4. A psychologist has studied the effects of room lighting on the ability of rats to solve a maze-learning problem. The independent variable in such a study is _____.

    (a) the numbers of errors made in the maze
    (b) the number of subjects tested
    (c) the responses, as measured by time needed to solve the maze
    (d) the room lighting

5. Both the control group and experimental group in a study are chosen so each group has 50 percent Protestants, 30 percent Roman Catholics, and 20 percent from other religions. The experimenter used _____ sampling technique.

    (a) random
    (b) stratified
    (c) accidental
    (d) naturalistic

6.   To collect information in a study, a psychologist hires an experimenter who does not know the purpose of the study and uses subjects who are not informed about the experiment's intent. Doing this _____.

    (a) illustrates use of single-blind control
    (b) shows use of a double-blind procedure
    (c) demonstrates the experimenter's attempt to make the study objective
    (d) both b and c are correct

7.   Which of the following can influence the performance of a fixed-action-pattern (FAP)?

    (a) sign stimulus
    (b) habituation
    (c) motivation
    (d) all of the above

8.   The sex of a human child is determined by _____ .

    (a) the chromosome carried by the male sperm cell
    (b) the chromosome carried by the female egg cell
    (c) the combination of chromosomes created in the zygote
    (d) all 46 chromosomes that form the embryo's cells

9.   Given: Father has characteristic *Ff* and Mother is *ff*, where *F* is dominant and *f* is recessive. What percentage of their children could *pass on* the recessive characteristic?

    (a) 25
    (b) 50
    (c) 75
    (d) 100

10. A spontaneous change in the genetic code, creating a permanent and often radical effect is called _____ .

    (a) crossing-over
    (b) a mutation
    (c) vacuum activity
    (d) eugenics

11. Suppose research has shown that a particular behavior can be learned only during a limited time period. The concept of _____ seems most appropriate to describe this situation.

    (a) nonspecificity
    (b) readiness
    (c) critical period
    (d) cognitive stages

12. A child is able to develop coordinated series of ideas, but to do so must relate them to observable events or objects. This child is probably in which of Piaget's stages of cognitive development?

    (a) sensori-motor
    (b) pre-operational
    (c) concrete operational
    (d) formal operational

13.   Development of all basic skills marks the end of which developmental stage?

    (a) infancy
    (b) early childhood
    (c) later childhood
    (d) adolescence

14.   As a child grows older, the influence of _____ is likely to become more important, while the influence of _____ generally decreases.

    (a) peers, significant adults
    (b) heredity, environment
    (c) prenatal stages, postnatal stages
    (d) readiness, critical periods

15.   The transmission of a signal through a nerve cell is called _____ .

    (a) excitatory potential
    (b) resting potential
    (c) action potential
    (d) graded potential

16.   Which of the following is part of the peripheral nervous system?

    (a) the cerebellum
    (b) the spinal cord
    (c) the autonomic system
    (d) the corpus callosum

17.   The endocrine system secretes _____ .

    (a) hormones
    (b) blood cells
    (c) into the blood stream and body cavities
    (d) *a* and *c*

18.   Sensation has taken place when _____.

    (a) the signal is picked up by the receptor
    (b) the action potential has passed through the sensory peripheral nerves
    (c) the signal has been recorded by the brain
    (d) a response has been made by an effector

19.   Color vision is generally best when the image is focused upon _____.

    (a) the cornea
    (b) the fovea
    (c) the rods
    (d) the cochlea

20.   The conversion of a stimulus into an action potential is described by the term _____.

    (a) dysfunction
    (b) reception
    (c) perception
    (d) transduction

21.   Seeing ○ as a circle represents _____.

         (a) closure
         (b) grouping
         (c) perceptual constancy
         (d) figure-ground relationship

22.   If you read the sentence "Sigmund Fraud was a founder of psychology," and you do not spot
       any errors, you have demonstrated the principle of _____.

         (a) set
         (b) perceptual constancy
         (c) subliminal perception
         (d) contrast

23.   A person who misinterprets a stimulus that actually exists has experienced _____.

         (a) an hallucination
         (b) an illusion
         (c) subliminal perception
         (d) extrasensory perception

24.   Most dreams appear to take place during _____.

         (a) stage 4 sleep
         (b) non-REM sleep
         (c) REM sleep
         (d) transcendental states

25.   External controls of consciousness include _____.

         (a) use of surgical procedures
         (b) meditation
         (c) biofeedback
         (d) both (*b*) and (*c*)

26.   Psychology has as its purposes the prediction or control of behavior. How are these
       alike? How do they differ?

           Prediction and control both allow psychologists to investigate the principles governing be-
       havior. They differ in that prediction usually refers to the psychologist's ability to anticipate
       naturally occurring events, while control refers to situations in which the psychologist manipulates
       the circumstances and therefore the observed responses.

27.   One of the students in Mrs. Hodge's class has had trouble "keeping up" with the rest of the
       class. Mrs. Hodge decides to try to find out why. What kind of psychologist would she ask
       to help?

           Mrs. Hodge would ask a school psychologist to evaluate the student's problems. This might
       involve psychological testing, diagnosis, and counseling for that student.

28. A psychologist has tested the effects of room color on the activity level of children playing in the room. What kinds of extraneous or irrelevant variables might the psychologist try to control in such an experiment?

The size of the room, the consistency of lighting, the temperature of the room, unusual noises, interruptions, and the like are all examples of the extraneous or irrelevant influences that might affect the results obtained.

29. In some experiments, the subjects are temporarily misled about the purposes of the investigation. In others, neither the subjects nor the data-collecting experimenters know the intent of the study. What are the names for these experimental conditions, and why are they used?

When only the subjects do not know the real purposes of the experiment, it is called a single-blind procedure. When neither the subjects nor the active experimenters know the real purposes, the procedure is called a double-blind.

Both techniques are used to try to avoid biases that might influence the results of the experiment. It is hoped that by using such procedures the experimenter can isolate the effect of the independent variable upon the dependent variable in the experiment.

30. Suppose that a particular species of bird seemed to develop longer wings over succeeding generations. What explanation might be given in terms of Charles Darwin's theory?

Darwin believed in natural selection, or "survival of the fittest." Apparently, the birds that develop longer wings are more likely to be able to survive. Thus, over generations, long-wing characteristics are found, while shorter-wing characteristics "drop out."

31. What are some of the causes of mental retardation? Can anything be done to prevent the birth of mentally retarded children?

Mental retardation may result from some genetic imbalance (such as Down's syndrome) or some environmental variable (such as insufficient oxygen supply during the prenatal period). These have been identified as leading causes of mental retardation. Genetic counseling or appropriate prenatal care may help prospective parents avoid having mentally retarded children.

32. Why must psychologists be careful in applying the "schedule" of a particular developmental scale to a particular child?

Developmental scales provide information about the typical or average child. However, any one child has particular characteristics unique to her or him, and the individual differences among children must be recognized.

33. For what age group are the terms *sensori-motor stage, infancy,* and *oral stage* used?

All three terms describe events of the first two years following birth. *Sensori-motor* is the term used by Piaget to describe cognitive events of the period; *infancy* describes the physical and motor development of the period; and *oral stage* was Freud's designation of the personality during that period of time.

34. At least in theory, moral development progresses through three stages. What would behavior of the third stage be like?

In the third stage, a person accepts standards because of self-understanding and the development of principles and a conscience. This behavior is considered "beyond" moral behavior that occurs simply because of rewards and punishments or because of duty.

35. The firing of a neuron has been described by the "all-or-none principle." What does this principle state?

The all-or-none principle describes the response of a neuron to a precipitating stimulus. If the stimulus value is great enough, an action potential is generated and travels throughout the length of the neuron. No signal can start and then "die" part of the way through the neuron.

36. What explanation is there for the human being's superiority over other organisms in the abilities to communicate, generate thoughts, and create ideas?

Researchers have been able to "map" some of the functions of the cerebral cortex. Their findings indicate that only a small percentage of the cortex's total area is involved with sensori-motor functions; a much larger area seems to control communication and memory processes. "Lower" animals do not have such a highly developed cerebral cortex.

37. What are the findings and purposes of split-brain research?

Split-brain research has investigated the functioning of the cerebral hemispheres when the connections between them are temporarily disrupted or permanently destroyed. These studies reveal the differences in function for the two hemispheres, allow the investigation of hemisphere dominance, and provide information regarding the transfer of information from one hemisphere to the other.

38. Why is sensation said to occur in the brain?

Sensations are not registered or "recorded" until the signal has reached the sensory area of the cerebral cortex. A signal is picked up by a receptor, transduced into an action potential, transmitted through the sensory peripheral nervous system into the cerebral cortex, where it is then interpreted as a sensation.

39. Working in a chicken-processing plant, Rose finds she soon adjusts to the peculiar odor associated with chickens. Her reaction represents what psychological principle?

Rose is showing sensory adaptation. Her sensory sensitivity has adjusted to the amount of stimulation, the type of stimulation, and the consistency of that stimulation.

40. Standing at attention during a military review, a soldier notices that it is somewhat difficult to maintain perfect balance. Why?

It is likely that several factors have combined to affect the soldier's balance. The position of attention may have put unusual demands upon the kinesthetic senses by having the body held in a rigid position. The soldier's position may also have restricted visual referents and limited touch reception or vestibular reception. Any or all of these might affect balance and help create the soldier's problem.

41. There are several different kinds of perceptual constancies. All of them, however, share a common principle. What is it?

Perceptual constancies show that an experienced organism's response to stimulation remains the same even when the stimulus is placed in different circumstances. Thus, a square is seen as a square even when it is viewed at an angle, and the yellow car is seen as yellow, even in unusual lighting.

42.   In a drawing of a golfer striking a drive, the viewer is led to focus upon the person. The tee, the trees, the fairway, and other aspects of the drawing surround the person, but are not prominent. What principle describes this relationship between the person represented and the other components of the drawing?

This is the figure-ground relationship. The person (figure) is made to stand out from the background (ground) so that the viewer's focus is on the golfer and not on the other parts of the drawing. This can be accomplished by placement of the figure, size, contrast, or many other factors.

43.   Suppose, in the same drawing, that the artist includes some double-image lines and "sweep" lines around the arms. What is the artist attempting to accomplish?

These lines would be used to try to give the impression of movement. In a static presentation such as a drawing, the use of apparent movement is an attention-getting device.

44.   How are sensory deprivation and sensory overload alike? How do they differ?

Sensory deprivation and sensory overload represent the two ends of the sensation continuum: unusually low and unusually high levels of stimulation, respectively. The response to sensory deprivation is often to try to generate more stimulation. The response to sensory overload is frequently sensory adaptation.

45.   Explain why professional athletes sometimes have difficulty adjusting their sleeping and eating schedules to their playing schedules.

Each person establishes what are called circadian rhythms, or a biological clock. When playing schedules disrupt eating and sleeping routines (as they are likely to do with day and night games being played in several time zones) the athletes may have considerable difficulty adjusting.

Answers to Problems 1–25

1. (c)	6. (d)	11. (c)	16. (c)	21. (a)
2. (b)	7. (d)	12. (c)	17. (d)	22. (a)
3. (a)	8. (a)	13. (b)	18. (c)	23. (b)
4. (d)	9. (d)	14. (a)	19. (b)	24. (c)
5. (b)	10. (b)	15. (c)	20. (d)	25. (a)

Chapter 9

Motivation

Motivation may be defined as *conditions which initiate, guide, and maintain behaviors*—usually until some goal is reached or the response has been blocked. Motivation seems to play a part in all behaviors.

9.1 THE MOTIVATION CYCLE

Some motives appear in cycles. The *cycle of motivation* follows a three-part repetitive chain: (1) a *need* or drive builds; (2) *instrumental responses* are made as attempts to reach some goal to satisfy the need; and (3) once the *goal* has been reached, *relief* from the need follows. Often, the relief is only temporary, and the cycle may start again.

EXAMPLE 1. An obvious illustration of the motivation cycle is the sequence of hunger, finding and eating food, temporary relief, hunger again, and so on. The repetitive nature of the motivation cycle can be shown for many different motive conditions, and the time span for the cycle may vary.

9.2 VARIABLES AFFECTING THE MOTIVATION CYCLE

While the motivation cycle itself seems rather simple, it may be altered or modified by several types of variables.

Assessment of Motivation

The strength and quality of a motive condition may be estimated in one of two ways. First, an estimate of strength of motivation can sometimes be made by determining how long it has been since the motive was last satisfied. This period of time represents the *deprivation* the person experiences. In experiments, psychologists may manipulate deprivation in order to influence a subject's motive condition.

A second means of estimating the strength of motivation is to observe particular behaviors and infer from them a subject's motive condition. This method depends on naturalistic observation, and requires that the observer has had some previous knowledge that associates a certain kind of behavior with a particular motive condition.

EXAMPLE 2. Parents of a very young child are able to estimate when their child is hungry by finding out how long it has been since the child was last fed. They may also estimate a child's hunger by observing certain behaviors (such as crying) that are associated with hunger.

Adaptation of Response

Many motives promote nonproductive responses, which do not serve the instrumental purpose of leading to a goal. In many cases, a person will have to make a behavioral adjustment, so that different instrumental responses are made and the cycle can be completed.

EXAMPLE 3. A young child may find that banging on the table with a spoon or shouting at a parent does not serve to get the parent to bring food. The child may have to adjust his or her behavior—perhaps by learning to ask politely for food—in order to satisfy the motive condition.

Goal Specificity

Not all satisfiers (goals) are viewed as equally desirable. A person who appears to prefer a certain goal over others—even when the others would satisfy the motive condition adequately—is exhibiting *goal specificity*.

EXAMPLE 4. Parents feeding a very young child may find that the child expresses preferences very noticeably, even when communication by language has not yet developed. For example, the child may spit out the carrots but gulp down all the green beans.

9.3   GENERAL PRINCIPLES OF MOTIVATION

It is difficult to determine just how many different types of motives exist. It is sometimes impossible to make a simple distinction between unlearned motive conditions and learned motive conditions. Furthermore, it is sometimes impossible to determine the origins of motives. Despite these difficulties, certain principles seem to apply to many, if not all, motive conditions.

Instinct, Need, and Drive

Instinct, need, and *drive* are three terms used to describe motive conditions. An *instinct* is defined as an innate condition that regularly provokes a specific, complex response from all members of a certain species when a distinctive stimulus pattern is presented. A *need* is sometimes described as a deficit or imbalance. A need may be physiological (such as a need for warmth) or psychological (such as a need for achievement). A *drive* is either the state resulting from the physiological need or a general wish to achieve some goal.

Functional Autonomy

Some responses to a motive condition may persist even after the original motive condition ceases to exist. In such a case, the response itself becomes a motive. This is called *functional autonomy*.

EXAMPLE 5. Ask almost any "confirmed" smoker if smoking was enjoyable when it was first started. The answer you will probably get is no. Very few people started smoking because they found it truly pleasurable. Rather, they smoked at first because it brought social approval of some kind. However, smoking becomes self-motivating, so much so that the individual eventually may smoke even when it is socially disapproved.

Relationship of Motivation to Performance

A general relationship of motivation to performance is shown by the graph in Fig. 9-1.

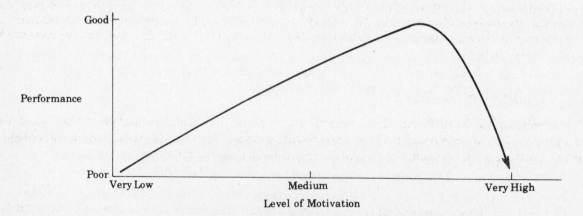

Fig. 9-1

The exact maximum level of motivation that will yield the best performance will vary from task to task, but the general research finding is that performance will be poorer if the motivation level is lower *or* higher.

EXAMPLE 6.   Students are familiar with the effects of motivation on performance. The student who does not care at all about a course often does poorly. The student who cares, but keeps it under control, does well. The student who cares too much (and "clutches") often does poorly.

9.4   UNLEARNED MOTIVES

Some *unlearned motives* are called *survival motives* because they must be satisfied if an organism is to continue to live. The list of survival motives is short: hunger, thirst, the need for air, the need to maintain body temperature, the need to relieve fatigue, and the need to eliminate body waste products. The responses which satisfy these motives are eating, drinking, breathing, sheltering, sleeping, and eliminating.

One additional unlearned motive condition, that of pain, appears to be unlearned, but is *not* a survival motive. It is possible to live without relief from pain for many years, while relief of any of the other unlearned motives must occur relatively soon or death will occur. In the case of the survival motives the time span may vary from minutes to weeks, depending upon which motive is involved. However, relief is essential in all cases, while it is not for pain.

Homeostasis

Many of the body processes that operate to satisfy the unlearned motives are automatic in nature. The body regulates itself in an attempt to maintain an internal physiological balance. This balance is called *homeostasis*.

EXAMPLE 7.   A weight-reduction diet makes use of the body's tendency to make homeostatic adjustments. When individuals who are overweight reduce their food intake, they create an energy deficit. To make up for this deficit, the body will burn stored fats. This, in turn, will lower the weight and thus make the diet successful. (*Note*: You are always on some kind of diet. The question is, is the diet a good one or a bad one for you?)

Response Variability

Satisfaction of the survival motives is essential, but the type of satisfaction may vary from person to person and from time to time. The amount of variability differs depending upon which motive is being discussed, but all show some flexibility in terms of what responses and goals will complete the motivation cycle.

EXAMPLE 8.   Someone living in Pennsylvania would recognize a need for some type of shelter at least during part of the year. Maintaining body temperature simply could not be done unless shelter was available. The response that would satisfy this need might range from living in a tent and insulated sleeping bag to living in a thirty-room mansion. Many motives besides the need to maintain body temperature would influence the choice of shelter.

9.5   COMBINATION MOTIVES

Psychologists have found that some motives, called *combination motives* result from the combined effect of unlearned and learned characteristics. Other motives cannot be classified as either learned or unlearned; that is, their origins remain in debate.

Sex

Sex is probably the best example of a combination motive. Some aspects of sexual development and sexual response—such as onset of puberty or the time needed for recovery between one ejaculation and the next—are physiologically determined. Other aspects of sexuality—such as standards of attractiveness or acceptable sexual practices—are a function of social learning. As a result, any one individual's sexual motivation results from a combination of physiological and social influences. (*Note*: Sex is not classified as a survival motive. Survival of the species depends upon sexual activity, but survival of an individual does not.)

Maternal Behavior

Maternal behavior is another combination motive. Hormonal flow influences maternal behavior, but so do social standards.

Stimulation Needs

Stimulation needs refer to the levels and types of sensory or perceptual activity an individual requires. These requirements for stimulation appear to be both unlearned and learned. Stimulation needs include motives such as the need for activity, the need for variety, and the need to satisfy curiosity.

EXAMPLE 9.   Some psychologists have been very concerned about the effects of educational television shows on children. The psychologists suspect that such shows create a need for very high levels of stimulation in children who are presented with educational materials. Although the psychologists realize that a minimal (unlearned) level of stimulation is essential if learning is to occur, they fear that the preschool-age child will come to expect a (learned) level that cannot be duplicated or maintained in the school setting.

Contact Comfort

Contact comfort is one motive whose origins have remained in debate. Contact comfort is the apparent need of the young to have soft, warm, cuddly things to which they may cling. It is still impossible to definitively state whether this need is an unlearned, inborn reaction or the result of associating such stimuli with other rewarding activities, such as feeding.

EXAMPLE 10.   A "special" blanket or stuffed animal may provide a young child with contact comfort. The reasons why the blanket or animal are so special, however, are not yet clearly defined. (It is possible this motive influences some adult behavior, also.)

9.6   LEARNED MOTIVES

Learned motives are often called *social motives* because they develop from social (environmental) interactions. In many societies, these become the predominant motives because survival needs are satisfied readily and easily. Learned motives generally develop as a result of societal rewards and punishments and include motive conditions such as the need for achievement, the need for friendship or affiliation, the need for dominance, and the need for relief from anxiety. None of these are necessary for survival and none seem to have an unlearned component, yet all may become very important determinants of behavior. (*Note*: Needs such as those described above probably exist because of some psychological deficit, but direct demonstration of such needs has not been accomplished.)

It should be kept in mind that the list of learned motives given in this section is incomplete. (A complete list of all learned motives would be exceedingly long.) Several unmentioned learned motives that have been studied are needs for play, understanding, aggression, and autonomy.

Need for Achievement

One of the most extensively researched of learned motives is the *need for achievement*. Individuals who seek a very high standard of performance for themselves have probably internalized achievement as a personal goal. However, they probably developed their need to achieve because of the social approval of success or the punishment of failure.

Much research on achievement needs has been conducted by using the *Thematic Apperception Test* or some other similar projective task. (See Chapter 17.) A person taking such a test is confronted with ambiguous pictures and is asked to describe them or tell stories about them. These stories or descriptions are supposed to reveal the subject's need for achievement. Most of the studies have been conducted with male subjects, although recent investigations have tried to identify achievement and fear-of-success motivations in women as well.

EXAMPLE 11.   In an early investigation of sex differences in attitudes toward achievement, male subjects were asked to respond to a statement describing a male who was the top student in his medical school class, and female subjects were asked to respond to a statement describing a female who was at the top of her medical school class. Almost all males responded favorably to the top male student; that is, they said the man's achievements would result in positive aftereffects. By contrast, the majority of the females indicated that the woman's success would lead to difficulties, particularly loss of femininity or social rejection. Subsequent research has questioned this result, but this technique for studying achievement motivation continues to be used.

Need for Dominance

The *need for dominance* is satisfied by being able to direct others' behavior. This may be accomplished by persuasion, suggestion, command, or some other means. No matter which technique is employed, successful control over others' responses is the intended goal.

Need for Affiliation

Another highly researched learned motive is the *need for affiliation*, the need to experience attachment to others through friendship, sociability, or group membership. Closely related to the need for affiliation is the motive for *dependency*—that is, reliance upon others. Affiliation and dependency appear to correlate with a number of other behaviors, including performance in testing situations and reactions to anxiety.

EXAMPLE 12.   In one research study, college students were observed as they awaited receiving an electric shock. During this waiting period, the students showed signs of anxiety and a marked tendency to prefer to wait with others rather than to wait alone. Apparently, the need for affiliation grows as the need to relieve anxiety grows.

Need for Relief from Anxiety

Social learning may create problems, which in turn create anxiety until they are solved. The need to relieve such anxiety may serve as a motive condition, causing a person to seek responses that will reduce the anxiety and solve the problem. Rather than seeking out something positive, an anxious person is motivated to get away from something negative.

9.7   CONFLICT

More than one motive condition may be operating at any given moment. Sometimes the motive conditions are compatible with each other, but at other times they may be incompatible. Psychologists call this latter situation a *conflict*. Several different types of conflict situations exist.

Approach-Approach Conflict

One of the milder and more easily resolved conflicts is the *approach-approach conflict*, a situation in which a person must choose between two or more positively-valued persons or objects. A conflict arises because only one of several possible positive responses can be chosen.

EXAMPLE 13.   Suppose you are in a resturant where dessert is included in the price of the dinner. You can choose only one dessert from the list of chocolate parfait, lemon meringue pie, strawberry shortcake, and hot fudge sundae. If you like more than one of the desserts listed, you are experiencing an approach-approach conflict.

Avoidance-Avoidance Conflict

An *avoidance-avoidance conflict* exists when a person is confronted with a choice between two or more negatively-valued persons or objects. Occasionally, the person will withdraw entirely from the situation rather than choose.

Approach-Avoidance Conflict

An *approach-avoidance conflict* occurs when an observer is confronted with a single person, object, or event that has both positive and negative qualities. The relative strengths of these opposing qualities must be weighed by the observer before a resolution can be reached. *Multiple approach-avoidance conflicts* are found in situations where there is more than one stimulus and each has both positive and negative values.

EXAMPLE 14. Suppose someone who was on a weight-reduction diet was confronted with the menu described in Example 13. This person would see any one choice of dessert as both positive (how good it would taste) and negative (how many calories it has). The menu would thus create a multiple approach-avoidance conflict for the dieter.

9.8   THEORIES OF MOTIVATION

Four well-known theories of motivation that attempt to explain motive conditions are humanistic theory, psychoanalytic theory, social-learning theory, and activation-arousal theory.

Humanistic Theory

The basis of the humanistic theory of motivation is a *hierarchy of needs*, suggested by the psychologist Abraham Maslow. A simplified summary of this hierarchy is as follows: (1) physiological needs (survival motives); (2) safety needs (security motives); (3) belongingness needs (affiliation and acceptance needs); (4) esteem needs (status and achievement motives); (5) self-actualization needs (to become what one is capable of becoming).

Each level of needs must be at least partially satisfied before the next will become important to an individual. The humanistic psychologist sees self-actualization as the ultimate goal of every person.

Psychoanalytic Theory

Sigmund Freud is given credit for psychoanalytic theory. Freud viewed motivation as largely unconscious and frequently an expression of aggressive or sexual desires. These might be expressed openly or in some symbolic form such as dreams or "slips of the tongue." (See Chapter 19 for a more thorough treatment of psychoanalytic theory.)

Social Learning Theory

Social-learning theorists propose previous learning as the major source of motivation. The success or failure of particular responses leads to an understanding of what will produce positive or negative consequences and a desire to repeat successful behaviors.

Personal experience is not mandatory for social learning to occur; learning by observing some other person succeed or fail may be sufficient to produce motive conditions. (See Chapter 13.) Moreover, rewards or punishments may be either external or internal.

Activation-Arousal Theory

Activation-arousal theory proposes that any organism has a typical, normal, appropriate level of arousal and that behavior will be directed toward trying to maintain that level. This means that if environmental stimulation is too high, behaviors will occur to try to reduce arousal; if stimulation is too low, an increase of arousal will be sought.

EXAMPLE 15. A possible explanation of why a person might seek the anxiety-arousal of a sky-diving situation may be found in this theory. The person may have a typically high level of arousal and use activities such as sky-diving to keep arousal near or at this norm.

Solved Problems

9.1   Your child's teacher calls you one afternoon and tells you that your child has been "acting up" periodically in class. Apparently, your child continues to misbehave until the teacher has to stop whatever else is being done with the rest of the class. The teacher asks why the child persists in misbehaving. Having studied some psychology, you answer, "It's just an example of the motivation cycle." The teacher asks you to explain. How would you describe the motivation cycle?

The motivation cycle starts with some initial drive or need. This is usually followed by an instrumental (goal-seeking) response and, if the motive condition is strong enough, the responding continues until the goal is reached. Once the goal is achieved, there is relief. This relief is often only temporary; when the motive strength again builds up, the cycle may begin once more.

In this case, perhaps the child needs attention or social recognition from the teacher. If this is lacking in everyday activities, the need continues to grow until the child *has* to find a way to get attention. Disruption is the instrumental response, the goal is satisfied (temporarily) and does not reappear until the motive strength has once again increased.

9.2   Why does the child in Problem 9.1 misbehave (rather than do something else) in order to get attention?

Very simply, because it works. Generally, most organisms are able to make adjustments or adaptations to conditions to allow satisfaction of a motive condition. In this case, apparently, bad behavior gets attention while good behavior doesn't.

9.3   The other children in the class in Problem 9.1 try to stop your child's misbehavior, but it continues until the teacher says or does something. Why is that?

The misbehaving child is showing goal specificity. Just as not any food will satisfy a hunger drive in most cases, not any attention appears to work in this situation. The child seems to want the *teacher's* attention particularly.

9.4   How can one estimate whether a motive exists and how strong it is?

Estimates of motivation can be made in two ways. One way is to determine how long it has been since the motive was last satisfied; this period of time represents the deprivation the subject has experienced. The other way of estimating motivation involves observing behavior and estimating what the motive must have been to provoke that behavior; this method involves naturalistic observation of the subject and inferring from such observation.

9.5   Does deprivation automatically create a motive condition?

In some cases, deprivation automatically creates a compelling motive condition. For example, if you were deprived of air, you would be intensely motivated to try to correct the situation. However, other kinds of deprivation do not create motive conditions. If you were deprived of a trip to Cleveland, you might not feel deprived and motivated. In other words, deprivation does not necessarily create a motive condition.

9.6   *Instinct, need,* and *drive* are all used to describe motivational situations. What does each
            of these terms mean?

            An *instinct* is defined as an inborn condition that automatically triggers specific complex
            behaviors from all members of a certain species when a particular stimulus is present. A *need* is not
            automatic; it has been described either as a physiological imbalance or something more general, such
            as a social need for affection. A *drive* is viewed as the state resulting from the physiological or
            psychological deficit, or, more generally, as a desire to reach some goal.

9.7   What is functional autonomy?

            On occasion, a response is first made as an instrumental response, used to try to satisfy some
            motive condition. As the response is made repeatedly, the person comes to appreciate the response
            for its own sake. When the response becomes motivating in and of itself, functional autonomy has
            occurred. An example of this might be jogging, which is first done to try to get into condition, but
            later is appreciated just for the pleasure it brings.

9.8   Suppose a tennis player says to her coach, "I was so 'up' for the match that I played very
            poorly." What principle of motivation is the tennis player describing?

            In general, it seems that a person's performance will improve as motive level increases, but only
            up to a point. When the level of motivation surpasses this point, the person's performance can be
            expected to deteriorate. The tennis player in this example may have been over-motivated. Her
            performance might have been better had she not been so "up" for the match.

9.9   What motive conditions have to be satisfied in order for people to survive?

            The so-called *survival motives*, each of which must be at least partly satisfied if a person is to
            continue living, are: hunger, thirst, the need for air to breathe, the need to maintain body tempera-
            ture, the need to relieve fatigue, and the need to eliminate waste products from the body. To survive,
            a person must satisfy each of these motives—some very quickly, others with less immediate
            demand. (For example, a person cannot survive without air for more than a few minutes, but can live
            several days without sleep or several weeks without eating.)

9.10   Describe some of the adjustments the human body itself may make automatically in order
            to satisfy the survival motives. What name is given to the physiological state the body
            attempts to maintain?

            When the body gets too warm, it perspires in order to cool off. When the body is too cold, it
            shivers to warm up. If a person needs liquid and has ingested none for some time, the body's stored
            liquids are used and dehydration begins. When fatigue becomes intolerable, sleep is inevitable, such
            as in a state of exhaustion. All of these processes represent the body's attempts to maintain
            homeostasis, or internal physiological balance. (*Note*: The motive condition is described as the need
            or drive, while eating, drinking, sleeping, eliminating, breathing, and sheltering are the responses
            made to satisfy these motives.)

9.11   All of the survival motives are unlearned. What other motive is unlearned but not
            classified as a survival motive?

            The need to relieve physiological pain is unlearned, but not included in the list of survival
            motives. This is because one *must* satisfy the survival motives within some time period or die, while
            it is possible to live with pain for an entire lifetime.

9.12   Do all human beings satisfy their survival motives in the same way?

            The amount of variability depends upon the particular survival motive being discussed. All
            people breathe in order not to suffocate, just as all people sleep and all people eliminate waste

products. It can also be said that all people eat, but one person may adhere to a "meat and potatoes" diet while another is a strict vegetarian and a third lives only on intravenous feeding.

9.13	Problem 9.12 suggests that a person may show goal specificity in satisfying a survival motive. May a person also show functional autonomy in satisfying a survival motive? Furthermore, may learned motives play a part in determining how a person satisfies a survival motive?

The answer to both questions is yes. For example, a person may have to wear clothing in order to maintain an adequate body temperature in a cold climate. This survival motive—the need to keep warm—is unlearned. However, the person may be satisfying certain learned social motives in selecting a wardrobe. Also, the choice of clothing may be satisfying in and of itself—in other words, in selecting a particular wardrobe, the person may be showing functional autonomy.

9.14	Is sex a survival motive? Explain your answer.

The best answer is "yes and no." If one talks about survival of the species, the answer is yes. However, the survival of an individual does not depend on sexual activity.

9.15	Don't humans have unlearned sexual responses? Why shouldn't sex be classified as un-learned?

Sexual response, to some extent, is unlearned. Certain physiological processes are relatively automatic and appear if appropriate stimulation starts the responses. However, learned variables also strongly influence human sexual activity. These variables may differ from one group to another, depending on a particular society's standards of such things as beauty or sexual morality.

9.16	Sexual motivation is a combination of unlearned and learned factors. Name some other combination motives.

Several other motives seem to be both unlearned and learned. Maternal behavior, which is affected by both hormonal flow and social standards, seems to be both learned and unlearned. Contact comfort, the apparent need for something soft and warm to cuddle, that is shown by young children, also seems to be both learned and unlearned. Stimulation needs also fall in the category of combination motives.

9.17	Why are stimulation needs classified as combination motives?

Stimulation needs are a combination of unlearned and learned factors. The study of sensory deprivation (see Section 7.3) has shown that if a minimal level of stimulation is not present, a person will try to increase stimulation (it has been suggested, in extreme cases, by hallucinating). Such behavior appears to be unlearned. However, research has also indicated that the individual who has been rewarded in stimulating circumstances will seek out those circumstances again and again. These latter responses appear to be the result of learning.

9.18	Are learned (social) motives more important in modern developed societies than they are in underdeveloped societies?

Probably. Most people in modern developed societies do not have to worry much, if at all, about the unlearned (survival) motives: these people have adequate food, drink, shelter, sleep, the opportunity to breath, and the opportunity to eliminate body waste products. As a result, learned behaviors, which are influenced by societal rewards and punishments, become predominant in a person's life. In a society that does not offer satisfaction of the basic survival motives (particularly for food and liquids), the learned motives might not predominate.

9.19   Why is achievement sometimes called a "masculine" characteristic?

There are basically two reasons for this. One is that most of the first 25 years of research on achievement was done using males as subjects. The second reason is that initial research using female subjects concentrated on the idea that females feared success. (It was believed that a female showing high achievement risked social rejection and/or loss of femininity, while success motives in males were seen in a more positive light.) More recent research indicates that these results may be very situation-specific rather than exclusively related to sex.

9.20   Dominance, affiliation, and anxiety relief have been classified as learned motives. What conditions might lead to the development of such motives?

Such motives might be necessary for survival; for example, you might avoid someone who had a fatal communicable disease, or you might want to affiliate yourself with a person who would protect you in a dangerous situation. It is much more likely, however, that these motives result from social pressures. Dominance over others may lead to rewards, affiliation with others may give a person an "in-group" feeling, and relief of anxiety is frequently relief from society-produced problems, getting away from difficulties and establishing a more tolerable condition.

9.21   A college athlete achieved All-American status in football and baseball. Professional teams in both sports sought to sign him to a contract. Confronted with two lucrative offers, he could not decide which to take. What psychological term describes this athlete's situation? What resolution might be expected?

The athlete is faced with an approach-approach conflict, in which both possible choices are attractive to him (or positively valued). The resolution would be to choose the sport that seemed to be most favorable—perhaps football because of the immediate membership on a major league team or perhaps baseball because a longer career in sports could be expected.

9.22   Name two other common forms of conflict and give examples of each.

Two other common conflicts are avoidance-avoidance conflicts and approach-avoidance conflicts. *Avoidance-avoidance* involves two unpleasant choices, such as when a person must spend Saturday morning either cleaning house or doing the laundry. *Approach-avoidance* conflicts exist when a single choice has both pleasant and unpleasant possibilities. Studying may result in good grades, but it is also hard work and may keep a person from doing other, more pleasant, things. (In addition, a person may be faced with a multiple approach-avoidance conflict, in which there are several choices and each has both positive and negative aspects. For example, buying a car may represent a multiple approach-avoidance conflict. Each car you might buy has positive features, such as good mileage or good looks; but each car may also have negative features, such as a high price or a high insurance payment.

9.23   How are conflicts resolved?

In general the resolution of all conflicts is essentially the same: the most dominant motive "wins out," and the person chooses accordingly. However, in the case of an avoidance-avoidance conflict, the person may sometimes choose a third alternative, that of "leaving the field." The person in Problem 9.23 might spend Saturday morning sleeping rather than cleaning or laundering, thus withdrawing altogether from the conflict situation.

9.24   Imagine a person opening the door of an apartment and greeting another person, who is a new acquaintance. The person who opens the door is looking forward to the visit from someone who may turn out to be a good friend. What need does this person have, and where in Maslow's humanistic hierarchy does this need fall?

This person's need is for affiliation, which would be approximately in the middle of Maslow's humanistic hierarchy. The person's physiological and safety needs apparently are not uppermost at the moment, but affiliation or belongingness are currently important. At this moment, the person does not seem to show need for self-esteem or self-actualization.

9.25 Suppose the host greets the visitor with "I'm so mad you're here" when really intending to say "I'm so glad you're here." How might a psychoanalytic theorist interpret this slip of the tongue?

Psychoanalytic theory places heavy emphasis on the influence of unconscious motives related to sex or aggression. In this case, the host may be unconsciously annoyed by the visitor's interruption. The aggressive greeting could be seen as an instance of unconscious motives affecting behavior.

9.26 Now imagine that the person at the door is selling magazines. Suppose the tenant is able to firmly but politely refuse to listen to the sales pitch the salesperson wants to make. What might a social learning theorist say about this response?

Social learning theory proposes that motivations are a function of past learning experiences. Successful responses and those that produce unfavorable consequences lead to an understanding of what will produce rewards and/or punishments. Apparently, this individual has had previous experience with door-to-door sales attempts and has learned the appropriate responses to satisfy the motive of not wanting to be disturbed. The past experience need not have been personal; learning by observing someone else successfully cope with the situation may lead to modeling. Additionally, the reinforcements need not be external, but may be self-initiated and self-regulatory.

9.27 Finally, suppose the person opening the door really has no intention of buying any magazines, but simply asks the salesperson to come in so that there can be some conversation. How would an activation-arousal theorist interpret such behavior?

It appears the person wants to increase the level of arousal in the apartment. Asking the salesperson to come in is a way of increasing activity and bringing the level of arousal in the apartment closer to what is desired.

Key Terms

Approach-approach conflict.   A situation in which a subject must choose between two stimulus situations, both of which have positive values.

Approach-avoidance conflict.   A situation in which a subject must decide whether to go toward or away from a single stimulus situation that has both positive and negative values.

Avoidance-avoidance conflict.   A situation in which a subject must choose between two stimulus situations, both of which have negative values.

Conflict.   A situation in which two or more incompatible motive conditions are operating at the same time.

Contact comfort.   The need of many young organisms to have something warm and soft to cling to; apparently a combination motive.

Cycle of motivation.   A proposal explaining many motive situations as a sequence of need, instrumental response, goal, and relief; the cycle often repeats itself.

Deprivation.   Doing without; in motivation, often measured in terms of time since the motive was last satisfied.

Drive.   The state resulting from physiological need; less specifically, the general wish to reach some goal.

Functional autonomy.   A situation in which a response which was made originally to satisfy some motive becomes motivating in and of itself.

Goal.   In motivation, the satisfier of a motive condition.

Goal specificity.   The desire to satisfy a motive condition with a particular reinforcement rather than with any reinforcement that would satisfy.

Hierarchy of needs.   A proposal, by the psychologist Abraham Maslow, that arranges motives in an order of importance; those lower in the hierarchy must be satisfied before the higher ones can be satisfied.

Homeostasis.   A state of physiological balance.

Instinct.   An innate (inborn) condition that regularly provokes specific, complex responses from all members of a species when a distinctive stimulus pattern occurs.

Instrumental response.   A response leading toward a goal.

Learned motives.   Conditions that result from experience and initiate, guide, and maintain behaviors; often called *social motives*.

Motive.   A condition that initiates, guides, and maintains behaviors.

Multiple approach-avoidance conflict.   A situation in which a subject must choose between two (or more) stimulus situations, each of which has both positive and negative values.

Need.   A physiological deficit; less specifically, some condition for which satisfaction is desired.

Stimulation needs.   A class of motives in which a person seems to require certain levels of sensory or perceptual stimulation.

Unlearned motives.   Conditions that are inborn or innate and that initiate, guide, and maintain behaviors.

Chapter 10

Emotion

Emotion is a complex state of the organism, generally characterized by a heightened state of arousal and personal feelings.

10.1 GENERAL CHARACTERISTICS OF EMOTION

The judgment of emotion is largely a subjective matter. (This is true both for the person experiencing the emotion and for someone else who is judging that person's experience.)

Stimulus Identification

Because so much subjectivity may be involved in judging someone else's emotions, it is usually necessary to identify the stimulus that generated the response in order to make an accurate evaluation of the emotion being expressed.

EXAMPLE 1. Suppose you were looking at a picture of a 35-year-old man. You can see only his head, neck, and shoulders, and tears streaming down his cheeks. Are the man's tears an emotional response? And if so, what emotion do they represent? If the man is chopping onions, this probably is not an emotional response. If the response is emotional, however, it may be a reaction to a sad event or to a very happy one. Without seeing the stimulus, it is often difficult to tell the type of emotion that is being expressed.

Emotion as a Response

The concept of emotion as arousal and feeling implies that emotions are responses to the provoking stimuli. However, this internalized reaction may serve as only the first part of a chain of events that leads to an externalized (observable) response. In other words, emotion may become a stimulus for further responding.

Emotion as a Motivator

The internal reactions a person experiences may provoke additional responding. When this occurs, emotion serves as a motivator. The entire chain of reaction becomes: (1) an emotion-producing stimulus leading to (2) an emotional response (internal); (3) this emotion acts as a motivating stimulus, which results in (4) an expression of emotion (external).

When emotion is considered as a motivator, the same principles discussed for motivation (see Chapter 9) apply to emotion. Particularly, the relationship between the level of emotional state and performance will follow the inverted-U pattern illustrated in Fig. 9-1 (page 106).

EXAMPLE 2. Imagine that you are working on a term paper for a class. When you go to the library to locate a particular reference for your paper you find that someone has cut and removed the pages you need. Naturally, this fact is frustrating (an emotion-producing stimulus) and you feel angry (an internal response). Your external reaction may vary with the strength of your anger. If the missing article was not too important, you would probably just look for others. If it was fairly important, you might flush somewhat and mutter about the situation, but then get on with your work. If it was very important and no substitute would do, you might slam the book closed and go into a rage, yelling at the librarian and forgetting entirely about working on your paper.

Indicators of Emotion

There are three different indicators of emotion that are frequently used to identify the emotion expressed and the level of arousal and feeling being experienced. These are the personal reports of the person, the observed behaviors of that person, and evidence of physiological reactions accompanying the emotion.

Personal reports.   While outward response may not reveal a person's feelings or arousal, that person may choose to express an emotion by speaking or writing about it.

Observed behaviors.   Gestures, postures, facial expressions, movements, and other such responses may be used to help understand the emotion being expressed.

Physiological indicators.   Changes in heart rate, breathing pattern, blood pressure, pupil size, EEG pattern, or galvanic skin response (GSR) are measures often interpreted as indicators of emotions.

EXAMPLE 3.   Imagine a professional golfer preparing to tee off in a very important playoff match. Stopped by a reporter and asked, "How do you feel?" the golfer might respond, "OK. Relaxed," or "Scared to death." This personal report might be confirmed or disconfirmed by observations made by the reporter: is the golfer smiling or frowning, breathing normally, or flushed and sweaty? The reporter might interpret all these indicators—spoken, observed, and physiological—and then decide how the golfer did feel.

Anthropomorphism and Parsimony

Two cautions about observing emotions should be kept in mind. First, one should not interpret the behaviors of lower organisms in terms of human emotions. (Attributing human characteristics to a lower organism is called *anthropomorphism*.) It should be avoided, especially when some other explanation of the organism's behavior is sufficient.

EXAMPLE 4.   When a dog is given food, it will often wag its tail. It is more appropriate to say that the dog has responded with tail-wagging than to say that the dog was "happy."

The second caution about observing emotional behavior is that if a simple, or *parsimonious*, explanation is adequate for a given situation, one should use it in preference to a more complicated explanation.

EXAMPLE 5.   Economy of explanation is desirable *only* if the explanation is as good as or better than the more complicated alternative. Recall the discussion of sensation in Chapter 6. The sensing of a stimulus can be explained as a function of three major factors: motivation, probability of the stimulus, and "noise." The sensing of a stimulus can also be explained, however, by the single factor of threshold value. In this case, the latter (parsimonious) explanation is not as good as the more detailed explanation.

10.2   BASIC TYPES OF EMOTIONS

Most languages contain many words and descriptive phrases associated with emotions. However, general consensus has led to the acceptance of three basic types of emotions: fear, anger, and pleasure.

Fear

Fear can be viewed first as a *response* to some fear-producing stimulus. For example, the response may be one of doubt, hesitation, dread, dismay, or even horror. This response is provoked by some occurrence that might be variously described as frightening, alarming, startling, or terrifying. In turn, the fear response might then serve to motivate further behavior, such as escape, attack, or panic.

Fear-producing stimuli seem to change in importance as a person grows older. What is sudden, unexpected, and perhaps frightening to a child may not be at all fear-provoking to an adolescent or an adult. On the other hand, some fear-producing stimuli that affect adolescents and adults—particularly in social situations—may not provoke fear in a young child.

EXAMPLE 6. A 2-year-old in a nursery might have little worry about burping in front of the other children. However, an adolescent with a little gas might dread just such an event occurring in front of his or her peers.

Occasionally, fears can become so severe that they take on irrational but compelling properties. When this happens, the fear is called a *phobia*. Phobias are often established in a manner comparable to classical conditioning. (See Chapter 11.)

EXAMPLE 7. Suppose an individual was involved in an accident that took place in a small, enclosed space. Such a space may become associated with pain in this person's mind, and the person may become claustrophobic (that is, fearful of enclosed spaces). Virtually all of the enclosed areas that the individual might encounter after the accident would most likely be perfectly safe, but the previous experience produces intense fear reactions and therefore an avoidance of such spaces.

Anger

The emotional reaction of anger may vary from being modestly "worked up" to being bitter, enraged, or infuriated. Such reactions are provoked by displeasing or frustrating stimuli. Of course, as with other emotions, these reactions may serve to initiate additional responding, perhaps in the form of hostility, aggression, or regression.

Pleasure

Pleasure ranges from simple reactions of delight or fun to ecstatic experiences of love. In general, pleasure reactions are generated by the presence of a favorable or approach stimulus of a goal. Subsequent expression of pleasure may take such diverse forms as smiling, laughing, or hugging and kissing.

Variations and Combinations

It appears to be possible to describe most other emotional situations as either variations of or combinations of these three basic emotions. The intent is not to limit the richness of our vocabulary in representing emotional circumstances, but rather to simplify explanation of how and why emotions occur.

EXAMPLE 8. It is easy to think of how an exasperated person behaves. The upset and disgust, accompanied perhaps by bullying or blustering behavior, may be the result of anger (from some frustration), fear (of exposure of social inadequacy), or pleasure (derived from getting someone else to "give in").

10.3 EXPRESSION OF EMOTIONS

An emotion is an internal event, but it may in turn provoke external evidence of itself. These external responses vary, depending upon a number of factors, including mode of expression, previous experience, and age.

Modes of Emotional Expression

Several types of responses may reveal emotions: personal reports, observable behaviors, and physiological indicators all can provide information on the emotion a person is experiencing. It should be noted, however, that contradictions may appear. For example, a person may verbally report one type of emotion when body position, gestures, and other reactions indicate some other emotion.

Previous Experience

One of the most influential factors on the expression of emotions is past experience. Typically, any given society or subculture develops stereotyped reactions that are deemed appropriate for certain emotion-producing situations. While these may vary considerably from one group to another, certain reactions (such as smiling when happy or crying when sad) appear to be quite universal.

One very important aspect of previous experience appears to be the opportunity to observe some meaningful model. Quite frequently, emotional expressions will imitate those shown by a model, especially if the model is seen as an important or significant person. (See Chapter 13.)

Age Differences

The emotional experiences a person has seem to accumulate, so that noticeable changes seem to take place as a person grows older. Several patterns appear quite general. An older person is likely to show more restraint or control in the expression of emotions. Along with this, there is a tendency for the emotional expressions that do occur to be more verbal and less physical. Furthermore, as a person grows older, one can expect her or him to show increasing complexity and differentiation of emotional states.

EXAMPLE 9. A young child is very likely to show fear often, possibly by crying or withdrawing. Adults, on the other hand have learned to try to hide their fear reactions and put up a "good front." Correspondingly, the young child will be much more likely to strike out physically when angered. The angry adult is more likely to speak out or gesture rather than strike.

10.4   SPECIAL TOPICS IN EMOTIONS

Research on emotions has led to practical applications of certain findings and explanations of special problems.

Lie Detection

One practical application of the study of emotions has been the attempt to develop dependable lie-detection techniques. Research has substantiated that emotion-producing situations can often be detected by measuring physiological responses such as heart rate, respiration rate, or GSR, even when personal reports or observed behaviors do not give any indication of an emotion.

The theory of lie detection depends on the thesis that a person who is telling the lie is in an emotion-producing situation. Thus physiological indicators of emotion can be used to judge whether or not a person is telling the truth. It must be realized that interpretation of results from such tests must be made very carefully because many situations other than lie-telling may also be emotion-producing. Indeed, research studies have so far not been able to establish distinct patterns of physiological indicators associated with precise emotional states.

Psychosomatic Disorders

Physical illnesses brought about by psychological causes are called *psychosomatic disorders*. The extent or severity of a psychosomatic illness may range from a mild headache to severe paralysis, depending upon the provoking stimulus. The physical illness symptoms are present, but there are no accompanying physical causes.

EXAMPLE 10. A touch of nausea before a big exam may be psychosomatic in nature. The pressure of business may produce excessive stomach acidity and eventually ulcers. The need to attract or maintain attention may generate skin rash. All of these and many similar situations reveal possible psychosomatic illnesses. (*Note*: These reactions could also be the result of flu, malfunctioning glands, and an allergy, respectively. It is necessary to determine the cause before making any decision.)

Learned Helplessness

In certain kinds of unpleasant, emotion-producing situations, some individuals may come to believe that an unpleasant consequence is inescapable or inevitable. In such cases, these people may accept what are considered unalterable consequences, and demonstrate the kind of behavior psychologists have labelled *learned helplessness*. Of course, it may be possible to continue to work against the situation, but the apparent certainty of the result keeps these people from making serious attempts to help themselves.

EXAMPLE 11. An individual who previously suffered from a physical affliction which prevented some kind of response may continue to fail to make the response even after the physical disorder has been corrected. The helplessness of the previous period "carries over," and the response is not made even when it is again possible.

10.5 THEORIES OF EMOTION

The earliest attempts to explain emotions were the James-Lange theory and the Cannon-Bard theory.

The James-Lange Theory of Emotion

The James-Lange theory is named for two individuals (William James, an American psychologist; and C. Lange, a Danish psychologist) who independently developed the same basic idea at about the same time. The theory proposed that stimuli produced bodily changes that, in turn, generated felt emotions. This theory thus suggested that stimuli were first keyed to physical responses and only afterwards were interpreted as emotion.

The Cannon-Bard Theory

A later theory, the Cannon-Bard theory of emotion proposed that a stimulus is received by the cortex, recognized as emotion-producing, and sent to activate lower brain centers in the hypothalamus and limbic system. From this portion of the brain, signals are then sent out simultaneously to both external muscles and internal organs and back to the cortex. The muscles and organs make the physiological reactions to the emotion, while the cortex perceives the signal as the emotion. Thus, the theory proposed that physiological and psychological reactions occur at the same time.

Cognitive and Attribution Theories of Emotion

More recent investigations into emotions have stressed the interaction of cognitive (intellectual) and physiological (bodily) influences. These theories emphasize the influence that thought processes can have on the emotion being felt by a person. Physiological arousal alone is not seen as the sole determinant of emotion, and a person's appraisal and labelling of a situation have a great effect on the emotion the person experiences. Cognitive and attribution theories place emphasis on an individual's ability to perceive cause-and-effect relationships between various situations and emotional experiences.

EXAMPLE 12. A person might explain depression as a result of not sleeping enough, not being able to visit with close friends, or not getting a raise when one was expected. In each case, the symptoms might be very similar, but the emotion attributed to quite different causes.

On occasion, a sharp difference may exist between a person's first interpretation of an emotional event and what has been called the *secondary appraisal*. Secondary appraisal usually occurs some time after the initial emotion-producing event. The person may attribute the emotion to some cause completely different from what was first proposed.

Solved Problems

10.1   Suppose that members of the hiring committee of the history department of a university are gathered to discuss the candidates they interviewed. One of the committee members comments about a particular candidate by saying, "Well, that one certainly seemed very emotional!" Several other committee members agreed. What kind of information was probably used in making this judgment?

Three different kinds of information might have led to the committee member's remark: (1) the candidate may have given a personal report of experiencing emotion; (2) the member may have observed behavior that appeared to be the expression of emotion; or (3) there may have been some physiological indicators that seemed to indicate the candidate was in an emotional state.

10.2   One committee member responds by saying "Gee, I didn't think that at all. Can you be more specific?" An immediate reaction from one person is, "Didn't you see how the nervousness showed? All those little gestures, the strange movements—that person was really emotional!" Explain why the two members of the committee differ in their interpretation of the behavior. What seems to be the most important factor in making *any* decision about whether or not an emotion has been expressed?

Judgment of emotion is largely *subjective*. What is considered as emotional gesturing or movement by one person may seem perfectly calm or normal to another. Additionally, the context of the actions is very important. The most important factor in judging emotional expression is to know what stimulus provoked the reaction being observed.

10.3   Quite frequently, emotions are said to produce a state of arousal. What kinds of physiological indicators are used to measure this arousal?

Several physiological indicators may be used to measure arousal. These include EEG, galvanic skin response (GSR), heart rate, blood pressure, respiration rate, and pupil size.

10.4   Is it possible to use these physiological measures in some sort of practical application?

The most famous practical application of physiological indicators of emotion is the "lie detector." The effectiveness of the device depends on the theory that telling a lie is an emotion-producing experience: although the observed behavior (the subjects verbal statement) may not reveal the lie, the physiological indicants will reveal that the answer given may have been a lie. (*Note:* More recent work in this area has attempted to include variation in the speech pattern recorded as a voice print in order to determine when a lie has been told.)

10.5   We often say that someone "gets angry" or "gets scared" when something occurs. Such phrases suggest that emotions are responses. However, we also often say things like, "I couldn't do anything because I was so scared." The implication of this kind of statement is that the emotion was a stimulus that prevented responding. Can these two different views of emotion—as a response and as a stimulus—be reconciled?

The explanation comes by realizing that there must be a stimulus which "keys off" the emotion. Thus, "getting scared" occurs because some stimulus provokes the fear reaction. This, in turn, may serve to stimulate additional responding. The emotion is first a response that may then serve as a motive condition, which is a stimulus.

10.6   Are the effects of emotions comparable to the effects of other motive conditions?

In general, emotions affect behavior in the same manner as other motive conditions do, and the completion of the motivation cycle can be expected. Additionally, the inverted-U curve predicted for the relationship between motivation and performance can be expected when emotion is considered as the motivator.

10.7   Suppose a dog barks, jumps, spins, and generally shows a high level of activity when you begin to open a can of dog food. Is it correct to claim that the dog is "happy" in this situation?

Psychologists must constantly guard against anthropomorphizing, or attributing human characteristics to lower organisms. To say a dog is "happy" is to attribute a human emotion to it, and psychologists prefer simpler explanations. Perhaps a psychologist would view the dog's behavior as a conditioned response. (See Chapter 11.)

10.8   Consider the dog's behavior as described in Problem 10.7. What principle would psychologists be using in choosing the simpler explanation rather than the more complicated one?

In psychology, the generally accepted approach is to use the most economical interpretation of an event that will account for the phenomenon observed. This is referred to as the law of *parsimony* and would apply here.

10.9   A young child may often show fear of strange objects or events, especially if they are unexpected. The same young child, however, seldom shows fear of embarrassment or rejection. Just the opposite is frequently true of older children and adults. Explain these differences in emotional response.

Two variables appear to be important in determining these differences in emotional reactions. In the young child's situation, much perceptual learning (understanding) is left to be accomplished. Sudden, unexpected stimuli may produce fear because they are not understood. Adults, too, may be frightened by unexpected events or strange objects, but adults have generally had much more experience with such events. However, experience has also taught the adult about social embarrassments and rejections that may occur if inappropriate behaviors are shown. For example, fears concerning body odor or similar factors may be quite compelling for an adult, but have little or no effect on a young child.

10.10   Suppose an adult shows an abnormally extreme concern about body odor, showering four or five times each day, changing clothes each time, and using special soaps, deodorants, and so forth. What explanation might be given for such behavior?

This kind of compulsive behavior (see Chapter 21) is representative of a *phobia*—an intense, compelling fear. Phobias develop from learning experiences, often when previously neutral stimuli (in this case body odor) become paired with fear-producing stimuli (perhaps fears of social rejection). It is likely that an individual could learn a phobia for almost anything if the neutral stimulus were paired with one that produced fear.

10.11   Basing your answer on the solution to Problem 10.5, explain why a common psychological cliché, "Frustration leads to aggression," really represents a two-step process.

Frustration is the stimulus that provokes an emotional response. The appropriate label for such a response is anger. Anger, in turn, serves as the motivational stimulus for additional responding, which in many cases may take the form of aggression. Thus, the cliché really should say, "Frustration leads to anger, which in turn leads to aggression."

10.12   Does the cliché, even in its modified form, always hold true?

No. Frustration does *not* always lead to aggression, especially in cases where aggression might actually create more problems for the person. Two other possible reactions to frustration include regression (exhibiting more child-like behaviors than would normally be appropriate) and displacement (showing aggression, but directing it towards an "innocent" stimulus rather than the one producing the frustration). (See Chapter 19 for a discussion of these and other ego defense mechanisms.)

10.13 Explain how modeling may be the source of either fear or anger.

Modeling (imitation) is usually based on the behavior of significant others. For example, a child exposed to models who show fear of certain stimuli or anger at other stimuli is likely to adopt similar responses. It should be noted that the significant others or events a child imitates may be actual or fictitious, with the latter including stories, television shows, or movies.

10.14 Why is it that when a group of people finish singing a difficult song, hear a joke, or observe a young child try to learn to ride a bicycle, they may smile or laugh?

The reaction is probably one of pleasure, outwardly expressed as a smile or laugh. The basis of the emotion of pleasure seems to be the attainment of some goal. In each of these situations, some motive probably is satisfied—perhaps achievement for the song, social acceptance for the joke, and affection or pride for the child.

10.15 Envy has often been used as a label for an emotional reaction. Show how the concept of envy may be viewed as a variation and combination of the three basic emotions: fear, anger, and pleasure.

Envy implies an emotional state in which a person wishes to have what someone else has. This may have resulted from fear of never being able to attain the particular goal or frustration, in the sense of wanting something unattainable. Furthermore, envy might provide pleasure by allowing the person to express such thoughts and thus achieve some reinforcement or goal, perhaps social support from others who feel the same way.

10.16 Suppose Sarah is 6 months old, Sally is 6 years old, and Sandy is 16 years old. Describe how all three might react to being shown and then given a very attractive present.

Sarah probably coos and smiles, reactions that appears to be innate in almost all children presented with pleasurable stimuli. Sally might be likely to run to the present, and laugh, jump, and then hug and kiss both the present and the person who gave it to her. Sandy probably says "Thank you," accepting the present with a smile and any appropriate gestures—such as a handshake, hug, or kiss—depending on who gave it.

10.17 How influential are societal restraints on the expression of emotional feelings?

While all children appear to show innate patterns such as cooing and smiling to a pleasure-producing object or event, it is also true that all societies appear to teach some forms of restraint on emotional expression. These may vary widely from one culture to another, but typically follow a pattern in which increasing age results in decreasing physical response, increasing verbal response, and increasing control, complexity, and differentiation.

10.18 How do verbal and nonverbal responses sometimes reveal contradictions in emotional expression?

Problem 10.4 showed one instance of this: when the person tells a lie, his or her words may not reveal this fact. However, the person's physiological reactions may.

Other responses, such as body posture, facial expressions, or certain gestures, may be equally revealing. Correspondingly, even when nonverbal cues are not readily apparent, verbal slips (see Problem 9.28, for example) may reveal emotional attitude.

10.19 Can one expect emotional expression to follow a certain pattern in a particular culture?

Indeed, society does appear to impose restrictions upon the expression of emotions. The "usual" expression becomes the stereotype of what is appropriate in the situation for any given group. It should be recognized that such expressions are very situation specific; that is, what is an appropriate expression of emotion in one situation may be totally inappropriate in another.

10.20   Bobby has asthma. His breathing difficulties seem to be associated particularly with feathers. His parents take care to avoid exposing Bobby to feathers in any form: they do not take him on trips to the zoo, they do not use feather pillows, and they have no pet birds in their home.

One day Bobby is taken to a museum on a school trip. Passing a marble sculpture of several birds, Bobby suddenly has a severe asthma attack. Does this incident provide evidence for interpreting Bobby's asthma as a psychosomatic illness?

Psychosomatic disorders are physical illnesses brought on by psychological causes. The immediate evidence indicates that Bobby's reaction is psychosomatic because it was provoked by sculptured, marble feathers that could not possibly contain allergens. It is likely this may be a generalized response which originated from some conflict Bobby had previously experienced with feathers.

10.21   Imagine walking out of a theatre and onto a sidewalk and then turning a corner. Suddenly you are confronted with a very tall individual wearing a Halloween gorilla costume and screaming at you. Interpret your probable reaction according to the James-Lange theory of emotion.

The James-Lange theory proposed that the stimuli (the gorilla suit and scream) automatically triggered bodily changes (perhaps jumping back, gasping, or running), and that the perception of these bodily changes is the emotion which you felt.

10.22   What interpretation would be given to the situation in Problem 10.21 if the Cannon-Bard theory of emotion were employed?

The Cannon-Bard theory of emotion states that the felt emotion and the physiological reaction to the stimuli are triggered simultaneously. Thus, the sensory stimuli received by the individual are interpreted by the cortex, and a signal is sent to activate lower brain areas (the hypothalamus and limbic system). At the same time, messages are also transmitted to the internal organs and the muscles, producing the physiological reactions to the emotion.

10.23   What kind of attribution might be made for the responses shown in the situation described in Problem 10.21?

This would depend upon the person's interpretation of the situation and the social stimuli surrounding the event. The person might say, "I jumped and gasped because I was scared," or "I jumped and gasped because I was surprised," or "I jumped and gasped because it was so funny." Certainly these three reasons differ, and any one person would most likely choose one of them over the other two.

10.24   Again, consider the situation described in Problem 10.21. What kind of secondary appraisal might a person make after the first emotional reaction to the "ape"?

After jumping, gasping, or running and reaching relative security, a person might make a secondary appraisal and say, "Gee, why did I run? That was probably just some joker on the way to a party. That was sort of silly." This secondary appraisal might be followed by a feeling of relief.

Key Terms

Anger.   One of the three basic emotions; a response of heightened arousal in the class of rage or hostility.

Anthropomorphism.   The attribution of human characteristics to objects or nonhuman organisms.

Attribution.   Ways of giving causes to the acts of other people or oneself.

Cannon-Bard theory of emotion.   A theory proposing that emotion consists of simultaneously-occurring physiological and psychological reactions to an emotion-producing stimulus.

Emotion.   A complex state of the organism, usually marked by a heightened state of arousal and the feelings accompanying that condition.

Fear.   One of the three basic emotions; a response in the general class of anxiety or dread.

Galvanic skin response (GSR).   A change in the electrical resistance of the skin as a result of the autonomic changes that produce sweating.

James-Lange theory of emotion.   A theory proposing that emotion-producing stimuli generate physical reactions, which in turn are perceived as felt emotions.

Learned helplessness.   The acceptance of what seem to be the unalterable consequences of a situation, even if change may be possible.

Lie detector.   A device that measures physiological reactions such as heart rate or GSR; these reactions supposedly reveal when the responder has lied.

Parsimony.   Economy of explanation; a parsimonious explanation is preferred to a more complex one if both explain a situation equally well.

Phobia.   An intense, compelling fear.

Pleasure.   One of the three basic emotions; a response ranging from mild delight to ecstasy.

Psychosomatic disorder.   A physical illness brought about by a psychological cause.

Secondary appraisal.   A reinterpretation of the causes of an emotion; may change the explanation from the one that was first proposed.

Chapter 11

Classical Conditioning

Psycholigists are concerned with learning and particularly with the different factors that influence acquisition, retention, and use of learned responses.

11.1 DEFINITION OF LEARNING

Learning is defined as a relatively permanent change in behavior that occurs as a result of experience. This definition implies there is *acquisition* of a response and retention of that response once it has become a part of an organism's behavior. (*Note*: Psychologists study several different forms of acquisition, including classical conditioning, instrumental conditioning, or learning through modeling. They also measure the retention of such learning in numerous ways. Chapters 11 through 16 explore these aspects of psychology.)

Learning and Maturation

The definition of learning given above stresses the effect of experience. The definition does not mean to diminish the importance of physical maturation; indeed, physical development may be a necessary condition for learning to occur. However, physical development alone is not sufficient; for learning to take place, an organism must have experience.

EXAMPLE 1. Very young children (six months old, for example) do not have enough development to be able to speak a language. Only when they are older can they begin to learn to speak. However, in the absence of the right kinds of experience—including appropriate models, practice, and reinforcement—even a much older child (such as an adolescent) will not speak a particular language.

Learning-Performance Distinction

It must be recognized that learning and performance are not necessarily the same. A person's observable behavior (or performance) will not always reveal what the person has learned.

EXAMPLE 2. A young child who gets lost in a large crowd at a sports stadium may cry, but be unwilling to talk. A callous observer might react by saying, "The kid doesn't even know his name." Actually, the child may have committed to memory his name, address, and telephone number. However, the child may additionally have been taught not to speak to strangers, and this latter learning may keep him from responding to questions he knows how to answer.

11.2 CLASSICAL CONDITIONING

Classical conditioning is a process in which an organism learns to respond in a particular way to a stimulus that previously did not produce the response. This stimulus, which was once "neutral," becomes response-producing because it is paired (or associated) with another stimulus that does produce the response.

Classical conditioning also is called *respondent conditioning* or *Pavlovian conditioning*. The term *respondent* implies that the learned response is elicited involuntarily from the subject rather than produced by the subject in a voluntary (or operant) manner.

The term *Pavlovian conditioning* gives credit to the Russian physiologist Ivan Pavlov (1849–1936), the first person to investigate classical conditioning extensively. Pavlov devoted over thirty years of his career to the study of this type of learning.

The Classical Conditioning Paradigm

A stimulus that is originally neutral and comes to be response-producing is called a *conditioned stimulus* (abbreviated as CS). The stimulus that produces the response on the first trial and each trial after is called the *unconditioned stimulus* (UCS).

The response elicited by the UCS is called the *unconditioned response* (UCR). Eventually, the same type of response will occur at the presentation of the CS; this response is called the *conditioned response* (CR). A diagram representing classical conditioning appears in Fig. 11-1.

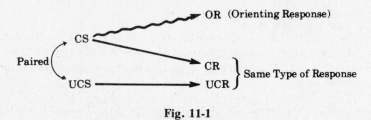

Fig. 11-1

The *orienting response* (OR) indicated in Fig. 11-1 often occurs on the first few trials. The subject responds by determining where the stimulus comes from or what stimuli are presented.

EXAMPLE 3. In his original investigation, Pavlov used dogs as subjects. He found that presentation of meat powder (UCS) would cause the dogs to salivate (UCR). Pavlov then paired the ringing of a bell (CS) with the presentation of meat powder. This pairing soon led the dogs to salivate at the sound of the bell (CR). The OR in this situation occurred in the first few trials, when the dogs turned their heads in an attempt to determine where the bell was located.

Inter-Stimulus Interval

A paired CS and UCS may occur exactly together, or there may be a time interval between them. The time between the onset of the CS and the onset of the UCS is the *inter-stimulus interval* (ISI). The word *contiguity* is used to describe this relationship between the presentation of the CS and UCS.

EXAMPLE 4. The Pavlovian experiment described in Example 3 may be conducted with several different kinds of contiguity relationships:

Simultaneous. The bell and the meat powder are presented at exactly the same time.

Delayed. The bell comes on first and remains on until the meat powder is presented.

Trace. The bell comes on and goes off before the meat powder is presented.

Backward. The meat powder is presented before the bell is rung.

Temporal. The bell is never rung. The CS in this situation would be a constant time period, such as five minutes. (The meat powder would be presented every five minutes.)

11.3 EXTINCTION

Extinction in classical conditioning is the procedure of presenting the CS alone (without the UCS) for repeated trials. The word extinction is also used to refer to the result of such a procedure, in which the CR returns to its original (preconditioning) level.

EXAMPLE 5. In Pavlov's experiment (Example 3), extinction was produced by repeatedly sounding the bell without presenting the meat powder. Eventually, the dogs stopped salivating at the sound of the bell. That is, the CR (salivating) returned to its original, preconditioning level.

Extinction as a Measure of Response Strength

Resistance to extinction is one measure of the strength of a CR. In general, it is felt that the greater the resistance to extinction, the greater the strength of the established CR. In the absence of the UCS, a "strong" CR would persist for many trials in which only the CS was presented. A "weak" CR, on the other hand, would be extinct after a few trials in which only the CS was presented.

Asymptote

Repeated presentations of the paired CS and UCS often produce a CR that *approaches* a maximum strength. This "leveling-off" of CR strength near some maximum is called the *asymptote* or *asymptotic value* of the response strength.

Effect of Partial Reinforcement on Extinction

Partial reinforcement occurs when the CS is paired with the UCS on some, but not all, of the trials. A partial reinforcement situation is described in terms of a percentage; for example, if the CS is paired with the UCS on half the trials, the subject experiences 50 percent reinforcement.

Research has shown that a CR acquired under partial reinforcement conditions is more resistant to extinction than is a response established under continuous (100 percent) reinforcement. This finding is called the *partial reinforcement effect* (PRE).

EXAMPLE 6. Suppose two dogs were conditioned to make the salivation response to the sound of the bell. One dog was trained in a continuous reinforcement situation, while the other heard the bell on every trial, but was presented meat powder on only some of the trials. The CR of the latter dog would be more resistant to extinction than would be the CR of the first dog. (*Note*: Several theories have been proposed as explanations of the PRE. No one theory has gained general acceptance, but the general finding still holds: partial reinforcement results in greater resistance to CR extinction.)

11.4 SPONTANEOUS RECOVERY

Imagine a situation in which a CR appears to be extinguished. If, following a period of rest, the CS is again presented (alone, with no UCS present), the CR will sometimes reappear. This is called *spontaneous recovery* of the response. The strength of the CR will not be as great as it was originally, before extinction, but partial recovery of the CR will occur.

EXAMPLE 7. Suppose the CR of one of Pavlov's dogs was extinguished and the dog was kept out of the experimental setting for several days. If the dog was then placed again in the experimental setting, it would salivate (CR) at the sound of the bell (CS). Evidence of salivation under these circumstances would indicate spontaneous recovery of the dog's CR.

11.5 STIMULUS GENERALIZATION

Stimulus generalization is demonstrated when a CR is made not only to the original CS, but to other stimuli that are similar to the original CS. Stimulus generalization that is based on the physical properties of a stimulus is called *primary stimulus generalization*.

Human beings, who have a command of language and other symbols, are able to show another form of stimulus generalization, called *secondary stimulus generalization*. A human CR may be given not only to the original CS, but to other stimuli that are judged similar because they have the same meaning as the original CS.

EXAMPLE 8. One of Pavlov's dogs might salivate to both a bell and a similar sounding chime. Humans may show comparable primary stimulus generalization by responding to a variety of automobile horns, all of which may sound similar.

However, humans also have the capacity to make the same response to stimuli that do not have similar physical properties but have equivalent meaning. Thus, humans may respond in the same way to stimuli such as the following:

Raise = *Rays*.   When spoken, the same sounds yield primary stimulus generalization.

Lift = *Raise*.   Secondary stimulus generalization based upon word meaning.

Lift = *Elevator*.   Secondary stimulus generalization if one is familiar with British use of the words.

11.6   DIFFERENTIATION (DISCRIMINATION)

A subject who gives the CR to a particular CS but does not respond to similar stimuli shows *differentiation* (or discrimination).

Concept of a Continuum

A subject who responds to the original CS *only*, and not to any other stimuli, shows complete stimulus differentiation. If the subject gives the CR indiscriminately to all stimuli, complete stimulus generalization has occurred. These two extremes can be seen as the ends of a *continuum*; responses to some—but not just one stimulus or all stimuli—represent the middle points between these two poles.

EXAMPLE 9.   Pavlov's dogs would have shown complete stimulus generalization if they salivated to any noise. If, on the other hand, the dogs responded to the original bell but no other similar sounds, they would have shown complete differentiation. Pavlov showed that when dogs were forced to make choices (that is, differentiate) between two stimuli that were very similar, they sometimes showed signs of confusion and distress. Pavlov called this phenomenon *experimental neurosis*. (See Chapter 21.)

Response Generalization

Response generalization occurs when a subject gives not only the original response, but other similar responses, to the original CS. In other words, one stimulus elicits an entire class of equivalent responses.

EXAMPLE 10.   A group of people are shown a new product which they admire. Their responses might include exclamations such as "Fantastic!" or "Gorgeous!" or "Wonderful!" or "Magnificent!" These exclamations illustrate response generalization in that they are equivalent responses given to a single stimulus.

11.7   HIGHER-ORDER CONDITIONING

When the strength of the CR is near its maximum value, the CS that elicits the CR may take the role of a UCS. A new pairing could then be established, in which a new CS would be paired with the well-established CS. Repeated presentation would lead to the elicitation of the same type of CR by presentation of the new CS alone. This is called *higher-order conditioning*.

EXAMPLE 11.   Assume that Pavlov's pairing of the ringing bell and the meat powder had been presented many times, so that the dog's salivation response was very well established. Subsequently, pairing a tapping noise with the bell might lead to higher-order conditioning. Repeated tap-bell pairings would then yield a salivation response to the tapping noise alone.

Higher-order conditioning is sometimes used when the pairing of the original CS with the UCS may produce difficulties because of distraction or incompatability; it is then hoped that the CR can be produced by the second CS. The first CS–UCS pairing allows the eventual desired conditioning.

It should be noted that each new-CS–old-CS pairing is both a conditioning trial for the new CS–CR attachment and an extinction trial for the old CS–CR link. A weakly-established original CR may extinguish before the new bond can be formed.

11.8 SPECIAL EXAMPLES OF CLASSICAL CONDITIONING

The principles of classical conditioning can provide interesting perspectives on other psychological principles. Two of these are the development of secondary (conditioned) reinforcers and the topic of phobias.

Secondary Reinforcement

Secondary (conditioned) reinforcers are developed when a previously neutral stimulus (CS) is paired with a reinforcement (UCS) and the CS takes on reinforcing properties. Quite frequently, secondary reinforcers are verbal stimuli that become meaningful as reinforcers only after pairings of this sort. (*Note*: Secondary or conditioned motivation can be established in a similar manner. See Section 11.8.)

EXAMPLE 12. Being told by a teacher that your work is "excellent" may serve as a reinforcer. Yet if you had never learned the word *excellent* or had learned it in a context where it was paired with poor performance and punishment, the meaning would be lacking or different, and the word would not be reinforcing.

EXAMPLE 13. Money is a secondary reinforcer. Humans learn to accept money as a reinforcer because they know that money can in turn be used to purchase other secondary reinforcers, or primary reinforcers such as food or heat.

Phobias

Phobias are intense, compelling fears thought to be established in the same manner as other classically-conditioned responses. A previously-neutral stimulus (CS) is paired with a fear-producing stimulus (UCS), and the CS comes to take on fear-producing (motivating or emotional) attributes.

EXAMPLE 14. Imagine stepping into an elevator that plunged twenty floors before the emergency brake saved you from crashing at the bottom of the shaft. It is probably easy for you to understand that your next confrontation with an elevator might be highly fear-producing. The previously neutral stimulus (the elevator) has taken on fear-producing qualities because of the single (CS–UCS) pairing.

Solved Problems

11.1 Does a child's physical growth and development ensure that learning will take place? Will a child who has learned a particular response always be able to perform it?

Simply maturing (growing up) is not enough to guarantee that learning will take place. Physical development may, in many cases, be a necessary condition for learning, but it is not sufficient. Learning results from experience and may or may not come to pass depending upon whether or not the experience occurs. There is a difference between learning and performance. A child may learn a response and yet be unable to perform it. (Conditions of the moment may prevent the child from revealing what she or he has learned.)

11.2 Are all learning processes the same?

Some of the characteristics of all learning processes are the same. For example, experience is always necessary if learning is to take place, and all learning results in relatively permanent changes in behavior. However, the actual acquisition of learned responses may result from several different types of learning processes. Psychologists study these processes—such as classical conditioning, instrumental conditioning, and learning through modeling—in an attempt to understand the various types of acquisition situations.

11.3   The acquisition of a response in classical conditioning often is described as involuntary. Why?

The classical conditioning situation involves the pairing of an originally neutral stimulus with a response-producing stimulus. Both stimuli are presented to the subject, and a "forcing" of the response occurs. In effect, the subject does not have a choice of what response will be made, nor to what new stimulus the response will be attached.

11.4   Classical conditioning also has been called *respondent conditioning* or *Pavlovian conditioning*. How did it get these labels?

The word *respondent* implies the involuntary nature of the subject's response in classical conditioning. It is in contrast to a subject operating in a voluntary manner upon the environment, which is characteristic of operant, or instrumental, conditioning. (See Chapter 12.)

Classical conditioning is also sometimes called Pavlovian conditioning in honor of Ivan Pavlov, a Russian physiologist who first explored many of the principles of classical conditioning. (His studies concerned the salivary responses of dogs.)

11.5   Playing in the backyard one day, three-year-old Sam is on a swing when a rabbit suddenly appears out of the bushes and startles him. He slips off the swing, falls against the sandbox, and hurts his arm. Sam cries from the pain. Later, after calming down and having a bandage put on his arm, Sam returns to the backyard; while he is standing in the grass, another rabbit hops into view. Sam begins to cry. Identify the UCS, UCR, CS, and CR in this situation.

The UCS is the pain. It is response-producing, and in this case generates the UCR of crying. The CS is the appearance of the rabbit. Presumably the rabbit's appearance was originally a neutral stimulus; however, it came to be paired with the pain and later produces the CR—crying at the sight of the rabbit.

11.6   In Problem 11.5, both the UCR and the CR are crying. Does this mean the UCR and CR are always the same?

No. The UCR and CR are the same *type* of response, although they may differ either quantitatively or qualitatively. For example, Sammy's crying in response to the pain might be classified as sobbing, while the later crying (at the sight of the rabbit) might be called whimpering, and the quantity of tears may differ.

11.7   Repeated pairings of a CS and UCS usually lead to a well-established CR which approaches a maximum value. What is this maximum value called? After repeated pairings, what usually happens to an OR (orienting response)?

A CR that is nearing its maximum value is said to be approaching its *asymptote*. Usually an OR is short-lived and drops out after the first few trials (once the subject becomes somewhat accustomed to the presentation of the stimulus).

11.8   The inter-stimulus interval (ISI) represents the presentation arrangement or contiguity of the CS and UCS. If the line in Fig. 11-2 depicts the onset of the UCS, sketch lines for the CS that illustrate the relationship between the CS and UCS for delayed, trace, backward, and simultaneous classical conditioning situations.

Fig. 11-2

Figure 11-3 illustrates the relationship between the UCS and CS in each ISI relationship.

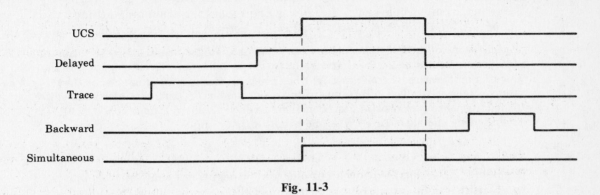

Fig. 11-3

11.9 Sketch a line (similar to the ones in Problem 11.8) illustrating temporal conditioning.

A set time span serves as the CS in temporal conditioning. Thus, only a line for the UCS is needed, as in Fig. 11-4. (The intervals between each appearance of the UCS should be equal.)

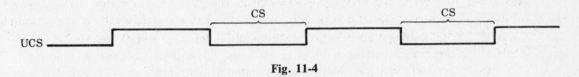

Fig. 11-4

11.10 Refer to Problem 11.5 again. Suppose Sam's parents recognized his fear of rabbits. What would they do in order to extinguish his response to rabbits?

Extinction of a classically-conditioned response involves repeated presentation of the CS alone. The result of such a procedure is that the CR strength returns to its original (preconditioning) level. In Sammy's case, repeated presentation of a rabbit without the accompanying pain should lead to the cessation of crying in the presence of the rabbit.

To facilitate this, Sam's parents might want to institute a counter-conditioning procedure. This probably would mean pairing something positive (such as fondling or candy) with the sight of the rabbit. This would create a new classically conditioned CR to replace the old one.

11.11 Observing the speed with which Sam's crying response is extinguished is one way of measuring the strength of the response. Explain.

In general, it is assumed that CR strength will be revealed by the amount of time or number of trials necessary to extinguish the response. Very short extinction represents a weak CR, while longer extinction means the CR was stronger.

11.12 Refer to Problem 11.5 again. Suppose that a year has passed and the next spring has arrived. On the first really lovely day, Sam's parents set up the swing once again, and Sam immediately begins to play. After a while, however, he comes into the house sniffling just a little bit. Questioning reveals that Sam has once again seen the rabbit. What principle explains Sam's response?

Sam has shown spontaneous recovery of the CR (crying). Presentation of the CS following extinction and a period of rest may elicit the CR once again. Sam's response is typical of those observed in spontaneous recovery because the strength of the response is not as great as the original CR. (Sam is only sniffling, not crying uncontrollably.)

11.13 After World War II, many residents of countries that were bombed expressed great hatred for and fear of the sound of low-flying planes. When questioned as to why they so disliked the sound, many people said, "You never knew whether a bombing attack would be a bad one or not." Explain how these responses illustrate the effect of partial reinforcement.

The sound of the low-flying planes was often associated with damage, destruction, or death, but not always. Bombs could fall harmlessly in fields, lakes, or remote regions, or they could be "duds." Furthermore, the planes might be only on reconnaisance missions, or they might not be enemy planes at all. The uncertainty of the result produced a partial reinforcement effect, making the fear response *very* resistant to extinction. Even years later, comparable aircraft sounds would generate fear and hatred even when no bombs were falling.

11.14 Problem 11.13 illustrates how an unpleasant or negative situation could persist because of the partial reinforcement effect (PRE). Can PRE also be found in a pleasant or positive situation?

The partial reinforcement effect is not limited to only unpleasant occurrences. For example, although not all cocktail parties are fun, some may be. The link a person establishes between cocktail parties and fun will probably be maintained even if some parties are not very pleasant.

11.15 Suppose you have attended several cocktail parties that were fun. Then you receive an invitation to another such party from hosts who had never before asked you to a party. Even though you have never been to one of their parties, you anticipate having a good time. What principle does your expectation illustrate?

This situation illustrates stimulus generalization; you are responding not to the stimulus to which your reaction was originally conditioned, but to another similar stimulus.

11.16 Distinguish between (1) responding in the same manner to the sound of a bell and the sound of a buzzer and (2) responding in the same manner to the words *bell* and *gong*.

If the same response is made to the sound of a bell and a buzzer, primary stimulus generalization has been shown. (The subject has made like responses because the *physical* properties of the stimulus were similar.)

If the same response is made to the words *bell* and *gong*, secondary stimulus generalization has been demonstrated. (The subject responds in a like manner because of the *meaning* of the two words, even though their physical properties differ.)

11.17 Suppose you receive invitations to two different parties that are to be held the same evening. You immediately accept the invitation to the party at which you expect good food, drinks, and companionship. You also send regrets to the host of the other party. (In the past, this person's parties have been boring, full of business talk, and with poor food and drink.) Your decision illustrates what psychological principle?

In the past, invitations from both hosts were probably neutral stimuli. However, one has been paired with pleasure while the other has been associated with boredom. Thus, you have developed a distinction between these two similar stimuli. This illustrates differentiation (discrimination).

11.18 Suppose the line in Fig. 11-5 represents all the possible shades of blue. (To the right, the blue becomes paler and paler until it is white; to the left, the blue becomes darker and darker until it is black.) Now suppose that a person has been conditioned to respond to the color blue. How would you illustrate this person's responses if the person showed: complete stimulus generalization; complete stimulus differentiation; and some in-between result?

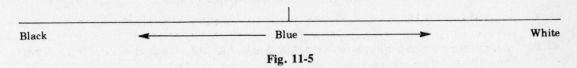

Fig. 11-5

The three lines in Fig. 11-6 illustrate possible response patterns for a person conditioned to respond to blue.

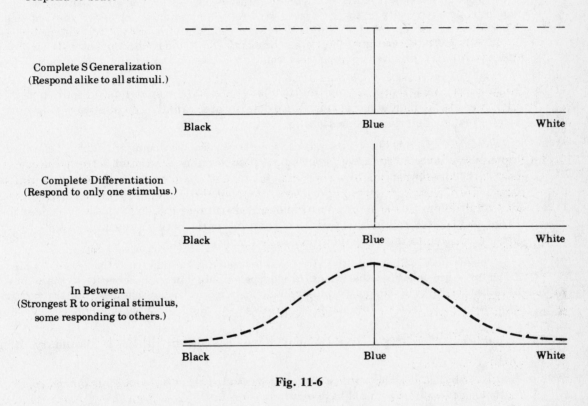

Fig. 11-6

11.19 Distinguish between stimulus generalization and response generalization.

Stimulus generalization is giving one response to several similar stimuli. Response generalization is giving several similar (or equivalent) responses to one particular stimulus.

11.20 For several months during the summer, the family dog has come running to the kitchen whenever it hears the sound of the electric can opener. In some instances, this sound has meant that food would soon be put into the dog's dish. (This is a partial reinforcement situation). Later that year, the dog's owner must turn on the kitchen light just before using the can opener. Now the dog runs to the kitchen whenever the light comes on. What has happened?

The dog's behavior is a result of higher-order conditioning. Originally, the sound of the can opener was the conditioned stimulus (CS_1), and the food served was the unconditioned stimulus (UCS). The chance pairings of the light (CS_2) with the sound of the can opener (CS_1) have led to the conditioned response being produced by the light as well as by the sound. This may occur even though the light was never paired directly with the food.

11.21   Higher-order conditioning is the establishment of a CS_2–CR pairing. What may happen to the CS_1–CR pairing during such conditioning?

Each CS_2–CS_1 pairing simultaneously represents a conditioning trial for the establishment of a CS_2–CR pairing and an extinction trial for CS_1–CR. If the CR is not strong the CS_1–CR pairing may be extinguished.

11.22   Any language contains words that are used as conditioned reinforcers. Explain what would be necessary to make the phrases "bad boy" or "bad girl" be pleasant, positive reinforcers.

Words are at first neutral (to a very young child, for example). They acquire meaning only by being paired with other stimuli. To make the phrases "bad boy" or "bad girl" positive reinforcers, it would be necessary to pair these phrases with rewarding or pleasant circumstances. Repeated association of the phrase (CS) with the reward (UCS) should produce conditioned reinforcement. (*Note:* The phrases given here are in English. They could have been rearranged into *dab oby* and *dab rilg* and, if paired appropriately, could then take on reinforcing properties.)

11.23   Fran shows an intense, compelling fear of spiders. If a spider is present, her anxiety increases markedly and her performance deteriorates rapidly. Explain how this fear could be the result of classical conditioning.

A spider (CS) probably was paired with some strong fear-producing stimulus (UCS) one or more times in Fran's past. Fran's fear (a phobia) resulted when the association between the two stimuli became well established.

11.24   Reread Problem 10.20. Bobby's asthma appears comparable to Fran's fear as described in Problem 11.23. Explain how this is so, then interpret Bobby's reaction to the sculptured birds according to the principles of classical conditioning.

The feathers (CS) apparently have been associated with some UCS that produced breathing difficulty. Although this actually may have happened once (but not necessarily, as the asthma may have been used by Bobby as an attention-getting device), Bobby has now illustrated stimulus generalization by reacting not only to real feathers, but also to a statue that represented feathers.

11.25   What kind of reaction would Bobby have to show to illustrate secondary stimulus generalization?

If Bobby had an asthma attack when someone *talked* about feathers, birds, or the like, secondary stimulus generalization would have occurred.

Key Terms

Acquisition.   The process by which an organism makes a response part of its behavioral repertoire.

Asymptote.   The "leveling off" of response strength as it approaches its maximum value.

Backward conditioning.   In classical conditioning, a trial in which the onset of the UCS occurs before the onset of the CS.

Classical conditioning.   The acquisition procedure in which a previously neutral stimulus is paired with a response-producing stimulus until the neutral stimulus elicits the same type of response; also called *respondent conditioning* and *Pavlovian conditioning.*

Conditioned reinforcer.   See *secondary reinforcer.*

Conditioned response (CR).   In classical conditioning, the response elicited by the CS; usually similar to the UCR.

Conditioned stimulus (CS).   In classical conditioning, the stimulus that was originally neutral and comes to be response-producing.

Delayed conditioning.   In classical conditioning, a trial in which the onset of the CS precedes the UCS, with the CS staying on at least until the UCS has occurred.

Differentiation.   Responding to the original stimulus, but not to the other, similar stimuli.

Discrimination.   See *differentiation*.

Experimental neurosis.   When a differentiation is made very difficult, yet is forced, a subject sometimes exhibits neurotic patterns; first pointed out by Pavlov.

Extinction.   In classical conditioning, both the procedure of presenting the CS alone repeatedly and the result of this procedure, which returns the CR to its original (preconditioning) level.

Higher-order conditioning.   A conditioning procedure in which a new CS is paired with a well-established CS from a previous instance of classical conditioning; the new CS comes to elicit the same type of CR.

Inter-stimulus interval (ISI).   The time between the onset of the CS and the onset of the UCS.

Learning.   A relatively permanent change in behavior as a result of experience.

Orienting response (OR).   In classical conditioning, any of a number of adjustment responses made when the CS first occurs.

Partial reinforcement.   In classical conditioning, when the CS is presented on every trial, but the UCS occurs on only some of the trials.

Partial reinforcement effect (PRE).   The finding that responses conditioned under partial reinforcement are more resistant to extinction than are those conditioned under continuous reinforcement.

Performance.   The responses that an organism actually shows; may or may not reveal what the organism has learned.

Primary stimulus generalization.   Stimulus generalization based upon the physical properties of the stimulus.

Response generalization.   Responding to the original stimulus not only with the original response, but with other similar responses.

Secondary reinforcer.   When a previously neutral stimulus is paired with a reinforcer and comes to take on reinforcing properties.

Secondary stimulus generalization.   Stimulus generalization based upon the subject's knowledge of language or some other type of symbol.

Simultaneous conditioning.   A classical conditioning procedure when the ISI equals zero; that is, the CS and UCS occur at the same time.

Spontaneous recovery.   A phenomenon in which, after a period of rest following extinction, the CR reappears when the CS is presented alone.

Stimulus generalization.   Responding not only to the original stimulus, but to other, similar stimuli.

Temporal conditioning.   A classical conditioning procedure in which the UCS occurs at regular intervals; these regular intervals are treated as the CS.

Trace conditioning.   A classical conditioning procedure in which the onset *and* cessation of the CS occurs before the UCS is presented.

Unconditioned response (UCR).   In classical conditioning, the response elicited by the UCS.

Unconditioned stimulus (UCS).   In classical conditioning, the stimulus that is response-producing on the first and every other trial.

Chapter 12

Instrumental Conditioning

Instrumental conditioning is a learning process that involves changing the probability of a response by manipulating the consequences of that response. An *instrumental response* is defined most simply as a response that leads to a goal.

Instrumental conditioning is also called *operant conditioning* or *Skinnerian conditioning*. The term *operant* is used because instrumental responses are frequently operations upon the environment. The term *Skinnerian* gives credit to the work of B. F. Skinner, a leading investigator of the many principles of instrumental conditioning.

12.1 CHARACTERISTICS OF INSTRUMENTAL CONDITIONING

Instrumental conditioning is concerned with the acquisition and retention of instrumental responses as well as the elimination of undesired responses.

The Instrumental Response

An instrumental response is a voluntary response made by an organism. These responses may be learned in a sequence (or *chain* of behavior) so that the end result is attainment of a desired goal.

Contingency of Reinforcement

Generally, instrumental conditioning occurs in situations where the actual delivery of a reinforcement depends upon the appropriate responses being made. This is called the *contingency* of the reinforcement upon the response.

EXAMPLE 1. Suppose a salesman is told that he must make a certain number of sales before he will receive a bonus payment. This is a contingency situation. The completed sales are the *instrumental responses*, the money is the *reinforcement*, and delivery of the bonus money is contingent upon the successful completion of the sales.

Noncontingent Reinforcement

An organism may link a particular response and reinforcement when such an association is inappropriate. The result may be the development of a *superstitious behavior*, in which the organism performs as if the response will produce the reinforcement. In fact, no contingency actually exists.

EXAMPLE 2. People involved in sports often show supersitious behaviors. A coach wears a particular plaid coat on a night when his team wins a very convincing victory. Although the coat in no way influenced the result of the game, the coach may continue to wear it at games as long as a victory streak continues.

Law of Effect

E. L. Thorndike proposed the *Law of Effect*, which stated that a response followed by a satisfying stimulus or by the termination of an annoying stimulus will become conditioned. Sub-

138

sequent research has generally supported this proposal. (These contingency situations have come to be called, respectively, *positive reinforcement* and *negative reinforcement*. See Section 12.6.)

12.2 COMPARISON OF INSTRUMENTAL AND CLASSICAL CONDITIONING

There are two major differences between instrumental and classical conditioning: how voluntary the response is and how identifiable the stimuli are in each situation.

Voluntary Response

In general, instrumental conditioning involves responses that are voluntary or emitted by an organism, while classical conditioning involves responses that are involuntary or elicited from the organism. Instrumental conditioning does not involve forcing the response being studied, while the response of interest in classical conditioning is forced by the unconditioned stimulus.

Stimulus Identification

In classical conditioning, both the conditioned stimulus and the unconditioned stimulus are readily identified, and the association of the CR to the CS can be easily studied. By contrast, in instrumental conditioning there is no identifiable UCS that forces a response nor CS to which the response becomes attached. The key relationship in instrumental conditioning is not between stimuli, but rather between the response and the reinforcement.

12.3 ACQUISITION OF INSTRUMENTAL RESPONSES

Several factors are important in the acquisition of instrumental responses, including how this acquisition is initiated, measured, and extinguished.

The Cumulative Record

The most common means of determining whether or not an instrumental response has been conditioned is to use a *cumulative record* of that response. A cumulative record simply indicates the number of satisfactory responses made in a given time period.

EXAMPLE 3. A type of apparatus used very frequently in operant conditioning is called an *operant conditioning chamber* (or popularly, a *Skinner box*). A basic form of this is represented in Fig. 12-1.

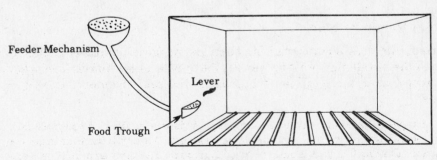

Feeder Mechanism

Lever

Food Trough

Fig. 12-1

An untrained and hungry laboratory rat that is placed in equipment such as this may eventually learn to press the lever, which in turn will activate the feeder mechanism and cause pellets of food to be delivered to the food trough. A cumulative record of the lever-pressing responses might be illustrated as in Fig. 12-2.

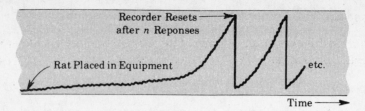

Fig. 12-2

Shaping

Shaping is the reinforcing of closer and closer approximations of a desired response. In some cases, it may be necessary to encourage the first response, so that it may be reinforced and begin the progression of shaping.

EXAMPLE 4. When a naive rat is placed in an operant conditioning apparatus, it often is possible to speed the acquisition of the lever-pressing response by using a shaping procedure. With a remote control apparatus, the experimenter can reinforce the rat's approaches to the lever, any indications of interest in the lever, placing a paw on the lever, and finally pressing the lever—a sequence of responses that leads to the appropriate response.

EXAMPLE 5. Language learning frequently involves shaping. At first a child's approximations of a desired word are reinforced, as are the better and better attempts produced later. At first, a child may say "Baaaaa," followed by "Brrrr," "Bud-da," and finally "butter."

Extinction

Extinction in instrumental conditioning is accomplished by terminating the delivery of reinforcement following the response. The result of this procedure should be a decrease in the rate of responding until it reaches the preconditioning level.

EXAMPLE 6. Suppose a rat has been conditioned to make the lever-pressing response in order to receive food pellets. Extinction is accomplished by simply turning off the feeder mechanism so that additional responses will not lead to the delivery of food pellets. Although the rat may continue to respond for some time, the expected change in response rate should be observed eventually. A cumulative record of extinction might be illustrated as in Fig. 12-3.

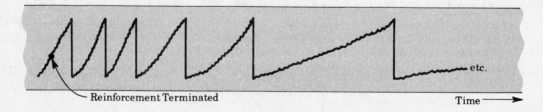

Fig. 12-3

12.4 PARTIAL REINFORCEMENT EFFECT

Generally, the effect of partial reinforcement in instrumental conditioning is the same as in classical conditioning—that is, partial reinforcement leads to greater resistance to response extinction than continuous reinforcement. In addition, certain special effects of the PRE in instrumental conditioning have been studied extensively.

Schedules of Reinforcement

Partial reinforcement has been investigated by arranging the contingency conditions according to several different principles. These various arrangements have been termed *schedules of reinforcement.*

Schedule Characteristics

Four variables appear most important in determining basic schedules of reinforcement These are (1) *fixed* arrangement, where the schedule never changes; (2) *variable* arrangement, where the schedule may change, although usually around some average value; (3) *ratio* scheduling, which is based upon the number of responses made; and (4) *interval* scheduling, based upon time.

Basic Schedule Formats

There are four basic schedule formats, as follows:

Fixed Ratio (FR).   The reinforcement is contingent upon the subject making a certain number of responses (or *n* responses). This number remains constant throughout the procedure.

Fixed Interval (FI).   The reinforcement is contingent upon a correct response being made at the end of a specified time interval. This time interval never varies.

Variable Ratio (VR).   The reinforcement is contingent upon the subject's responding. However, the number of responses required varies from trial to trial, usually in a random pattern. (There may be an average number of responses required, but this will not be readily apparent to the subject.)

Variable Interval (VI).   The reinforcement is contingent upon the subject's giving a correct response at the end of a period of time, but this time period changes, usually in a random fashion. (There may be an average amount of time, but this will not be readily apparent to the subject.)

EXAMPLE 7.   The rat in the operant conditioning chamber might demonstrate one of the four basic schedules as follows:

FR: The rat must make 10 lever presses before a food pellet will be delivered to the trough. The speed or pattern of responding does not matter, as long as 10 responses are made.

FI: The rat must make one correct response at the end of a 30-second interval. Responding is not required at any other time during the interval, and the interval never changes.

VR: The rat is reinforced after 3, 13, 7, 10, 7, 15, 17, 10, and 5 responses. While this pattern averages 10 required responses per reinforcement, sometimes fewer are needed, while at other times many more must be made before the reinforcement will be given.

VI: The rat is reinforced when a correct response is made at the end of 15-, 27-, 45-, 30-, 33-, 10-, 30-, and 50-second intervals. Although the average time is 30 seconds, the interval may be either shorter or much longer.

Expected Performance

Each of the basic schedules of reinforcement will usually produce a particular or distinctive pattern of responding, as follows:

FR.   Bursts of responses closely matching the required number of responses will be followed by brief pauses just after the reinforcement is delivered.

FI.   No responding or very slow responding during the early part of the interval will give way to a high rate of responding just as the interval nears completion.

VR. A constant, high rate of responding can be expected as the subject learns that more responses mean more reinforcements; however, the subject is unable to determine how many responses must be made for each reinforcement.

VI. A slow, steady rate of responding occurs. (The rate of responding is not important, but responding at the end of each interval is required.) The subject "protects" against missing an interval by continuing with the steady performance.

EXAMPLE 8. The cumulative record of responses under each of the four basic formats would tend to look like the results shown in Fig. 12-4. (*Note*: Each "hash mark" denotes delivery of a reinforcement.)

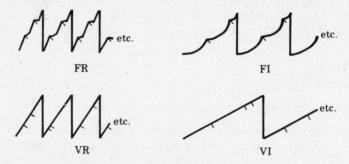

Fig. 12-4

More Advanced Schedules

Combinations or variations of the basic schedules lead to more complex schedules of reinforcement, including *multiple schedules, compound schedules,* and *concurrent schedules.*

A multiple schedule requires the subject to satisfy two or more independent schedules that are presented successively, each in the presence of some cue stimulus. A compound schedule reinforces a single response according to the requirements of two or more schedules operating at the same time. A concurrent schedule reinforces the subject when two or more responses are made to satisfy two or more schedules at the same time.

EXAMPLE 9. "Locker-room language" may be most appropriate when a person is actually in a locker room, only somewhat appropriate when out for a night with the fellows, and totally inappropriate when attending a church social. The different social settings serve as discriminative stimuli for what is essentially a multiple schedule of reinforcement.

EXAMPLE 10. The rat may be required to respond to an FR schedule within a FI limit. The reinforcement is not delivered unless the appropriate number of responses is made during the interval *and* the correct response is given at the end of the interval. (This is called a *conjunctive schedule*, a type of compound schedule.)

12.5 GENERALIZATION AND DIFFERENTIATION

In some instrumental conditioning situations, discriminative cue stimuli indicate to the subject when responding is appropriate or inappropriate. These are not considered conditioned stimuli because they do not elicit specific responses, but they do serve as signals for the general class of instrumental responses.

Stimulus Generalization

Just as in classical conditioning, stimulus generalization is shown when the subject responds not only to the original (discriminative) stimulus, but to other similar stimuli; in other words, the same operant response is made in several similar situations.

Differentiation

Differentiation occurs when the organism distinguishes between the original discriminative stimulus and other similar stimuli, making the instrumental response in the presence of the original stimulus, but not to other similar stimuli.

12.6   REINFORCEMENT CHARACTERISTICS

A major factor in instrumental conditioning is the delivery of reinforcement following responding. Several characteristics of reinforcement have been studied, including positive reinforcers, the effects of aversive stimuli, various conditions of learning or feedback serving as reinforcers, and delay of reinforcement.

Positive Reinforcement

Positive reinforcement means that the presence of a particular stimulus serves to strengthen or maintain a response.

Aversive Stimuli and Negative Reinforcement

An *aversive stimulus* is one the subject finds noxious or unpleasant. *Negative reinforcement* means that the *removal or absence* of a particular stimulus (usually an aversive stimulus) serves to strengthen or maintain a response.

EXAMPLE 11. With a grid-type floor in the operant conditioning chamber, it is possible to deliver an electric shock to the rat. The electric shock can be terminated by pressing the lever. The electric shock is the aversive stimulus while the termination of the shock is a negative reinforcement which strengthens or maintains the lever-pressing response. (*Note*: Almost everyone would find electric shock aversive, but many other stimuli may be judged aversive by some and not by others. Previous experience may be important in determining the properties of a stimulus situation.)

Escape, Avoidance, and Punishment

In Example 11, the lever-pressing response terminated the aversive shock. Such a response represents *escape behavior*; that is, responding that removes an already-present aversive stimulus. *Avoidance* responding means that an organism responds in a way that keeps an aversive stimulus from being delivered. *Punishment* occurs when a response leads to or is followed by an aversive stimulus.

It should be recognized that punishment situations usually involve a contingency relationship; that is, the aversive stimulus occurs because the response was made. However, occasionally, an aversive stimulus may occur contiguously with some response although no contingency exists. In such cases, a superstitious relationship may develop. (See Section 12.1.)

EXAMPLE 12. Behavior as simple as running may fit all three categories of escape, avoidance, or punishment. If the aversive stimulus of a rain shower is present, one may run to escape from it. If one fears heart trouble, one may run for conditioning with the hope of avoiding later physical difficulties. An athlete who misbehaves may have to "run laps," a punishment situation.

Other Classifications of Reinforcement

In the previous chapter, the development of a conditioned reinforcer was described. (See Section 11.8.) In this type of learning, a previously neutral stimulus takes on reinforcing properties. Two other special cases of reinforcement are feedback and using a response as reinforcement.

Feedback occurs when a subject is informed of the results of a response. The feedback may serve as either reinforcement, lack of reinforcement, or punishment for the response, increasing or decreasing the likelihood that the response will be made again.

Using a *response as reinforcement* may be accomplished by making performance of that response contingent upon performance of some less probable response.

EXAMPLE 13.   Using a response as reinforcement sometimes has been called "Grandma's Rule." A child may be informed that an "if-then" contingency situation exists: only when a particular low-probability response (such as shoveling snow from the driveway) has been completed will a high-probability response (such as going sledding) be allowed. Sledding thus serves as a reinforcement for snow-shoveling.

Delay of Reinforcement

Delay of reinforcement means that, although a contingency relationship between a response and reinforcement does exist, some time elapses between the completion of the response and the delivery of the reinforcement. In general, the effect of delay of reinforcement is to reduce learning efficiency.

12.7   USES OF INSTRUMENTAL CONDITIONING

There are many possible uses for instrumental conditioning in family life, education, business, clinical and counseling psychology therapies, animal training, and other areas. Two examples of the practical applications of such principles are in programmed learning and behavior therapy.

Programmed Learning

Programmed learning is an instruction or review technique in which material to be learned is presented in successive, well-planned steps. (The material may be presented in a textbook format, by a teaching machine, or possibly with a computer.) Subjects are expected to respond to a certain problem and then check to determine if the answer they have given is correct or incorrect. The answer provides feedback or reinforcement, generally immediately (a no-delay situation).

Two varieties of programs are *linear programs* (in which each person follows the same program in the same sequence) and *branching programs* (in which the sequence may vary, depending upon the answers given). Linear programs make certain that all subjects study the same material, but may prove boring to some or too difficult for others. Branching programs allow each person to investigate the most important areas according to the responses made, but not all people study the same materials and follow-up may be more difficult.

Behavior Therapy

The basic premise of *behavior therapy* is that acceptable responses will be reinforced and unacceptable responses will be extinguished or suppressed, sometimes by using both nonreinforcement and punishment. Such a technique does not place high value on understanding the causes of behavioral symptoms, but it has been beneficial in creating responses that are socially acceptable and thus in helping patients return to a relatively "normal" life. (See Chapter 22.)

Solved Problems

12.1 Consider where you are sitting as you read this problem, and suppose you are hungry. Briefly describe the instrumental responses you would have to make to reach a goal that would satisfy your motive.

Depending on where you are reading at the moment, the sequence of instrumental responses might be: (1) stand; (2) walk from where you are to the coffee room; (3) remove money from your pocket; (4) pay for a doughnut; and (5) sit at a table to eat. The actual eating of the doughnut is called a *consummatory response*, while the preceding responses are instrumental responses, made because they lead toward the desired goal.

12.2 Instrumental conditioning also has been called *operant conditioning* or *Skinnerian conditioning*. Why?

The term *operant* implies the organism's ability to operate upon the environment. This is in contrast to respondent conditioning, in which the organism's response is a reaction to stimulation from the environment.

Instrumental conditioning is called Skinnerian conditioning because of the influence of B.F. Skinner, an American psychologist who developed theories and techniques that greatly expanded knowledge of instrumental conditioning.

12.3 Why is instrumental conditioning described as a contingency situation?

Instrumental responses are voluntary responses that lead to a goal or reinforcement. Unless the response is made, the reinforcement will not be attained. Thus, the reinforcement is dependent upon, or contingent upon, performance of the response.

12.4 Do contiguous response-reinforcement associations mean that a contingency relationship will be established?

Contiguous response-reinforcement situations do not necessarily indicate that a contingency relationship will be established. Contingency means that the reinforcement is dependent upon the response being made, while contiguity refers only to the fact that the response and reinforcement occur together. When the organism performs a response that happens to be followed by a noncontingent reinforcement, it is possible that a superstitious behavior may be created.

12.5 Contingency implies that the instrumental response becomes conditioned because it is followed by the reinforcement. What principle was proposed as a general explanation for such situations?

The Law of Effect proposed that when a response led to either a satisfying state of affairs or the removal of an annoyance, that response would become conditioned. This principle was first set forth by E. L. Thorndike very early in the development of the psychology of learning and it has been supported quite well ever since.

12.6 Suppose that Sonja, an eight-year-old, found that keeping her room clean meant that her mother would praise her behavior and sometimes offer her special treats. Why would this behavior be classified as instrumental learning rather than as classical conditioning?

There are two major differences between a response that is classically conditioned and one that is instrumentally conditioned. First, in Sonja's case the response is not forced or elicited, but rather voluntary or emitted. Second, there is no clear-cut CS in operant conditioning to which the response become attached. Sonja's voluntary response to a general stimulus situation is instrumental, rather than one which is classically conditioned.

12.7   In attempting to lose weight, many people are told to record everything they eat and calculate the number of calories consumed each day. This allows them the opportunity to observe the decrease in caloric intake or fluctuations in eating behavior as days pass.

As their eating behavior comes nearer to that which will produce a loss of weight, any weight loss that has already occurred will serve as reinforcement for the responding. What principles of instrumental conditioning may be used in describing this situation?

The change in eating behavior toward better approximations of a desirable diet represents shaping. The associated weight loss and maintenance of a new, more desirable weight level serve as reinforcements for this correct responding. Recording the caloric intake from day to day represents a cumulative record of responding.

12.8   Young children often learn to operate upon their environment (that is, their parents) by crying. This seems particularly true at times when the children do not want to go to bed, although they are very tired and in need of sleep. What parental response is necessary to eliminate this type of crying.

The parents should *not* respond. By reacting, the parents would be reinforcing the crying. By not reacting, the parents initiate an extinction procedure, which if carried through will lead to elimination of the crying. Consistency is necessary, however, because an occasional reaction to the crying will serve as partial reinforcement and make the response very resistant to extinction. Likewise, punishment may suppress the response, but not eliminate its recurrence at some later date.

12.9   In the previous problem, the partial reinforcement effect is described in the same fashion as in classical conditioning. Is this effect of the PRE the same in both classical and instrumental conditioning?

The effect of the PRE is the same for both classical and instrumental conditioning situations: partial reinforcement results in greater resistance to extinction than continous reinforcement does.

12.10   Briefly explain the variables that are considered most basic in establishing schedules of reinforcement.

The variables that seem most important in the determination of schedules of reinforcement are: whether the schedule is fixed or variable and whether the schedule is based upon a ratio of responses to reinforcement or on an interval of time. Fixed schedules do not change, with the same amount of time or the same number of responses throughout. Variable schedules may change, although frequently an average number of responses or amount of time is used. Ratio schedules are based upon a number of responses, while interval schedules are based upon some time period.

12.11   A student seeking to make some extra money finds a job painting shutters for a construction firm. The student is told that the work can be done at whatever time fits best into the school schedule and that the wages paid will be ten dollars each time twelve shutters are completed. Analyze this situation in terms of schedules of reinforcement.

The important consideration is the payoff. Ten dollars is given after twelve shutters are completed, a fixed ratio circumstance where a certain consistent amount of responding is rewarded with a monetary payoff.

12.12   Bingo is a game that is popular with many groups. Often, observation of such a group will reveal players who simultaneously keep track of two or more cards during any one game. Such behavior reflects a particular schedule of reinforcement that probably has produced the PRE. Which schedule is this?

The multiple-card Bingo player shows a variable ratio schedule of reinforcement. As more responses (that is, cards) are made, the chances of getting a payoff are increased. However, there is no guarantee that after a certain number of responses are made, a payoff will occur. Thus, an inconsistent schedule based upon responses (rather than time) means this is a VR schedule of reinforcement.

12.13 The student attending a class where the instructor gives unannounced ("pop") quizzes should probably study according to one of the schedules of reinforcement. Which one?

Unannounced quizzes may occur at any time. Therefore, the student needs to be ready for one in any class and should study a little bit each day in anticipation of a possible exam. This is a variable interval schedule of reinforcement, where the payoff comes after a certain amount of time, but the time periods may vary.

12.14 In many classes students are assigned a term paper. While the paper may be completed and turned in at any time during the course, it *must* be finished by a given date. Responding to complete such an assignment illustrates which schedule of reinforcement?

This is a fixed interval schedule of reinforcement. The work must be completed within a specific period, but not at any specific time within that period. (*Note*: Psychologists often refer to the "typical" pattern of responding for such assignments as the "term-paper effect." No matter what length of time is allowed, many students complete their work with desperate "all-nighters" the day before the paper is due. This burst of responding at the end of the interval is comparable to that produced by the lever-pressing rat.)

12.15 An English instructor says, "You are to write four themes within the next three weeks. You may turn them in whenever you wish within that period, but failure to complete them all means no credit will be given for any." What is the reinforcement arrangement in this case?

This is a fixed ratio within a temporal limitation and is called a *drh*, or differential reinforcement of high rates of responding. The responses are reinforced provided the necessary number occurs before the time has elapsed. This is an example of a compound schedule of reinforcement.

12.16 An interlocking schedule (another example of a compound schedule of reinforcement) may demand that the number of responses increases as the length of time since the previous reinforcement increases. Why might such a schedule create a major problem for children learning to read?

The required number of responses for reinforcement may become exceedingly large very quickly. If first-grade children do not produce the appropriate responses to begin with, the ever-increasing demands of second and third grade will mean those same children will fall more and more behind the children who are able to keep up.

12.17 The electric flash units used by many photographers make a peculiar whining sound as they recharge just after being used. This noise continues until the unit is once again ready to flash. Experienced photographers learn to wait until the noise terminates before attempting to take another picture. What principle is illustrated by such behavior?

The photographer's behavior illustrates differentiation in an instrumental situation. The response made (taking pictures) is an instrumental response leading to a goal (getting some good prints or slides). By waiting until the whining sound has finished the photographer is able to discriminate between an appropriate time to respond and an inappropriate time to respond.

12.18 Young children seem to learn quite early in life that when an adult says the child's first name in a particular manner, the child better "shape up" or trouble may follow! The child learns the appropriate instrumental response to avoid trouble, and uses it in all situations where a cue of this type is given. The child's behavior illustrates what principle?

By performing the same instrumental responses to several similar (but not identical) stimuli, the child shows stimulus generalization. In this case, the generalizing is beneficial, keeping the child from getting into trouble in a number of different situations.

12.19 Suppose the child described in Problem 12.18 does not respond appropriately. The adult decides to try to discipline the child by restricting the child's playtime and confining the child to one room. The child is then given the opportunity to act in an acceptable fashion, and the adult assures the child that good behavior will mean the end of confinement. Analyze this situation according to the principles of instrumental conditioning.

There are a number of interrelated principles in this example. The child's misbehavior leads to punishment when the adult restricts the child's activity. The confinement is an aversive stimulus. The child is given the opportunity to make an escape response by acting in an acceptable fashion and, if this occurs, will receive a negative reinforcement when the aversive stimulus is removed. (*Note*: Discipline does not mean punishing, but rather, teaching. The wise adult would not only lift the confinement ruling, but also praise the appropriate responses.)

12.20 Suppose the child in Problem 12.18 keeps himself or herself from getting into trouble. What type of responding is this?

The child makes avoidance responses. Having learned how to keep the aversive stimuli from being administered, the child is able to avoid getting in trouble. (*Note*: Many adults claim that children have an uncanny knack for knowing just how far they *can* go and still not be in trouble. This represents quite sophisticated differentiation.)

12.21 The rat receiving a food pellet for pushing the lever in the operant conditioning chamber and the child receiving praise for appropriate behavior are two examples of the same principle. What principle is this?

Both situations illustrate the principle of positive reinforcement. The instrumental response is followed by a stimulus which, when present, strengthens or maintains the response. (*Note*: Praise is a conditioned reinforcer. See Section 11.8.)

12.22 People learning to play a musical instrument can usually tell when the sound they make is good or bad. That is, the sound informs the players of how well they have mastered the instrument, and this information may affect the players' future responding. What principle is illustrated by this example?

Information about the consequences of a response is called feedback. When feedback affects future responding, it serves as reinforcement. Feedback may help to strengthen or maintain certain responses or, perhaps, extinguish others.

12.23 In Problem 12.19, the child's confinement was described as an aversive stimulus. In another situation, an adult might attempt to influence a child's behavior in another way, such as by saying, "As soon as you have cleared the table, you may go out and play." How does this latter situation differ from the confinement example given before? What principle is illustrated?

In this case, one response is being used to reinforce another. A low probability response (clearing the table) will be performed so that a high probability response (playing) may follow. This is a positive reinforcement condition, while the termination of confinement represents negative reinforcement.

12.24 Teachers are quite frequently accused of failing to show concern for students because they assign and collect papers, but do not return them to the students for long periods of time. Students often claim that such a practice reduces learning efficiency. One psychological principle seems to explain why the accusation probably is correct. Name the principle and explain how it fits this situation.

The principle is delay of reinforcement, which states that if there is a long period of time between response and reinforcement, and especially if that period is unfilled, learning efficiency will diminish considerably. In this instance, the feedback from the teacher would serve as reinforcement (or punishment), and the long delay reduces performance.

12.25 Older children often tease their younger sisters and brothers. Parents, annoyed by such actions, often try to discourage this kind of behavior. Describe how the concepts of instrumental conditioning, punishment, escape responses, and avoidance responses might all fit into an explanation of the parent's and child's behavior.

One way of reducing the teasing would be to extinguish those responses and reinforce other, more appropriate ones. Conditioning might be used in conjunction with punishment, such as when the parent says, "If you torment that child, I'll . . . " and establishes a potential punishment condition.

An older child who is placed in a punishment situation may seek a response to reduce or eliminate that punishment. Thus, the older child would show escape behavior, which would lead to a negative reinforcement—the removal of an aversive stimulus. The child who successfully makes an adjustment in responding, so that the aversive stimulus is not administered, is showing avoidance behavior.

12.26 Fred, Betty, Sally, and John have decided to learn to play bridge. They go to a bookstore and buy a "teach-yourself" book. Each uses the book in turn, but when they get together for the first time, they find they have read different parts of the book. A quick investigation shows they have followed different directions, depending upon the initial responses each person made. What kind of book did they have?

This probably was a programmed learning text that used a branching program. If each reader gave a different initial response, each would have been directed to a different section of the book. Had the book been written with a linear program, all four would have followed the same sequence and studied the same program.

12.27 Many children leave their clothes, toys, books, bicycles, and dolls wherever they wish. Briefly describe how parents might act in order to change such behavior in their children.

The parents could use a system of reward, punishment, and extinction based upon the principles of instrumental conditioning. This would essentially be a behavior modification program.

Probably the first step in this case would be to stop picking up for the child; that is, eliminating reinforcement for careless or sloppy behavior. This extinction procedure might be combined with punishment when such behavior was evident and reinforcement for appropriately neat behavior.

It is important that the child be made a part of this program at all times. Parents who occasionally clean up for the child will be giving the child partial reinforcement for sloppiness, and this will make the child's careless behavior very resistant to extinction.

12.28 Suppose the child in Problem 12.27 shows extremely sloppy behavior. How might the principle of shaping be important in modifying the child's behavior?

Shaping, or reinforcing closer and closer approximations of the desired behavior, is a principle used frequently in instrumental conditioning. In this case, a parent at first might ask nothing more than that the child bring indoors any clothes or toys left outside the house. Later, the parent would attempt to refine the child's behavior even more, perhaps by encouraging the child to put dirty clothes in the laundry basket or toys in the garage or closet.

Key Terms

Aversive stimulus.   Any stimulus the organism judges to be noxious or unpleasant.

Avoidance response.   Any response an organism makes in order to keep from experiencing an anticipated aversive stimulus.

Behavior therapy.   The use of instrumental conditioning procedures to help create socially acceptable behavior.

Branching program.   Those programmed learning situations in which progress through the program depends on the subject's responses; the program may vary for each subject using it.

Compound schedules.   Partial reinforcement schedules in which a response is reinforced according to the requirements of two or more schedules that operate at the same time.

Concurrent schedules.   Partial reinforcement schedules in which two or more responses are made to satisfy two or more schedules at the same time.

Contingency.   In instrumental conditioning, a situation in which reinforcement is not delivered unless certain responses are made.

Cumulative record.   The tally or record of appropriate or satisfactory instrumental responses made in a given time period.

Delay of reinforcement.   A period of time between the response and reinforcement in a contingency situation.

Discriminative stimulus.   A cue stimulus that indicates when it is either appropriate or inappropriate to make an instrumental response.

Escape response.   Any response made by an organism in order to get away from an already-present aversive stimulus.

Feedback.   An organism's knowledge of the results of its response.

Fixed schedules.   Partial reinforcement schedules that remain unchanged.

Instrumental conditioning.   A learning process that involves changing the probability of a response by manipulating the consequences of that response; also called *operant conditioning* and *Skinnerian* conditioning.

Instrumental response.   A response leading toward a goal.

Interval schedules.   Partial reinforcement schedules in which reinforcement is delivered after a response that has been made at the end of a given time period.

Law of effect.   Thorndike's proposal that a response followed by the presence of a satisfying stimulus or the termination of an annoying stimulus will become conditioned.

Linear program.   Any programmed learning situation that progresses in the same way for each subject.

Multiple schedules.   Partial reinforcement schedules that require the subject to satisfy two or more independent schedules that are presented successively, each cued.

Negative reinforcement.   A type of event in which the removal or absence of a stimulus condition strengthens or maintains a response.

Noncontingent reinforcement.   Reinforcement that follows a response but is not dependent upon that response.

Operant conditioning chamber.   An apparatus used for experimental testing of instrumental conditioning; several varieties exist.

Positive reinforcement.   A type of event in which the presence of a stimulus condition strengthens or maintains a response.

Programmed learning.   A special learning technique that usually involves small steps, immediate feedback, and a high level of reinforcement for performance.

Punishment.   A type of event in which delivery of an aversive stimulus is contingent upon a certain response.

Ratio schedules.   Partial reinforcement schedules in which the reinforcement delivered is based upon the number of responses made.

Schedules of reinforcement.   Ways of arranging partial reinforcement in instrumental conditioning situations.

Shaping.   Reinforcing closer and closer approximations of a desired behavior.

Superstitious behavior.   When an organism performs as if a particular response causes reinforcement, but in fact there is no contingency.

Variable schedules.   Partial reinforcement schedules that can change, usually around some average value.

Chapter 13

Learning by Modeling

Learning by modeling has also been called *observational learning, learning by imitation, no-trial learning, vicarious learning, identification learning*, and *social learning*. No matter which label is used and which particular emphasis is stressed, the basic premise of learning by modeling is that one person or animal observes the behavior of another and is then able to perform some or all of that observed behavior.

13.1 COMPARISON TO OTHER LEARNING FORMS

Learning by modeling differs from classical conditioning and instrumental conditioning in several important ways, including species limitations, the significance of reinforcement, and the importance of the type of response made.

Limitations by Species

Imitative behavior is limited to some extent by species membership. Animals as well as humans are able to demonstrate learning by modeling, but in most cases can only imitate activities that are within the skill range of their species and that are appropriate to their species' pattern of behavior. (There are limitations on the types of learning an organism can accomplish through classical conditioning or instrumental conditioning, but the limitations of species' membership on learning by modeling seem more rigid. Fewer animals appear to learn by modeling than by classical or instrumental conditioning.)

Effect of Reinforcement

Reinforcement appears to facilitate learning by modeling rather than to force a response, as in classical conditioning, or to develop a contingency relationship, as in instrumental conditioning. An imitated response is more likely to remain in the behavioral pattern if it is followed by reinforcement. However, the imitated response gets into the behavioral pattern because it has been observed, *not* because of the reinforcement. In other words, reinforcement serves only as a motivating condition for learning by modeling.

Importance of Modeled Responses

For the safety of the learner or others, some responses are best learned through modeling. In some cases, forcing a response is impossible, and learning by shaping an instrumental response might place the learner, teacher, or others in unreasonable jeopardy.

EXAMPLE 1. Learning to shoot a pistol or rifle could be accomplished by classical or instrumental conditioning techniques. However, such techniques might turn out to be very dangerous. In classical conditioning, for example, a learner's orienting responses might result in an unintentional firing of a weapon; and in instrumental conditioning, the trial-and-error shaping of an appropriate response might very well be time-consuming and unsafe. By contrast, the correct, safe use of a weapon could be modeled with relative safety and speed.

13.2 TYPES OF MODELING

Modeling may take place in several different ways, although the basic premise is the same in all cases.

Live Modeling—Observation

Perhaps the most common form of learning by modeling is the direct observation of a live model by the learner. This usually occurs in social situations, involving individuals with whom the observer has frequent contact (such as parents, teachers, or peers).

(*Note*: One theory of learning and personality development is called Social Learning Theory, or SLT. One very important consideration in SLT is what person is available to be modeled.)

Vicarious Learning

Vicarious learning occurs when an observer not only is able to note the response the model makes, but is also able to observe the consequences of that response. The actual response *and* the resultant reinforcement or punishment are observed together with the vocal, postural, or facial gestures that may reveal the model's emotional reactions. The observer does not actually make the response at this point, nor does the observer receive directly any reinforcement or punishment. However, the vicarious experience can serve to arouse the observer and may influence later responding.

EXAMPLE 2. You may easily recall vicarious learning if you have ever observed someone else suffer a very painful burn. For example, suppose you have watched a friend lean against an electric range where one of the surface units has just been turned off. You no doubt saw the nasty burn which your friend received. This was sufficient to arouse your anxiety and understanding, and you did not have to lean on the hot unit and also get burned in order to know that it could hurt you. This is a case of vicarious suppression of a response; situations involving positive reinforcement for the model may lead to vicarious *facilitation* of a response.

Symbolic Learning—Verbal Modeling

Some modeling depends on verbal representation of a behavior rather than an observation of an actual behavior. More than any other single characteristic, this ability distinguishes humans from other species and makes a human's behavioral range so broad. Activities represented in verbal codes can be retained (or stored) for later use. As guides for the imitation of appropriate responses, they may considerably reduce the time and effort involved in learning a certain behavior.

EXAMPLE 3. Suppose you discovered a time-saving short-cut from your home to a local theater. You could use a verbal description to represent this path to a neighbor. In effect, that neighbor will be modeling your behavior, but no direct observation of the "short-cut" is necessary. The neighbor relies instead on a sequence of verbal guides, such as, "Left on McKenzie until you reach Riverside, then right to Bittersweet. . . . "

Pure Imitation

Some modeling involves exact imitation of another's response. In some cases, this may mean there has been imitation without understanding. That is, the response is copied, but the meaning of the response is not recognized by the imitator.

EXAMPLE 4. Sometimes pure imitation leads to humorous situations. Many stories have been told about children singing Christmas carols without learning the correct words. However, when one listens carefully, the children may be singing about "Round John Virgin" or "Hark the hairless angels sing." These are good attempts at imitative modeling, but are obviously done without understanding.

13.3 FACTORS INFLUENCING MODELING

The fact that someone is exposed to a particular behavior does not guarantee that the behavior will be modeled. A number of factors influence whether or not learning by modeling will occur.

Attention

The single most important factor in learning by modeling is *attention*. It is necessary that the observer *attend to* the behavior being shown by the model. Lack of attention may result in partial or incorrect modeling, or no learning by modeling at all. Attention may be affected in turn by many factors, such as those that influence perception. (See Chapter 7.)

Proximity

Attention must be directed toward a model if observational learning is to take place. In general, the observer is most likely to select as a model someone who is close by rather than someone remote. This means that parents, other close relatives, and good friends, for example, are much more apt to be chosen as models than are strangers. (See, however, Example 7.)

Model Status

Research has shown that observers are selective in their choice of models. This selectivity seems to be based upon the status of the potential model, including such characteristics as the position the model holds, the role the model plays, the power or influence the model has, and the ability of the model to communicate.

Most evidence supports the findings that high-status models are more likely to be imitated than are low-status models. While the determination of status may vary according to the observer, position (such as parent, teacher, or minister), role (such as leader of a peer group), or power (such as the right to administer or withhold reinforcements) are important factors in the direction of attention. Combined with the model's ability to communicate, these factors incline the observer toward or away from the model.

EXAMPLE 5. Junior high school students are often very favorably impressed by teachers who are able to talk in the idiom and at the level of the students and still manage to teach. Such teachers are recognized as "special" and are usually held in high esteem by the students. If such a teacher suggested that certain kinds of behavior such as smoking were inappropriate, the students might stand a good chance of adopting the suggestion. If such a suggestion were put forth by a low-status teacher, the students might not follow it.

EXAMPLE 6. Suppose a high school teacher walks into a classroom every day and begins his presentation by saying, "Now today, children...." Such a method of address might lower the teacher's status in the eyes of his students. (High school students do not expect to be treated like children, and they will have a strong tendency to discredit an instructor who treats them that way.)

It should be noted that even "strangers" could act as models if they are accorded status through publicity in the mass media. Observers may have never met the model personally, but could still confer on the model very high status.

EXAMPLE 7. Television has made it possible for most of us to observe the behaviors of people with special abilities. Thus, we may attempt to model some of our behaviors on the behaviors of gourmet cooks, singers, or tennis players we have seen and heard on television.

It must be recognized that it is the observer who grants status to a model. Each observer may choose differently, depending upon the qualities he or she judges most important.

Influence and Power

An *influence* is defined as a change in a person's attitudes or behaviors that originates in another person or a group. Two distinct types of influence have been identified: *independent influence*, in which a change occurs because the message itself is persuasive; and *dependent influence*, in which a change results from the social characteristics of a model or group. *Power* is defined as *potential influence*. A model's status may be significantly affected by both the influence and power that an observer perceives in the model.

Cognitive Control

The previous paragraph implies that influence and power are *external* events that can have an important effect on an observer. *Cognitive control* is the observer's *internal* control, which results from verbal learning or other types of learning the observer has experienced.

EXAMPLE 8.   Research on the personality and behavioral characteristics of presidential assassins has shown that almost every assassin was at least partially under internal, delusional control. Inner voices, irrational beliefs, and a sense of "heroic destiny" helped bring the assassin to the point of committing the act. Furthermore, seclusive attitudes tended to keep these people from being exposed to corrective social influences. While this may be considered an extreme or bizarre example, it illustrates the extent to which internal control may supercede external power or influence.

13.4   RETENTION

For learning by modeling to be successful, the observer must be attentive to the model and retain a memory of the model's behavior to be used at a later time. (Retention is fully discussed in Chapter 15.) The observer may retain a particular visual image or a verbal representation of the model's behavior. As mentioned previously, verbal modeling allows a model to present an almost unlimited range of behaviors to an observer, even when actual demonstration of those activities is not possible. Visual images may be very strong, and in some cases almost impossible to keep from conscious memory, but the extent of retention and later transmission of a model's behavior may depend on the observer's language development.

EXAMPLE 9.   Architects often have a "feel" about a particular building—yet may be unable to express this to the client. In such a case, the visual image is stronger than the architect's ability to express it. Quite frequently, the architect will construct a model of the structure, putting the images into a three-dimensional form that can then be discussed, revised, and eventually shown to the client. This process may be repeated several times during the development of plans for the building, and it is sometimes possible for the client to learn to imitate the behavior of the architect: the client, after a while, may be able to visualize changes in the plan without actually seeing them in a revised model.

13.5   REINFORCEMENT AND PUNISHMENT

As mentioned earlier, reinforcement facilitates learning by modeling but is not necessary for modeling to occur. The same holds true for punishment: it may be used to encourage learning by modeling, but it does not guarantee that such learning will take place.

Reinforcement or punishment may affect an observer through vicarious learning. (See Section 13.2.) The observed effects of other's behaviors can be very important, and observers may develop attitudes of self-arousal or self-reinforcement based upon the behaviors and reaction they have seen in models.

Self-Arousal

A person who observes others succeed, fail, or perhaps be punished for a particular activity may retain an image or verbal representation that can be recalled at some later time and serve as a motivating stimulus.

EXAMPLE 10.   One need never have spoken to a large group of people in order to feel fearful of public speaking. Most people, in fact, feel somewhat anxious by just thinking about such a situation. Simply observing the public-speaking experiences of others is often enough to create the anxiety.

Self-Reinforcement

Observers may establish standards for their own performance on the basis of what the model appears to accept. There may be some sort of interaction, however: if the model is judged as a low-status person, for example, the observer may try to set higher standards; if the model is seen as a high-status person, the observer may accept lower standards.

Relationship of Vicarious Reinforcement to Actual Reinforcement

Vicarious reinforcement (through learning by modeling) seems to be quite helpful in many situations for learning a new, previously untrained response. However, vicarious reinforcement is unlikely to maintain that response because the learner will come to expect actual reinforcement.

EXAMPLE 11. Having observed a salesperson use a particular technique and be highly rewarded, you might attempt to imitate the same behavior. If your efforts were not rewarded, however, you would probably not continue to use this technique, particularly if you continued to see the other person being rewarded.

13.6 SPECIAL CONCERNS OF LEARNING BY MODELING

The discussion of modeling in this chapter has so far been largely confined to cases in which one observer attends to the behavior of *one* model. It should be recognized, however, that over a period of time a person will tend to blend the actions of several different models. Thus, a personal style of behavior, which differs from the behavior of any one model, will emerge.

It is very difficult to determine just how much influence any one model has had on a person's behavior. However, even if percentages of influence cannot be decided, the fact that multiple influences played a role in any one person's behavior is hard to dispute.

Socialization and Conflict

Learning by modeling is the source of many social behaviors. The attitudes and behaviors modeled in and reinforced by certain cultures or subcultures are adopted at an early age, and are often maintained throughout life.

A person who grew up in one culture or subculture may, of course, observe behaviors from another, and may even take these other behaviors as models. This could create a conflict for the person. The resolution of such conflict will in part be determined by the strength of the two behaviors: the stronger or more valued of the two would most likely be adopted.

EXAMPLE 12. Teenagers often find themselves in serious conflict situations. Their peer group may claim and demonstrate that smoking marijuana is an acceptable and desirable activity. In most cases, a conflicting set of standards would be shown by the parents. In such a situation, the teenager will have to decide which model to imitate. Such choices are not easy, particularly because anxiety over possible rejection (by the peer group) or punishment (by the parents) will occur.

Inhibition and Disinhibition

Learning by modeling has been used to make response patterns more or less probable by using the model's activities as a guide for the observer. If the observer is performing some response that is judged inappropriate, a model experiencing very negative or aversive consequences for such behavior or a model experiencing positive consequences for a contradictory behavior may be used. If the observer is unwilling to act in a given situation, a model who does act and experiences positive consequences may be used. The basic purpose of these conditions is to try to inhibit those responses judged inappropriate or "release" the observer from inhibitions regarding behaviors which would be appropriate.

These principles have been adopted, in part, into a therapeutic technique known as desensitization. Modeling often play a very important part in a patient's approach toward more normal behavior. (See Chapter 22 for a discussion of this therapeutic technique.)

Solved Problems

13.1   In both classical conditioning and instrumental conditioning, there is an important relationship between the desired response and reinforcement. In learning by modeling, is reinforcement considered important? What is the major emphasis of learning by modeling?

Reinforcement is important in learning by modeling, but not for the same reasons it is important in classical or instrumental conditioning. Reinforcement neither forces a modeled response (as in classical conditioning) nor serves as a *necessary* condition (as in instrumental conditioning). Instead, reinforcement in learning by modeling *facilitates* a subject's response. The major emphasis of learning by modeling is that the subject observes some response and then tries to imitate that response.

13.2   What are some of the other names given to learning by modeling, and what do they imply?

Learning by modeling has been called both *observational learning* and *imitative learning*. In addition, it has been called *vicarious learning* because of the indirect nature of the learning experience in some situations. Also, Social Learning Theory (SLT), has been proposed to explain modeling because it emphasizes the role of the model and the relationship of the observer to the model. Two other terms, *identification learning* and *no-trial learning*, have also been used. The former suggests that subjects identify themselves with models; the latter implies that modeled behavior is not necessarily based on trial-and-error learning.

13.3   Many young children who listen to birds sing find they cannot imitate exactly the sounds they hear. What principle of learning by modeling is demonstrated by this attempt at imitation?

To some extent, learning by modeling is species-specific. In other words, behaviors of a given species cannot always be copied by another species. Many psychologists believe that the capacities for both perceiving a behavior and for reproducing the behavior are innate. While some overlap may appear to exist (for example, certain birds can imitate human speech) many forms of responding are limited exclusively to a given species.

13.4   Why is modeling considered the "best" kind of learning technique for certain behaviors, such as swimming or driving an automobile?

When compared to other forms of learning, modeling is most efficient and least dangerous. For the two behaviors mentioned, there are no readily available stimuli to force the correct response, thus ruling out classical conditioning. Furthermore, shaping closer and closer approximations of a desired response may be a part of learning either behavior, but some initial model seems necessary to avoid what might be tragic errors. In both cases, providing a model helps insure a relatively high level of safety for the learner.

13.5   Suppose a professional golfer crouches over a 4-foot putt, strokes the ball, and watches as it curls toward the cup, dips in, and then pops out. The golfer drops the putter, a pained expression crosses her face, she throws her arms toward the sky, and finally exclaims, "Why me?" The spectators groan in accordance, and many show similar expressions of displeasure. What principle of modeling behavior does the spectator's reactions illustrate?

The reactions shown by the spectators illustrate vicarious experience. The golfer conveyed her own emotional reactions with her gestures and what she said. These displays aroused similar strong emotional reactions in the observers. (Many vicarious learning situations do involve emotional reactions, but emotions are not a necessary condition for vicarious learning. What is important is that the observer learns a response from the activity of the model without actually experiencing what the model experienced.)

13.6 Distinguish between these situations in which a parent shows a child how to ride a bicycle and those in which a parent tells a child how to ride a bicycle.

Showing the child the appropriate sequence of responding is live modeling. Telling the child how to ride is symbolic learning through the use of language. In the latter case, it is essential the child be able to understand the descriptions if a successful response pattern is to follow.

13.7 Young children sometimes embarrass their parents by using foul language at socially inappropriate moments. Such responses probably illustrate what principle?

Foul language at the wrong time (which may be any time) could indicate pure imitation, or modeling without understanding. The children may learn the words, but not the meaning, with the result sometimes being very surprising.

13.8 What single factor, more than any other, determines whether or not learning by modeling will take place?

A person cannot learn by modeling if there is a lack of attention to the important aspects of the model's behavior. Attention must occur, or learning by modeling will not. Simple exposure to a model will not insure learning, as the subject may ignore the model entirely or ignore the essential features of the model's behavior.

13.9 People often say things like, "Well, look at her friends! How can you expect her to act differently?" Such statements are representative of an important aspect of learning by modeling. What is it, and how does it affect the responses learned?

In many cases, a person may center his or her attention on close associates. With the repeated opportunities for observation and modeling, this person is likely to act in a manner similar to the manner of these close associates.

13.10 Quite frequently, amateur athletes attempt to look and act in ways similar to those displayed by professional athletes. What is the basis for the amateur's imitation?

The professional athlete is judged to be an expert in a given sport. As such, the professional is accorded a role of prestige or high status by the amateur. This fact, combined with the fact that the consequences of the professional's behaviors are viewed as favorable, often leads the amateur to imitate the professional's behavior.

13.11 How do advertisers attempt to capitalize on the kind of imitation described in Problem 13.10?

Professional athletes (and others in "highly visible" occupations) are imitated enthusiastically. Advertisers try to benefit from this by utilizing a generalization effect: the advertiser hopes the buying public will assume that the "star's" expertise in one area must somehow carry over into other areas. Thus, the movie star may advertise baking products or the professional athlete may advertise clothing. The advertisers hope that the imitative behaviors will produce purchases of these products, even though there is no evidence that the "star" truly has extensive knowledge of the particular product.

13.12   The high-status models described in Problem 13.10 and 13.11 are public figures. Are all significant models public figures?

       No. Public distinction is not necessary for a person to be judged a significant model. The only crucial fact is that the observer believes that the model is important or holds high status. For example, parents, close relatives, or friends who do not command public attention may serve as very important models.

13.13   Suppose that the model being observed is not judged as having status, but the message being presented is recognized as important or persuasive. What terminology differentiates this situation from one where the message is accepted because the model is seen as prestigious?

       If the social characteristics of the model make the message persuasive or effective, the term *dependent influence* is used; that is, the success of the message depends upon who presents it. When the message itself is persuasive, the term *independent influence* is used.

13.14   What distinction can be seen between the actual change in one person's behavior because of imitation of some model and the *possibility* that some change may occur because of the actions of the model?

       An actual change that originates because of the actions of a model is called an *influence*. The *potential* for change that exists because of the prestige or status of the model is called *power*. Power may or may not be used; but when it is used, it will lead to influence of some other person's actions.

13.15   How do observers determine which model is important?

       Observers often determine which model is important or holds status on the basis of the power the model seems to have. (For example, children may learn to imitate parents because the parents have the power to control important sources of pleasure for the child.) In addition, observers may select models who seem to be rewarded for their behavior. (For example, amateur athletes may imitate highly paid and popular athletes.)

13.16   Fred has been asked to get the family boat off the trailer and into the lake. This is the first time Fred has done this. (His older brother Tom always performed this task in the past.) Somehow, in attempting to release the boat from the trailer, Fred has allowed it to overturn, and then in righting it he has managed to swamp the craft so it almost sinks. At this point, his parents rush to the scene and say, "How could you let this happen when you've seen Tom do this hundreds of times?" Fred dejectedly answers, "I guess I didn't remember." What important aspect of modeling is demonstrated by Fred's difficulties?

       Attention to the model is considered the most important requisite in learning by modeling. Retention of what has been observed ranks a close second. Either Fred has not attended to what his older brother did, or he has not retained it. (A person cannot be influenced by a model's actions if the person has no memory of those actions.)

13.17   Once they have calmed down and retrieved the boat, Fred's parents (Problem 13.16) decide to teach Fred the correct procedure for releasing the boat from the trailer. They patiently explain each step, trying to get Fred to picture just how each step is performed and to learn a series of key phrases that describe the process. Eventually, Fred becomes very capable at launching the boat. (He is able both to picture how it should be done and to recall the important phrases.) Fred's success represents what aspects of the retention process?

       Fred's retention includes both images and verbal representations of the task. Well-established images can be retrieved at will, and often are so powerful that they are difficult to exclude from retention once a cue stimulus has been given. Verbal coding of events allows considerable facilitation of later performance of an observed behavior because it allows a great deal of information to be carried in an easily stored form. For example, Fred does not *have* to recall images of each step; instead, he may code certain statements that allow him to reproduce the correct sequence of steps.

13.18   Lower organisms do demonstrate learning by modeling, but humans seem to have a much greater capacity for such an activity. Why is this? What limitations might exist for humans?

Humans have an immense capacity for language learning. This means that humans can make verbal representations of a model's behavior that can be retained for long periods of time. Moreover, this gives humans the ability to pass on information to others who did not observe the original activity of a model.

Humans have the most advanced language skills, although other organisms show evidences of some language development. (See Chapter 16.) Humans therefore have the greatest opportunity for verbal or symbolic modeling. Modeling through language is probably limited only by the language development of the particular person involved.

13.19   Humans are quite capable of producing mental images or thoughts that serve as motivational stimuli. Describe this concept of self-arousal.

Observations of the behavior of others often is accompanied by the learning and retention of images and verbal representations of the events. These may carry over to a later period, when recall serves as a motivator for behavior. For example, humans are able to generate thought processes that will produce nausea, or sexual arousal, or even anger by recalling the observed activities of others. Thus, self-arousal in some cases may be a function not of one's own behavior, but of the previously observed responses of some other person.

13.20   A recent research study investigated subjects who were shown a videotape of aggressive behavior that is ordinarily disapproved. However, the aggressive behavior shown on the tapes went unpunished. The subjects shown these tapes were as likely to imitate the aggressive behaviors as were subjects shown a videotape which depicted the same behaviors being rewarded. What term describes this situation, and what explanation seems to fit these circumstances?

The subjects are experiencing vicarious reinforcement; that is, they are able to see the positive results of the normally disapproved responses. In the latter videotape, the responses yield direct positive reinforcement, while in the first situation, the absence of anticipated punishment apparently indicates permissiveness and reduces fears that might otherwise accompany such behaviors. This fear reduction seems to serve as a negative reinforcement, with the removal of the aversive stimulus (fear) strengthening the likelihood of modeling the observed behaviors.

13.21   Suppose, instead, that the videotape in Problem 13.20 had shown the aggressive responses being punished. What would be the expected effect on subjects who observed such tapes?

Vicarious observation may influence behavior in both facilitative and inhibitory manners. Thus, the punishment noted here would be likely to reduce the potential modeling of responses. Research studies have shown that observed responses that are consistently punished produce almost no imitation.

13.22   Suppose a psychologist is hired by a business firm to determine ways to sustain the high rate of production by the firm's workers. It is unlikely that the psychologist would recommend that workers be allowed to observe rewards given to selected fellow workers. Why?

Vicarious reinforcement of responses seems to be a fairly effective way of helping an individual acquire a new, previously unlearned response. However, the motivational effects of vicarious versus actual reinforcement favor the actual reinforcement. The unrewarded workers might at first be motivated to imitate the rewarded workers, but in the long run they may resent the other workers or the firm's management.

13.23 Suppose the workers receiving direct reinforcement in Problem 13.22 had the opportunity to observe the reinforcements given to other workers. Would this tend to enhance performance?

This is a tricky problem. If the workers observe reinforcements comparable to or below what they are receiving, they may feel superior and continue to perform well. If they see reinforcements they are not yet receiving, but realize the possibility of achieving these at some time in the future, they may strive to reach that end. However, if the workers observe reinforcements being given to others and these reinforcements appear to be unattainable for themselves (and especially if these are given for comparable or inferior work), the result may be a deterioration of performance. The vicarious reinforcement may serve as a standard for judging actual reinforcement, and thus produce satisfaction *or* discontent, depending upon the evaluation made.

13.24 Could vicarious reinforcement establish in a person his or her own standards for reinforcement?

The solution to this problem depends on the status of the model being observed. If the observer holds the model in high respect and sees that the model is unwilling to accept the mediocre performance of a response, the observer is likely to adopt similar standards for the behavior. The observer may attempt to match or imitate the model's responding and reward herself or himself only when such standards have been achieved. (It should be noted that low standards accepted by a high-status model may become the standards accepted by the observer.)

13.25 "He acts *just* like his father" is probably only a partially accurate statement. Why?

Unless the son's behavior has been restricted tremendously, it is exceedingly unlikely that his environment has been exactly comparable to that of his father. Moreover, even if many of the son's behaviors are modeled after the father, research has shown that the son may be unable to imitate all of his father's responses. The son's responding is more apt to be based upon the adoption of a combination of several models' attributes. Careful observation of the son's behavior would probably reveal characteristics in imitation of his mother, other relatives, significant peers, and other models.

13.26 Adolescents often find they have difficulty starting conversations with members of the opposite sex. They often remark, "What should I say?" or "How do I start?" Explain how learning by modeling may help solve their dilemma.

One of the many applications of learning by modeling is in the area of disinhibition. When someone has a need for reducing anxiety associated with a particular reasonable behavior, presentation of a successfully coping model to imitate will often reduce inhibition and make it much easier for the observer to use similar responses, thus reducing the anxiety. In the teenager's situation, copying the attitudes and actions of successfully interacting peers may reduce the inhibitions related to such conversations. (*Note*: Observation of unsuccessful models who were previously held in high status may raise anxiety levels and increase inhibition.)

13.27 Suppose a person is confronted with the behavior of two highly valued models (for example, a parent and a member of the clergy) and that their behaviors differ somewhat. What kind of situation is this? What kind of behavior might be expected from the observer?

This is a conflict situation. (See Section 9.7.) The observer may make a comparison and possibly a choice between the two somewhat different responses. Resolution of a conflict of this nature may depend upon the strength of status of each model. If one is much more important to the observer than the other, responding is likely to favor the more highly valued model's style. If the models are equivalent, the observer may adopt a combination of attitudes, reflecting selected aspects of each model's actions.

Key Terms

Dependent influence.   A change in a person's attitudes or behaviors that occurs because of the social characteristics of a model or group.

Disinhibition.   In modeling, observing a response and learning that the response is appropriate to a given situation.

Independent influence.   A change in a person's attitudes or behaviors that occurs because a perceived message itself (rather than the sender of the message) is persuasive.

Influence.   A change in a person's attitudes or behaviors that originates in another person or group.

Inhibition.   In modeling, observing a response and learning that the response is inappropriate to a given situation.

Live modeling.   One organism copying a behavior of another organism that is physically present and observed.

Model status.   The standing or position accorded the model by the observer.

Modeling.   The observation and subsequent incorporation and display of a response or response sequence; other names for modeling are *observational learning, learning by imitation*, and *identification learning*.

Power.   In modeling, potential influence.

Self-arousal.   In modeling, a motive condition that arises out of the observation and retention of the behaviors of others.

Self-reinforcement.   In modeling, the satisfaction of standards that have been established by observing others' behaviors.

Symbolic learning.   In modeling, learning a behavior without actually observing it; verbal descriptions are used to establish the modeled response.

Vicarious learning.   The experience of observing and understanding another's response and the consequences of that response.

Chapter 14

Variables Affecting Acquisition

The learning process can be divided easily into two subcategories: the *acquisition* of new materials and the *memory* of those materials as measured by later retention. This chapter is concerned primarily with variables that influence the initial learning, or acquisition, phase. Chapter 15 is a discussion of the variables affecting memory, or retention.

14.1 SELECTION OF LEARNING MATERIALS

One important factor in determining what materials will be learned is *attention*. If a subject does not attend to the materials, the chances of learning are markedly reduced. (See Section 13.3 for additional discussion of this phenomenon.) Several features of the attention process appear important in determining the extent and success of acquisition.

Sensory Gating

Sensory gating is a process in which the brain sends messages to some of the sensory systems to decrease the amount of information they treat; at the same time, the brain allows other sensory systems to remain fully functioning. This seems to be a physiological analogy to the concept of *selective attention*, in which the subject pays attention to certain aspects of the environment while ignoring (or giving less attention to) others.

Sensory gating does not imply total blockage. The sensory systems not "featured" at the moment continue to operate, and if an unusual stimulus occurs, the focus of attention may change rapidly.

EXAMPLE 1. An author, sitting at a desk, may concentrate on the words on a page, while "damping" other sensations such as the noise of a fan in the office or an automobile outside. However, if the fan suddenly begins to make strange noises, the author's concentration on the words is apt to be broken, and auditory sensitivity is likely to increase. (As an experiment, try shifting your own sensory attention right now—what sounds can you recognize that you were ignoring moments ago?)

Parallel versus Sequential Attention

Parallel sensory processing occurs when several stimuli are being acted upon simultaneously by the brain. This type of processing is usually incomplete and seems to represent only an elementary stage in the acquisition of new materials.

Sequential attention is a higher level of sensory processing, in which each unit of information is treated separately and in a sequence. The subject gives special attention to each sensation, and the careful processing of each results in the acquisition and retention of information.

Feature Extraction

In effect, the sensory system selects which incoming stimuli are to be processed. The next stage of acquisition appears to be establishing meaning for these stimuli. This is done by what is known as *feature extraction*, or the identification and "decoding" of the most relevant aspects of the stimuli.

EXAMPLE 2. Feature extraction would be important in determining that an r was an r and not a t or a Γ. Careful inspection reveals that there are distinguishing characteristics (features) that can be recognized (extracted) so that the observer will respond, "That's an r," rather than, "That's a t," or "That's a gamma."

14.2 CHARACTERISTICS OF THE LEARNER

The qualities a learner brings to a situation may affect how acquisition progresses.

Individual Differences

Just as there appear to be individual differences in physical development, the influence of motivation, the expression of emotions, and many other behaviors, there are individual differences in acquisition abilities. Indeed, many of these above-mentioned factors may serve to influence the progress of acquisition.

EXAMPLE 3. Many interactions of these factors may be observed. A person who is highly motivated to become a professional singer may be tone deaf. Another, who cares little about singing, may have "perfect pitch." Such differences will be reflected in their abilities to learn to sing. A person whose capabilities, interests, and opportunities all blend and lead to a successful career is truly fortunate.

Preparedness

Some psychologists have argued for a concept of *preparedness* as an influence on acquisition. These psychologists believe that some organisms have evolved so that they are prepared for acquisition of certain types of materials, unprepared for learning others, and possibly predisposed *not* to learn still others. Such a concept might explain why some types of learning seem to occur so easily, while other types proceed with great difficulty, at best.

EXAMPLE 4. The concept of preparedness might help explain language learning by chimpanzees. (See Chapter 16.) Research studies have indicated that chimpanzees are almost totally unable to imitate human speech. They are able, however, to acquire and use American Sign Language (ASL). It seems that gestural communication has evolved for chimpanzees, while oral communication has not.

14.3 THE LEARNING CURVE

Psychologists have attempted to illustrate the progress of acquisition with pictorial or graphical representations of performance plotted as a function of time or of trials. These representations are called *learning curves*. (One must keep in mind, however, that performance is not always an accurate indicator of learning.)

EXAMPLE 5. One might be interested in the accuracy of pitching horseshoes as a function of number of hours of practice. The performance measure used could be the number of ringers made, which would be plotted against practice time. Different subjects might show quite different patterns of performance, as illustrated in Fig. 14-1. Each of these lines would be called a "learning curve," although subject D doesn't seem to be learning at all.

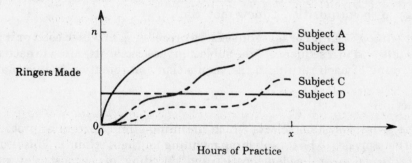

Fig. 14-1

Plateau

Occasionally, during the course of the trials, the learning curve will "flatten out," and no apparent progress will be made. Following this period, performance once again improves. This period of no improvement, preceded and followed by periods of improvement in performance, is called a *plateau* in the learning curve.

Asymptote

When a subject achieves maximum or near-maximum performance, the learning curve levels off. This final leveling of the curve is called an *asymptote*. (*Note*: The asymptote may be less than the maximum that some subjects could achieve, but is maximum or near-maximum for the subject being tested.)

Incremental versus One-Trial Analyses

A continuing controversy in the psychology of learning is the debate as to whether learning of any given unit of information takes place in small, cumulative steps (increments) or in a single acquisition experience (one-trial learning). Although research evidence seems to favor the incremental interpretation, some dispute continues because contradictory results do exist.

14.4   GENERAL FACTORS INFLUENCING ACQUISITION

Educators and psychologists have devoted much time and effort in an attempt to determine the factors that help or hinder acquisition of new materials. Some of the most important findings are reported in this section.

Overlearning

Suppose some criterion of performance (such as one perfect recitation of a poem) is used to represent learning. (Once a subject has recited the poem perfectly from memory, learning has been achieved.) Any practice that occurs *after* this criterion has been reached is called *overlearning*. Overlearning is usually reported as a percentage of the time or number of trials needed for original learning.

EXAMPLE 6.   Suppose a subject took 16 trials to learn a list of nonsense syllables (consonant-vowel-consonant sequences such as YOF, which do not make a word). If the subject then continued to practice the correct order of this list for 8 more trials, 50 percent overlearning would have occurred.

Research has shown that the law of diminishing returns seems to operate for overlearning. While 50 percent overlearning usually results in a significant improvement in a subject's acquisition and retention of material, 100 percent overlearning helps some more, but not tremendously. Overlearning beyond 100 percent (such as 24 overlearning trials in Example 6, which would equal 150 percent) seems to result in little additional improvement. (*Note*: Overlearning helps increase acquisition and retention of responses, but one must be careful to determine that the responses being practiced are the desired ones.)

Knowledge of Results—Feedback

Any information about the effect of a response is called *knowledge of results* (KR), or *feedback*. Two findings indicate the importance of KR in acquisition situations: KR leads to faster acquisition of new materials, and immediate KR is often more beneficial than delayed KR. It appears that in many circumstances, the subject treats KR as if it were reinforcement, and delay of KR is equivalent to delay of reinforcement. (See Section 12.6.)

Distribution of Practice

In general, the *distribution* of practice—so that blocks of acquisition trials are interspersed with rest periods—seems to improve acquisition performance. When acquisition trials are massed together, performance suffers.

EXAMPLE 7. A practical application of this principle occurs in study situations. Acquisition of new materials seems to proceed more easily if studying is divided into study sessions and breaks. (Of course, this assumes the study segments are not too short and the breaks are not too long.)

Whole-Part Distinction

Efforts to acquire new materials may be attempts to acquire all of the material to be learned at one time (the whole method) or only segments of the material at one time (the part method). In the part method, a subject may divide the material into several units, studying each separately and trying to bring them all together only after each has been learned individually. The subject may also incorporate an "add-on" technique, in which one unit is learned, then a second is added to it, etc. This latter method is called the progressive-part method.

Research indicates that the choice of whole, part, or progressive-part methods may best be made by analyzing the materials to be learned. Certain tasks seem to lend themselves more to one type of procedure than to another.

EXAMPLE 8. Diving provides a good example of how method selection may depend upon the task to be learned. A simple forward dive from a standing position is usually taught by using the whole method. A running approach may be practiced as a separate skill and then be connected with the dive. More sophisticated dives, such as a somersault with a full twist, might best be practiced by using the progressive-part method.

Active versus Passive Approach

Careful study of the acquisition of new materials has shown that a subject who plays an active role in acquisition generally shows better performance than does a passive subject. Educators have translated this result into a "recitation-reading" comparison, showing that active discussion of new materials is likely to promote acquisition of those materials, while a more passive, reading-only approach is less likely to do so.

One aspect of an active approach to learning involves the concept of *warm-up*. It appears that for some tasks, an initial period of adjustment and introduction is necessary before acquisition can take place. A learning curve revealing warm-up effects might be illustrated as in Fig. 14-2.

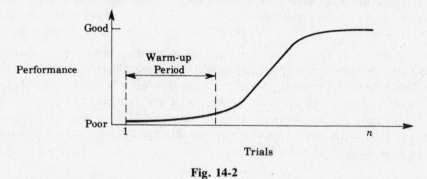

Fig. 14-2

Primacy and Recency Effects

Two fairly common influences on acquisition are the primacy and recency of the materials being learned. *Primacy* refers to those materials that are presented first in a series; *recency* refers to the items presented last. In general, the primacy and recency effects tend to encourage acquisition, whereas presenting materials in the middle of a series does not.

Context

A context can influence acquisition in two basic ways. First, the meaning of the material to be learned may be inferred from the use of that material in a particular setting. And second, associations that promote acquisition may result when certain materials are presented in a particular setting. (This latter phenomenon is sometimes referred to as *state-dependent learning*.)

EXAMPLE 9. Suppose you did not know the meaning of the "word" *abvoc*. However, in conversations with others you find that abvocs are cute, that some abvocs cry, wet, and have moving parts, and that children love abvocs. Such statements might provide sufficient information to allow you to develop a meaning for abvoc.

EXAMPLE 10. State-dependent learning is the principle applied when the cast of a play moves its rehearsals to the theater in which the production is to be presented. (This is often done when a dress-rehearsal is held.) It is hoped that the cast will be more likely to remember their lines and perform correctly because there is no difference between the rehearsal setting and the actual performance setting.

14.5 VERBAL LEARNING

Word usage, the basis for verbal learning, appears to be a species-specific behavior for humans. The extent of human communication appears almost boundless because of this unique capacity. Language skills will be treated later (Chapter 16); the focus here is on techniques for studying and factors that influence verbal acquisition.

Methods of Study

Three techniques are used commonly in verbal learning studies. In *serial learning*, the materials are presented in order and must be learned in that order. In *free recall*, the materials may be learned (and later produced) in any order the subject prefers. In *paired-associate learning*, a particular stimulus is linked with a particular response; given the stimulus, a subject must be able to make the correct response.

EXAMPLE 11. Suppose subjects are presented with the following list of nonsense syllables: YOF, NAH, GIP, TEC, XUH, ZEM. In serial learning, the subjects would be required to learn the correct letter sequences of each item and to give YOF first, NAH second, etc. Free recall would require the correct letter sequences to be learned, but any item could be given first, second, or in any other position in the sequence.

EXAMPLE 12. A paired-associate task might use numbers as stimuli and the nonsense syllables as responses: 43–YOF, 22–NAH, 68–GIP, 97–TEC, 14–XUH, 50–ZEM. Subjects are required to learn the appropriate pairings and give the correct response when presented with a stimulus.

Factors Influencing Verbal Learning

Psychologists have studied the factors that influence acquisition of verbal materials. Some of the most important influences are presented here.

Similarity.   Certain verbal materials are learned easily and retained because they are similar to previously learned materials. In verbal learning, *similarity* may be based upon physical similarity (primary stimulus generalization), similarity in meaning (secondary stimulus generalization), or similarity that arises from some personal association the subject makes.

Meaningfulness.   Research has shown that verbal materials judged meaningful are more likely to be learned and retained than are materials that are judged less meaningful. (*Meaningfulness* is defined as the number of associations evoked by the material being learned.)

In paired-associate learning, the meaningfulness of the *response* seems to be learned to be an especially important variable. The pairing of a "high-meaning" stimulus and a "low-meaning" response is more difficult to learn than the pairing of a "low-meaning" stimulus and a "high-meaning" response. In other words, acquisition and retention are easier with "low-high" (or "high-high") pairings of stimulus and response than "high-low" (or "low-low") pairings.

Other features of the materials that appear related to meaningfulness include *pronounceability* (more easily pronounced items are learned more readily than items that are difficult to pronounce); *discriminability* (how distinctive the item is); and *frequency* (how commonly used the item is). It should be noted for this last factor that frequency of word usage differs for written language when compared to spoken language. Thus, mode of presentation may be important as well.

EXAMPLE 13. In Examples 11 and 12, the nonsense syllable TEC would be more likely to be learned than the nonsense syllable XUH. TEC has a higher meaningfulness value (based on studies of associations), is more easily pronounced, and is relatively easy to discriminate. Furthermore, in English, the letter sequence TEC is found more frequently than the sequence XUH.

Imagery. Imagery refers to the quality of a stimulus that evokes "mental pictures." In general, it is easier to create mental images for concrete stimuli rather than abstract stimuli. Better learning, in the form of more rapid acquisition, can be expected for high-imagery stimuli rather than low-imagery stimuli. This seems especially true in paired-associate situations, where high-imagery stimuli benefit the learning of pairs.

EXAMPLE 14. It is easy to illustrate imagery values by simply trying to create mental pictures representing words such as *basis* and *women*. These two words are used frequently in both written and spoken English, but differ considerably in how easily they can be translated into mental pictures.

Organization. Organization is a factor that can influence both the acquisition and recall, and may be imposed either by the material itself or the learner. More organization, if it is sensible and does not contradict other factors of the materials, usually leads to improved acquisition and recall. This appears to be especially true if the learner takes an active part in developing the organization of the material.

14.6 TRANSFER OF TRAINING

Transfer of training (also called *transfer of learning*) occurs when the learning of one set of materials influences the later learning of another set. Some psychologists claim this is the most important learning principle that can be applied to educational situations.

Testing Transfer of Training

The experimental design used to test transfer of training is as follows:

	Step 1	*Step 2*
Experimental Group:	Learn Task A.	Learn Task B.
Control Group:	Put in time.	Learn Task B.

Both groups are as alike as possible before the experiment begins. (See Chapter 2 for a discussion of experimental methodology.) To avoid possible biases because of warm-up or fatigue effects, the control group is kept busy doing some unrelated task during Step 1, while the experimental group is learning Task *A*.

The test of transfer comes in Step 2. If the experimental group learns Task *B* more easily than the control group (that is, in less time, with fewer trials, or with fewer errors), *positive transfer* has occurred. *Positive transfer* means the learning of one task has facilitated the learning of the second task. If the experimental group has more difficulty than the control group in learning Task *B*, *negative transfer* has occurred. (Learning Task *A* has hindered the learning of Task *B*.) If both groups learn Task *B* equally well, *no transfer (or neutral transfer)* has occurred.

EXAMPLE 15.   Learning to play the piano would probably lead to positive transfer when one started to learn to play the organ or harpsichord. However, learning to play the piano might hinder learning to play the drums. (Negative transfer might occur because the manual skills developed in piano-playing are very different from those required for drumming.) Finally, learning to play the piano would probably have no transfer to learning how to speak Spanish.

Learning to Learn

A person may learn general principles rather than specific items of information and then use these general principles in later learning situations. In such a case, the subject has learned to learn. *Learning to learn* (also called *learning sets*) takes place when the subject has learned how to go about doing a task and has been able to transfer this knowledge to a later learning situation.

EXAMPLE 16.   A thief might show learning to learn in a series of break-ins. Having learned the general principles of how to force a lock, the thief may apply the principle to each new lock confronted, determining the specific technique that works for each.

14.7 LEARNING WITHOUT AWARENESS

One final concern in the acquisition of new materials is whether or not the subject is consciously aware that learning is occurring. Some researchers have suggested that changes in behavior as a result of experience may be demonstrated without the subject's recognition of these changes. Unfortunately, unqualified proof of this hypothesis has been difficult to provide, and controversy regarding the possibility of learning without awareness continues.

EXAMPLE 17.   In one famous study of learning subjects were asked to speak individual words. Without identifying the nature of the study, the experimenter reinforced only plural nouns. The rate of plural nouns spoken was measured to determine if a change occurred, and subjects were later questioned regarding their knowledge of the reinforcement conditions. In some instances, the rate of plural nouns spoken did increase, and the subjects claimed not to have recognized the reinforcement conditions. However, the possibility of bias in responding could not be completely controlled, and the results remain debatable.

Solved Problems

14.1   Musicians have been known to become so involved with the performance of a piece that they are totally unaware that a part of the stage setting has fallen during the concert. Such an incident is an extreme example of what principle?

This kind of occurrence is an example of selective attention, where the person is able to concentrate on a particular sensory message and block out other stimuli. (Selective attention is seldom as absolute as that of the musicians described above; an unusual stimulus—such as the piece of falling scenery—may often bring about a change in attention, at least temporarily.)

14.2   The careful processing of incoming information seems to differ from the general reception of sensations. How? What effect does careful processing have on the acquisition of materials?

The careful processing of incoming sensory information seems to occur in a sequential manner; that is, one item at a time is processed. In the general reception of sensations, processing is not as detailed or complete, and a number of stimuli are dealt with at the same time. It appears that if more than an elementary or rudimentary understanding of the materials is desired, sequential presentation will facilitate acquisition. Simultaneous presentation means that attention will have to be devoted to many stimuli, so that each single stimulus cannot be fully processed.

14.3   Suppose you were attending a concert. Your hearing might be considered the most important sense at the time, even though other sensory channels continued to work. What principle does this demonstrate?

One form of selective attention is called *sensory gating*. Certain sensory receptors (in this case, those of hearing) are fully active, while the brain sends messages to the other receptors to reduce the amount of information they handle. The emphasis of the sensory gating process may shift from one type of sensation to another. For example, if the odor of a perfume was present during the concert, it might be ignored; the odor of a burning curtain, however, might change the sensory selectiveness quite rapidly.

14.4   While listening to an orchestra concert, you may find that you concentrate not only on the music, but on the particular sounds produced by one of the instruments. You may do this because you want to learn to play that part or because you are especially interested in how that part blends with the others. What name is given to your ability to concentrate on and listen to one instrument? Can you have this ability in more than one sensory channel?

By choosing to concentrate on a particular instrument, you are showing *feature extraction*. Essentially, this is a first step in determining what a message means and how it fits into the overall sensory reception. The same sort of process may operate in other situations, such as when you are reading. If a line of this solution appeared as fe–t–re extr–ct—n in a s–ns–ry ch—n– l," you would probably understand it. The context and the fact that the letters reproduced did represent the basic features of the words would give you enough clues to decipher the message.

14.5   A wild rat is exposed to a new food in the garbage dump. It eats some, becomes quite sick several hours later, and never eats that type of food again. Some psychologists believe that the rat's behavior illustrates an evolutionary principle? What principle is this?

The rat's behavior illustrates what some psychologists have called *preparedness*. The term implies that evolutionary development has made it possible for the rat to make the association between the new food (perhaps the odor or taste, a CS) and the later illness (UCS) despite the long interstimulus interval.

Research has shown that such aversions are quite selective, so that noises or lights in the dump will not serve as effective conditioned stimuli, but odor or taste will. It has also been suggested that an organism may be prepared, unprepared, or contraprepared for the acquisition of certain types of learning.

14.6   In Chapter 4, emphasis was placed upon the concept of individual differences in physical development. Does this concept have any place in the theory of learning acquisition?

Research evidence supports the idea that there may be individual differences in learning acquisition. In part, these may be a function of the differences in physical development, particularly for the acquisition of rudimentary motor behaviors. Thus, generalizations about learning abilities may be inappropriate because of differences among subjects.

14.7   Sketch the "learning curves" that would represent the difference between the belief that learning takes place in one trial and the belief that learning is an incremental process.

See Fig. 14-3.

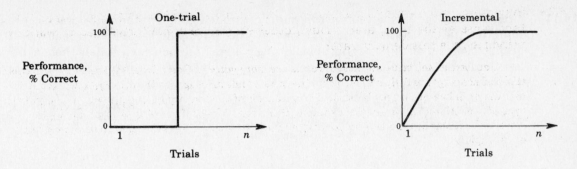

Fig. 14-3

14.8 A famous study of learning to interpret Morse code showed that the subjects first learned to understand each separate letter, held this level for a while, then somewhat suddenly seemed to be able to receive whole words. The resultant learning curve showed this pause before the new technique was grasped. What is this pause called?

The pause, which is called a *plateau*, is illustrated in Fig. 14-4.

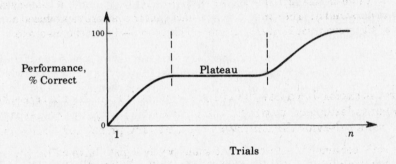

Fig. 14-4

14.9 Suppose, in the study reported in Problem 14.8, the research was terminated just before the plateau period was completed. Instead of being called a plateau, what label might have been assigned? Why?

If the study had been stopped prematurely, the plateau period might have been seen as an asymptote. Asymptotic performance occurs when the subject seems to have reached maximum (or near-maximum) values for the response being measured. (In this case, previous knowledge of the abilities of other learners might have kept the study going because higher levels of performance could be expected.)

14.10 Why is the commonly accepted phrase, "Practice makes perfect," probably inaccurate, but representative of an important aspect of acquisition?

Practice does not necessarily make perfect—practice makes *permanent*. It may be that the response being practiced is not altogether correct, yet it is reinforced enough to become a part of the subject's behavior repertoire. As more and more practice is devoted to a given task, the subject is likely to experience overlearning, making acquisition (and subsequent retention) of the response more probable.

14.11 In recent years, golfers have used computer-controlled golf simulators for practice. In the simulator, the ball is struck against a specially designed panel that gives a readout telling the direction and distance of that shot. Some golfers find such devices help them maintain their skills or learn new skills. Such a machine operates according to what learning principle?

Each shot is "judged" by the machine for direction and distance, thus providing the player with *knowledge of results* (or *KR*). This immediate *feedback* may be particularly helpful if the player wishes to try to learn a new grip, stance, or swing pattern.

14.12 People who are studying or otherwise working often take "coffee breaks." What principle of learning are they putting to use when they take such breaks?

The principle being shown is the distribution of practice. In general, distributing practice into practice sequences and rest sequences seems to facilitate learning. Thus, "coffee breaks" probably facilitate study or work performance as compared to working straight through.

14.13 Two students have to memorize a poem that each will have to recite in front of the class. One practices each stanza separately, memorizing one at a time and not trying to recite the entire poem until all the stanzas have been learned. The second learns the first stanza, then repeats the first while learning the second, and continues adding each successive stanza in this manner until the entire poem is learned. Distinguish between these two methods of learning.

The first student is using the part method of learning, while the second is using the progressive-part method. While both are part methods and differ from trying to learn the whole poem at once, the two methods differ in the amount of practice given to each stanza. The first student devotes enough time to each stanza to learn it. The second student not only learns each stanza, but because of the progressive-part, or add-on, technique, experiences overlearning for the earlier stanzas.

14.14 Guides describing how to study, counselors' suggestions, and practical experience all tend to favor certain attitudes toward trying to acquire the materials used in a school course. One attitude, in particular, stresses the *active approach* toward learning. What does this mean? What are some examples of this approach?

The active approach means that the learner actively takes part in the learning process. Research evidence indicates that being active in an attempt to learn is usually more beneficial than remaining passive. Examples of active studying include underlining and making notes while reading (rather than just reading) and trying to answer questions about the material (rather than just reviewing it).

(*Note:* The wise student incorporates into study patterns many of the other previously mentioned principles: using overlearning, distributing study sessions, seeking knowledge of results, finding warm-up techniques, and determining whether whole or part techniques will work better.)

14.15 Betsy has represented her law firm at a conference in another city. When she returns home, she is asked about the people she met. As she tries to name them and recall the sequence of meetings, she finds she is able to remember only those who greeted her at the start of the conference and those she was with at the end. (She has difficulty remembering some of the others.) What principle of acquisition does Betsy's pattern of recall illustrate?

This pattern of recall illustrates two principles of acquisition: the importance of *primacy* of some material and the *recency* of other material. Research results support the findings that materials presented first and last are more apt to be learned (and therefore remembered) than those presented during some middle period.

14.16   Suppose Betsy (Problem 14.15) is interrupted by her questioner and told not to worry about the sequence of meetings. She is asked only to try to recall as many names as she possibly can, in any order she pleases. What assumption about her learning has the questioner apparently made?

> Betsy's attempt to recall the names in order was a serial, or ordered, task. The questioner seems to have determined that Betsy can't recall the names in order, and therefore suggests she switch from serial recall to free recall. Associations other than order might help Betsy remember more of the names she learned.

14.17   A famous professional athlete is known to have an interesting technique for maintaining a good relationship with his followers. Upon first being introduced to someone, he tries to have his picture taken with the person. He keeps a copy of that picture and writes the name of the person on the back. These pictures are catalogued by geographical region, and each time the athlete returns to a given area, he looks again at the picture and learns or relearns the names that go with the faces. (The athlete expects to meet some of these people again and wants to be able to greet them by name.) The athlete's behavior represents what type of learning technique?

> Trying to connect the names with the faces is an example of paired-associate learning. This differs from Betsy's attempts to recall names (in the previous two problems) because the athlete must make a correct association between a stimulus and a response, while Betsy need only remember the response. Her acquisition involved responses only, while his involves stimuli and responses.

14.18   On one occasion, followers of the athlete were vacationing in Florida and decided to attend one day's competition. When the athlete met these people, he experienced temporary confusion and had some difficulty recalling their names. Finally he said, "You belong in my Ohio file, not the Florida one!" What principle did his statement illustrate? What kind of acquisition situation was involved?

> More than just face-name paired-associate learning had occurred. At least one additional paired-associate had developed, between Ohio and the people. This incident illustrates the effect of *context*; that is, learning takes place within a given context and recall may be based on these associations as well as the stimulus-response pairing. Similarly, the athlete might recall names when greeting the people at a competition site, but be unable to remember those names if a chance meeting happened in an airport. (This is an example of state-dependent learning.)

14.19   One day, attempting to show his students that people really think differently, a third-grade teacher asked the class to "write a word that is like the word *horse*." Responses from three of the students were *house, pony,* and *Charlie*. How might a verbal learning psychologist interpret these responses? Was the teacher's point made?

> The teacher's request is a test of similarity. The three responses made show how individuals may interpret such a request in quite different manners. The response *house* was made because the word itself looked like *horse* (primary stimulus generalization). The response *pony* showed similarity in meaning (secondary stimulus generalization). The response *Charlie* was a personal similarity; perhaps the child had a horse named Charlie. Words may be judged as similar for many reasons that depend on an individual's previous experience.

14.20   Two candidates on the same ticket (perhaps for governor and lieutenant governor) would probably not say, "We complement each other," even though it would be a reasonable remark. Why not?

> The problem here is one of discriminability. The word *complement*, meaning one candidate acts as the other's counterpart, is too close to the word *compliment*. If the listeners failed to discriminate between these two words, their reaction might be, "Sure, you say nice things about each other so that

you'll be elected." Thus the word *complement* would probably be avoided because it has a low discriminability value.

14.21   To start this problem, take a moment to create a "mental picture" of something you like. Having done this, try to analyze what it was you pictured and why you could form such a good image. Do you like honesty? What is the difference between the image you created and an attempt you might have made to picture honesty?

It is very likely you created an image of some concrete concept rather than an abstract one. Perhaps your image was of a favorite person, a hot fudge sundae, or a place you enjoy visiting. Even if you admire honesty greatly, you would probably not choose to form a mental image of such an abstract concept. Concrete terms are understood, learned, and remembered partly because of their high imagery values. Abstract concepts are somewhat more difficult to picture mentally.

14.22   In learning the names of the streets of a big city, young children are sometimes taught phrases such as, "The names of presidents run east and west, and the names of states run north and south." What principle is involved here? What learning procedure appears to maximize the benefits of this principle?

Cues of this nature provide *organization* of the material to be learned. In general, greater organization makes learning easier. Maximizing the effects of organization can be accomplished by arranging the learning experience so that the learner "discovers" the concepts or categories for organization. Compared to passive acceptance of categories, active organization of concepts results in faster learning and improved retention. Thus, the teacher may try to have the students themselves discover the "president-state" organization of the streets by having them look at a map.

14.23   Psychologists and educators spend many hours and dollars trying to design school curricula so that each step in a learning program leads logically to the next. Why?

The obvious answer is that programs are designed in this fashion to try to maximize the students' learning experiences. The principle involved is positive transfer of training. If curricula are designed carefully, it can be expected that many of the students' learning experiences will make succeeding learning easier to accomplish. In a sense, the learning process is a series of "steps," and students must take them in the proper sequence if learning is to be efficient.

14.24   Suppose that when you prepare to study you follow a set routine of study techniques regardless of the material to be learned. What learning principle would your study habits represent?

Learning general principles that are then applied in a number of different situations is called learning to learn. In this situation, your general principles of how to study are applicable to many different types of subjects.

14.25   Suppose three-year-old Terry comes home one day and tells his parents that his "preference" for dinner that evening would be hot dogs. His parents are quite surprised—not by the choice, but by the fact that he has used the word *preference*. They ask him where he learned it, and his answer is, "Oh, I don't know, I just know it." If such learning really did take place, it might be evidence for learning in what kind of condition? Why is this controversial?

Terry's learning might represent learning without awareness. However, this is a controversial concept because it is very difficult to define awareness, difficult to determine if Terry was aware while learning but has forgotten the circumstances, and difficult to present any research evidence that supports the concept of learning without awareness in an unqualified manner.

Key Terms

Acquisition.   In learning, the attaining of a response that becomes part of the behavioral repertoire of the organism.

Asymptote.   In a learning curve, the point at which the performance has approached near maximum and begins to "level off."

Discriminability.   In verbal learning, how distinctive one item is from others.

Feature extraction.   Identification of the most important aspects of a total stimulus configuration.

Free recall.   A process in which learned materials are later recalled in any order the subject chooses.

Imagery.   The ability of a stimulus to evoke "mental pictures."

Knowledge of results (KR).   Any information about the effect of a response; also called *feedback*.

Learning curve.   A graphic representation of the change in performance as a function of time or number of trials.

Learning to learn.   A general form of transfer of training; learning the general principles of how to go about performing a task.

Meaningfulness.   In verbal learning, the number of associations evoked by material that is being learned.

Memory.   The storage and later measured retention of a response that was previously acquired.

Negative transfer of training.   When the learning of one task increases the difficulty of learning a second task.

Nonsense syllable.   A consonant-vowel-consonant sequence that does not make a word.

Overlearning.   The amount of practice occurring after a performance criterion has been reached.

Paired-associate learning.   A learning technique in which particular stimuli are linked with specific responses.

Parallel attention.   Sensory processing when several stimuli are attended to simultaneously.

Plateau.   In a learning curve, a period of little or no change in performance preceded and followed by periods of performance improvement.

Positive transfer of training.   When the learning of one task facilitates learning of a second task.

Preparedness.   An evolutionary concept regarding the organism's readiness to learn; used to try to explain why some learning occurs easily while other learning may be quite difficult.

Primacy effect.   In learning, the finding that materials presented first will be acquired and remembered well.

Pronounceability.   In verbal learning, the characteristics of a word that make it either difficult or easy to pronounce.

Recency effect.   In learning, the finding that materials presented last will be acquired and remembered well.

Selective attention.   A sensory state in which an organism attends to certain aspects of the environment while ignoring others.

Sensory gating.   A brain process that reduces the input into certain sensory systems while allowing other systems to remain fully functioning.

Serial learning.   Learning in which materials are presented in a particular order or sequence that must be followed.

Sequential attention.   Sensory processing in which single units of information are treated in succession.

State-dependent learning.   The association of learned materials with the environment in which they were learned.

Transfer of training.   The effect of learning one task upon the learning of another task.

Warm-up.   Any of a number of experiences that serve to prepare an organism for performance of a response.

Chapter 15

Retention and Forgetting

In previous chapters, a distinction was made between acquisition of new materials and retention of them after they have been learned. This chapter focuses on this latter aspect, the retention of learned material.

15.1 DEFINITIONS

Several different terms are used when discussing retention. *Retention* is thought of as the storage of learning over some period of time, called the *retention interval*. *Memory* includes both retention (storage) and *retrieval*, which is getting the response out of storage. If for some reason the subject is unable to produce the response at the end of the retention interval, *forgetting*, the loss of retention or the inability to retrieve, has occurred.

Information-Processing Approach

Retention can be evaluated with what is called the *information-processing approach*. Psychologists interested in trying to represent human learning functions in terms of computer programming have analyzed the learning process as an input—processing—output sequence. By knowing the stimuli to which the subject is exposed and the response the subject later makes, they hope to program computers to simulate the learning process and thus better understand acquisition, retention, and retrieval.

EXAMPLE 1. Computers have been programmed to play games as simple as tic-tac-toe or as complex as chess. The computer can play quite well and, in fact, will never lose (but may tie) at tic-tac-toe. However, computers cannot yet duplicate an expert chess player's ability. It appears the latter game requires both retention and creativity (see Chapter 16) of an order computers cannot yet attain.

15.2 DIFFERENT TYPES OF STORAGE

While debate has not completely resolved the question of what types of storage humans may have, a fairly widely accepted theory proposes three: sensory storage, short-term storage, and long-term storage.

Sensory Storage

The basic notion of *sensory storage* is that items are held in an unprocessed sensory form before being "read out," categorized, or interpreted. This kind of storage is thought to last for only a short period of time, although the length of the retention interval may vary (from hundredths of a second to several seconds) depending on the sensory process involved. The theory proposes that materials are either processed from sensory storage into short- or long-term storage or they are lost or discarded.

EXAMPLE 2. An ingenious investigation of sensory storage makes use of a *tachistoscope*, a device that can control the time of a visual stimulus presentation in fractions of a second. Subjects are given a very short exposure (perhaps one-tenth of a second) to a stimulus item. This is followed by a very brief delay interval, and then a marker (such as an arrow) indicates what part of the stimulus item is to be recalled. The subject

177

does not actually see the image projected by the tachistoscope at this point. Instead, the subject "sees" a *visual trace* of that image. Research of this type has shown that visual trace persists for less than 2 seconds.

Short-term Storage

Short-term storage extends from 1 to 30 seconds after exposure to a stimulus item. Initial processing of the material, in which information is taken from sensory storage, takes place during this period. Short-term storage is viewed as a temporary or interim period. It is one step past the unprocessed sensory storage, but if further processing does not take place, the material will be lost or discarded.

EXAMPLE 3. Suppose a newspaper has neglected to print the starting times for a movie you particularly wish to see. You might call the theater to get that information. (Looking in the telephone book, you would find the correct number, dial it, and wait for your call to be completed.) The processing necessary to make the call requires only short-term storage; the number is quickly used and discarded. If one hour later you were asked for the theater's number, you would probably not remember it.

Long-term Storage

Long-term storage occurs when materials in sensory storage or short-term storage are processed, rehearsed, and encoded or otherwise treated for retention over a period of more than 30 seconds (and maybe for thirty years). As long as initial acquisition does take place and the person maintains the ability to make the appropriate response, items in long-term storage may have unlimited retention intervals.

EXAMPLE 4. You probably can recall an event from your childhood. Perhaps you remember a happy moment, such as receiving a special present from your parents; or maybe you remember a sad incident, like the death of a favorite pet. All such memories are retrieved from long-term storage.

Just what processes are involved in long-term storage (or, for that matter, in sensory or short-term storage) remains a matter of conjecture. Apparently, activity in the central nervous system is required, and memories are somehow stored in the brain. Just what changes take place, however, has not yet been determined.

15.3 MEASURES OF RETENTION

Psychologists have devised a number of different ways to evaluate retention. Each is an attempt to retrieve and measure information held in storage.

Recognition

In *recognition* measures of retention, the subject is presented with the correct answer, usually as one of a number of available answers. The subject then responds by selecting the answer he or she thinks is correct. The objective scoring of such tests is possible because a result, such as the number of correct answers, can be determined without the possibility of scorer bias.

EXAMPLE 5. Matching or multiple-choice questions are usually recognition tests of retention. Suppose you are asked, "Name the city represented by a baseball team named the Red Sox: (a) Boston, (b) Cincinnati, (c) Kansas, or (d) Chicago." You should select answer (a), recognizing that it is the correct answer, and eliminate the others.

Recall

In *recall* measures of retention, a minimum cue statement or question is presented and the subject is required to supply additional information. (Correct or incorrect answers are not presented before the subject responds.)

EXAMPLE 6. Essay questions and "completion" questions are often recall tests of retention. For example, suppose you are asked, "What are the names of the major-league baseball teams in Cincinnati, Kansas City, and Chicago?" No selection of names is furnished; the respondent is expected to generate the answers without any additional prompting. (The answer would be the Cincinnati Reds, the Kansas City Royals, and the White Sox *and* Cubs in Chicago.)

Relearning

In some situations, subjects may have to *relearn* materials they have learned before. The amount of time or the number of trials required for relearning may then be compared to the amount of time or number of trials required for original learning. Measurement of retention can then be computed in terms of the *savings score* shown in relearning:

$$\text{Savings score} = \frac{\text{original learning} - \text{relearning}}{\text{original learning}}$$

By multiplying this value times 100, one arrives at a percentage to report as retention.

EXAMPLE 7. On Wednesday, it takes Fred 20 minutes to memorize a vocabulary list for one perfect recitation. On Friday, when he is tested for retention, Fred relearns the list perfectly in 5 minutes. Thus, his savings score (retention) is 75 percent:

$$\text{Savings score} = \frac{20 - 5}{20} \times 100 \text{ percent}$$

$$= \frac{15}{20} \times 100 \text{ percent}$$

$$= 75 \text{ percent}$$

Comparison of Retention Measures

It is important to recognize that an estimate of retention may vary, depending on the measure of retention that has been used. Because of the differences in presentation and scoring, recognition tests should never give a zero value for retention, while recall measures may. Relearning, however, may show a negative score if the time or number of trials necessary for relearning exceeds what was required for original learning.

EXAMPLE 8. A subject might be taught the names of all the major-league baseball teams. Having accomplished this, the subject might then learn the names of all the major-league hockey teams. Later, when retention for baseball team names was tested, a recognition test using matching might yield a score of 45 percent, recall might be 20 percent, and relearning might be −7 percent. The last result might occur because of the subject's great difficulty in getting the New York City teams correct, switching back to Mets and Yankees from Rangers and Islanders.

Qualitative Measurement

One seldom-used measurement of retention (at least in psychological investigations) is called *qualitative measurement*. Qualitative measurement involves a more subjective judgment than any of the previously-mentioned techniques, and it often requires literary, artistic, or musical ability. As a result, memory sometimes is not as important as skill and the evaluator's judgment, and conclusions regarding retention may be difficult to make.

EXAMPLE 9. A famous study of ability to reproduce a drawing started with an original drawing like the one shown in Fig. 15-1.

Fig. 15-1   **Fig. 15-2**

The first subject saw this drawing and, from memory, attempted to duplicate it. The second subject saw the drawing made by the first subject and, from memory, attempted to duplicate it. The tenth subject's attempt looked something like Fig. 15-2. Each subject's recollection of the previous subject's drawing contained some slight distortion, and the cumulative result of these distortions resulted in a considerable change.

15.4   THE CURVE OF FORGETTING

Early in the history of psychology, a German named Hermann Ebbinghaus devoted much of his career to studies of acquisition and retention processes in verbal learning. One conclusion he reached has remained relatively unchallenged: the general pattern for loss of retention is that greatest loss will occur soon after acquisition, with the rate of loss diminishing after that. This is represented by what has come to be called the *curve of forgetting*, shown in Fig. 15-3.

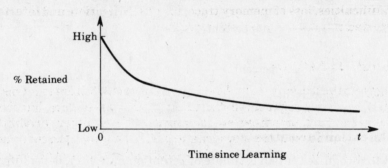

Fig. 15-3

While the general form of the curve seems to hold for many cases, the exact level and shape may vary somewhat, depending upon individual variables such as motivation, materials learned, or amount of rehearsal.

Reminiscence

The acquisition of some tasks often produces accompanying fatigue, which may become pronounced if the acquisition trials are massed together rather than distributed. As a result, tests of retention that are given following practice and a subsequent period of rest may yield better performance than will those given immediately after practice is completed. The increase in performance after practice *and* a rest period is called *reminiscence*. (*Note*: This assumes no change in motivation or reinforcement conditions that might produce a similar jump in performances.)

The von Restorff Effect

An especially distinctive stimulus that is inserted into any part of a serial list will be learned and remembered very well. The remainder of the items in the list will show a fairly typical position in the curve of retention—the first- and last-learned will be remembered better than those in the middle of the list. This phenomenon is called the *von Restorff effect* (or sometimes the *isolation effect*). It is illustrated in Fig. 15-4.

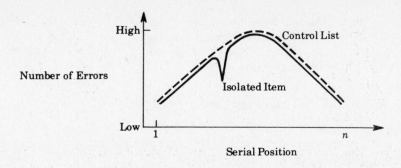

Fig. 15-4

EXAMPLE 10. Suppose a group of subjects is asked to memorize the items in the following list: "Horse, cow, mouse, dog, bicycle, cat, sheep, pig." The von Restorff effect would be shown if the subjects tended to learn and retain the one distinctive item—"bicycle"—better than they learned and retained the others in this list.

15.5 THEORIES OF FORGETTING

No single theory of forgetting has gained predominance in psychological literature. Theories based on retrieval difficulties, loss of memory trace, lack of motivation, and interference have been proposed and supported in part by research results.

Forgetting as Failure to Retrieve

One theory suggests that forgetting is the result of a person's failure to retrieve materials that are already stored. The theory suggests that acquisition has taken place, but that poor organization in storage, poor prompting, inappropriate motivation, or some other variable keeps the person from performance that would reveal the stored materials. Changes in the cue, suggestions for new ways to organize the material, or other alterations in attempting retrieval have often shown that the subject's performance can improve considerably.

EXAMPLE 11. A young child who is asked to ". . . replicate the design you saw," may appear to have no recollection of the stimulus. However, if the request is changed to, ". . . draw me a copy of the picture you just saw," the child does much better. In this case, a change of cue makes the task much more comprehensible.

Forgetting as Fading of the Memory Trace

Another theory of forgetting proposes that loss of retention occurs because of the disuse of learned materials. Failure to call upon the memory trace means that the trace will somehow "fade," and the memory will eventually be lost. To counteract this "fading," a subject must practice. Evidence for this theory comes from research studies in which the typical "curve of forgetting" (see Section 15.4) appears even though there is no indication that anything except the passage of time has contributed to the loss of retention.

EXAMPLE 12. Highway restaurants sometimes entertain their waiting customers by putting puzzles on the tables. One of these involves a triangular-shaped arrangement of golf tees, where all but one hole in the block of wood holding the tees is filled. The task is to try to "jump" one tee over another, always removing the one that has been jumped, until only one tee remains. Customers find this challenging and somewhat difficult, but often discover a pattern that allows them to succeed and repeatedly practice this successful solution.

Returning to such a restaurant and being confronted once again with such a puzzle, many customers reach for it confidently only to find that they cannot remember the solution they previously found. Statements such as, "I *knew* how to do this. . . . Now just a moment," are fairly common. Because it is doubtful that other puzzles of this nature have been encountered in the interim period, it would appear that the trace of the previous solution has faded through disuse. However, it could be very difficult to determine if some other contributing factors might have been operating in addition.

Forgetting as Distortion of the Memory Trace

Another theory suggests that forgetting occurs because of distortions of the memory trace. This theory suggests that some materials incorporated into memory are only partially accurate and that inappropriate descriptive labels are attached to them. In either case, the altered meanings of stored materials will make accurate recollection impossible. Again, some research evidence supports such a conclusion: when inaccurate labels are provided for learned materials, distorted memories may result.

Motivated Forgetting

The psychoanalytic theory of *repression* suggests that some forgetting comes to pass because a person wishes to forget something. Originally proposed by Freud, this view suggests that forgetting is one means by which an individual can "protect" his or her personality. (The label for such protections is *ego defense mechanisms*—see Chapters 19 and 21 for a more thorough discussion.)

Freud believed that readily accessible memories were found in the *preconscious*. Memories that might arouse great anxiety were pushed "deeper" into memory, into the *unconscious*, where they could not be called forth easily. Repression was likely to put memories into the unconscious, but Freud believed that such memories continued to influence behavior in the form of *unconscious motives*.

While experimental evidence to support the notion of repression has not been produced, repression has been used in case histories to account for forgetting.

EXAMPLE 13. One clinical case history can illustrate how repression occurs and how it affects behavior. Hilda, a young girl, misbehaved badly one day and ran away from her parents. In the process, she fell into a rushing stream and ruined her best clothes. Although she was hurt and in need of attention and comfort, her parents did no more than punish her. The memory of this day became very anxiety-producing for Hilda. She eventually managed to repress her conscious memory of these events, but unconscious aftereffects persisted. The key stimulus appeared to be the rushing water, and as Hilda grew older she found comparable stimuli (such as a running shower) very anxiety-producing. Fortunately, she was able to uncover the repressed memory and ultimately overcome her fears.

Forgetting as a Result of Interference

One of the best documented theories of forgetting is based on the idea that loss of retention results from interference from other materials. This has been studied with what are known as proactive inhibition and retroactive inhibition experimental designs. In each case, the question investigated is what effect one learning task will have upon the retention of some other learning.

Proactive inhibition. The experimental design for *proactive inhibition (PI)* is as follows:

	Step 1	*Step 2*	R E S T	*Step 3*
Experimental Group:	Learn *A*.	Learn *B*.		Test *B*.
Control Group:	Put in time.	Learn *B*.		Test *B*.

If, when the material of Task *B* is tested, the control group does better than the experimental group, it may be concluded (assuming no experimental flaws exist) tht PI has taken place. That is, the Task *A* materials interfered with the later retention of Task *B* materials.

Retroactive inhibition. *Retroactive inhibition (RI)* is studied using the following experimental design:

	Step 1	Step 2	R E S T	Step 3
Experimental group:	Learn 1.	Learn 2.		Test 1.
Control group:	Learn 1.	Put in time.		Test 1.

Again, if the control group performance is significantly better in Step 3, Task 2 learning has interfered with the retention of Task 1. (*Note*: Most research on both PI and RI has studied interfering or inhibiting effects in an attempt to determine reasons for loss of retention. If one learning made retention of the other appear easier, however, the word *facilitation* would be used.)

EXAMPLE 14. Learning names to go with faces may eventually lead to either PI or RI when similar-looking people are involved. Recalling a first-learned name when a second would be appropriate is an instance of PI. If the second-learned name is called forth when the first is appropriate, RI is shown. (This is a difficulty people in "public" jobs, such as teaching or selling, often encounter.)

15.6 SPECIAL ISSUES IN RETENTION

Retention is not without its unusual aspects. Two of these are called the tip-of-the-tongue phenomenon and confabulation.

Tip-of-the-Tongue Phenomenon

Retrieval of information from long-term storage is sometimes not readily accomplished. For example, you may sometimes feel ready to give the desired answer only to find you cannot (thus the name *tip-of-the-tongue phenomenon*). Quite frequently, approximations of the answer are attempted. (For example, was that animal an ascot? Asclot? Osclot? No, it was an ocelot.) Similar sounds, number of syllables, or the same initial letter may be used in attempts to determine the correct response. Such a memory search is not random. Because of similar meaning, words such as *tiger, puma,* or *jaguar* might come to mind as you try to thing of *ocelot*.

Confabulation

Confabulation is a memory error that occurs under conditions of high motivation. Asked to recall a particular event, people very anxious to do so may manufacture a report that seems appropriate. In such a case, the person may believe that the report is true even when it contains combinations of several recollections or mixtures of fact and fiction. Questioned about such errors, subjects frequently cannot identify the mistakes.

The most obvious cases of confabulation are found in brain-damaged patients, but it is probable that everyone confabulates to some extent, retrieving some "key" features and "filling in" the rest.

Solved Problems

15.1   A college teacher wanted to demonstrate the relationship of retention to forgetting. To do this, the teacher instructed her students to listen to a series of numbers and pay very close attention. When the list was completed, the teacher asked one student to name those numbers in the series that he had forgotten. The student immediately responded by saying, "Forty-three, twenty-two, fifty-eight . . ." until he realized he didn't know what numbers he'd forgotten. What point does this incident demonstrate?

The student's response showed that one cannot tell what one has forgotten, only what one has remembered. Thus, psychologists never measure forgetting directly; they measure retention and assume that what was not retained has been forgotten.

15.2   Is memory different from retention?

Retention is the storage of material over some period of time. Memory is a more inclusive term, implying that materials have passed through the acquisition phase of learning, have been stored, and are available for retrieval.

15.3   What is the information-processing approach to the study of retention?

Basically, the information-processing approach is an attempt to draw analogies between human mental processes and the processes of computers. The learning of material is seen as an input—processing—output sequence, with acquisition occurring at the input stage, storage occurring during the processing stage, and retrieval (the measurement of retention) as output. Psychologists who attempt to imitate human functions by using computers hope that by analyzing the computer's input, output, and processing phases they will develop a greater understanding of what goes on during human learning.

15.4   Suppose you are sitting in a totally darkened room. Someone else is in the room and waves a lighted cigarette in a figure-eight pattern. What do you see, and why?

What you are likely to "see" is a tracery of light rather than a single moving point of light. Although the entire figure-eight probably is not recorded at one time (unless the other person is moving the cigarette at a very rapid pace), at least part of the figure seems to be present. (You may "see" this even though you realize there is only one moving point of light.) The explanation of this is that you are holding a sensory storage of the moving stimulus, and thus see a visual trace of the path along which it is moving.

15.5   Your daughter is getting married. At the reception, you stand in line and meet for the first time many of her friends and many of her husband's relatives and friends. A short while later in the reception, an acquaintance of yours comes over, points to one of these people, and asks who she is. You find you are unable to recall the woman's name, although you heard that name only a few minutes ago. Why?

The explanation is that you have held the name in short-term storage but have not processed it for longer retention. Short-term storage usually is defined as a 1- to 30-second period during which the stimulus item may be used. After that period, however, the item is rapidly discarded or blocked. (The information is processed from sensory storage into short-term storage, but does not go any further than that.)

15.6   A study by three psychologists showed that many people were able to recall names and events from their high-school days as much as 30 or 40 years later. Their accuracy, as checked against documentation from yearbooks, was quite high. What storage process is involved here? What limitations exist?

The ability to recall items over such a long period of time indicates long-term storage of the materials. This is the third stage of processing, following sensory storage and short-term storage, and may be almost limitless, depending upon the type of information retained. Thus, names or events may be recalled with great accuracy, while learned motor movements might not.

15.7   Look at Question 1 in Examination I (p. 98). What type of question is it?

It is a recognition question, in which a correct answer is presented along with several incorrect answers. The subject's task is to identify that correct answer. This kind of question usually can be objectively scored—the number of correct answers or a percentage of correct answers can be reported.

15.8   Look at Problem 15.2 (p. 184). What type of question is it?

This question measures recall. The question provides a minimal cue, and the subject must provide all the additional information. No correct (or incorrect) answers are available to the subject before responding begins.

15.9   John and Frank are participating in the same verbal learning experiment. Their task is to learn a serial list of nonsense syllables until they can make one perfect recitation from memory. John requires 16 trials to accomplish this, while Frank takes 10 trials. One week later, both subjects are brought back to the laboratory to relearn the same list. John needs 8 trials for relearning, and Frank requires 6 trials. What does the experimenter conclude about the retention shown by the two subjects?

The experimenter's conclusion is that John seemed to retain more of what he learned originally. The conclusion is based upon the relearning measure of retention. John's savings score was 50 percent, $100 \times (16 - 8)/16$, while Frank's saving score was 40 percent, $100 \times (10 - 6)/10$. It should be noted that Frank's acquisition of the materials progressed more rapidly than John's did. However, the concern here is with retention, not acquisition.

15.10   Suppose a professor gives a class the chance to choose the method of retention measurement that will be used on their final examination. If the students want to start the test with the biggest possible advantage, which measurement of retention will they choose?

The class should choose recognition tests. As long as they are not penalized for guessing, they can anticipate receiving some credit for correct answers chosen by chance. For example, with four-choice multiple-choice questions, students might get 25 percent correct just by guessing. A recall test may produce a zero percent retention score, while a relearning measure (which probably would not be used in a classroom setting) can actually produce "minus savings," such as when relearning takes longer than original learning. (*Note*: Some instructors recognize the differences described above, and they adjust the scale so that no actual advantage exists for any one measure.)

15.11   Suppose a person is told a story that begins with the sentence, "One night, three fellows went to a picnic and played quoits. . . ." Later when the person is asked to retell the story, he begins, "One day, three guys went on a picnic and played games. . . ." What accounts for the change?

Attempts to duplicate stories, music, or drawing often result in changes in performance. Perhaps the most frequent of these is to make the imitation of the original more "normal," or more like what is usual in the environment of the respondent. Thus, in this answer, *night* changes to *day*, *fellows* become *guys*, and *quoits* become *games*. Occasionally, some unusual stimulus will be embellished rather than made more common. In this case, for example, *quoits* might "stick" in the respondent's pattern, but become "a daring contest of quoits!"

15.12 A very famous study in psychology has come to be known as the "sleep-waking" study. Subjects were trained for a task, then measured for retention at various intervals afterward. In half the cases, the subjects went about normal daily activity following training (waking condition), while the other half rested or slept following training (sleeping condition). Activity, as opposed to sleeping, appeared to interfere more with retention. Sketch the "curves of forgetting," with appropriate labels, for these two groups.

See Fig. 15-5. Both groups showed the "typical" curve of forgetting, with the most rapid loss of retention (or "decay") occurring soon after learning. In addition, the loss for the waking group was greater than the loss for the sleeping group.

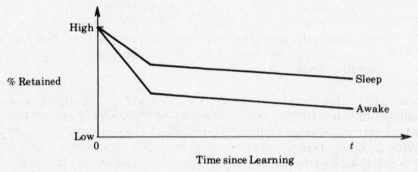

Fig. 15-5

15.13 A student has been preparing for a typing test. He has practiced feverishly for many hours in order to increase both his accuracy and speed. The night before the test, the student practices for several hours, then does one final practice test and measures both accuracy and speed. The next morning, at the actual test, the student performs considerably better than in the previous night's test. What phenomenon describes this result? What is one possible explanation of this, and could there be other explanations?

The phenomenon in which retention performance is better than any previous practice performance is called the *reminiscence effect*. The explanation usually given is that during the rest period, fatigue effects are dissipated and, as a result, performance levels increase. This explanation is given frequently for reminiscence of motor tasks, especially when the rest period follows massed practice sessions. An alternate explanation is possible: the student's better performance on the test may also be a result of changes in his motivation.

15.14 A grandfather and granddaughter are talking about elementary school. The grandfather is asked, "Well, what was it like when you were in grade school?" He responds, "You know, I don't remember too much of that anymore except that it was fun and that my third-grade teacher was named Mrs. Wakenhut. Was she ever nice!" When asked if he can remember any of his other teachers, the grandfather finds he cannot. His recall of Mrs. Wakenhut's name seems to illustrate what principle of retention?

It can be presumed that the grandfather learned the names of all his elementary-school teachers quite well. His recall of Mrs. Wakenhut, but none of the others, may illustrate the von Restorff effect, in which one distinct response is remembered, in the right place and in the midst of many others that are not recalled.

15.15 One popular notion is that we never forget anything that has happened to us; that is, everything is "stored away" somewhere in memory. What theory of retention seems to support this idea? Is there evidence to support the theory?

The theory of memory that supports this notion is based upon the concept of failure to retrieve. The theory suggests that the memories are indeed present, but lack of organization, proper cues, or some other variable keeps us from producing the memory. Research studies have shown that when stimulus cues are altered to generate new attempts at retrieval, many additional responses can be generated. Also, electrical and chemical stimulation of certain areas of the brain sometimes generate memories that otherwise seem to have been lost.

15.16 Arriving early for his piano lesson, Charlie is surprised to find his teacher practicing scales and other basic exercises. When he asks why the teacher is practicing such "simple stuff," the answer he gets is, "Why, if I didn't, I might forget how to play them!" The teacher's answer shows a belief in which theory of forgetting?

The teacher seems to think that memory depends upon use, while forgetting will occur with disuse. This theory proposes that memory is held as a trace, which may fade if it is not renewed periodically. (*Note*: such a theory would help explain the "curve of forgetting" shown in Problem 15.12.)

15.17 Look at the three drawings in Fig. 15-6. Subjects in one group were told that drawing *a* resembled a tree. Subjects in a second group were told that drawing *a* resembled a light bulb. Later, in an attempt to reproduce drawing *a* from memory, the first group of subjects tended to make drawings like *b*, while the second group's drawings tended to look like *c*. What theory of forgetting explains these results?

(*a*)　　　　　　(*b*)　　　　　　(*c*)

Fig. 15-6

The theory is that forgetting may occur because changes or distortions may develop with the passage of time. In this experiment, the potential distortions are provided by the experimenter. The *meaning* first attributed to a stimulus is likely to determine (at least in part) how it will be recalled later.

15.18 When she was fired from her sales position, Susan reacted by saying, "I just can't understand it. Why, I remember how well I did with that customer from Portland, and then there was the other one from Yorktown. My goodness, I shouldn't have been fired." Suppose you knew that Susan had great difficulty with a customer from Chesterfield and had lost an important customer from Ashfield. What theory of memory and forgetting might then be used to explain her response?

Susan's responses seem selective: she remembers the favorable circumstances and forgets the unpleasant ones. Such forgetting is called *motivated forgetting* and is attributed to repression, a psychoanalytic concept that proposes that some memories are deliberately forgotten in order to help protect one's self-image. This concept was stressed by Freud and many of his followers as a possible explanation of what they called *unconscious motives*.

15.19 A series of experimental investigations in verbal learning has shown that if subjects learn various responses from one conceptual category (such as the names of vegetables) and are asked to recall these after a short-term storage period, performance will decline with succeeding trials. Additionally, if after several such trials the response material changes in conceptual category, recall percentage improves. The improvement is related to how much difference appears to exist between the original materials and the new items. Figure 15-7 is a graphical representation of these results. In the first three trials, subjects were asked to memorize lists of vegetables. In the fourth trial, they were asked to memorize either another list of vegetables or names of fruits or sports.

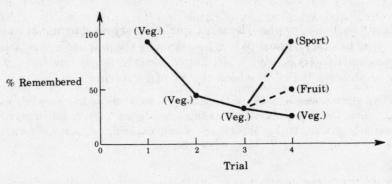

Fig. 15-7

What theory seems to explain the decline in performance for the second and third trials? How does this same principle help account for the results of the fourth trial?

The decline in performance can be attributed to proactive inhibition (PI), in which the learning of earlier material interferes with the retention of later learned material. The apparent release from PI on the fourth trial is greater for the sports words than for the fruit words because there is less conceptual overlap between vegetables and sports than there is between vegetables and fruits.

15.20 Lucky enough to receive an overseas travel grant, Professor Pritchard first spent three months studying in France. Then he moved to Barcelona, Spain for three more months. As he prepared to leave Europe, Pritchard returned briefly to Paris, where he found that he often used Spanish phrases instead of French. How does the interference theory of forgetting help account for his trouble?

Pritchard's difficulties illustrate retroactive inhibition (RI), in which new learning (Spanish) interferes with retention of previously learned material (French). Both RI and PI studies support the concept that forgetting may occur because of the inhibiting or interfering effects of materials other than those being tested.

15.21 Return to Problem 15.12 and look at the "curves of forgetting" for the sleeping and waking groups. The "decay" theory helps to explain the shape of the curve. But how does interference theory seem to account for the difference in the performance level of the two groups?

Retroactive inhibition appears to be important in this study. The sleep group has little or no opportunity to be exposed to materials that may interfere with later retention; this group learns and then goes to sleep. The waking group, on the other hand, may experience many interfering or inhibiting situations after learning. (It is assumed that both groups had an equal opportunity for PI effects before the study started, so RI seems to account for the differences found.)

15.22   An experimenter who uses the relearning method to test retention might find that subjects show a negative savings score. Using the principle of retroactive inhibition, account for such "negative savings."

The explanation of negative savings could be that some interfering learning took place during the period between the measurement of original learning and the relearning test. If sufficient interference developed, the relearning of the original task could be more difficult than the original learning itself was.

15.23   A subject is given some cues and asked to recall the name of a particular famous actress. The subject's first response is "Fairbanks." The experimenter tells the subject that this is incorrect, and actually is the name of a famous actor. The subject then pauses for a moment and says "Fairborn, Fairburn, Burnbank, and Fairheart." Finally the subject responds correctly with "Bernhardt." The sequence of these responses illustrates what pattern of retention?

The subject's responses seem to illustrate the "tip-of-the-tongue" phenomenon (TOT). Searching through stored memories, the subject selects names which approximate the category (acting), the correct number of syllables (two), and similar sounds (such as *burn* and *heart*), before determining the correct answer. It is unlikely the subject would have chosen a name such as *Jones* because it carries none of the appropriate characteristics.

15.24   A hypnotized person who was asked to describe his first bike-riding experience produced a rather lengthy and detailed description. When compared to actual evidence, the description proved to be inaccurate in a number of respects. What has happened? What is this called?

This phenomenon is called *confabulation*. The person apparently is highly motivated to produce a "good" description and, if he is unable to remember actual details, he generates some that seem to be appropriate. In some cases, later analysis of confabulation by the subject does *not* reveal which parts are true and which are made up. (The person apparently is unable to distinguish fact from fiction, and believes the entire story.)

Key Terms

Confabulation.   A memory error that occurs under conditions of high motivation; the subject may be unable to distinguish between accurate and inaccurate recollections.

Curve of forgetting.   The graph plotting the percentage of learned materials retained as a function of time since learning; generally shows that most loss of retention occurs soon after acquisition.

Forgetting.   The loss of retention or the inability to retrieve a stored memory.

Long-term storage.   Retention of a stimulus for more than 30 seconds; materials from sensory or short-term storage are processed or encoded for this type of storage.

Memory.   The storage and later measured retention of a response that was previously acquired.

Proactive inhibition (PI).   The effect of some *previous* learning upon the retention of some later learning.

Recall.   A measure of retention in which a subject is given only a minimal cue and must produce the requested materials.

Recognition.   A measure of retention in which the correct answer is presented to the subject, who must select it from among several alternatives.

Relearning.   A measure of retention in which the time or trials necessary for the second learning of a task are compared to the time or trials necessary for original learning; see also *savings score*.

Reminiscence.   An improvement in performance following a rest period given after practice of a task.

Repression.   Motivated forgetting; one of the defense mechanisms proposed by Freud.

Retention.   The storage of learning over some period of time.

Retention interval.   The period of time between acquisition of a response and retrieval of that response from storage.

Retrieval.   The process of bringing materials from storage.

Retroactive inhibition (RI).   The effect of some *later* learning upon the retention of some previous learning.

Savings score.   A percentage that expresses the difference between the time or number of trials required for original learning as opposed to the time or number of trials required for relearning.

Sensory storage.   The very brief retention of a signal in its unprocessed sensory form.

Short-term storage.   Retention of a stimulus for a 1- to 30-second period; during this period, some initial processing takes place.

Tachistoscope.   An instrument designed to allow very brief presentations of visual stimuli.

Tip-of-the-tongue phenomenon (TOT).   When retrieval (usually verbal) from long-term storage seems almost possible, but cannot quite be accomplished.

Unconscious motives.   Information that is held in memory and continues to influence responding but is not recognized at a conscious level by the person.

von Restorff effect.   When an exceedingly distinctive stimulus within a list is remembered very well as compared to its surrounding items; also called the *isolation effect*.

Chapter 16

Thinking, Problem-Solving, and Language Development

Once psychologists gained some knowledge of the processes of acquisition and retention in learning (see Chapters 11–15), a number of them turned to consideration of the uses of learning. Many areas have been investigated, with several emerging as major aspects of study. This chapter concentrates on three of these: thinking, problem-solving, and the development of language.

16.1 THINKING

Thinking is symbolic mediation, or the use of symbols to span the time interval between presentation of some external stimuli and the responses made to them. Thinking is an internal, personal process, often attributed to activity of the mind. Thinking cannot be observed directly, but must be presumed from observable behaviors.

EXAMPLE 1. One college instructor is known to demonstrate the individuality and "hiddenness" of thinking to classes by asking the entire class to ". . . think of the dirtiest word you can!" The instructor then points out that unless one of the students calls out the word, there is no way for any member of the class to know what choice another made. However, one of the students could speak, write, or gesture in such a way as to indicate his or her thought. The other students could then interpret this as representative of the student's thinking.

Directed versus Autistic Thinking

Much of our thinking occurs in attempts to solve problems. Such thinking is called *directed thinking*, implying that the thinking occurs for a purpose. Thinking that uses symbols in a seemingly aimless fashion, as in some forms of daydreaming, is called *autistic thinking*.

Symbols

A *symbol* is any stimulus that has become a commonly accepted representation of some object, event, action, or idea. A symbol may take any form or any meaning, as long as there is general agreement that the symbol stands for some other particular thing.

Concepts

Concepts are symbols that summarize or generalize attributes typical of several objects, events, actions, or ideas that are dissimilar in other important aspects.

EXAMPLE 2. Concepts may have different levels of generality, while symbols are usually quite specific. For example, the word *horse* would be considered a very general concept, referring to an entire class of animals. The word *thoroughbred* represents a more limited concept within the general class of horses. The name *Secretariat*, in this context, is a symbol for one particular horse.

Types of Concepts

Concepts are classified as *simple* when they represent a single stimulus property. (For example, all things are either blue or not blue.) Concepts are *complex* when more than one stimulus property is considered simultaneously.

Complex concepts take several forms. *Conjunctive* concepts are defined by the simultaneous presence of two or more properties. *Disjunctive* concepts may also be based upon two or more properties, but any one property or a combination of properties is adequate to satisfy the concept. *Relational* concepts establish a relation between two properties.

EXAMPLE 3. The various types of complex concepts can be illustrated by considering beverages. The word *highball* represents a conjunctive concept because to satisfy (or fit into) the concept a drink must have at least two properties: the presence of alcohol *and* some other fluid (such as water or soda). The word *beverage* itself is a disjunctive concept because any one of a number of drinks (such as water or beer or milk) or a combination of drinks (such as coffee with milk) satisfies the concept. Any comparison—such as the statement, "Milkshakes are thicker than sodas,"— expresses a relational concept.

Concept Hierarchies

Almost all concept classifications contain a number of items. When asked to report the items in a conceptual class, most people will start with their strongest associations and then continue to add items until they can think of no others. The resultant list represents a *concept hierarchy*, in which there is some kind of ranking of the members of the concept category.

EXAMPLE 4. If asked to list modes of transportation, most Americans would start with items such as *automobile, plane, bus, train*, or the like. Lower in the list (and thus in the hierarchy) might be words such as *rickshaw, dogsled*, or *sampan*. (A person from another culture would probably have a very different hierarchy.)

Developing Concepts

Concepts do not simply spring, completely developed, into a person's consciousness. Generally, it is necessary for a learning process to occur. Often, this learning process involves hypothesizing about the concept category, testing that hypothesis, revising the understanding of that concept on the basis of the test results, reformulating the concept, and then repeating the process.

People appear to use various kinds of strategies in developing concepts. In some cases, they may consider all stimulus attributes simultaneously (a *wholistic* approach). In other circumstances, they may consider only one characteristic at a time (a *partistic* approach).

Representations of Thinking

As mentioned earlier, thinking is a personal and private event unless a person represents the thought processes in some observable way. Research on thinking has shown that there are two very common thinking processes, *inner speech* and *imagery*. Inner speech occurs when a person makes verbal representations of thought processes. Imagery occurs when a person recalls or generates sensory stimuli. Investigations of inner speech or imagery usually depend on verbal reports of the processes made by subjects.

16.2 PROBLEM-SOLVING

A major consideration in the study of learning has been *problem-solving*. Problem-solving occurs when an individual or group establishes some goal and seeks ways to reach that goal. As previously indicated, the thought processes involved in trying to solve a problem are called *directed thinking*, while aimless daydreaming or fantasizing is called *autistic thinking*. Directed thinking is consciously motivated and is therefore affected by the motive conditions that influence other kinds of behaviors. (See Chapter 9.)

The Problem-Solving Sequence

Careful research of the process of problem-solving has disclosed a fairly common sequence of events leading to the goal. Generally, the steps seem to be as follows:

Recognize there is a problem. Not being able to understand that there is a problem would stop the process at this point.

Define the problem accurately. This seems to involve recognizing concepts that are pertinent to the problem. If the key concepts are not available, the problem may not be solved.

Produce hypotheses about the problem's solution. Based upon the concepts selected in the previous step, guesses about how to resolve the problem are developed.

Test the hypotheses. Each hypothesis should be either confirmed or disconfirmed. While several may solve the problem, it is often possible to select the single best hypothesis.

EXAMPLE 5.   The sequence of events leading to a goal could be easily demonstrated if you wished to drive to a particular city. Suppose you wanted to go to University Park, Pennsylvania from Pittsburgh. If you did not realize that you didn't know the route, you might drive aimlessly and only arrive by chance. However, once you recognized the problem, you might then seek out the relevant concepts (for example, route numbers or distances), consider alternate possibilities, do some calculating to determine which might be the best route, and finally select one.

While this example is fairly straightforward, it should be recognized that the same sequence might apply to a problem as complex and subtle as a personality difficulty or an emotional disturbance. An individual must first recognize there is a problem, then determine the key concepts necessary for solving the problem, and finally complete the problem-solving process as described.

Reasoning

Reasoning is a type of thinking in which a person tries to solve a problem by incorporating two or more aspects of past experience. Not all reasoning takes the same form. *Programmatic reasoning* is said to exist when already-existing systems of thought are used. *Generative thinking* involves the creation of new systems of thought.

Reasoning is a difficult process to study. Much of the process is internal and may not be recognized by either the researcher or the subject.

Variables Affecting Problem-Solving

Problem-solving is a kind of performance, and it is subject to some of the same influences that affect other types of behavior. For example, variables such as motivation and past experience will influence problem-solving performance.

Motivation.   The inverted-U curve of performance described in Section 9.3 is seen also for problem-solving. Very low levels of motivation yield poor problem-solving performance. As motivation levels increase, so too does performance, but only up to some point. (Very high levels of motivation will usually yield poor performance.) In addition, a particular motivation may influence a subject's attention, directing the subject to certain problems or aspects of the environment and away from others.

Past experience.   Previous experience may predispose a subject to respond in a certain manner when trying to solve a problem. In discussing this phenomenon, psychologists usually distinguish between a *habit,* which implies a long-term tendency to respond in a certain manner, and *set*, which is the temporary tendency to respond in a certain fashion.

EXAMPLE 6.   The recent fad of installing and using citizen's band radios in personal automobiles can be used to illustrate the difference between habit and set. Most of the people who use these radios employ a special language when broadcasting, but they do not talk in this same manner when not broadcasting. Rather, they return to a more "normal" or typical form of talking. The use of the special CB dialogue represents a *set*, a temporary tendency to respond in a certain way in a particular situation. Out of that situation, the people returned to their *habitual* form of conversation.

One form of set that has been studied extensively is called *functional fixedness*. This occurs when a subject is unable to see any other use for an object except its normal or usual one, although some novel response might be both useful and appropriate for solving the problem at hand.

EXAMPLE 7.   In a famous research investigation of functional fixedness, two strings were suspended from the ceiling of a room. One string was near a corner of the room and the other was near the center, and a pair of pliers was available. The subject's task was simply to tie the two strings together. However, the strings were not long enough to allow the subject to hold one and be able to reach the other, even when using the pliers to grasp the end of one string.

Those subjects who viewed the pliers only as grasping objects could not solve the problem. (These subjects were said to show functional fixedness.) On the other hand, some subjects were able to use the pliers in a different manner: they tied the pliers to the end of the central string and started it swinging in a pendulum motion. It was then easy for them to go to the corner, grasp the other string, and catch the swinging string when it came near enough. In other words, by using the pliers as a weight (and not a grasping tool) they were able to solve the problem.

Insight

Insight is the term used to describe the phenomenon in which a problem is posed, followed by a period of no apparent progress in solving the problem, and then a sudden solution. The key characteristic of insight is the suddenness of the solution: a swift determination of a hypothesis that can be confirmed. Insight seems to be very personal and is difficult to describe as a psychological process.

Creativity

One special consideration in problem-solving is *creativity*, which is shown when a subject generates an original, productive, and unusual solution to a problem.

Psychologists make a distinction between *convergent thinking*, in which the subject is seeking a known solution to a problem, and *divergent thinking*, in which a subject is attempting to generate a novel or different solution to a problem. (Divergent thinking is a type of creative thinking.)

Research into the relationship of creativity and intelligence has shown that there is little or no correlation between the two. Apparently, the mode of thinking is more important to creativity than is the amount of intelligence.

EXAMPLE 8.   In attempting to measure creativity, psychologists have generated many different types of tests. One of these involves presenting the subject with a minimal visual cue and asking the subject to complete the drawing. For example, the subject might be shown drawing *a* in Fig. 16-1. and be asked to complete it. A response such as drawing *b* would be judged much less creative than a response such as drawing *c*.

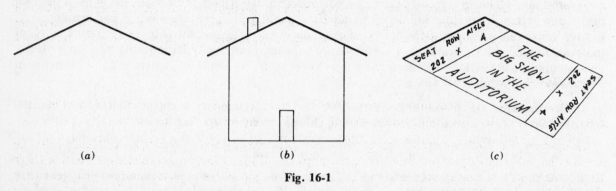

Fig. 16-1

Simulation

In an attempt to identify the processes involved in problem-solving, some psychologists have turned to the use of the computer. Given a knowledge of the input (stimuli) to which the subject is responding and the output (responses) the subject makes, these psychologists attempt to program the computer to *simulate* this functioning. They then study the program in an attempt to analyze what processes must be involved. (Studies of this nature are generally more successful when the problem is one requiring convergent thinking rather than divergent thinking.)

16.3 LANGUAGE DEVELOPMENT

Language development is one of the major areas in the study of learning. Psychologists who study this area are called *psycholinguists*, and they are interested in the relationships between an organism and its language. Their work covers the acquisition, structure, and usage of language.

Signs versus Symbols

Signs and symbols are both signals, or stimuli that can be used for communication. They differ in that a *sign* has meaning because of its very nature, while a *symbol* has its meaning because a number of people (or other organisms) have chosen to accept that meaning. Any agreed-upon designation (a word, drawing, gesture, etc.) may serve as a symbol.

EXAMPLE 9. If you made a noise like the sound of a cow, you would be using a sign, a stimulus that has meaning because it corresponds (at least somewhat) to the sound naturally made by a cow. Writing or saying the word *moo*, however, would be using a symbol. The word *moo* does not duplicate the naturally-occurring events, but has only come to have a meaning that is generally accepted.

Written versus Spoken Language

The development of language in humans generally progresses in at least two different forms, written and spoken language. Written language depends upon the visual presentation of words, while spoken language depends on the production and reception of sounds.

In general, word usage in written language differs somewhat from word usage in spoken language. Words are used with different frequencies, are arranged differently, are repeated more often in spoken language, and generally take a more casual form in spoken language and a more formal form when written.

Expressive versus Receptive Language

Expressive language is defined as words that convey a message. *Receptive language* defines what is understood from the words used. Expressive and receptive language may not be the same thing; that is, the message-producer may intend to convey one message while the message-receiver may interpret the same words in a quite different manner.

EXAMPLE 10. Multiple meanings for words may make it particularly difficult for communication to occur. For example, the word *bread* had at one time at least two meanings: it meant both a food and money. When a message-producer said, "Wow, I sure would like more bread," the receiver could understand the statement in at least two ways.

Word Development and Usage

Psycholinguists have studied the construction and use of words in great detail. These investigations have resulted in the development of the following terms and findings:

Phonemes. *Phonemes* are the basic sound components of a spoken language. Young children seem to have the ability to produce phonemic patterns of many languages, but soon learn to limit their patterns to those appropriate to the language being learned. Most analyses suggest that English has about 45 phonemes.

Syllables. While phonemes are the basic units of speech, they are not what are "heard" or concentrated upon by the producer or receiver. Instead, the producer or receiver concentrates on *syllables*, which are composed of one or more phonemes.

Morphemes.   *Morphemes* are defined as the smallest meaningful unit of a language. Not all syllables are morphemes, because not all syllables have meaning when they stand alone. A morpheme may contain one or more syllables.

EXAMPLE 11.   The words *wing* and *taking* can be used to illustrate the difference between a syllable and a morpheme. *Wing* is a single-syllable word that is also a morpheme. The word *taking* has two syllables, but the *ing* syllable cannot be considered a morpheme because it does not have meaning by itself.

Words.   Phonemes, syllables, and morphemes may be considered the structural components for words. *Words* are the symbols used in a language.

Phrases, clauses, and sentences.   Word combinations build phrases, which in turn may be developed into clauses or sentences. Sentences may have several clauses, but when they do, the receiver's typical pattern is to treat each separately.

Surface Structure and Deep Structure

Psycholinguists have looked at how the arrangement of words may vary and what effect this has upon the meaning being conveyed. The arrangement of the words has come to be called the *surface structure* of the language, while the meaning being transmitted is called the *deep structure*.

EXAMPLE 12.   Two sentences such as, "Glenn took the test," and "The test was taken by Glenn," have the same meaning or deep structure, although their surface structure is different. One could alter the meaning of the second sentence by substituting the word *purse* for *test*, so that it would read, "The purse was taken by Glenn." This would leave the surface structure almost the same, but alter the deep structure considerably.

Development of Language Rules

It is beyond the scope of this book to consider the many different rules that exist for any one language. However, it is appropriate to note several findings that seem to hold for the development of most languages. In general, children in all cultures learn the rules for language at about the same age and in approximately the same sequence. In addition, children of all cultures tend to make word usage and grammar errors that require them to learn both rules and exceptions to rules.

Behavioristic versus Cognitive Interpretations

A controversy in the study of language development has produced two different explanations for *why* a child learns a language. The *behavioristic* approach suggests that language develops because the child learns it in the same manner as any other learning; that is, because of classical conditioning, instrumental conditioning, and modeling. Emphasis is placed upon reinforcement of language patterns.

The *cognitive* approach contends that the child is born with capabilities for developing language and that simple exposure to some language is sufficient for language to be learned.

There are supporting research studies available for both viewpoints, although some evidence, particularly in the spontaneous production of new word combinations by children, tends to favor the cognitive approach.

Language for Animals

Again, this is a topic that can only be touched on in this book. Extensive research on language development in lower organisms (especially the chimpanzee) has shown that while lower organisms have little or no success learning written or spoken language as humans know it, they can be taught to communicate using American Sign Language or other symbolic forms. Rather extensive vocabularies have been developed, along with some grammatical understanding. Communication using the specially trained symbols has occurred between the lower organisms and humans and has been attempted between one member of the species and another (e.g., one champanzee and another).

Solved Problems

16.1   Perhaps one of the most difficult problems psychologists have is to define the concept of thinking. What makes a definition of thinking so hard to achieve?

   The greatest problem is that thinking is essentially an internal or "hidden" process. It cannot be observed directly, but must be inferred from other, measurable behaviors. Although often attributed to activity of the mind (mental processes), no direct record of the mind can be achieved.

   We cannot observe mental processes directly, but we can make inferences about thinking on the basis of subsequent performance. Thinking is thought of as a mediational process, bridging the gap between stimulus and response by use of symbols, images, or concepts. (*Note*: The input—processing—output analysis mentioned in Chapter 15 would seem to apply here. Thinking would fall in the processing stage, and computer programming could be used in an attempt to simulate the events that occur during thinking.)

16.2   Not all thinking is aimed at being productive. What distinction do psychologists make between productive and nonproductive attempts?

   Much thinking is referred to as *directive thinking*, thinking conducted with the intent of reasoning, problem-solving, creating, or pursuing some other goal. Nondirected or nonproductive thinking has been called *autistic thinking*. Generally, this type of thinking is conducted without intent, as in an aimless daydream or fantasy.

16.3   Consider the words *San Francisco* and *city*. Which term is a symbol, and which is a concept?

   In this problem, *San Francisco* is a symbol because it is a one-of-a-kind label for a particular city in California. The word *city* is a concept because it can be used to summarize or describe many places, including San Francisco. (In general, concepts are symbols representing common characteristics shared by events or objects that are otherwise different.)

16.4   Individuals who are deaf often use means of communication other than speech. Explain how their patterns of communicating are comparable to the use of symbols in speech.

   A symbol is simply some agreed-upon designation that has come to stand for an object, event, action, or idea. The gestures of American Sign Language (ASL) are symbols just as much as written or spoken words are. (Another similar example would be the Braille type used by many blind people: the raised dots are symbols of letters or numbers.) The key characteristic of a symbol is that it has an accepted meaning, and not that it has a particular form.

16.5   A visitor from Germany was taken to see her first baseball game. Her American host believed he had ample knowledge to explain the game. During the course of the evening, the host realized how difficult it was to explain what seemed to be very simple concepts. For example, the host described a strikeout by saying, "Well, three strikes and the batter is out." When asked to describe a strike, the host had a good deal more trouble. Why?

   The concept *strikeout* is a simple concept, while the concept *strike* is instead a disjunctive concept (a kind of complex concept).

Strikeout is a simple concept because any combination of three strikes results in a strike-out. However, the definition of *strike* is much more complicated. A strike may be a missed swing, an umpire's decision about a pitch not swung at, a foul ball if there are fewer than two strikes, a foul tip held by the catcher if there are already two strikes, or a foul bunt if the batter already has two strikes. These are all mutually exclusive events that are represented by a single disjunctive concept; that is, the concept requires that the action need satisfy only one of these criteria in order to qualify as a strike.

16.6   Think again about the situation described in Problem 16.5. A base-on-balls, or walk, occurs when the batter gets four balls. Explain how *base-on-balls* is a simple concept, while *ball* itself is a conjunctive concept.

Base-on-balls is a simple concept because any combination of balls adding up to four means that the batter may go to first base. However, a *ball* is a conjunctive concept because it requires more than one criterion to be satisfied. The pitch must be judged by the umpire as being outside the "strike zone" *and* it must not be swung at by the batter. If either criterion is not satisfied, the pitch cannot be called a *ball*.

16.7   We often use phrases such as "heavier than," "shorter than," or "more muscular than . . ." in attempting to distinguish between two people. What kind of concept do these phrases illustrate?

Any relationship between two aspects of a situation may be described by a *relational* concept. The important consideration is that there is a comparison of a common characteristic they share. Thus, both people have some weight, but one is judged heavier than the other.

16.8   Suppose your knowledge of baseball was quite limited, but you were interested in learning about the game. Perhaps without realizing it, you might start formulating hypotheses about the meaning of the words *strike, ball, double-play,* and *sacrifice fly*. You would check each observation you made against your hypotheses of what those words meant. Your "hypothesis-check-revise-check again" approach reveals something about concept formation. What is it?

This testing of ideas to help formulate concepts shows that strategies are often used in concept development. Not all strategies are the same; you may consider all the attributes you have been able to identify and incorporate them into your hypothesis (a wholistic approach) or consider one attribute at a time (a partistic approach). Either way, your attempts to understand may be more effective (and perhaps less embarrassing) than just making guesses.

16.9   Take a moment to think of a list of *fruits*. Having done this, consider which ones you listed first and which came later. Now really try to stretch your recall to include as many as you can. Were the fruits you thought of first ones that are fairly common? Did you find you could add more to the list after you tried again? What principle is illustrated by your performance? What does it mean?

If you are like most people, your answer to the first two questions was yes. You did name fruits you consider common and you could add more when you tried. Your performance showed what is called a *concept hierarchy*. In a concept hierarchy, the associations between the concept and items given at the beginning of the list are very strong, while those toward the end of the list are much weaker. (Thus, most Americans respond first with *orange* or *apple* rather than *kumquat* or *pomegranate*.)

16.10   Asked to describe a building in another city, Brian finds he has difficulty. He says, "Gee, I can 'see' it perfectly. Let me think for a second how to describe it to you." He pauses, seems to consider the problem, and then tries to say what the building is like. Brian's behavior emphasizes what differences in two kinds of thinking?

Brian's ability (or claim) to be able to "see" the building perfectly indicates thinking by using imagery rather than words. His wish to pause for a moment and consider seems to show the need to use inner speech, while his response, when finally given, shows verbal thinking. Both the use of images and inner speech are fairly common to thinking, but to be able to know what is being thought, some performance (usually with words) must be observed.

16.11   What is problem-solving?

A *problem* exists when one has defined a goal and seeks some way of achieving that goal. *Problem-solving* seems to involve motivated thinking, that is, thinking which is activated, directed, and maintained in the hope of accomplishing a goal. It can be distinguished from aimless (non-goal-oriented) thinking, such as daydreaming or fantasizing, which is also called *autistic thinking*.

16.12   Suppose you are preparing a special dinner and have just put a cake in the oven. You then step outside for a moment to cut some parsley from your garden. When you return to the door, you find that you have locked yourself out. Obviously, you have a problem. According to the analysis of problem-solving, what sequence of events is likely to occur now?

Most problem-solving seems to follow a fairly standard sequence. In this case, there may be a brief interlude before problem-solving begins while you express the emotion of anger, but once past that, the progression may be as follows: (1) to define the problem accurately; (2) to consider which concepts are most relevant for solving the problem; (3) to create hypotheses about how to solve the problem; and (4) to test and confirm (or disconfirm) which hypothesis solves the problem best. Thus, your thinking could be: (1) This door is locked. (2) Are all the doors locked? How about the windows? Does anyone else have a key? Will I have to break in? (3) My guess is there is something unlocked, and I'll be able to get it open and get in, or I'll go next door and call my wife. (4) Well, let's try these ideas and see what happens.

16.13   The question of solving problems is sometimes a question of *reasoning*. What types of reasoning have been suggested by psychologists? Why does each have inherent difficulties that may make understanding the process difficult?

Reasoning has been divided into reasoning by using systems, or *programmatic reasoning*, and reasoning by formulating systems, or *generative thinking*. Logical thinking is an example of the first type of reasoning, requiring the use of already-established conventions or rules for the solution of a problem. On the other hand, generative thinking requires the creation of new thought processes, or new ways of looking at or solving the problem.

Both styles of reasoning are difficult to study because many of the processes are internal or "hidden" and may not be available either to the investigator *or* the person being studied. Computer simulation has been used to try to analyze programmatic reasoning, and some description of both logical and illogical reasoning is possible, but psychologists have had little success determining the processes used in generative thinking.

16.14   In design class one day, the architecture students were given what their instructor called a "creativity" project. The class started at one o'clock, and the students had until five to produce a record jacket cover for untitled music which the instructor played for them. The projects were graded by the instructor at the end of the class. Cheryl, who found this a stimulating and interesting problem, got an A. Steve, who was bored and could not see how this project was relevant to architecture, got a C. And Beth, who had been having difficulties with this class, got very excited and upset by this assignment and got a C. Explain the performance of these three students.

Problem-solving is similar to every other kind of performance in that it will be influenced by motivation. The expected performance on a task can be predicted as a function of the level of motivation being experienced, and the inverted-U curve of performance (see Section 9.3) is usually found. Steve, Cheryl and Beth fit this prediction very nicely, as illustrated in Fig. 16-2.

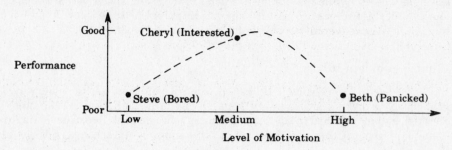

Fig. 16-2

16.15 As you have read this book, you you probably expect it to be well written in grammatically correct English. Past experience with books has created a habit, and reading at this moment should be reinforcing the belief that this book does not contain errors in grammar and spelling. But did you notice that there were *two* errors in the first sentence of this problem? Why do most people miss one or both of the mistakes? Having just missed these two, would a person be likely to miss other errors that occur soon afterwards? What about later?

Habit and set seem to cause the mistakes. Past experience has generated an expectation that current events usually reinforce. However, having been tricked, the reader would develop a new set, or temporary tendency to respond, so that another similar error would probably be caught. (The set might get altered or dissipated over a period of time, so that later stronger habits would again determine the reader's chance of spotting the errors. We used this type of item previously in Solved Problem 7.20. Did you get caught again?)

16.16 Given a flower pot, a stick, a flag, and two thumbtacks, Fred was asked to make a flag which would stand up straight. After much puzzling, he finally admitted that he could not accomplish the task. His best effort looked something like Fig. 16-3.

Fig. 16-3   Fig. 16-4

Joyce took one look at the same problem and said, "You're missing the obvious!" She then simply turned the flower pot over and used the drainage hole in the bottom to support the flag, thus making the flag stand perfectly straight as in Fig. 16-4. What principle explains Fred's failure to solve this problem?

Fred's problem is explained by the principle of *functional fixedness,* a special type of set that makes a person unable to "see" alternate uses for an object. Fred could only envision using the pot right side up, while Joyce, apparently not troubled by functional fixedness, used it upside down, as a stand or pedestal.

16.17 Suppose you are given the following sequence of numbers, "2, 2, 4, 12, 48, . . ." and are asked what numbers will follow. You may find that reasoning does not immediately produce a solution. Then suddenly, after continued study of the sequence, you get an "Aha!" feeling as you spot the principle involved. How do psychologists describe this type of mental process?

This "Aha!" experience is called *insight*, the sudden discovery of a hypothesis that can be confirmed. Such an insight can be described to others, but the actual process of having an insight appears to be a personal experience that is not often easily taught to others.

(*Note*: The sequence is based on the following: the first number, 2, is multiplied by 1; that result is multiplied by 2; the next result is multiplied by 3; and so on.)

16.18 Psychologists have used computers in an attempt to make them match human mental processes. What is this sort of attempt called? Why is it more successful for some kinds of behaviors than for others?

Trying to make the computer match the human's thought processes is called *simulation*. If a person's thinking has followed some programmatic sequence, the computer can often duplicate it. On the other hand, if the person's thoughts have been of a generative nature, the computer may not be able to simulate them. Convergent thinking can usually be simulated by a computer because a known end-product is being sought; divergent thinking is much more difficult to simulate because a creative process is taking place, and the goal of the thinking pattern may not be apparent.

16.19 Is convergent thinking always noncreative? Is divergent thinking always necessary for creativity? How important is intelligence in creative thinking?

Convergent thinking is often noncreative, but it may be used as a "gathering" device to collect information that will be used eventually in a creative solution. Divergent thinking, in which a variety of thoughts are generated and arranged in novel patterns, does seem to be a crucial aspect of creativity. Such thinking may even be autistic thinking or fantasizing, rather than an intentional or directed processes.

It is interesting to note that a minimum of intelligence is probably necessary for successful creative thinking, but there does not appear to be a strong correlation between creativity and intelligence. The types of thinking the individual shows seem more important than the level of intelligence.

16.20 Why is the smell of an onion classified as a sign, while the word *onion* is classified as a symbol?

Both a sign and a symbol are signals and, as such, may be used for communication. A sign has acquired meaning because its inherent characteristics establish a relationship between it and some naturally occurring event. In this case, the odor of the onion and the presence of that particular vegetable are related. A symbol has meaning only because the meaning has been agreed upon. There is no reason why an onion *has* to be called an onion. The letters might be rearranged to spell *ninoo* and, if accepted or agreed upon generally, *ninoo* would become the symbol representing that vegetable.

It should be noted that while written and spoken words are the most commonly used symbols for communication, other symbols also exist. For example, the gestures of American Sign Language (ASL) used by deaf persons, the Braille alphabet used by blind persons, and international traffic signs are all used for communication.

16.21 In what ways do written language and spoken language differ?

The most obvious difference is that written language uses letters, while spoken language uses sounds. But many other differences exist. Different words are used, they are arranged differently, and a person's spoken vocabulary is usually more limited and more repetitive than his or her written vocabulary. The messages conveyed by the two forms often differ both in content and intent. Spoken language tends to be more casual and direct, while written language is often more formal and more carefully regulated by grammatical conventions.

16.22   A student was assigned the project of developing a psychological test that could be used to measure retention skills. The student chose to test 8-year-old children for their memory of certain designs. The student would show the children a design for a specified length of time, and then remove it and have the children attempt to draw what they had seen. The student's instructions to the subjects were, "Study the design carefully. When I take it away, take your pencil and make a facsimile of the design." Many of the subjects did not understand what was expected. Can you explain why?

Most 8-year-olds do not understand the word *facsimile*. While the student apparently felt this word was descriptive, the subjects did not. The student's intent was to produce expressive language, that is, words that convey a message. But in this case, the key word chosen did not convey the message to the subjects.

16.23   An English-speaking person would probably have little or no difficulty pronouncing the word *jolly,* but a native Spaniard would be very likely to say the same word as "ho-yee." Why?

Not all languages make use of the same phonemes. As the basic components of spoken language, phonemes allow linguists to distinguish between one language and another or among speech patterns within the same language. The Spanish language does not make use of sounds exactly like the sounds represented by *j* and *ll* in English. In fact, such sounds may be virtually unpronounceable for a Spaniard not trained in English.

16.24   Morphemes and syllables are slightly different. What distinguishes the two?

Syllables are the basic unit to which we attend when we hear a spoken language. Syllables are often combinations of phonemes, and serve as the smallest speech pattern normally produced. Not all syllables are meaningful by themselves. Linguists have developed the concept of morphemes to represent the smallest *meaningful* units of language. Morphemes are made up of one or more syllables, but cannot be separated into smaller units and maintain meaning.

16.25   Consider the following two sentences: "Kraig drove the car," and, "The car was driven by Kraig." How are these sentences similar? How do they differ? What terms do linguists use to describe these similarities and differences?

Both sentences have the same meaning, but they are constructed differently. Linguists would say that both sentences have the same deep structure (meaning) but different surface structures (constructions).

Suppose, in the second sentence, that the word *at* is substituted for *by*. The sentence would then read, "The car was driven at Kraig." Notice how the surface structure remains about the same, but the deep structure changes considerably.

16.26   A bright 4-year-old has learned the plural of the word *mouse*. It intrigues the child that there are not several *mouses,* but several *mice.* One day, this same child hears her mother referred to as her father's "spouse." Later, she asks her parents if they are "spice." Her behavior illustrates what aspect of language development? Is this comparable for all languages?

Language acquisition begins with the learning of single words, advances to combining those words, modifying the words, and developing the rules of the language. While the rules of various languages differ considerably (for example, in the placement of adjectives or gender of words), children do seem to learn the appropriate rules for their particular language at about the same time and in approximately the same sequence. In this case, the child's question shows an error that indicates that rule learning is taking place, but is not yet completed.

16.27   A major controversy regarding language acquisition centers around the differences between the behavioristic interpretation and the cognitive viewpoint. Briefly describe the major differences between these two views.

The behaviorist viewpoint stresses the acquisition of language based upon reinforcement principles, typified by classical and operant conditioning and modeling. In contrast, the cognitive approach proposes that there are innate or inborn mechanisms for processing language. In this latter view, exposure to language is sufficient for language development to occur. (Reinforcement is not seen as a necessary condition.) The cognitive viewpoint states that rules will be learned in approximately the same sequence by all normal children.

One telling point in favor of the cognitive (or inborn) interpretation is that children are able to produce unique constructions never before heard or reinforced. Some evidence seems to support the idea that these inborn mechanisms need to be stimulated before the child reaches adolescence, or language may not develop.

16.28   Early research by psychologists attempting to teach chimpanzees to speak proved almost totally fruitless. Later, attempts to teach American Sign Language or other symbolic codes were quite successful. Why the difference? Were the later successes truly representative of teaching language to lower organisms?

The difficulty with the early studies was that the researchers were trying to use a mode of communication which could not be accomplished by the chimpanzees, perhaps for physiological reasons. When later investigators switched to a more compatible system, language learning progressed fairly rapidly.

These latter studies did represent teaching language to lower organisms. The format did not involve the use of written or spoken words, but as mentioned before, ASL or symbolic codes are forms of language and may be used for communication.

Key Terms

Autistic thinking.   Aimless thinking, such as fantasizing or daydreaming.

Complex concept.   A concept that represents more than one stimulus property simultaneously.

Concept.   A symbol that summarizes or generalizes the attributes of some objects, events, actions, or ideas that are otherwise dissimilar.

Concept hierarchy.   The "rank" of members in a concept category.

Conjunctive concept.   A complex concept based upon the simultaneous presence of two or more stimulus properties.

Convergent thinking.   Thinking aimed at finding a known solution to a problem.

Creativity.   In problem-solving an original, productive, and unusual approach to a task.

Deep structure.   The meaning transmitted by words used in a language.

Directed thinking.   Thinking that occurs for a purpose, as in problem-solving.

Disjunctive concept.   A complex concept based upon the simultaneous consideration of two or more stimulus properties, but in which the presence of any one stimulus property is adequate to qualify the stimulus as an instance of the concept.

Divergent thinking.   Thinking devoted to finding a new or different (previously unknown) solution to a problem.

Expressive language.   Words that convey a message.

Functional fixedness.   A type of set in which a subject is unable to use some object in a novel manner.

Generative thinking.   The creation of new systems of thought.

Imagery.   Internal representations of visual stimuli.

Inner speech.   Internal representations of verbal stimuli.

Insight.   In problem-solving, the phenomenon in which a subject knows the problem, has a period of no apparent progress, and then suddenly finds a solution.

Morphemes.   The smallest meaningful unit of a language.

Phonemes.   The basic sound or inflection components of a spoken language.

Problem-solving.   The recognition and establishment of some goal, followed by attempts to reach that goal.

Programmatic reasoning.   Reasoning using already-existing systems of thought.

Psycholinguistics.   The study of the relationship between organisms and their language; concerned with the acquisition, structure, and usage of language.

Reasoning.   Attempts to solve a problem by combining two or more aspects from past experience.

Receptive language.   What is understood from words that are used.

Relational concept.   A complex concept based upon the relation between two features of a stimulus situation.

Set.   The temporary tendency to respond in a certain manner.

Sign.   A signal that has inherent meaning because its characteristics are related to naturally occurring events.

Signal.   Stimuli that can be used for communication.

Simple concept.   A concept concerned with a single property only.

Simulation.   Attempts to use a computer program to duplicate the processing (thinking) stage in problem-solving.

Surface structure.   The arrangement of words in a language.

Syllables.   The smallest speech units to which the receiver usually attends.

Symbol.   Any specified stimulus which has become a commonly-accepted representation for some object, event, action, or idea.

Thinking.   A personal process of symbolic mediation, often attributed to the mind.

Examination II

For each of the first twenty-five questions, circle the best answer. (The correct answers appear on page 210.)

1. Functional autonomy refers to _____.

    (a) the reduction of cognitive dissonance
    (b) the principle of homeostasis
    (c) the satisfaction of survival motives
    (d) the concept of a self-reinforcing response

2. Children at the beach are often seen running toward the waves, only to shy away from the water at the last possible moment. Their behavior probably illustrates _____.

    (a) an approach-avoidance conflict
    (b) an approach-approach conflict
    (c) an avoidance-avoidance conflict
    (d) a multiple approach-approach conflict

3. In the hierarchy of needs proposed by humanistic psychologists, the highest level is called _____.

    (a) belongingness
    (b) self-actualization
    (c) esteem
    (d) safety

4. When a person chooses not to vote and says, "My vote doesn't matter, they'll do whatever they want anyway," the principle illustrated is _____.

    (a) phobic reaction
    (b) autonomic depression
    (c) psychosomatic disorder
    (d) learned helplessness

5. The use of a lie detector depends upon _____.

    (a) trapping the subject into making contradictory responses
    (b) identifying the lie from changes in physiological responses
    (c) spotting nonverbal gestures which reveal the lie
    (d) determining the subject's subjective appraisal of arousal

6. If an observed emotional reaction seems restrained, verbal, and relatively long-lived, the respondent was probably _____.

    (a) Susan, age 3
    (b) Sally, age 10
    (c) Sarah, age 30
    (d) not enough information to determine

7. In a classroom demonstration, the instructor has a student sit on the desk in front of the class and hold her head still. A bellhop's bell is sounded and followed by a puff of air into her eye from a quickly squeezed empty syringe. Soon the student begins to blink when the bell sounds. In this example, the UCS is _____.

    (a) the air puff
    (b) the sound of the bell
    (c) the desk
    (d) the empty syringe

8. When tested for a reaction to the word *horse*, a subject answers *ride*. Later, when tested to the word *Pony*, the subject again answers *ride*. Giving the same response to these two stimuli illustrates _____.

    (a) primary stimulus generalization
    (b) secondary stimulus generalization
    (c) confabulation
    (d) spontaneous recovery

9. Forward trace classical conditioning occurs when _____.

    (a) the CS comes on and stays on until the UCS goes off
    (b) the CS and UCS come on together
    (c) the CS comes on and goes off before the onset of the UCS
    (d) the UCS comes on before the CS

10. A coach who tries to get a player to come closer and closer to a particular movement needed in the sport is probably using _____.

    (a) respondent conditioning
    (b) programmed learning
    (c) shaping
    (d) punishment

11. A rat being reinforced on a fixed ratio of fifteen (FR = 15) is being reinforced _____.

    (a) every 15 seconds
    (b) for a response after each 15-second period
    (c) following a UCS presented each 15 seconds
    (d) for a certain number of responses

12. If removal of some stimulus strengthens or maintains a response, it is probably correct to say _____.

    (a) that punishment has occurred
    (b) that positive reinforcement has occurred
    (c) that negative reinforcement has occurred
    (d) that a noncontingent reinforcer has been established

13. Sandra has found that spraying her skillet with a special preparation keeps food from sticking when cooked. Sandra's response illustrates _____.

    (a) an avoidance response
    (b) an escape response
    (c) an approach response
    (d) a punishing response

14. The effect of reinforcement on modeling appears to be _____.

    (a) facilitation of learning
    (b) establishing a contingency
    (c) forcing a response
    (d) developing a superstition

15. A child's use of derogatory phrases without any apparent understanding is most likely an example of _____.

    (a) vicarious learning
    (b) pure imitation
    (c) lack of attention
    (d) respondent conditioning

16. Power is defined as _____.

    (a) cognitive control
    (b) dependent influence
    (c) independent influence
    (d) potential influence

17. In a learning curve, a plateau occurs when _____.

    (a) the performance has reached a final peak
    (b) a level period of performance is preceded and followed by performance improvement
    (c) a negatively-accelerated performance curve has been obtained
    (d) one-trial learning has been observed

18. Which of the following combinations of factors should produce the best acquisition of a respondent in a subject?

    (a) overlearning, massed practice, passive attitude
    (b) overlearning, massed practice, active attitude
    (c) no overlearning, distributed practice, passive attitude
    (d) overlearning, distributed practice, active attitude

19. When the learning of one task makes it more difficult to learn the next task _____.

    (a) positive transfer has taken place
    (b) overlearning has been observed
    (c) learning without awareness has occurred
    (d) negative transfer has taken place

20. If Robert took 15 trials to learn a list of words and later relearned the same list in 6 trials, his savings was _____ that of Lois, who learned in 20 trials and relearned in 8 trials.

    (a) greater than
    (b) the same as
    (c) less than
    (d) cannot tell from the information given

21. Repression is defined as _____.

    (a) an increase in performance following a period of rest
    (b) going back to a more child-like attitude
    (c) motivated forgetting
    (d) confabulation

22. When the pattern for the experimental group in an experiment is Learn Task 1, Learn Task 2, Rest, Test Task 2, _____ is probably being studied.

    (a) transfer of training
    (b) retroactive inhibition
    (c) proactive inhibition
    (d) the von Restorff effect

23. Listing words such as *baseball* or *football* before giving words such as *hurling* or *cricket* would represent _____.

    (a) the respondent's concept hierarchy
    (b) a wholistic approach to concepts
    (c) a disjunctive concept
    (d) autistic thinking

24. Creating new systems of thought is _____.

    (a) generative thinking
    (b) programmatic reasoning
    (c) simulation
    (d) surface structure

25. A morpheme is _____.

    (a) a phrase's meaning
    (b) a phonemic syllable
    (c) typically divided into clauses
    (d) the smallest meaningful unit of langauge

26. Describe the concept of homeostasis and explain how it is related to survival motives.

Homeostasis is defined as internal, physiological balance. The body attempts to maintain this balance automatically. The adjustments which are made by the body are in keeping with its survival needs—for example, perspiring when body temperature begins to get too high or "passing out" when exhausted.

27. Why must some motives be treated as combination motives?

Research, so far, has revealed that some motives, such as sex, seem to contain both learned and unlearned components and that other motives, such as contact comfort, simply cannot be classified as learned or unlearned. Thus, it is necessary to refer to some as combination motives.

28. What is meant by the concept of "fear of success"? How has this been studied?

Fear of success refers to a subject's belief that achievement may lead to problems. This has been studied primarily as a feminine characteristic; that is, success for females may lead to loss of femininity or social rejection and thus is to be feared. Extensive research on this motive in males has not yet been completed.

29. Why is an adult's emotional expression often described as "restrained"?

Adult emotional expression is often described as "restrained" simply because it is—at least in comparison to that of a child. Adults tend to be less physical, show reduced outward expression, and are more able to control emotional expression than are children.

30. Describing an incident later, Larry says, "I was so mad I could have spit nails. I couldn't think of what to say!" Explain this reaction in terms of emotion, motivation, and performance.

The emotion is anger at a very high level of intensity. Larry's reaction is comparable to other behaviors performed under high levels of motivation; that is, performance is poor. (He was unable to speak.) Later, when calmer, Larry probably could think of lots of responses that would have been appropriate.

31. Why is extinction considered both a procedure and a result?

The two aspects of extinction are essentially inseparable. Removal of the reinforcement condition creates the extinction procedure and leads to the result of the response returning to its preconditioning level.

32. While bending over to smell some flowers, Randy is stung by a bee. How would you test later to see if Randy had become classically conditioned in this situation?

Assuming the bee sting was painful, a later test for classically conditioned response would be to have Randy get near to the flowers again and observe his reactions to identify any expression of fear, such as withdrawal or crying. The CS is the flowers; the UCS is the bee sting; the UCR would be the reaction to the pain; and a CR would be some comparable reaction.

33. Faced with a highly exciting situation, a worker is simply unable to complete a job even though he has previously learned it well. In terms of learning, what has happened?

This worker's reaction illustrates the learning-performance distinction. Performance does not necessarily reveal learning. This is once again an example of overly high levels of motivation leading to poorer performance.

34. "Horseplayers" often seemed to be hooked on gambling. In terms of schedules of reinforcement, explain why.

Betting on horse races is an example of variable ratio reinforcement: the more often a bet is made, the more likely a "win." But no gambler wins all the time. The successes and failures represent a partial reinforcement condition, and research has shown that partial reinforcement leads to greater resistance to extinction than does continuous reinforcement.

35. Describe the differences between punishment and escape conditions.

Punishment occurs when an aversive stimulus follows a response and a contingent relationship exists. Escape is found when a response allows the subject to get away from an aversive stimulus; that is, the contingency is between the response and a negative reinforcement.

36. What is the most typical way instrumental conditioning is measured?

Instrumental conditioning is measured by determining a cumulative record of responses. This is a record of the number of appropriate responses made during a given period of time.

37. Learning by modeling has some advantages over other forms of learning. What are some of these advantages?

Learning by modeling is advantageous to other forms of learning (for example, trial-and-error) because it can keep the subject from dangerous, embarrassing, or otherwise difficult situations that might create serious problems.

38.   If your friend tells you how to bake some delicious cookies ("Add two cups of flour, then one teaspoon of vanilla, etc.") and you follow that recipe successfully, you have demonstrated a particular kind of modeling. What kind?

This is symbolic modeling—particularly verbal modeling. Without actually seeing your friend perform any of these steps, you are able to duplicate the performance and make the cookies.

39.   Suppose you were asked to recall the names of couples who dated when you were in high school. In terms of verbal learning, what are you being asked to do?

This task would represent a paired-associate task (e.g., Jack went with Grace). Note that this is also a test of long-term retention rather than short-term storage or sensory storage.

40.   An auto mechanic who repeatedly follows a patterned approach in trying to discover the problem with a car illustrates what learning principle?

This demonstrates learning to learn, or the learning of general principles that are then applied to specific situations. The mechanic hopes that this will be a positive transfer situation.

41.   What is an asymptote? Why is the term used when describing incremental learning?

An asymptote refers to a level of performance that appears to be near the maximum for a subject. In incremental learning situations, performance generally keeps improving until the asymptotic level is reached.

42.   Sports fans are sometimes accused of confabulation. Why might this be true?

Fans are usually highly motivated to respond favorably to "their" team. Thus, fans may dispute a strike called on one of "their" batters or a foul called on one of "their" linebackers or recall fantastic plays which never actually happened.

43.   What role might sleeping play in the retention of learned materials?

A subject who sleeps after learning avoids the possibility of encountering interfering materials. This would mean the subject would avoid retroactive inhibition, and better retention could result. Furthermore, sleeping may be viewed as a rest period separating periods of learning, and periods of learning alternated with rest periods are more effective than massed learning.

44.   Can a hand gesture be a symbol?

A symbol is simply any stimulus that has come to have a commonly accepted meaning for something else. Any gesture may be a symbol, as long as there is general agreement about what the gesture represents.

45.   In terms of grammar, what is the difference between these two sentences: "The bird left the nest," and "The rat left the nest."

The two sentences differ slightly in surface structure and greatly in deep structure. The choice of the word *bird* or *rat* would have considerable effect on the meaning of the sentence.

Answers to Problems 1–25

1. (d)	6. (c)	11. (d)	16. (d)	21. (c)
2. (a)	7. (a)	12. (c)	17. (b)	22. (c)
3. (b)	8. (b)	13. (a)	18. (d)	23. (a)
4. (d)	9. (c)	14. (a)	19. (d)	24. (a)
5. (b)	10. (c)	15. (b)	20. (b)	25. (d)

Ch

Psychological Testing and Measureme...

One of the first applications of psychological principles was in the development of psychological tests for predicting such things as school success or mental fitness. For example, Alfred Binet and others developed the first standardized intelligence tests in the early 1900s.

This chapter concerns itself with the important characteristics of a good test, the uses and abuses of tests, and some of the basic forms of psychological tests that have been developed. Chapter 20 deals specifically with intelligence and creativity, which many tests measure.

17.1 CHARACTERISTICS OF A GOOD TEST

Psychologists have identified four characteristics that seem to be most important for a good test. These characteristics are reliability, validity, standardization, and objectivity.

Reliability

Reliability refers to the consistency with which a result will be obtained when either identical or supposedly equivalent forms of a test are used. In testing, perfect consistency cannot be expected, but a high degree of reliability is essential. It would be impossible to make accurate or meaningful predictions from the results of an unreliable test.

Validity

Validity means that a test measures what it claims to measure; that is, a valid test predicts what it intends to predict. A test may have several validities, for example, a high validity for the prediction of scholastic success in literature courses but a much lower validity for predicting success in mathematics courses.

It is very important to identify just what a test *does* measure. Improper use of tests may lead to inaccurate predictions and, therefore, faulty counseling or guidance.

Comparison of Reliability and Validity

It is necessary to note that a test may be highly reliable, but invalid. This can occur when a test measures something consistently, but does not measure what it claims to measure. However, a test that is valid will also be reliable. (If the test measures what it intends to measure, then it will have to do this with fairly high consistency; otherwise the test would not predict accurately.)

EXAMPLE 1. Suppose you were shown "Keiner's Test of Intellectual Skills," which consisted of summing up the following three physical measurements: (1) the circumference of the subject's head; (2) the length of the subject's nose from tip to eyebrow; and (3) the distance separating the centers of the subject's two eyes. You will probably realize that this test could have very high reliability, yet very likely be totally invalid. This example is purposely absurd, but the principle it illustrates is important—it is possible for a number of people to take specified measurements from one subject and obtain the same results from (or measurements of) that subject, thus showing the test's reliability. However, such measurements may be completely inappropriate for the purposes stated, and thus have no validity. Test developers constantly guard against the possibility that their tests may be either unreliable or invalid.

211

Standardization

Standardization refers to how the testing is carried out. All aspects of the testing procedure, including the administration of the test and the scoring and evaluation of the results should follow the same pattern each time the test is given. If the testing procedure is not standardized, differences among the test performances of the subjects may be the result of variations in test procedures, and not an accurate indicator of differences among the subjects.

Norms. One way to standardize test results is to establish *norms*, which are scores obtained from groups of people who have taken the test. Once norms have been determined, performances by others taking the same test (in the same manner) can be compared to the norms.

EXAMPLE 2. College students who expect to go to graduate school often have to take the Graduate Record Exams (GRE) or a comparable test and submit the scores along with their applications. A copy of the scores is sent to each student, along with norms for the test. Thus, the students know what their absolute GRE scores were and how these scores compared to those obtained by others taking the same tests. Often, these are reported as percentile values. (A percentile is the point below which a certain percentage of the population falls. For example, a person who scored in the sixty-fifth percentile would have done better than 65 percent of the people who took the test.)

Norms versus criterion orientation. Norms are frequently helpful in interpreting the results of psychological tests, but on occasion they may be misleading. In such cases, it may be better to use a *criterion*, or an absolute standard, to evaluate a subject's performance.

EXAMPLE 3. Suppose you were assigned the task of determing how much aptitude for mathematics a particular child had. Depending on the situation, you might use either a normative scale or a criterion scale of measurement. For example, suppose the child attended a special school for children with high aptitudes for mathematics. You might then avoid the norm approach because your subject, in comparison to others in the special school, might not seem to have much aptitude for math. (The norms in this school would be very high, and the child you studied might score in a deceptively low percentile.) Thus, caution must be exercised in interpreting test results and in choosing standards of measurement.

Norms and stereotypes. Because norms are established on the basis of test results and are often reported as statistics, they sometimes take on the "ring of truth" for the naive reader. They can, however, be misinterpreted. For example, a person may look at a norm and follow this train of reasoning: "(1) if this is the average or typical score of a group of people and (2) one person is a member of that group, then (3) this score must be typical of that person." The test results *may* be typical of that person, but the norm does not provide any assurance that it is so.

Objectivity

Objectivity means that an observer's or measurer's biases or prejudices play no role in observation or measurement. (All measurements are made in a neutral or dispassionate fashion.) Observers who allow bias to influence their judgment or measurement are described as *subjective* rather than objective.

EXAMPLE 4. In some cases, the person administering, scoring, and evaluating a psychological test is not told why the subject is being tested. This is done so that the person will not form preconceptions. It would be inappropriate, for example, for the teacher who has complained about a student's behavior in class to then give a personality test to that student. Instead, the test should be given by someone who is neutral and will proceed in an objective fashion.

17.2 TYPES OF PSYCHOLOGICAL TESTS

In theory, any test of a behavioral characteristic could be called a psychological test. Several of the most important types of psychological tests will be discussed here.

Achievement and Aptitude Tests

Achievement tests are designed to measure what a person has accomplished up to a given point in time. *Aptitude tests* are designed to predict what a person may accomplish in the future if given appropriate training. Both of these types of testing are based on the concept of *ability*, which is a person's potential for acquiring a skill. (Achievement tests show how well a person has acquired skills up to now, while aptitude tests indicate how well a person might acquire skills in the future.)

(*Note*: In a sense, *all* ability tests are achievement tests, showing only how well the person does on a given test at a particular time. However, the purposes of achievement and aptitude tests differ, and psychologists try to design aptitude tests that measure basic skills that do not require any specific knowledge.)

Scholastic versus vocational tests. There are two major types of aptitude tests: *scholastic* aptitude tests (which are used to predict future successes in academic pursuits) and *vocational* aptitude tests (which are used to estimate future successes in employment situations).

EXAMPLE 5. Scholastic aptitude tests that are based exclusively on vocabulary skills predict quite well how a student may react to additional academic training. However, such a test might be almost totally inappropriate for checking physical proficiencies or psycho-motor abilities, for which tests of muscular strength, manual dexterity, and coordination should be used instead. Thus, a psychologist has to design a testing program that is suited to the particular task being evaluated. (*Note*: The tests of physical proficiencies and psycho-motor skills sometimes are referred to as tests of *noncognitive* abilities. Quite frequently, both cognitive and noncognitive abilities are tested when a person applies for a job.)

Personality Tests

Personality tests are designed to try to determine what is typical of an individual or what the person usually does. (Generally, these tests are related to some theory regarding the structure of personality and therefore attempt to measure traits or characteristics specified by that theory. The basic principles of personality are considered in depth in Chapters 19 through 21.) There are several different ways of evaluating personality, including paper-and-pencil tests, projective tests, situational tests, and techniques such as interviewing.

Paper-and-pencil tests. Paper-and-pencil tests usually used for personality evaluation consist of a questionnaire containing statements to which the individual can respond with answers such as "yes, maybe, no" or "true, false, cannot say." In other cases, a subject is given a list of adjectives from which to choose those that he or she feels are self-descriptive.

Projective tests. In projective personality tests, the subject is usually presented with a series of ambiguous stimuli and asked for a description of or a story about each. The theory of these tests is that the person will reveal some personality characteristics by introducing them into (or projecting them onto) the stimulus provided. The two most widely known projective tests are the Thematic Apperception Test (TAT), which uses a series of twenty monochrome pictures, and the Rorschach Test, which uses ten inkblots (some of which have color). Scoring techniques have been developed to try to help maintain some objectivity when using these tests.

EXAMPLE 6. The "inkblot" shown in Figure 17-1 is not taken from the Rorschach Test, but it is similar to the type of figures used in the test. The subject is shown the figure and asked, "What could this be?" or "What does this remind you of?" After responding to the entire set of figures, the subject goes back through the cards and points out what part of each inkblot determined the response.

Other personality evaluations. Two other general categories of personality evaluation deserve mention. These are interviews and situational tests.

Interviews are face-to-face encounters between people. They may be conducted in order to gather the same information as might be obtained by using a paper-and-pencil test. However, interviews give the interviewer a chance to expand on questions asked or probe answers the interviewee gives.

Fig. 17-1

In situational tests, a person is placed in a previously planned situation and is expected to react. The responses made by the person are evaluated as a means of determining his or her personality characteristics.

EXAMPLE 7.   Several years ago, a favorite situational test in employment interviewing consisted of offering the candidate a cigarette and a light, but not providing an ashtray. The reactions of the candidate to the growing length of ash and the lack of a place to dispose of it were observed in an attempt to determine something about that candidate's personality. As might be imagined, there are serious doubts about the reliability and validity of such "one-shot" tests of a personality.

Intelligence Tests

Intelligence tests are probably best described as a series of aptitude tests that predict scholastic abilities. They are the best known and most widely used psychological tests and have been quite thoroughly researched. Chapter 20 is devoted to a discussion of tests of intelligence and creativity.

Test Batteries

Psychologists may combine several different psychological tests into a series and present them to a person. Such a combination of tests is referred to as a *test battery*. The results from the various tests often are plotted as a *profile* of scores, which provides information used in counseling and guidance.

17.3   TESTING CONCERNS

Several variables must be taken into account when using psychological tests. Some of the most important are discussed in this section.

Individual versus Group Tests

One concern is whether each individual needs to be tested separately or not—sometimes data can be collected from a number of people simultaneously. Individual tests have the advantage of giving the psychologist a chance to closely observe the subject taking the test, and they are sometimes more sensitive than group tests as a means of evaluating special characteristics. On the other hand, individual tests are generally more expensive than group tests, and they often require a more highly trained administrator.

Group tests have the advantage of allowing large amounts of data to be collected quickly. They are also relatively inexpensive and usually do not require skilled administration. As a means of surveying a number of individuals quickly, they work fairly well, although it is difficult to keep accurate track of each subject's effort or motivation.

Speed versus Power Tests

Speed tests are tests that have a time limit as a significant variable. (Subjects are expected to do the best they can within a limited amount of time.) For all practical purposes, *power tests* have no time limits. Subjects are asked to give their best possible performances and not worry about the time involved.

Cross-sectional versus Longitudinal Investigations

Psychologists often need to compare the performances of subjects in various age groups. There are basically two ways of making such comparisons. *Cross-sectional investigations* are tests of different individuals in each of the age groups being studied. Data collection can take place fairly quickly, but matching samples from one age group to another may be difficult or impossible. *Longitudinal investigations* test the same subjects throughout the study, and thus matched samples are unnecessary. However, longitudinal studies take a much longer period of time to complete and tend to have a higher probability of subject loss because of the waiting periods between one testing session and the next.

EXAMPLE 8. Suppose a psychologist wanted to test the motor skills of children at ages two, four, six, eight, and ten. In a cross-sectional study, matched groups of children in each age group could be tested in a matter of days. A longitudinal study, on the other hand, would require a testing period stretched out over eight years.

Culture-free and Culture-fair Tests

It has long been known that an individual's cultural background can affect his or her performance on some cognitive ability and personality tests. Attempts have been made to create psychological tests that do not contain biases against or in favor of certain cultures or subcultures. *Culture-free tests* attempt to eliminate such biases totally, for example, with performance tests free of any cultural background influence. *Culture-fair tests* try to choose items that should be equally well-known by all cultural groups to be investigated. (*Note*: Most attempts at creating such tests have proved relatively unsuccessful.)

17.4   USES OF PSYCHOLOGICAL TESTS

Psychological tests are used for many different purposes. It must be remembered, however, that test results should be considered only advisory and that any other information available should be used in making either predictions or decisions. Several typical uses of tests are discussed here.

Selection

Probably the most common use for psychological test results is in the *selection* of individuals for academic or vocational positions. If there is more than one qualified applicant for a position, the person doing the hiring may administer tests to help in the selection process.

Counseling and Therapy

Ability tests and personality tests may be used by the psychologist who is attempting to aid an individual with guidance or therapy. The results obtained may help the psychologist formulate a plan for treatment of the individual or advise an individual about his or her abilities.

Legal Proceedings

Results from psychological tests are sometimes used in courts of law and other legal proceedings. For example, a court may have to make judgments of the sanity of a defendant in a criminal case.

Statistical versus Intuitive Judgment

A psychologist may make predictions or decisions based solely on some norm or criterion and the results of a test. In such a case, the psychologist has made what is called a *statistical judgment* based on the test. In other situations, the psychologist may use the test results *and* other pieces of information, including feelings or intuitions about the subject. In such a case, the psychologist has made what is called an *intuitive judgment* based on the total information.

17.5 ABUSES OF PSYCHOLOGICAL TESTING

Psychological testing has been questioned for a number of reasons, including the extent to which the tests can actually predict, the fairness of tests for all groups, the possibility that psychological tests invade a person's privacy, and the ways in which the results of tests are publicized or revealed.

Limited Prediction

Many of the predictions and decisions mentioned in Section 17.4 can be based on or aided by the results of psychological tests. However, psychologists and others with access to test results must realize the limitations of such scores and not attempt to rely upon them exclusively.

EXAMPLE 9. Intelligence tests are sometimes thought to provide results which may predict success in almost any aspect of behavior. Yet, research has shown that other variables—such as creativity, level of motivation, and psychomotor skills—may be as important or more important as indicators of future success. Basing predictions of success solely on intelligence scores is narrow-minded and inappropriate.

Test Fairness

As previously mentioned, attempts have been made to try to develop culture-free or culture-fair tests, but success has been limited. Thus, psychological tests may be misused if they are administered to a subcultural group for which they are inappropriate.

EXAMPLE 10. In an attempt to dramatize the lack of test fairness, a "ghetto" test was developed several years ago. Based upon the slang language of a particular subcultural group, the test showed how results could vary widely, depending on the kind of language used in the test.

Privacy

Privacy is invaded if the results of an individual's test are revealed without that person's knowledge or consent. (Merely administering a psychological test is not necessarily an invasion of privacy, and frequently serves the beneficial purpose of assisting an individual in making behavioral choices.)

Revealing Results

Anyone with access to the results of psychological tests should respect the privacy of those individuals who were tested, and should consider carefully the consequences of revealing test results. Government regulations that attempt to preserve privacy and limit access to test results have been enacted.

Solved Problems

17.1   Dr. Smith claims to have developed a short test that will measure musical talent. The test consists of five measurable tasks, including how frequently a subject can tap on a table in three seconds and how much pressure a subject can exert in clenching his or her fist. How reliable and valid is the Smith Test of Musical Ability?

   The test is likely to be quite reliable but not valid. It is reliable because the responses obtained from subjects would probably be consistent: the strength of a person's grip or the ability of a person to tap on a table quickly are not likely to change drastically from one test to the next. However, it is also probably safe to assume that hand strength or speed cannot be correlated directly to musical talent. Thus, the test would measure quite consistently, but not measure what it claimed to measure.

17.2   Another characteristic of a good test is standardization. What does this word imply about a test?

   In a sense, everything in a test that can be standardized should be standardized. The administration of a test and the scoring and evaluation of results should be done in the same manner every time the test is used. Variations in any of these procedures may yield test results that are not attributable to characteristics of the subjects taking the test, but rather to the way in which the test was conducted.

17.3   Anna transfers from one elementary school to another. The first school sends a letter to the second describing Anna as " . . . near the top of her class, one of our best students." When Anna starts in the second school, she is barely able to meet the standards set for her classmates and requires remedial tutoring in several subjects. How could a difference in the means of evaluation account for Anna's difficulty in the second school?

   The problem here may be that the norms used in evaluating Anna in one school may have been different from those used in the other. At the first school, Anna was indeed at the top of her class: when her performance was compared with the performance of others in her group, she appeared to be a good student. However, when she transferred to the second school, Anna could have been judged on the basis of other norms. (For example, the students in the second school might have been much further along in the acquisition of reading, writing, and mathematical skills.) Furthermore, the evaluation in the new school could have been criterion-based rather than norm-based: rather than judging Anna's performance in comparison to that of other students, the new school might have judged it against some absolute standard, or criterion.

17.4   How can the statistical establishment of norms lead to stereotyped descriptions of individuals?

   Statistics sometimes exert an undue influence on an observer's interpretations. (You may have encountered people who believe that anything established statistically must be right.) Using a norm as the basis for an assertion may lead to statements such as, "The average _____ does such-and-such and so-and-so." This, in turn, is followed by the stereotypical judgment, "Well, you are a _____, and they do such-and-such and so-and-so, so you must do these also." One must remember that norms reveal what groups of people have done. Norms are thus a collective report of behavior, and do not necessarily tell anything about what any one individual will do.

17.5   Students sometimes complain that two people in a class can give the same answer to an essay question and the instructor will score one answer higher than the other. If students are correct in saying that the two answers are the same, what characteristics of a good test has the instructor failed to satisfy?

   If previous work by the instructor has shown that the essay questions used on this exam were valid, reliable, and could be graded in a standardized manner, the instructor has probably failed to satisfy the criterion of objectivity. Apparently, some bias or prejudice has caused the instructor to make two different evaluations of the same answer. (*Note*: In defense of the instructor, it may be that bias was not involved and that fatigue or boredom with grading caused the discrepancy.)

17.6   What are the similarities and differences between achievement tests and aptitude tests?

Achievement tests are intended to measure performance development up to the time of testing. Aptitude tests are supposed to predict performance in the future. In reality, aptitude and achievement tests often are very much alike: they reveal what skills or abilities a subject has at a given point in time. However, their results are used differently.

17.7   When Fred is interviewed for a job, he is told that he is also expected to take several tests. He asks what kind, and the company representative replies, "Oh, some noncognitive ones." Fred is confused by this answer, and asks that the word noncognitive means. What answer is he given?

The company representative explains that they are interviewing Fred for a job that requires both scholastic (or cognitive) aptitude *and* noncognitive (or vocational) aptitudes. By checking his school records and the recommendations he has received, they are satisfied he has sufficient cognitive skills for the job. However, the company needs to make certain Fred has the perceptual-motor abilities and physical proficiencies necessary to do the job, and the noncognitive (vocational) aptitude tests are designed to measure just these qualifications.

17.8   Valerie applies for a job with the company described in Problem 17.7, and when she arrives for her interview, she too must take some tests. However, the tests are not all the same as those Fred took. One of Valerie's is a personality test, and she is told that there are no right or wrong answers—she should simply respond as she usually would.

These instructions reveal a major difference between aptitude or achievement tests and personality tests. What is the difference? Does the distinction always hold?

Because there are no correct or incorrect answers and because Valerie is asked to respond in her usual manner, the personality test is a measure of *typical performance*. On the other hand, in aptitude or achievement testing, a person is usually instructed to give the best possible responses, a measure of maximum performance. Thus, the distinction is between usual or typical responding and best or maximum responding.

One other point must be made about this distinction, however. While Valerie is instructed to respond typically on the personality test, she may feel, perhaps because of her motivation to get the job, that she ought to give some answers the evaluator will approve. The test may then become a measure of what Valerie thinks will be judged as the best response rather than Valerie's typical responding.

17.9   After taking the personality tests, Valerie asks the administrator why there were no inkblots or pictures. What answer is she given?

Valerie was probably given paper-and-pencil tests, not projective tests. Paper-and-pencil tests generally require the person to make choices among answers provided or to check a list of adjectives the subject believes to be self-descriptive. Some personality tests measure both normal and abnormal characteristics, while others are concerned with only normal characteristics. In projective tests, a person is presented with a series of ambiguous stimuli and asked to tell a story about or give a description of the stimuli. It is thought the person's responses reveal personality characteristics that are projected onto the ambiguous stimulus.

17.10 What other measures of personality, besides paper-and-pencil tests and projective tests, are used?

 The evaluation of an individual's personality is sometimes made through an interview. The advantage of such an evaluation technique is that it gives the interviewer an opportunity for additional probing and observation: subjects can be directly observed as they respond, and the interviewer can "steer" the interview toward points of special interest that may come up.

 A much less common technique of personality evaluation is called *situational* testing, in which a subject is brought into a predetermined environment and observed as he or she reacts. The responses of the subject are those interpreted by the observers.

17.11 Suppose several investigators wanted to study the relationship of age to intelligence. What would be some of the advantages and disadvantages of both cross-sectional and longitudinal studies in this investigation?

 Cross-sectional studies have the advantage of allowing the investigators to collect data very quickly. Cross-sectional studies also have limitations, however. For example, it may be difficult to accurately match samples at the different age levels being tested, the educational opportunities might have been significantly better for those of the younger age groups and scores obtained might be incorrectly interpreted as a decline in intelligence with increased age.

 Longitudinal studies have the advantage of testing the same subjects throughout the study. Thus, the differing educational opportunities that might have influenced the results in the cross-sectional investigation would not be an important factor. However, data collection in a longitudinal test is a *very* slow process, and there is a chance that many subjects might drop out over the course of the investigation.

17.12 Barney is given a series of vocational tests, each of which has a rather short time limit for completion. When he completes the tests, Barney complains that there wasn't enough time to complete each. What kind of test did Barney take? Why couldn't he be given more time?

 Barney took what are called *speed tests*, in which the time limitations are an important variable. These tests attempt to determine a subject's ability to perform correctly under the pressure of a time limit, and they are quite often used for vocational aptitude tests.

 Power tests, on the other hand, should have time limits that do not affect performance significantly. In other words, the vast majority of subjects should have more than enough time to complete the task. Thus, power tests are supposed to measure total capability without the additional consideration of time limits.

17.13 For counseling purposes, psychologists sometimes combine both scholastic and vocational tests into a series that measures several different aptitudes. What are these series of tests called? What kind of results are reported at the end of such a series?

 The series of tests often used for counseling purposes is called a *test battery*. The results obtained from the various tests are summarized by plotting what is called a *profile* of scores. By using these test batteries, counselors frequently can guide students or others into educational or vocational choices that should best suit their abilities.

17.14 Many colleges and universities require candidates for admission to take some form of standardized nationwide test so that the basic scholastic skills of all the candidates can be compared. Why are these standardized tests almost always group tests? When might a student be asked to take an individual test?

 Group tests are usually selected for surveying large numbers of people (such as all the candidates for admission to college in a given year) because they are relatively inexpensive, can be given to many people simultaneously, and are fairly easy to administer and evaluate. It is difficult, however, to assure the effort or motivation of each person taking the test.

A student might be evaluated with an individual test if the student had particular difficulties with classwork, if the student had particular physiological problems, or perhaps if the student was so exceptional that she or he asked for admission into a special program or asked to be given advanced placement. Such an individual test is generally more expensive because of the need for a specially trained administrator and/or scorer. However, an individual test may yield much more information about a subject's special qualities, and the person who administers such a test may have an opportunity to observe the subject's effort and motivation.

17.15   What is the difference between culture-free tests and culture-fair tests?

In a culture-free test, the questions or tasks are supposedly selected so that cultural differences will play no role in influencing the subject's response. In culture-fair tests, the questions or tasks the subject is to answer or perform are expressed in terms understandable to members of the subject's culture. Unfortunately, the results of culture-free and culture-fair tests have shown that they do not produce results significantly different from those produced in standard psychological testing. That is, at present there is probably no such thing as a truly culture-free or culture-fair test.

17.16   Suppose a high school student did not do very well on the nationwide test he took, yet the college he most wanted to attend accepted him, rather than another student who had better scores on the same test. Why would a college ask for such scores and then (apparently) not use them?

Test results are very seldom used as the sole basis on which admission decisions, or any other kind of decisions, are made. Other information is available and may be important. In this case, class records, recommendations, and the like would be used in conjunction with the test scores to make the admissions decision. In addition, some decisions are made on an intuitive basis rather than on a statistical one. Test results are not meant to be taken as absolute indicators of ability. A personal interview with the candidate or an essay he wrote may have signaled to an admissions officer some special quality the student possessed.

17.17   In what ways besides educational and vocational selection are psychological tests used?

Psychological tests have also been used in counseling or psychotherapy and in legal proceedings. In counseling and psychotherapy, the type of test used depends on the kind of help a person is being given: the counselor or therapist may use anything from a vocational aptitude test to various types of personality tests. In legal proceedings, test results may be used as evidence in cases where someone may be committed to a hospital or in cases where there is some dispute about the competence of someone who drew up a will, for example.

17.18   Suppose the high school student in Problem 17.16 was not accepted by his "first-choice" school and complained that the test—and all psychological tests—are unfair. What response could be given to such a complaint?

Most psychologists are willing to accept the conclusion that no test is entirely culture-free, culture-fair, or even conclusive. At the same time, however, they recognize that test results are seldom used as the only basis for the selection or admission. In and of themselves, tests may be unfair, and they cannot predict academic success perfectly; however, they must be used as *one* indicator of ability among many other indicators.

17.19   Are psychological tests by their very nature an invasion of privacy? Who should have access to the results of such tests?

A test, in and of itself, is not an invasion of privacy. Only abuses of testing and the results of tests can be considered invasions of privacy.

The rights of the individual must be protected, and coercion should not be used to force someone to take a test. Information on test results should be available to the person tested and distributed to others only after that person or a guardian has given permission. Great care must be taken in guaranteeing that psychological tests are not used to threaten individuals or to coerce them into doing what they would otherwise not do.

17.20   The answer to Problem 17.19 implies that a person should have a choice of whether or not to be tested. Why then should anyone ever choose to go ahead and be tested?

A psychological test may help someone make life choices, and in a way is no different from using a physical test to help make medical decisions or dietary choices.

Key Terms

Ability.   A person's potential for acquiring a skill.

Achievement test.   A test that measures what a person has accomplished up to a given point in time.

Aptitude test.   A test designed to predict what a person may accomplish in the future with additional training.

Criterion.   An absolute standard of performance used to evaluate a subject's performance on a test.

Cross-sectional studies.   Psychological tests administered at the same time to subjects from differing age groups.

Culture-fair tests.   Tests that try to use items that should be equally well-known to all subjects taking the test, regardless of their cultural or subcultural background.

Culture-free tests.   Tests which attempt to eliminate entirely the introduction of any biases created by cultural or subcultural differences.

Group test.   Psychological tests administered to more than one subject at the same time.

Individual test.   Psychological tests given by the test administrator to only one subject at a time.

Intelligence tests.   Tests designed to measure intelligence (see Chapter 19); usually consists of a series of aptitude tests that predict academic ability.

Intuitive judgment.   Decision based upon statistical data and other information, and the feelings of the psychologist giving a test.

Longitudinal studies.   Psychological tests administered to the same subjects at different times, often with fairly long periods of time between testing sessions.

Norms.   The scores, obtained by a representative group taking a particular test, that serve as the standard against which an individual's score can be compared.

Objective.   Free from bias or prejudice.

Paper-and-pencil tests.   Psychological tests that use written or check-type answers only.

Personality tests.   Tests designed to determine the attributes that are unique, enduring, and typical of a particular individual.

Power tests.   Psychological tests in which the time limit for completion is not considered an important variable.

Projective tests.   Personality tests in which ambiguous stimuli are presented to a subject who is asked to describe each or tell a story about each; supposedly, the reactions will reveal personality characteristics the individual has projected onto each stimulus.

Psychological testing.   The use of some measurement technique to try to assess a behavioral characteristic.

Reliability.   The consistency of results when a psychological test or other measuring technique is used more than once.

Rorschach inkblot test.   A projective test using ten inkblots as stimuli.

Scholastic tests.   Aptitude tests used to predict future performance in academic pursuits.

Scoring profile.   The presentation of a summary of the results collected from administration of a test battery.

Situational tests.   Personality tests in which the subject is placed in a prepared circumstance and is asked to react; the subject's responses are assessed for various personality characteristics.

Speed tests.   Psychological tests in which the time limit for completion is considered an important variable.

Standardization.   The process of testing with a consistent pattern, and the establishment of norms.

Statistical judgment.   Decisions based solely on statistical (or numerical or data-based) information.

Subjective.   Influenced by some bias or prejudice.

Test battery.   The combination of several different psychological tests into a series presented to a subject.

Thematic Apperception Test (TAT).   A projective test using twenty monochromatic, ambiguous pictures as stimuli.

Validity.   The capacity of a test to measure what it claims to measure (or predict what it claims to predict).

Vocational tests.   Aptitude tests used to predict future performance in a job or career.

Chapter 18

Statistics

Statistics is the discipline that deals with the collection, analysis, interpretation, and presentation of numerical data. This chapter is a discussion of the statistical techniques most commonly used in psychology.

18.1 PURPOSES OF STATISTICS

Statistics has two major purposes in psychology: (1) to summarize or simplify the data that have been obtained; and (2) to permit descriptions or inferences to be made from these data.

Descriptive Statistics

Descriptive statistics provide simplified or "shorthand" summaries of data. They are used to present the data collected in as concise a form as possible. In this chapter, frequency distributions, measures of central tendency, and measures of variability are some of the descriptive statistics discussed.

Inferential Statistics

Inferential statistics provide the means for evaluating relationships that exist within data obtained from a sample. Psychologists use inferential statistics when making predictions, often of the effect of some variable upon responses.

18.2 SYMBOLS USED IN STATISTICS

Several symbols are frequently used in statistical representations. Some of the most common are included in the following list:

$$N = \text{number of scores}$$
$$X = \text{score (or scores)}$$
$$M \text{ or } \overline{X} = \text{the mean or average score}$$
$$d = \text{the difference of a score from the mean}$$
$$\Sigma = \text{sum of}$$
$$D = \text{the difference in rank}$$
$$r \text{ or } \rho = \text{correlation}$$
$$SD \text{ or } \sigma = \text{standard deviation}$$

EXAMPLE 1. These symbols can be used in combination. Thus, the formula

$$SD = \sqrt{\frac{\Sigma d^2}{N}}$$

would be read as: The standard deviation (SD) is equal to the square root of the sum (Σ) of the squared differences of the scores from the mean (d^2), divided by the number of scores (N).

18.3 FORMULAS USED IN STATISTICS

There also are several formulas that are often used in psychological statistics. The following list presents the most common of these:

For calculating the mean:

$$M = \frac{\Sigma X}{N}$$

For calculating the standard deviation:

$$SD = \sqrt{\frac{\Sigma d^2}{N}}$$

For calculating the coefficient of correlation by the product-moment method:

$$r = \frac{\Sigma\,(d_x)\,(d_y)}{N\,(SD_x)\,(SD_y)}$$

For calculating the coefficient of correlation by the rank-difference method (where D represents a difference in rank for any one subject):

$$\rho = 1 - \frac{6(\Sigma D^2)}{N\,(N^2 - 1)}$$

Discussions of these formulas and examples of the use of each are presented later in this chapter.

18.4 FREQUENCY DISTRIBUTIONS

To be able to comprehend items of raw data, it is often necessary to arrange the data in a *frequency distribution*. This is accomplished by dividing the measurement scale of the data into *class intervals*, which are portions of the scale determined by the investigator. Thus, each item of data will fall within one of the class intervals set up by the investigator.

Frequency Polygons

Frequency polygons are line graphs that represent a frequency distribution.

EXAMPLE 2. An investigator studying the effects of room temperature on the performance of a task might plot a frequency polygon as in Fig. 18-1.

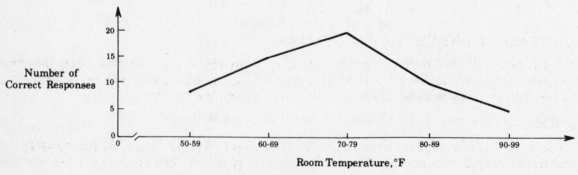

Fig. 18-1

Histograms

A *histogram* is a bar graph that represents a frequency distribution.

EXAMPLE 3. The data presented in Example 2 could also be plotted as a histogram, as in Fig. 18-2.

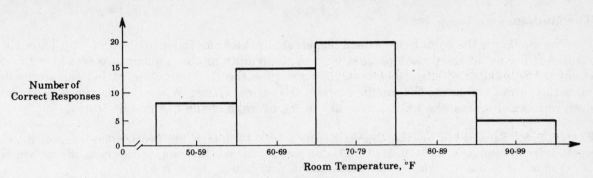

Fig. 18-2

Symmetry and Skew

Some frequency distributions have an equal number of scores (or other data) arranged in similar patterns on either side of the middle of the distribution. Such distributions are called *symmetrical distributions*. When the scores "bunch up" at one end of the distribution, the distribution is called *skewed*. Distributions may be positively skewed or negatively skewed, depending on where the "bunching" occurs. *Positive skew* means that most scores are found at the *lower* end of the measurement scale used; *negative skew* means that the majority of scores are found at the *upper* end (higher values) of the measurement scale.

EXAMPLE 4. The sketches in Fig. 18-3 illustrate distributions that are symmetrical, positively skewed, and negatively skewed. (Note that the "tail" of a skewed distribution is found at the end of the distribution that provides the label.)

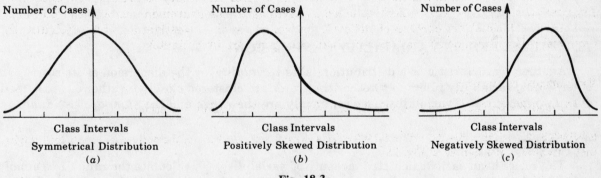

Fig. 18-3

18.5 MEASURES OF CENTRAL TENDENCY

A *measure of central tendency* is a statistical technique in which a single number that best represents a group of numbers is determined. Three different measures of central tendency are commonly used; they are called the *mean*, the *median*, and the *mode*.

The Mean

The *mean* is the average score for a distribution of scores. It is determined by adding up all the scores in the distribution and dividing by the number of scores. The formula for the mean is written as follows:

$$M = \frac{\Sigma X}{N}$$

EXAMPLE 5. Suppose you are given this set of scores: 14, 10, 12, 11, 15, 7, 8. To calculate the mean (M), you would divide the sum of the scores (ΣX) by the number of scores (N), as follows:

$$M = \frac{\Sigma X}{N} = \frac{77}{7} = 11 \; ans.$$

The Median

The *median* is the point below which 50 percent of the items in a distribution fall. Thus, the median is located at the fiftieth percentile of the distribution: the number of scores above it is equal to the number of scores below it. To determine the median one must list the scores in numerical order and locate the middle score in the series. (*Note*: When the distribution has an even number of scores, the median is equal to the average of the two middle scores.)

EXAMPLE 6.   Suppose you are given this set of scores: 10, 8, 17, 4, 11, 8, 12. To determine the median, you would order the scores (4, 8, 8, 10, 11, 12, 17) and identify the middle score. In this case, the median is 10. (You may also want to calculate the mean for this distribution; it, too, is 10.)

EXAMPLE 7.   Suppose another score was added to the distribution given in Example 6 so that the ordered series read as follows: 2, 4, 8, 8, 10, 11, 12, 17. In a distribution with an even number of scores, the median is equal to the average of the two middle scores. Thus, the median for this distribution is the average of 8 and 10, or 9. (You may want to verify that 9 is also the mean for this distribution.)

The Mode

The *mode* is the score that occurs with the greatest frequency within a distribution. The mode is the only one of the three measures of central tendency that may have more than one value.

EXAMPLE 8.   Examine again the distributions used in Examples 6 and 7. The mode for both distributions is 8. However, if one more score of 10 is placed in either distribution, each would become a *bimodal distribution* with modes of 8 and 10. (The reader may want to verify that if a score of 10 is added to the distribution found in Example 6, there is no change in the mean. But when a score of 10 is added to the distribution in Example 7, the mean equals 9 1/9.)

18.6   MEASURES OF VARIABILITY (DISPERSION)

Another characteristic of a distribution is its *variability*, or the dispersion of its scores. In other words, variability refers to whether the scores are clustered closely together or are spread out. Two measures of variability used commonly are the *range* and the *standard deviation*.

The Range

The *range* is an easily calculated measure of variability. To calculate the range, one simply subtracts the value of the lowest score from the value of the highest score. It should be noted that a range may give a misleading impression of a distribution in which all the scores but one are bunched closely together. If this single score's value is very different from the values of the other scores, the range may show great variability in the distribution when in fact there is very little variability.

EXAMPLE 9.   Using the distribution in Example 8, calculation of the range yields a value of 15 (17 − 2). (The reader may also want to determine the value of the range for the distributions given in Examples 5 and 6.)

The Standard Deviation

The *standard deviation* is a more sensitive measure of variability than the range because it takes into consideration every score, rather than just the extreme scores. A basic formula for the standard deviation is as follows:

$$SD = \sqrt{\frac{\Sigma d^2}{N}}$$

EXAMPLE 10. Using the distribution of scores found in Example 6, calculation of the standard deviation would progress as follows:

Score	d (Difference from mean)	d²
17	10 − 17 = −7	49
12	10 − 12 = −2	4
11	10 − 11 = −1	1
10	10 − 10 = 0	0
8	10 − 8 = 2	4
8	10 − 8 = 2	4
4	10 − 4 = 6	36

$\Sigma X = 70$
$N = 7$
$M = 10$

$\Sigma d^2 = 98$

$$SD = \sqrt{\frac{\Sigma d^2}{N}} = \sqrt{\frac{98}{7}} = \sqrt{14} = 3.742 \quad ans.$$

18.7 THE NORMAL PROBABILITY DISTRIBUTION

When many scores are collected and plotted on a graph, they often fall in a nearly symmetrical distribution called the *normal curve*. The normal curve is the graphical representation of the *normal probability distribution*, and an idealized version is shown in Fig. 18-4.

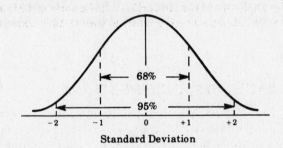

Fig. 18-4

The percentages shown are approximate, but do indicate that about 68 percent of any set of scores (or other numerically valued responses) will fall somewhere between the mean-plus-one standard deviation and the mean-minus-one standard deviation. Furthermore, 95 percent will fall between the plus-two and minus-two standard deviations from the mean.

Percentile Values

The normal curve (Fig. 18-4) can be redrawn to show what percentage of the scores falls between each indicator of deviation from the mean, as in Fig. 18-5.

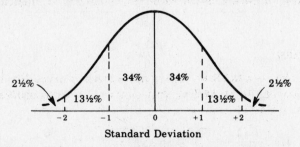

Fig. 18-5

It is then possible to determine the *percentile* values for a given score. For example, the mean score represents the fiftieth percentile (2½ + 13½ + 34 = 50). A score one standard deviation above the mean would be at the eighty-fourth percentile (2½ + 13½ + 34 + 34 = 84). A score one standard deviation below the mean would be at the sixteenth percentile (2½ + 13½ = 16). (More detailed representations of the normal curve can be found in statistics textbooks.)

Use of the Normal Probability Distribution

One of the most common uses of the normal probability distribution is in interpreting scores obtained. If the mean and standard deviation of a distribution are known, a score obtained from one subject can be compared to the distribution.

EXAMPLE 11.   If test results distribute in a normal curve which has a mean of 500 and a standard deviation of 100, a score of 600 is in the eighty-fourth percentile. That is, the subject's performance on the test was better than the scores of 84 percent of the people who took the test. It is also possible to determine from the curve that 95 percent of the subjects who took the test had scores between 300 and 700.

18.8   CORRELATION

Correlation refers to the relationship between two variables. A correlation may be shown graphically by using what is called a *scattergram*, or *scatter diagram*. A coefficient can also be represented numerically by calculating the *coefficient of correlation*. (Two common formulas for calculating correlation were given in Section 18.3.)

EXAMPLE 12.   A scatter diagram such as the one in Fig. 18-6 could be used to plot the results obtained from five subjects who performed both fine manipulation and gross manipulation tasks.

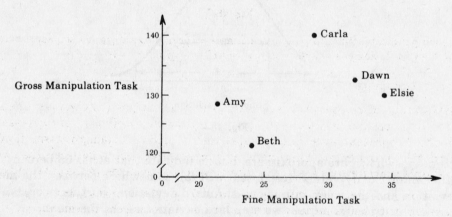

Fig. 18-6

Calculation of the *rank-difference* correlation was conducted in the following manner:

Subject	Fine Manipulation	Gross Manipulation	Rank Fine	Rank Gross	D	D_2
Amy	21	128	5	4	1	1
Beth	24	121	4	5	−1	1
Carla	29	140	3	1	2	4
Dawn	32	133	2	2	0	0
Elsie	34	130	1	3	−2	4

$$\rho = 1 - \frac{6\,(\Sigma D^2)}{N(N^2-1)} = 1 - \frac{6(10)}{5(24)} = 1 - \frac{60}{120} = +.50$$

Numerical Values for Correlation

No matter which formula is used for calculating a coefficient of correlation, the numerical values obtained will range from 0 (no correlation) to +1.00 *or* −1.00. If the correlation is positive (+0.01 to +1.00), the value of one variable increases as the value of the other increases. When the correlation obtained is negative (−0.01 to −1.00), the value of one variable increases as the value of the other decreases. The larger the absolute value of the correlation (regardless of sign), the better the predictions that can be made.

EXAMPLE 13. The scatter diagram shown in Fig. 18-6 and the correlation coefficient obtained in Example 12 both show a positive correlation. In general, the higher the value obtained for the fine manipulation task, the higher the value for the gross manipulation task. A negative correlation would be illustrated by the scatter diagram in Fig. 18-7.

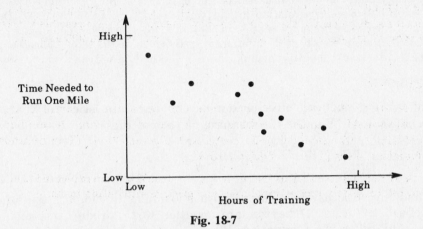

Fig. 18-7

The relationship indicates that the greater the number of hours of training, the shorter the time needed to run one mile. (The correlation coefficient obtained would be approximately −0.67.)

The Concept of Contingency

While the concept of *contingency* has been presented before (in Chapter 12), it deserves mention again. It is possible to calculate a fairly high positive coefficient of correlation (such as +0.75) that does not represent a meaningful relationship. This is because a correlation coefficient does not automatically indicate a contingent, or causal, relationship between the two variables studied. One should therefore use caution in interpreting the meaning of the obtained correlation.

EXAMPLE 14. It would be possible to calculate a correlation coefficient that showed a positive correlation between the ever-increasing height for the world's record in pole vaulting and the ever-increasing number of telephones in service in the United States. The value would be positive, yet the possibility of a contingent (causal) relationship is very small. (The interpretation would have to be that because more telephones were used, the record went higher; or, because the record went higher, more telephones were used. Neither interpretation seems reasonable, and additional investigation would probably reveal other causes for both increases.)

The Concept of Regression

In statistics, the word *regression* refers to the use of a previously obtained correlation and the values of one variable to predict the values of a second variable.

EXAMPLE 15. Insurance companies use the concept of regression to establish their rates. Premiums for automobile insurance vary according to the age and sex of the driver. Previous correlational studies have shown, for example, that male drivers between the ages of 16 and 25 have more accidents than do other drivers. Consequently, the companies will predict that a client who is a male within that age range has a greater likelihood of having an accident than do other drivers. The company will therefore charge a greater premium to insure this particular client.

18.9 SAMPLING

It should be noted that many statistics are calculated using the scores obtained from a sample of the population. Several different techniques for sampling were described in Chapter 2.

Solved Problems

18.1   What role do statistics play in psychology? What is the difference between inferential statistics and descriptive statistics?

Basically, statistics have two uses in psychology: (1) to simplify or summarize data that has been collected; and (2) to describe relationships between one set of data and another. Descriptive statistics basically serve the first purpose; that is, they are used to describe or summarize in a "shorthand" form data that has been collected. Inferential statistics serve the second purpose: they are used to describe relationships between or among various pieces of data and can be used to make predictions.

18.2   The following symbols are often used in psychological statistics: N, X, M or $\overline{X}$, d, Σ, D, r, or ρ, and SD or σ. What is the meaning of each of these?

See the list in Section 18.2 (p. 223).

18.3   In organizing data, psychologists often use formulas to compute the following: (1) the mean of a distribution; (2) the standard deviation; (3) the product-moment correlation; and (4) the rank-difference correlation. What is a formula used to compute each of these four?

See the list in Section 18.3 (p. 224).

18.4   Virginia has made a record of the number of miles walked each week by the thirty women in her dormitory. How might she plot a frequency distribution for this data?

A frequency distribution is simply a record of how many measurable cases or responses occur in each interval of preselected portions (or class intervals) of a measurement scale. In this case, Virginia decided to use class intervals of 5-mile segments. She obtained the following distribution (Fig. 18-8) from the thirty women in her dormitory.

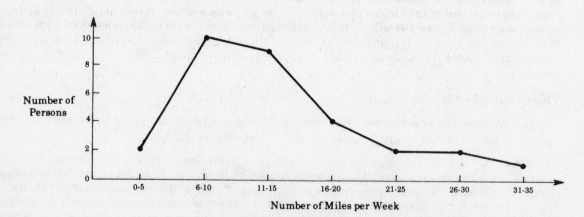

Fig. 18-8

18.5   A plot such as that in the solution to Problem 18.4 (Fig. 18-8) is called a *frequency polygon*. What would the same distribution look like if it were plotted as a histogram?

A histogram is a bar graph. The same distribution plotted as a histogram would look like Fig. 18-9.

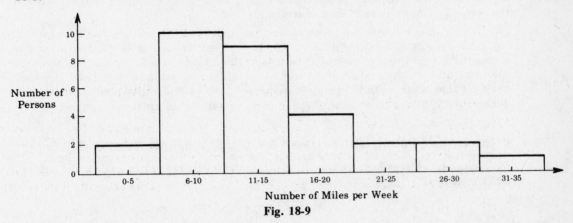

Fig. 18-9

18.6   Bennett decides to plot his golf scores for the previous summer's play. His distribution is shown in Fig. 18-10.

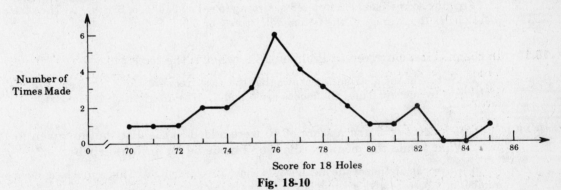

Fig. 18-10

One could characterize the frequency distribution shown in Bennett's frequency polygon by calling it "fairly symmetrical." What is a symmetrical distribution? What is a skewed distribution?

A symmetrical distribution is one in which the scores occur with roughly equal frequency on either side of the middle of the distribution. A skewed distribution is not balanced evenly; that is, more scores "bunch" at one end of the distribution or the other. The greatest number of Bennett's scores occur near the middle of this distribution. At either end, there are fewer scores.

Two different types of skew can occur. When the scores "bunch" toward the lower end of the scale, as in Virginia's distribution in Fig. 18-8, the distribution is said to be positively skewed. If the scores were to "bunch" at the other end, as in Fig. 18-11, the distribution is negatively skewed.

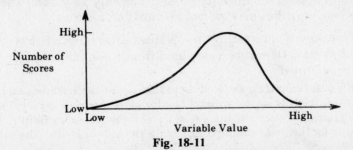

Fig. 18-11

18.7 What is a measure of central tendency? How does the mean represent a measure of central tendency? What are other measures of central tendency that are used fairly commonly?

A measure of central tendency is the number which best represents a group of numbers. (This number is the best prediction of a score that might be made by any one of the people represented by the scores that have already been collected.)

The *mean* is a measure of central tendency that gives the arithmetically calculated average score for the group. (To calculate it, the sum of all the scores is divided by the number of scores.) Other measures of central tendency are: the *median*, which is the fiftieth percentile score in the distribution (with an equal number of scores falling above and below it); and the *mode*, which is the score that occurs with the greatest frequency. (*Note*: There may be more than one mode in a distribution if two or more scores happen to occur with equal greatest frequency.)

18.8 Consider the following set of scores: 6, 10, 3, 5, 9, 5, 6, 4. What is the mean?

The mean (M) can be calculated by dividing the number of scores (N) into the sum of the scores (ΣX), as follows:

$$M = \frac{\Sigma X}{N} = \frac{48}{8} = 6 \quad ans.$$

18.9 In the distribution given in Problem 18.8, what is the median?

First the scores should be ordered according to value: 3, 4, 5, 5, 6, 6, 9, 10. Then the median is identified as the average of the two middle scores, or 5.5.

18.10 In the distribution given in Problem 18.8, what is the mode?

Inspection of the distribution shows that the most frequent scores are 5 and 6, and they occur with equal frequency. Thus, the modes are 5 and 6. (The distribution is bimodal.)

18.11 Suppose a score of 2 and a score of 10 were added to the distribution given in Problem 18.8. What would the mean, median, and mode be for such a distribution?

The new calculation of the mean would show ΣX equal to 60. This would be divided by 10, the number of scores, to give a value of 6.0 for the mean.

The median would remain the same, equalling the average of the two middle scores, 5 and 6. Thus, the median is 5.5.

By adding one more 10 to the distribution, three scores now occur with the same greatest frequency. Thus, the distribution is trimodal, with mode values of 5, 6, and 10.

18.12 Near the end of their senior year in college, two football running backs were in contention for the leading award given to college football players and were being heavily scouted by professional football representatives. One of the interesting considerations at which the scouts looked was the variation in yards gained with each carry. One of the backs went through his entire college career without ever losing a yard on any carry. At worst, he was stopped for no gain, but his longest gain was only 19 yards. The other back once lost 42 yards on one play, but also gained 98 yards on another.

The pro scouts' interest in these values illustrates what type of statistical consideration? What statistic can be calculated from the numbers given in this problem? What values are obtained?

In this case, the scouts are looking at a measure of variability and trying to determine if the scores cluster closely or scatter widely. One measure of variability is called the range, which is equal to the difference between the highest score and the lowest score in a distribution. The range of performance for the first running back is only 19 yards (19 − 0). The range for the second running back is 140 yards [98 − (− 42)].

18.13   Consider the following distribution of scores: 4, 5, 6, 7, 8, 9, 10. What is the value of the standard deviation?

The formula for the standard deviation is as follows:

$$SD = \sqrt{\frac{\Sigma d^2}{N}}$$

N is simply the number of scores in the distribution, or 7. The other variable in the equation, d, must be calculated for each score; (d is the difference between each score and the mean). The mean (M) is calculated as follows:

$$M = \frac{\Sigma X}{N} = \frac{49}{7} = 7$$

Thus, d and d^2 can be calculated for each score, and the squared differences can be summed to get Σd^2:

$X - M$	d	d^2
10 − 7	3	9
9 − 7	2	4
8 − 7	1	1
7 − 7	0	0
6 − 7	−1	1
5 − 7	−2	4
4 − 7	−3	9
		28

The values for M and d can then be substituted in the formula for the standard deviation:

$$SD = \sqrt{\frac{28}{7}} = \sqrt{4} = 2 \quad ans.$$

18.14   Interested in determining how well the speed limits were being observed on a heavily-traveled street, the city police set up a radar checkpoint and measured the speed of hundreds of cars that passed by. When they plotted all the values obtained, they found that the curve obtained closely approximated a normal probability distribution. What was the shape of the curve?

The normal probability curve is a symmetrical distribution, with most cases falling near the middle of the distribution and the "tails" tapering off sharply at the very high or very low scores (or speeds, in this case).

18.15   Repeated investigations have shown that the normal probability curve has certain properties. Suppose the police (Problem 18-14) found that the average speed of cars passing their checkpoint was 35 miles per hour and that the standard deviation had a value of 4. Sketch the curve they obtained, showing the appropriate percentages of the distribution.

The curve obtained would be similar to the one shown in Fig. 18-12.

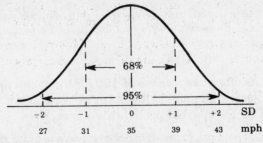

Fig. 18-12

This curve indicates that 68 percent of those cars passing checkpoint were going between 31 and 39 miles per hour and approximately 95 percent were included in the range between 27 and 43 miles per hour. It also can be determined that 2½ percent were going more than 43 miles per hour and another 2½ percent were traveling at less than 27 miles per hour. (These two last groups are in the "tails" of the distribution).

18.16 Another way to look at the normal probability curve is in terms of percentile values. Using the distribution given in Problem 18.15, calculate the value (or speed) at the fiftieth percentile. Also, at what percentile would a speed of 39 miles per hour fall?

It is sometimes convenient to recast the normal probability curve in terms of percentage, as in Fig. 18-13.

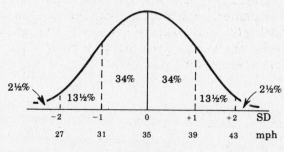

Fig. 18-13

Determination of percentile values can be made by adding percentage values from left to right; thus, the percentile value of 2½ is reached at the −2 standard deviation indicator; the sixteenth percentile is at −1; the fiftieth percentile is at the mean; the eighty-fourth percentile at +1; and the percentile value of 97½ is at the +2 standard deviation mark.

Solving the particular questions of this problem, the value at the fiftieth percentile is the mean value, or 35 miles per hour; and a speed of 39 miles per hour is located at the eighty-fourth percentile. (*Note*: Percentile values at other points on the curve have been determined and can be found by referring to a table of such values in a statistics handbook.)

18.17 Suppose you know that you have a normal probability distribution, with a value for the standard deviation equal to 6 points and a score of 52 at the sixteenth percentile. What is the mean of the distribution?

Using the same type of curve sketched in Problem 18.16, you can determine that the sixteenth percentile value is located one standard deviation below the mean. Therefore, if the score value at that point is 52, you add the value of the standard deviation (6) to determine the value of the mean, 58.

18.18 Using the same values given in Problem 18.17, what percentage of the group studied would fall between scores of 46 and 64?

The score of 46 is two SD units below the mean, while 64 is one SD above the mean. Adding the percentages between these two points, you find that 81½ percent of the group studied falls between these scores.

18.19 Intelligence tests often use a value of 100 for the mean and a value of 15 for the standard deviation. Subjects who score below 70 or above 130 are sometimes referred to as "exceptional." Based on the normal probability curve, does this label seem appropriate?

The subjects who score below 70 or above 130 are quite rare, composing the 5 percent which makes up the two "tails" of the distribution. Thus, the label "exceptional" is probably appropriate.

18.20   Several years ago, a professor at a western university calculated a relationship showing that as the measurements of the beauty queen from each year's pageant had increased, so too had the number of suicides in the professor's home city. What statistical method did the professor use? What caution should be heeded when interpreting this finding?

　　　The professor calculated the *correlation* between the beauty queen's measurements and the number of suicides in his city. The statistic may have suggested a relationship between the two phenomena, but it is necessary to recognize that this may not be an indication of causality, or a contingency relationship. (For example, in this case, causality could mean that the increasing measurements of the beauty queens led to greater numbers of suicides. Such a conclusion seems absurd, and no causality seems to exist here, even though a correlation does exist.)

18.21   Interested in determining how effective a student workbook was in helping students prepare for an examination, one teacher took the time to ask her students how many hours they spent studying the workbook and how much the student thought the workbook helped in preparation for the exam. The teacher then plotted the two graphs shown in Fig. 18-14. What are these graphs called, and what do they show?

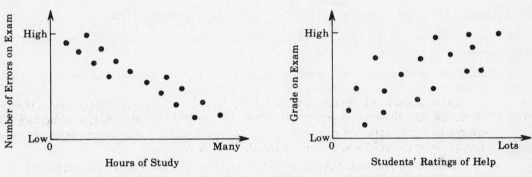

Fig. 18-14

　　　The plots are called *scatter diagrams*, or *scattergrams*. The scatter diagram relating hours of study to the number of errors on the exam shows a negative correlation; that is, the higher the value of one variable, the lower the value of the other. The scatter diagram relating the students' ratings of the workbook's helpfulness to the grade obtained indicates a positive correlation; that is, the higher the value of one variable, the higher the value of the other.

18.22   The values of the correlations determined for the relationships shown in the previous problem (18.21) were found to be −.68 and +.32. Which correlation is the better predictor?

　　　The negative correlation (−.68) would be a better predictor than the positive (+.32). Correlations may have any value from 0 to +1.00 or −1.00. The closer the correlation comes to an *absolute* value of 1.00 (either plus or minus), the more accurate the prediction that can be made from that correlation.

18.23   Suppose the teacher (Problem 18.21) used the information obtained from her scatter diagrams and correlations to make a prediction for the performance of some other class. By determining the number of hours of study each student reported, the teacher predicted the number of errors expected. Such a prediction, based upon knowledge of one variable's value and some previous correlation, illustrates what statistical procedure? Is this a fairly common procedure?

　　　Predictions of this nature illustrate the regression procedure, which is used fairly commonly. For example, admissions counselors correlate college entrance examination scores and the success of previous classes in college. These correlations allow the counselors to make predictions about the probable success of the members of each new class.

18.24 Interested in determining the correlation between the age of entrance into the armed forces and the length of time each person remains in the service, the government hires several psychologists to conduct the study. The psychologists explain they will select persons from each branch of the service to study this question. What is the term used to describe this selection procedure?

The procedure of selecting representative persons is called *sampling*. (There are several different ways of sampling; see Chapter 2.)

Key Terms

Central tendency.   A number that best represents a group of numbers.

Class interval.   Arbitrarily selected portions of a measurement scale; usually equal.

Contingency.   The concept of causality or dependency; indicates that there is a meaningful relationship between two variables.

Correlation.   The tendency of two (or more) variables to vary together (concomitantly); the numerical representation of the relationship between these two variables.

Descriptive statistics.   Measures or techniques that allow a summary portrayal of collected data.

Frequency distribution.   Graphic or tabular representation of the number of cases found in each class interval of a distribution.

Frequency polygon.   A line graph representing a frequency distribution.

Histogram.   A bar graph representing a frequency distribution.

Inferential statistics.   Measures or techniques that allow for the analysis or evaluation of relationships existing within a sample of data or between samples of data; can be used to make predictions.

Mean (M or $\overline{X}$).   The average score in a distribution of scores; calculated by summing all the scores and dividing that sum by the number of scores.

Median.   The middle score in a distribution of scores; the number of scores above and below it are equal, and the score is at the fiftieth percentile.

Mode.   The score that occurs most frequently in a distribution; there may be more than one mode in a distribution.

Negative skew.   When most of the scores of a distribution are found at the upper (higher) end of the measurement scale.

Normal curve.   The graphic representation of the normal probability distribution.

Normal probability distribution.   An idealized distribution based upon data collected from large samples; most scores are at, or near, the mean, with a few scores at the extremes; often used for making statistical inferences.

Percentile.   The point below which falls a given percentage of the total number of scores in a distribution.

Population.   The entire group from which samples may be chosen; *all* of a group.

Positive skew.   When most of the scores of a distribution are found at the lower end of the measurement scale used.

Range.   A measure of variability calculated by determining the difference between the highest and lowest scores in a distribution.

Regression.   Use of the knowledge of a previously obtained correlation and the value of one variable to predict the value of some other variable.

Sample.   A group selected from a population; the attempt should be made to make the sample as representative as possible of the population.

Scattergram.   The pictorial representation of a correlation.

Skew.   When the scores of a distribution occur with greater frequency at one end of the distribution.

Standard deviation (SD or σ).   A measure of variability based upon the differences of each score from the mean.

Statistics.   The discipline that deals with the collection, analysis, interpretation, and presentation of numerical data.

Variability.   The extent to which scores are dispersed in a distribution.

Chapter 19

Personality Principles

An individual's *personality* consists of those enduring attributes that are representative of his or her behavior. These attributes may be acquired because of the person's unique experiences or because of experiences shared with others. The attributes may also result from the influence of heredity, or the interaction of heredity and environment.

Several theories have been proposed to explain the acquisition of personality and to describe personality. After a brief review of the general factors influencing personality, these theories will be discussed.

19.1 GENERAL FACTORS INFLUENCING PERSONALITY

Regardless of the theory proposed to explain personality, two general factors are seen to influence personality development: a person's experiences within the environment and that person's hereditary background.

Environmental Experience

A person's experiences within the surrounding environment may have major effects upon the development of personality characteristics. These experiences may be *unique* to one person only or *common* to many people.

EXAMPLE 1. Imagine a man who lives in a fishing village and works on a fishing boat. The experiences of living in the village can be thought of as shared experiences, common to all the people who lived there. But suppose the man in question once spent several hours alone in the open sea after falling from a boat. In this respect at least, his experience is unique. The experience of being adrift may influence his personality in ways that would differ from the influences of the village experiences, which he shared with other people.

Hereditary Effects

The particular genetic pattern established at the moment of conception influences the personality characteristics a person will develop. In very obvious forms, inherited brain damage or birth defects may have pronounced influence upon the person's behavior. In addition, somatic (bodily) factors such as height, weight, skin coloration, the functioning of sense organs, and the like may affect personality development.

EXAMPLE 2. The sex of an individual is determined at the time of conception. Regardless of interests, both women and men have certain physiological characteristics that are unchangeable and will affect their behavior; for example, women can be impregnated, and men can impregnate; neither sex, however, can exactly duplicate the experiences of the other.

Interaction of Heredity and Environment

Many personality attributes result from the combined effects of heredity and environment. In most cases, it is difficult or impossible to assign percentages of importance to hereditary and environmental influences, but it is easy to see that the two do interact.

EXAMPLE 3. Diet provides a good example of this interaction at the many stages of human development. The mother's diet may affect the uterine environment, and thus influence the expression of the

238

hereditary characteristics in the embryo or fetus. Later, a person's diet may affect his or her weight, and thus personal appearance. This in turn may dispose the person to act in certain ways or lead others to react to the person in a particular manner.

Research on the Relative Effects of Heredity and Environment

Psychologists have attempted to determine the relative effect of heredity and environment in the development of personality. In general, it seems that the closer the relationship of two people, the more likely their personality characteristics will be the same. However, this tendency is affected by environmental circumstances. Thus, identical twins reared together are more likely to show similar patterns than are identical twins reared apart, but even twins reared apart would more likely be similar than would siblings who are not twins.

19.2 FREUD'S MOTIVATIONAL THEORY OF PERSONALITY

The best known theory of personality developed from the work of Sigmund Freud, a Viennese physician. In his theory, Freud put emphasis on the concept of mental illness and the use of psychotherapy to try to help people with problems. (See Chapters 21 and 22 for discussion of abnormal personality patterns and therapies.) A theory of personality emerged from Freud's attempts to develop successful therapy techniques.

The Structure of Personality

Freud believed that personality had three basic components: the id, the ego, and the superego. The personality was motivated throughout life by the fundamental drive called *libido*. Libido provided psychic energy that was devoted to the achievement of goals. Freud emphasized the underlying sexual nature of libido and believed that many of the goals sought for could be described as the seeking of pleasure.

The id. According to Freud, the *id* is the most primitive or instinctive part of personality. The id operates according to the *pleasure principle,* that is, seeking pleasure and avoiding pain regardless of societal beliefs or restraints. This means actions generated predominantly by the id are likely to be unsuppressed or restricted. (The behavior of young children often shows id control.)

The ego. In Freud's approach to personality, the *ego* is the problem-solving part of personality, which operates according to the *reality principle.* The ego seeks pleasure and avoids pain in rational ways that society approves. The ego thus seems to take the demands of the id and determines how to satisfy them in an acceptable manner.

The superego. The third component of personality, according to Freud, is the *superego.* The superego reminds the person of what would be ideal behaviors and what behaviors are totally unacceptable. The *conscience* is found in the superego.

EXAMPLE 4. Shopping in a supermarket, Louise, her teenage son, and her one-year-old daughter stop in the aisle beside the fruit display. Each is occupied, so that no one of them is watching the other. The daughter sees an apple, reaches out, picks it up, and begins happily munching; she simply seeks pleasure and satisfies the motive, having no idea she is doing something that might be called wrong. The son spots some grapes, thinks to himself that everybody else "rips off" the store a little, and takes a small handful and starts eating. Louise sees some peaches she would really like to have, but feels they are too expensive. Momentarily, she considers having a few weighed and priced, then putting some more in the bag after the grocery clerk has gone on to his next customer. However, she realizes this would be dishonest and decides to do without the peaches. Louise's actions reflect superego influence, her son seems to have been under ego control, and her daughter was under the control of motivation from the id.

Stages of Development of Personality

Freud proposed that the development of personality advanced through several *psychosexual stages*. In each of these stages, the libidinal energy found a particular focus. If the individual progressed through each stage without serious difficulties, a mature adult expression of libidinal energy could eventually be achieved. However, disturbances in the form of frustration or excessive gratification during one of the stages could lead to *fixation* at that stage, meaning that some of the libidinal energy of the adult would have to be used to satisfy responding appropriate to that stage rather than responding appropriate for an adult. A truly adult pattern of personality reflects the successful completion of each of the stages.

The oral stage.   The first psychosexual stage is called the *oral stage*. Libidinal energy centers around oral activities, particularly feeding and weaning. This stage lasts from birth into the second year of life. Fixation at this stage means that a high level of oral activity may be shown by the adult.

EXAMPLE 5.   Fixation at the oral stage may be represented by activities such as excessive gum-chewing, fingernail biting, talking, or eating. These behaviors are thought to occur because the person either has been satisfied too much during the oral stage or because the person has not had enough satisfaction during the stage.

The anal stage.   The *anal stage* is the second psychosexual stage, where the focus of libidinal energy centers around the external conflicts created for a child who is being toilet trained. The way the parents (or other significant adults) conduct toilet training will affect adult personality characteristics. Fixation at this stage may result in adult difficulties with the giving or withholding of love or approval, with stubbornness, and with conflicts between neatness and sloppiness.

The phallic stage.   In the *phallic stage*, the source of libidinal pleasure is in the genitalia. Characteristic behaviors at this time include exploration of the genitals, infantile masturbation, and interest in the anatomical differences between the sexes. Inability to achieve adult sexuality and responsiveness may result from fixation at this stage.

Freud believed this was the period when what he called the *Oedipal complex* (for boys) and the *Electra complex* (for girls) had to be resolved. Freud proposed that a child has sexual desires for the parent of the opposite sex and feels rivalry with the parent of the same sex. However, fear of punishment causes the child to identify with the parent of the same sex and to adopt similar behaviors. According to Freud, failure to complete this identification process may result in incomplete gender identity, difficulties in authority situations, or homosexuality.

The period of latency.   At the end of the phallic stage (about age 5 or 6), Freud believed the child entered a *latency stage*, when preoccupation with sexual concerns no longer existed. During this period, libidinal energies are reduced dramatically.

Adolescence and adulthood.   With the onset of puberty, a person goes into the final stage of development. At this point, the libidinal energies are rearoused, and the individual attempts to achieve adult sexuality. If there have been difficulties at earlier stages, the giving and receiving of adult (mature) love may be difficult or impossible to achieve.

EXAMPLE 6.   Suppose a person experiences considerable frustrations during the period of toilet training. It is possible that the residual fixations may cause the person to be stingy, stubborn, or extremely fussy. All such characteristics might prevail against the mature expression of giving or receiving love.

Ego Defense Mechanisms

Freud proposed that actions or events that offend the superego and do damage to one's self-image result in anxiety in the ego. To keep this damage and anxiety to a minimum, a person develops and uses *ego defense mechanisms* as a way of protecting the self. Some examples of ego defense mechanisms follow:

Repression.   The first step in all defense mechanisms (and thus the most prevalent of all) is *repression*, when the individual "forgets" anxiety-producing memories or keeps unacceptable desires from surfacing in the conscious. Sustained repression requires psychic energy, so if the material repressed is especially anxiety-producing, the individual may devote a great deal of energy to it. This may result in an abnormal personality pattern. (See Chapter 21.)

Rationalization.   A person who acts for a reason that is considered unacceptable may account for that action by claiming it was done for some other, acceptable reason. A person who behaves in this way is showing *rationalization*, the most commonly used defense mechanism after repression.

EXAMPLE 7.   Rationalization is sometimes demonstrated when a person who reads a pornographic magazine claims that he or she is reading it because of its "great literary content." Comparably, one person who crushingly defeats another in a game of tennis may claim to have done so in order to teach the loser to cope with defeat, when in fact the winner may have done so in order to increase his or her own sense of power.

Projection.   People who attribute their own unacceptable feelings to others are demonstrating *projection*. Projection may allow the person to express sentiments or beliefs that would produce anxiety if they were accepted as his or her own.

Displacement.   *Displacement* occurs when aggressive reactions are directed toward some "innocent" stimulus rather than the one actually producing anger. This is done because direct attack upon the hostility-producing stimulus is viewed as too stressful, and yet relief is desired.

Regression.   A person who adopts an attitude that is appropriate to a younger age level may be showing *regression*. Adopting a more childlike attitude may allow the person to avoid responsibilities and yet not "lose face."

EXAMPLE 8.   Older children often resort to "baby talk" following the birth of another child in their family. Direct attack toward the new baby would be inappropriate, but the regressive behavior may attract the parents' attention and thus help the older children maintain their feelings of self-worth.

Compensation.   Someone who feels deficient in some way may defend himself or herself by emphasizing some behavior that "covers up" the deficiency. This is called *compensation*, and it may take two forms. Using *direct compensation*, the person will emphasize behaviors that are specifically meant to be reactions to the felt deficiencies. Using *indirect compensation*, the person will stress behaviors that are not associated with the felt deficiency, but are rather substitutes.

19.3   OTHER MOTIVATIONAL THEORIES OF PERSONALITY

Freud was the first person to popularize what have been described as motivational theories of personality, but several other theories were developed by his associates or psychologists who came later. The theories of Jung, Alder, and Erikson serve as examples of these other motivational approaches.

Carl Jung's Theory

Carl Jung accepted many of Freud's explanations of personality, but differed with him on several important aspects. In comparison to Freud, Jung placed more emphasis on current events rather than childhood experiences and on social motives rather than sexual drives. Jung also proposed a quite different conception of the unconscious, suggesting that there were (1) the *personal unconscious*, similar to the unconscious proposed by Freud because it contained memories and repressed desires; and (2) the *collective unconscious*, which contained personality characteristics inherited from ancestors. This latter kind of unconscious carried traits that had developed over many generations to become typical of all people within a culture.

Alfred Adler's Theory

Alfred Adler also stressed social motivation rather than sexual drives. For Adler, the key to personality was a striving for superiority. Adler felt the person would recognize deficiencies, feel inferior, and then work to compensate for this inferiority. He also recognized that, unfortunately, society sometimes reinforces these felt deficiencies. Adler believed that when this happened, the person might develop an *inferiority complex*.

One other aspect of inferiority was that it might be *real*—that is, an actually-existing deficiency—or *imagined*—a felt deficiency that really does not exist. Either type of inferiority may motivate the person to try to compensate and seek superiority.

Erik Erikson's Theory

Erik Erikson tried to combine the Freud's emphasis on sexual drives with the emphasis on social motives stressed by other theorists. The result was an eight-stage theory characterized by a *crisis* that had to be resolved at each stage. The stages, along with the crises faced are as follows:

Oral-sensory stage: trust versus mistrust

Muscular-anal stage: autonomy versus doubt

Locomotor-genital stage: initiative versus guilt

Latency stage: industry versus inferiority

Puberty and adolescence: identity versus role confusion

Early adulthood: intimacy versus isolation

Young and middle adulthood: generativity versus self-absorption

Mature adulthood: integrity versus despair

In each crisis, the successful resolution of conflict will affect the ultimate psychological activity.

EXAMPLE 9. In Erikson's second stage, the child may have the opportunity to use and control musculature. If these attempts are successful, the child develops a sense of independence, adequacy, and self-control. However, if the attempts are limited or labeled as failures, a sense of inadequacy and lack of autonomy may develop. The feeling that develops then carries over to affect later psychological development.

19.4   TYPE AND TRAIT THEORIES OF PERSONALITY

Type theories of personality attempt to classify a person in a single *category* defined by one or more characteristics. Type theories began two thousand years ago and persist to the present day despite the realization by many psychologists that a single label cannot adequately describe a person's personality. A relatively modern version of a type theory was developed by Carl Jung. Jung proposed that there was a continuum of *introversion-extroversion* on which every person could be evaluated.

EXAMPLE 10. Extroversion, indicating how "outgoing" an individual is, depends a good deal on the environment in which the person is found. An extrovert in a monastery might be judged quite introverted by members of an acting company.

Trait theories try to categorize the personality on the basis of several observed behavioral characteristics. The decision regarding which characteristics to use in trait theories is often made on the basis of statistical analyses.

Factor Analysis

The statistical technique of *factor analysis* is frequently used to determine which characteristics best describe personality. Factor analysis reveals the correlations between various test items and allows common factors or traits to be determined. However, selection of the original items (perhaps questions or adjectives to be checked) is crucial, because the resulting factors identified will depend upon the material used. (See Problem 19.20.)

Body-Type Theory

One proposal that attempted to describe personality is known as the *body-type theory*. Individuals are classified in terms of their body types and personality characteristics. The three basic body types and their associated personality traits are as follows:

Endomorphy: a soft, fat body; and *visceratonia*: a cheerful personality desiring peaceful surroundings and acceptance by others.

Mesomorphy: a muscular and tough body; and *somatotonia*: a combative, straightforward personality.

Ectomorphy: a slim, frail body; and *cerebrotonia*: the restrained personality of an individual interested in academic pursuits.

19.5 LEARNING THEORIES OF PERSONALITY

Many psychologists attribute the acquisition of personality characteristics to learning. These psychologists have shown how classical conditioning (Chapter 11), instrumental conditioning (Chapter 12), and modeling (Chapter 13) may all be important in this acquisition.

Social Behavior Theory

Examples of the learning approach to personality are often classified as *social behavior theories*. The basic beliefs of such theories are that social behaviors are learned in the same manners as any other kinds of responses, that differentiation of social behaviors is learned according to the environmental circumstances that are present, and that these learned characteristics can be observed in everyday living.

Family and Peer Influence

In studying the effects of social behavior on the development of personality characteristics, psychologists have focussed attention on two major areas: the influence of the *family* and the influence of *peers*. General findings indicate that both sources are very important in disposing the person toward certain patterns of response. Furthermore, it seems that peer influences become relatively more and more important as a child grows older.

Conflict of Influences

Contradictory patterns of responding may be observed by a person, thus bringing different aspects of the personality into conflict. Resolution of such conflicts follows the same principles as in other conflict situations, with the strongest motive dominating the choice. (See Chapter 9.)

EXAMPLE 11.   While waiting in the check-out line of a discount store, Laverne sees one of her best girlfriends take a book from a boy's briefcase and slip it into her backpack. Laverne realizes her friend is stealing the book, but wonders whether or not to tell the boy about it. Her difficulty in deciding reflects the fact that she has learned that stealing is illegal and immoral, but she also has learned that one doesn't "tell on" good friends. When she chooses to say nothing, her inaction reflects the relative importance of the two values.

19.6 HUMANISTIC THEORIES OF PERSONALITY

Humanistic theories of psychology put emphasis on studying the whole human being and helping humans try to achieve their fullest potential. Subjective experience is considered as important as objective reports, and the unusual or exceptional is studied as well as the general or usual.

Rogers's Self Theory

Carl Rogers, a leading proponent of humanistic psychology, has developed a *self theory*, which stresses that the basis of personality is the human's wish to realize potentialities. Full realization would mean that individuals would be living in perfect accord with themselves and others. But full realization of potentials is dependent upon the atmosphere in which one grows up. Rogers would hope this atmosphere would reflect an attitude of *unconditional positive regard*, where individuals are valued, respected, and loved simply for what they are. Unfortunately, Rogers has found that most people seem to be raised in an atmosphere of *conditional positive regard*, where approval and respect are given for some, but not all, parts of behavior.

EXAMPLE 12. Conditional positive regard is shown when a parent claims on the one hand to love a child, but at the same time complains about that child's performance in school, making unpleasant remarks and perhaps even threats. The parent who is able to love the child and accept the child's abilities regarding school performance is showing unconditional positive regard, at least in this one situation.

According to Rogers, personality maladjustment occurs when a difference develops between a person's self-image and the reality of a situation. When a person is unable to incorporate new experiences into his or her self-image, anxiety may result and lead to the development of defenses against seeing the truth of the situation. Rogers would hope the person would have a more flexible self and be able to adjust to situations as they occur, thus avoiding personality maladjustment.

19.7 RESEARCH IN PERSONALITY

While it is beyond the scope of this outline to discuss research studies in detail, it is worth mentioning that study of personality is not all theorizing—it does include research studies as well. Information is gathered from clinical case histories, naturalistic observations, and laboratory experiments involving both humans and animals.

Solved Problems

19.1 During the years he was in junior high school, Manuel had a blood disease that kept him at home much of the time. The doctor told him to remain quiet, but Manuel was bored doing nothing and began sewing to fill his hours. When his classmates learned of his sewing abilities, many laughed and teased him about his "sissy" interests. However, when they saw the clothes Manuel made, they realized he was quite talented.

As an adult, Manuel became a respected fashion designer. When interviewed about his development, he described this junior high school period and attributed many of his personality characteristics to that time. Explain how this period provided both common and unique experiences that helped form Manuel's personality.

Common experiences are those shared by all the members of a culture or subculture. In Manuel's case, the attitudes toward sex roles apparently included the belief that males should not pursue sewing, which was labelled a "sissy" interest. However, another aspect of this same culture was to admire talent and creativity. Manuel's disease represented a unique experience, not generally shared by others in the culture or subculture. It created the circumstances that led to the time-filling task of sewing, which in turn led to development of an interest.

19.2 Bonnie and Becky were identical twins who, because of family difficulties, were raised in separate households. By chance, as adults, they happened to meet and were amazed by their similarities and their differences. They decided to attend a "twin convention."

While at the convention, Bonnie and Becky were able to compare their similarities and differences to those of other pairs of twins. Based upon past research findings how should

Bonnie and Becky probably compare to identical twins reared together and to fraternal twins?

Using research findings as a basis for prediction, the general expectation would be that Bonnie and Becky would show more differences than identical twins reared together, but more similarities than fraternal twins. The particular similarities and differences would depend upon the interaction of the characteristics they had inherited and the environments in which they were raised.

19.3   With the family gathered for Thanksgiving dinner, the grandparents are thrilled to have Christi, age 15 months sitting in her highchair right beside the table. As the meal progresses, there is a moment when the conversation pauses and, just at that moment Christi burps. The family is at first somewhat surprised, but then laughs and goes on with the meal. According to Freud's theory, Christi's behavior was a result of control by which part of the personality?

Christi's behavior was apparently controlled by the id. In general, behaviors under control of the id operate according to the pleasure principle, that is, seeking pleasure and avoiding pain, regardless of social sanctions. Loud burping is not considered socially acceptable in adults, but Christi had not yet learned this and could not be expected to learn it for a while.

19.4   Later, the grandfather in Problem 19.3 finds himself with the same need to burp, but does so in a muffled, polite manner. Using Freud's theory, explain the difference between the grandfather's response and Christi's response.

The grandfather, having long since learned what is socially approved or disapproved, muffles his burp so as to be polite. His behavior shows control by the ego part of the personality, operating according to the reality principle, which means seeking pleasure and avoiding pain according to what society accepts. The difference between grandfather's behavior and Christi's is in acting according to learned societal standards.

19.5   While working on his income tax return, Peter realizes that he has an opportunity to "hide" some income and not pay taxes on it. He considers what others in his society might do, but finally decides such behavior simply is not right. He declares the money and pays the taxes. According to Freudian theory, which part of the personality structure probably was operating when Peter made his decision?

It appears that Peter has made his decision according to the ideal standards he has learned, or perhaps the desire to not feel guilty if he did cheat. Such a decision is a function of the superego, which, according to Freud, houses the ideal standards and the conscience.

19.6   The pleasure-seeking drive was given a particular label by Freud. What was it? What were the general properties of this pleasure-seeking drive?

The pleasure-seeking drive was called *libido* by Freud, who believed it was a fundamental drive that motivated each person from birth until death. The essential feature of libido was that it had a sexual quality which, because of societal restrictions, could not be expressed directly. Instead, the libido had to find release in substitute or indirect fashions. These expressions begin in the first year of life, but change radically as the child matures and passes through what Freud called the psychosexual stages.

19.7   Not too many years ago, a famous actor had to undergo surgery for lung cancer. In the publicity releases at that time it was revealed the actor had been smoking five packs of cigarettes each day. How might Freud have explained this extremely heavy smoking?

Freud proposed that disturbances during childhood psychosexual stages could tie up libidinal energy so that as an adult the individual is fixated at a particular psychosexual stage. A fixated adult might then show behaviors appropriate to the childhood stage rather than mature or adult behaviors. In this case, the proposal would be that the actor was fixated at the oral stage, which occurs in the first two years, and expressed this with the very heavy smoking pattern.

19.8 Following the oral stage, Freud proposed two more childhood psychosexual stages. What were these called? What was the center for libidinal expression in each? What followed these stages?

After the oral stage, the two remaining childhood psychosexual stages were called the anal stage and the phallic stage. In the anal stage, pleasure resulting from excretion or retention of feces was the dominant characteristic. The phallic stage was characterized by libidinal expression generated by excitation of the genital areas. Freud proposed that a period of latency, or a quiet period for libidinal energies, followed the three childhood stages.

19.9 Is it possible that fixation at one of the childhood psychosexual stages will limit adult expression of libidinal energy?

Freud proposed that libidinal energy was "reawakened" with the onset of puberty. If the individual had progressed through the initial stages without significant disturbances, it was expected that mature, adult expression of libidinal energy could be achieved. However, fixation at one of the earlier stages would mean that some of the libidinal energy would be drained off to satisfy the fixation, thus leaving the individual with incomplete adult relationships.

19.10 Mr. Brewster had a bad day. The alarm clock didn't go off, he was late for work, and his boss yelled at him during the day. Later, he came out of his office to find that someone had hit and damaged his car but left no note or identification.

As Brewster pulled his car into the driveway that night, the family dog, Rex, ran to greet him. When Mr. Brewster stepped out of the car, he kicked the dog. His son Gerald happened to see this and ran toward his father saying, "Daddy, why did you *kick* Rex?" Mr. Brewster's response was, "He tried to bite me." He then turned and went into the house. In terms of the ego defense mechanisms proposed by Freud, what explanation might be given for Mr. Brewster's actions?

It is likely that Mr. Brewster built up considerable aggressive tendencies during his bad day, but really had no opportunity to release them. When he arrived home, Rex just happened to provide a good target, and Mr. Brewster illustrated *displacement*. That is, he released aggression toward an innocent object rather than the hostility-provoking stimulus.

When his son asked him about why he did this, Mr. Brewster responded with a second ego defense mechanism, *rationalization*. That is, he behaved as he did because of one motive, but attributed his behavior to another.

19.11 A psychologist finds that a new client presents a very strong "I'm fine!" attitude but sees problems in the behaviors of many others around her. For example, although she professes having no particular personal difficulties herself, she indicates that she and her father don't get along because "he's always angry at me." What kind of ego defense mechanism is this person probably using?

These responses may indicate *projection*, or seeing in others the motives which dominate the self. In this case, the woman may feel quite hostile toward her father but feel it is inappropriate to admit this. However, she finds she can talk about anger by projecting it onto the behavior of others, thus protecting her self image while still satisfying her need to discuss the topic.

19.12   Some adults discussing politics at a party begin to argue.   Finally, one of the group turns to Phyllis and asks, "How do you feel about that?" Phyllis responds by giggling and saying, "Oh, you don't want to ask that of a little girl like me!" The others in the group laugh and then pick up the discussion once more.   Phyllis continues to smile, but does not participate. Her response to the direct question may be an indication of which ego defense mechanism?

Phyllis's need to protect her self-image may have led her to show a form of *regression*, or the adoption of a childlike attitude.   Unable to answer the question and unwilling to admit it, the giggle and remark allowed her to escape from a possible confrontation or disagreement.

19.13   Two young men are the "weaklings of the beach." One of them joins a health studio, exercises religiously, and shows considerable success in muscle building, which he then shows off by strutting along the beach.   The other spends much less time at the beach and more and more time studying, eventually gaining a reputation for being very bright.   Both of these young men have illustrated an ego defense mechanism, although in different manners.   What is this mechanism? What are the two different expressions of that mechanism shown here?

Both men illustrate the ego defense mechanism of *compensation*, the overemphasis of a behavior to cover up felt deficiencies in some area.   The first young man shows *direct compensation* by his vigorous exercise ritual, while the second shows *indirect compensation* by selecting and pursuing a substitute goal.

19.14   In some people, a conflict may be so painful or anxiety-producing that it may be blocked entirely from conscious memory.   What did Freud call this? What may result?

Freud called this blocking from conscious memory, or motivated forgetting, *repression*.   A repressed conflict may persist, providing motivation from the unconscious and causing an individual to respond to it even though the source of motivation is not recognized at a conscious level.

19.15   Sitting on the porch one day, two mothers watched their children playing in the backyard.   The children's game involved a good deal of "make-believe" fighting, shooting, and falling down.   One of the women turned to the other and commented, "I certainly wish they wouldn't play those awful shooting games."

The second woman responded, "Well, it's not fun to watch, but I really think that's just part of growing up.   I think all children in every generation must play like that at some time." How would someone who had studied Jung's theories interpret this latter remark?

Jung expanded upon Freud's idea of the unconscious, dividing it into a personal unconscious (based upon one's own experiences) and the collective unconscious (which consisted of primitive experiences shared throughout history).   The second woman's remark would seem to show a belief that this collective unconscious might exist and serve as the motivational source for the aggressive games shown by each succeeding generation.

19.16   Although others respected his skills and felt he was a very good speaker, Carl did not think so.   He therefore enrolled in special speech-training classes, where he worked diligently to overcome what he felt were his shortcomings.   How might Alfred Adler interpret Carl's behavior?

One of Adler's major concepts was to put emphasis on the social factors in personality development.   A second important topic was the inferiority an individual might feel, either real or imagined.

In this case, Carl apparently has imagined his inferiority in speaking, but this has served as a motivation to make him seek special training.   Adler would interpret this as a compensation performed to try to overcome the perceived inferiority and satisfy Carl's striving for superiority.

19.17   Leonard, an adolescent, has taken on the role of "class clown," pulling practical jokes, tormenting people, and acting absurd in an attempt to get attention. If Erikson were analyzing these behaviors, what interpretation might he give?

Erikson's neo-Freudian psychoanalytic theory put emphasis on a sequence of crises which the individual must face and resolve. In Leonard's situation, the crisis is between identity versus role confusion. Apparently unable to resolve the identity crisis, Leonard has become confused and adopted a "negative" identity. Ultimate psychological functioning, according to Erikson, depends upon how well the person is able to resolve the conflicts at eight different specified stages.

19.18   In casual conversation, Joanne described Alice as "the most honest person I've ever met." A friend responded by saying, "Well, is that all? Isn't she anything but honest?" Joanne's reply was, "Well, that's really her distinctive characteristic." This conversation presents two different ways of trying to describe a personality. What are they? How are they alike and how do they differ?

Joanne's description best fits what is called a *type theory*. Her friend's approach is more like what is called a trait theory. Her concern is that several characteristics must be used to give an adequate description of a person's personality.

Both approaches are alike in that they try to describe personalities according to behaviors. (This differs from the emphasis on motives shown by the motivational theories.) They differ because a type theory proposes a singular explanation or description for personality, while a trait theory proposes several or many characteristics for describing personality.

19.19   Some individuals believe that fat people are jolly. What theory of personality does such a belief suggest?

Such a belief suggests a "body-type" theory of personality. The fat person (called an *endomorph*) is supposed to be cheerful and seek comfort and social approval. The endomorph's behaviors are described as the temperament of *visceratonia*. In such a theory, other body types are often linked with other personality traits. The *mesomorph*, a hard, well-muscled person, shows the temperament of *somatotonia*—aggressive, energetic, and direct. The *ectomorph* is tall, slender, and fragile or delicate. The temperament of the ectomorph is called *cerebrotonia,* with characteristics of withdrawal, inhibitions, and intellectualism.

19.20   As a class exercise, Dr. Lindquist had all his students respond to an adjective list by rating items they thought were descriptive of themselves. The complete lists were then turned in anonymously. Dr. Lindquist then used these response sheets to show the students how a factor analysis could be conducted. What did he say?

Dr. Lindquist's description of factor analysis showed the class two basic principles. First, the analysis was based upon correlations between items within the test. That is, if the students rated one item high did they also rate another, similar item high? And if they did not rate the first high, did they also not give a high rating to the second? When such correlational checks are completed, common factors or traits can be identified.

Secondly, a factor analysis is only as complete as the items put into it. For example, if Dr. Lindquist purposely left out all adjectives which related to being extroverted, he could have shown the class that the factor analysis totally missed that possible personality characteristic.

19.21   Social behavior theory emphasizes that personality characteristics are learned in the same manners as other learned responses. Using the family setting as a reference, give examples of how personality characteristics may be acquired through classical conditioning, instrumental conditioning, and learning through modeling.

Classical conditioning of a personality characteristic is easily demonstrated by describing acquisition of a phobia. For example, if the parents pair an originally neutral stimulus such as lightning with anxiety and fear-producing stimuli, the child may come to have intense, compelling fear of lightning. Instrumental conditioning may be shown by learning good manners. If the child makes an appropriate response, such as by saying "Please" or "Thank you," the parents may reward the child with praise. Thus, the good manners serve as instrumental responses leading to desired goals and become part of the behavioral repertoire. Modeling may also lead to the development of personality characteristics. For example, if the child observes the parent acting in an aggressive manner, the child may copy such behavior, especially if the parent seems to be reinforced for acting in this manner.

19.22 Parents are clearly an important influence on their children because they act as model and provide reinforcement. There is, however, another important source of influence on children. What is this source? How important is it?

    The other major source of reinforcement and models is the peer group. Studies have shown that as a child grows older, peer-group influence becomes more and more important. Peer-group and family influences seem most important when compared with other possible sources.

19.23 A fairly typical social problem might be represented by the student who is asked to join some friends in smoking marijuana. One set of values indicates that such behavior is inappropriate, unlawful, and not part of the family standards. A second set shows that smoking marijuana is acceptable and part of the peer-group standards. How might a student respond in this situation?

    Your answer to the question in this problem probably reveals what you believe is a reasonable solution to the problem or what you think the student would do, even if you do not think that response is correct. But the essential point of this is that the student is in a *conflict* and has to resolve that conflict. The development of personality characteristics may result from resolution of such conflicts, and the person may be described according to the choices which he or she makes. (Choices in conflict situations are usually made according to the principles outlined in Chapter 9.)

19.24 In a family where all the male members have been doctors and lawyers for several generations, Alan has decided he wants to become a forest ranger. Although his family claims to love him, they express great disappointment and disapproval with Alan's choice. Using the terminology developed by Carl Rogers, describe the attitude shown by Alan's family.

    Carl Rogers has distinguished between *unconditional* positive regard and *conditional* positive regard. The former means that all of an individual's actions will be respected and accepted, while the latter means that the response to some of the individual's actions will be warm and valued, but other actions will be disapproved. Alan's family represents this latter case. They love Alan, but disapprove of his choice of career. Rogers believed that an atmosphere of unconditional positive regard is necessary for a person to fully realize his or her potentialities. Thus, in this situation, Rogers might say that it would not be possible for Alan to fully realize his potentialities.

19.25 Margie is experiencing a conflict between what she feels is her self-image and criticisms her father is leveling at her. She believes she loves her parents, yet because of her father's attitude toward her style of dress, she is experiencing many feelings of hostility. According to Rogers, what are the two courses of action Margie may adopt as a result of this situation?

    Rogers proposed that the individual may either incorporate new experiences into an ever-changing and flexible view of self or perceive feelings as a threat to self-image, deny the feelings, and create a gap between reality and self-image. Margie either may recognize her feelings of hostility, admit them, and adjust her self-image to include such feelings, or she may deny the feelings and, according to Rogers, become maladjusted because of the discrepancy between her self-image and the reality of the situation. Rogers would prefer the first choice, believing that well-adjusted people are able to have an ever-changing self.

19.26   As a student in a class called The Psychology of Personality, Harland approaches the end of the quarter with some serious misgivings. His feeling is that study of personality has been primarily theoretical, and he finally asks his instructor if anyone has researched some of these ideas in an attempt to gather empirical evidence to support the theories. What response does Harland's instructor give?

  The instructor tells Harland that information leading to the development and support of personality theories has come from a number of sources. Some of it came from clinical case histories, some from naturalistic observations, and some from experimental studies. In the last category, there are many different examples, including studies such as Harlow's "surrogate mother" research using monkeys as subjects, Bandura's investigations of the modeling of aggressive behavior, or Bowlby's studies of separation anxiety. Harland finds out that there are many important sources for theorizing about personality.

Key Terms

Anal stage.   In Freud's theory of personality, the period when libidinal energy is expended to satisfy the conflicts created by being toilet-trained.

Body-type theory.   An attempt to predict personality by identifying the shape of the body and the characteristics that supposedly accompany that shape.

Cerebrotonia.   The personality accompanying ectomorphy; a quiet person interested in scholastic pursuits.

Collective unconscious.   In Jung's theory of personality, the part of personality that holds behavioral characteristics inherited from ancestors.

Compensation.   Emphasizing a behavior to account for or cover up some perceived deficiency.

Conscience.   In Freud's theory of personality, the part of the superego that reminds the person of what is *not* acceptable behavior.

Displacement.   Directing aggressive tendencies toward an innocent object rather than the one that produced the aggressive feeling.

Ectomorphy.   The body type describing a thin, fragile person.

Ego.   In Freud's theory of personality, the problem-solving part of personality, which operates according to the reality principle.

Ego defense mechanisms.   Actions or techniques that allow an individual to protect the self-image or cope with anxiety.

Endomorphy.   The body type describing the soft, rotund person.

Factor analysis.   A statistical technique involving the use of correlations to determine common factors or traits.

Fixation.   In Freud's theory of personality, the carry-over of effect from one of the psychosexual stages to the adult personality, so that the adult's libidinal energy must in part be expended to satisfy motives appropriate to the earlier stage.

Humanism.   An emphasis on positive, constructive human capacities; the basis for humanistic psychology.

Id.   In Freud's theory of personality, the most primitive or instinctive part of personality, operating according to the pleasure principle.

Inferiority complex.   From Adler's theory of personality, the concept that a person may experience feelings of deficiency and be reinforced in such a belief by others in society.

Introversion-extroversion.   Proposed by Jung, the continuum representing how responsive an individual is to stimuli within or outside of the self.

Latency stage.   In Freud's theory of personality, the period extending from the end of the phallic stage to the onset of puberty; during this period, libidinal energies are quiet.

Libido.   In Freud's theory of personality, the fundamental drive that provides psychic energy; has a basically sexual nature.

Mesomorphy.   The body type describing the muscular, rugged person.

Oedipal complex.   In Freud's theory of personality, when the child has sexual desire for the opposite-sex parent and rivalry with the same-sex parent; successful resolution occurs when the child identifies with the same-sex parent.

Oral stage.   In Freud's theory of personality, the period from birth into the second year of life, when libidinal energy is expended primarily to satisfy mouth-oriented activity.

Personal unconscious.   In Jung's theory of personality, the part of personality that holds memories and repressed desires.

Personality.   Those enduring characteristics that are representative of a person's behavior; they may be developed from unique or common experiences and the effects of environmental and hereditary influences.

Phallic stage.   In Freud's theory of personality, the period when libidinal energy centers in the genitalia; the period of the Oedipal complex.

Pleasure principle.   In Freud's theory of personality, seeking pleasure and avoiding pain regardless of social dictates; a property of the id.

Positive regard.   In Roger's theory of personality, the concept of acceptance by others; may be unconditional (unrestricted) or conditional (restricted).

Projection.   Attributing one's own unacceptable motives to others; seeing in others the motives which dominate the self.

Psychosexual stages.   In Freud's theory of personality, a series of phases in the development of personality.

Rationalization.   Acting because of one unacceptable motive while crediting that action to some acceptable motive.

Reality principle.   In Freud's theory of personality, seeking pleasure and avoiding pain in socially acceptable manners; a property of the ego.

Regression.   Acting in a manner appropriate to someone of a younger age.

Repression.   The use of psychic energy to keep anxiety-producing memories from conscious recognition; motivated forgetting.

Self theory.   A theory of personality based upon the human's desire to achieve complete realization of potentials.

Somatotonia.   The personality accompanying mesomorphy; an aggressive, direct person.

Superego.   In Freud's theory of personality, the part of the personality concerned with ideal behavior and what is not acceptable behavior (ego ideal and conscience).

Trait theory.   An attempt to categorize personality using the presence or absence of *several* characteristics.

Type theory.   An attempt to categorize personality by the presence or absence of *one* characteristic.

Visceratonia.   The personality accompanying endomorphy; a cheerful person seeking a passive, accepting environment.

Chapter 20

Intelligence and Creativity

The first standard measurements of intelligence were developed in Paris in the early 1900s by Alfred Binet, who was interested in predicting the academic success of school-children. Binet's test was later revised by Lewis Terman, of Stanford University, for use with children in the United States, and was released in 1916 as the Stanford-Binet Intelligence Test. A revised form of this test is still in use today.

20.1 DEFINITION OF INTELLIGENCE

Since 1916, a number of different tests of intelligence have been created, but no single definition of intelligence has gained dominance in the field. (Intelligence has been simply called that which intelligence tests measure.) Other definitions suggest that intelligence is composed of lasting personal characteristics that allow problem-solving; another definition explains intelligence as the combination of a person's inherited potential and measured performance.

20.2 MENTAL AGE

The Stanford-Binet test makes use of the concept of *mental age* (MA). If passed, each subtest in the Stanford-Binet test is worth two months' credit, with six subtests specified for each year level. The highest age at which *all* six subtests are passed is called the *basal age*. The subject is given credit for all years up to that age. The age at which no subtests are passed is called the *ceiling age*. No further testing is conducted once the ceiling age has been reached. Mental age is determined by totaling the number of months' credit accumulated by the subject.

EXAMPLE 1. Paul passes all 6 subtests at the seven-year age level, 5 subtests at age eight, 3 at age nine, 3 at age ten, 1 at age eleven, and none at age twelve. In this testing situation, Paul's basal age is seven, his ceiling age is twelve, and his mental age is nine years: $MA = (7 \times 12) + (12 \times 2) = 108$ months, or 9 years. The value obtained for mental age represents the performance which would be expected from the average person at that age. (See Problem 20.2.)

EXAMPLE 2. If Tina is tested and obtains a mental age of 108 months (9 years), she and Paul have the same mental age, regardless of their actual age. They both can be expected to perform at a level comparable to the average nine-year-old.

20.3 CONCEPT OF INTELLIGENCE QUOTIENT

Because not all subjects achieving the same mental age value on a test were the same age, a ratio was developed to try to express the differences implied by the observed performances. This ratio was called the *intelligence quotient* (IQ) and was equal to the value of the mental age divided by the *chronological* (or actual) *age* (CA) multiplied by 100.

$$IQ = \frac{MA}{CA} \times 100$$

EXAMPLE 3. In the previous examples, both Paul and Tina obtained a mental age value of 9 years (108 months). Paul is 9 years old, while Tina is 6 years, 9 months old. Using these chronological age values, Paul's IQ would be 100 while Tina's IQ is approximately 133. Calculations of these values would be as follows:

$$\text{Paul's IQ} = \frac{9}{9} \text{ or } \frac{108}{108} \times 100 = 100$$

$$\text{Tina's IQ} = \frac{9}{6\frac{3}{4}} \text{ or } \frac{108}{81} \times 100 = 133$$

Distribution of IQ Scores

When a sufficient number of IQ values have been obtained, the distribution of scores will approximate the normal probability curve (see Section 18.7), usually with a mean of 100 and a standard deviation of 15 or 16 points, depending upon the test used. (See Section 20.2.)

EXAMPLE 4. Using the standard deviation value of 16, which is used in the Stanford-Binet test, a person scoring 116 would be in the eighty-fourth percentile when compared to the total population, while the percentile value for someone scoring 68 would be two and one-half. (See Section 18.7 if this example proves difficult.)

Exceptional Subjects

Arbitrarily, those persons who obtain scores which differ from the mean by two or more standard deviations have been designated as *exceptional*. Those two or more standard deviations below the mean often are referred to as *mentally retarded*, while those two or more standard deviations above the mean are called *gifted*.

Mentally retarded. Simply designating a subject as a mental retardate because an obtained IQ value was two or more standard deviations below the mean has not proved to be an adequate description of the subject's capabilities. As a result, subgroups within the category of mental retardation have been developed. These subgroups, along with their IQ cut-off points, are as follows:

70–50: Mildly retarded (educable)

50–35: Moderately retarded (trainable)

35–20: Severely retarded (minimal skills)

20–0: Profoundly retarded (custodial care)

The gifted. The exceptional subjects classified as gifted are not divided into further subgroupings. Some studies have shown that subjects with very high measured intelligence (IQs of 180 or more) may have adjustment difficulties because they are misunderstood by parents or peers. But most research indicates that the gifted, as a group, are better adjusted and healthier than are people of average intelligence.

Ratio versus Deviation IQ

The concept of intelligence quotient was developed on the basis of work with the Stanford-Binet test, in which IQ was defined as a ratio of mental age to chronological age. However difficulties with using this ratio arise as subjects approach adult status: there is no way for the Stanford-Binet test to measure mental age in a way that would take into account the ever-increasing chronological age of a subject.

As a result, David Wechsler proposed the idea of *deviation IQ*, basing the reported IQ value on the normal probability curve. The Wechsler tests of intelligence have a mean IQ value of 100 and a standard deviation of 15. When the subject has completed the test, the administrator determines the obtained IQ by comparing the subject's performance against that of others at the same age and using the normal probability distribution for that age to establish the percentile and IQ score for the subject.

Group versus Individual Tests

As with other psychological tests, intelligence tests can be administered either to individuals or to groups. Individual tests are thought to be more sensitive and are used frequently when subject motivation may be suspect. However, they are more expensive to administer to subjects, require more training of the administrator, and require more time for the collection of data from a larger number of subjects.

Infant Intelligence Tests

A number of measures have been developed to try to assess infants' intelligence. These tests center around the evaluation of perceptual-motor skills such as turning, pointing, or following. Tests at later ages focus more on language skills, which cannot be used when testing infants. The result of this is that, with the exception of the very extreme cases, correlations between scores obtained on infant intelligence tests and later tests of intelligence are generally quite low.

20.4 COMPOSITION OF INTELLIGENCE

The composition (or structure) of intelligence has been described in several different manners. One quite common approach has been statistical analysis, while other proposals have attempted to separate intelligence into habitual and novel forms or to organize it according to developmental stages.

Factor Analysis

The statistical technique most often used to try to determine aspects of intelligence is factor analysis. The study of various problem-solving tasks and their solutions allows psychologists to identify characteristics of intelligence that seem to be correlated.

Thurstone's Factors of Intelligence

L. L. Thurstone used factor analysis to develop seven basic characteristics that appeared to make up intelligence. Thurstone identified seven aspects of intelligence, as follows:

Verbal comprehension: definition and understanding of words

Word fluency: being able to think of words rapidly

Number: being able to do arithmetic problems

Space: being able to understand spatial relationships

Rote memory: being able to memorize and recall

Perceptual: being able to grasp rapidly the similarities, differences, and details of objects or stimuli

Reasoning: being able to understand the principles or concepts necessary for problem-solving

In addition to these factors, it was suggested that there is a general factor (or G factor) that represents some general intelligence linking these separate characteristics.

EXAMPLE 5. In testing the space factor, the subject may be asked to try to find one figure "hidden" within a more complex figure. (See Fig. 20-1, where drawing (a) is "imbedded" in drawing (b).)

Other factor analysis studies led to the proposal that mental abilities could be "clustered" and arranged in a 120-factor model, as proposed by Guilford. No one analysis, however, has gained exclusive favor.

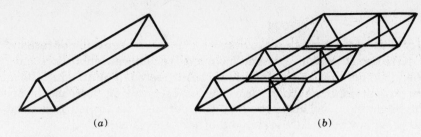

Fig. 20-1

Piaget's Stages of Cognitive Growth

The developmental sequence of cognitive growth proposed by Jean Piaget (discussed in detail in Section 4.5) has been used as an approach to understanding intelligence. The cognitive growth stages suggested are as follows:

Sensori-motor stage (birth to 2 years): understanding of sensations and basic cause-and-effect relationships

Pre-operational stage (2 to 7 years): conceptualization and representation by using language, drawings, or symbolic play

Concrete operational stage (7 to 11 years): logic tied to concrete things; series of ideas

Formal operational stage (11 years and above): use of abstract concepts and formal rules of thought and logic.

It has been proposed that an individual's intelligence can be estimated by comparing the particular characteristics of the person with the sequence proposed by Piaget.

Crystallized versus Fluid Intelligence

In an attempt to describe intelligence some psychologists have distinguished between crystallized and fluid intelligence. *Crystallized intelligence* is observed in the application of what has been learned already; this use of intelligence tends to become habitual or unchanging. *Fluid intelligence* is seen in the ability of a subject to adapt or adjust to new and different situations. Fluid intelligence is thought to be flexible and used when the person is confronted with previously unencountered problems.

EXAMPLE 6. Being able to solve word usage problems, such as fill-in-the-blank definitions would require reliance upon previous learning and thus the use of crystallized intelligence. However, solving anagram problems requires both knowledge and flexibility, and thus fluid intelligence. Completing the sentence "Wearing apparel for a foot is called a _____," requires crystallized intelligence, while recognizing that the letters in the word *shoe* can be found in the word *honest* requires more mental flexibility, or fluid intelligence.

20.5 RELATIONSHIP OF INTELLIGENCE TO OTHER FACTORS

Much research regarding measured intelligence has been devoted to trying to establish the relationships between intelligence and social or cultural or physical variables. Some of these variables are discussed in this section.

IQ and Heredity

Research studies have shown that, in general, the closer the genetic relationship of individuals, the greater the similarity of their measured intelligence. This is comparable to the finding for other personal characteristics such as personality. (See Chapter 19.)

IQ and Age

The stability of measured intelligence over a lifetime has been a major research area. Results of the research have been contradictory and have led to a general conclusion that IQ stability will depend upon the life experience of the individual being tested. For an adult, IQ may rise, remain the same, show a general increase or decrease, or increase or decrease in specific areas only. Changes in IQ seem to be influenced by the person's continued familiarity with testing situations, type of employment, life style, and other experiences.

IQ and Gender

Comparisons of the measured intelligence of males and females have shown that overall IQ values are approximately the same. (Intelligence tests are usually geared to avoid an overall bias favoring one sex or the other.) Studies of subtest results, however, have shown noticeable differences in performance related to sex. In general, females score higher on subtests involving vocabulary skills, perceptual details, and manual dexterity. Males often are found to perform better on mechanical, numerical, and spatial tests.

EXAMPLE 7. Suppose the problems presented in Examples 5 and 6 were used as parts of an intelligence test. As a group, females would probably do better on the anagram (word) task, while males would probably do better on the identification of the "imbedded" figure. (The reader might want to test this simple hypothesis by timing speed of response for both tasks by groups of people from each sex.)

IQ and School Success

Intelligence tests were originally intended to predict how much students would profit from additional academic instruction, and they have suited this purpose better than any other for which they have been used. Predictions are not perfect because of the influence of variables such as motivation, health, family circumstances, and the like, but IQ scores are found to correlate with academic performance in the range of $+0.30$ to $+0.75$.

IQ and Expectations

An interesting facet of the measuring of intelligence or the use of IQ values as predictors is that it is possible that the results may be influenced by the expectations of the user. This unintentional bias may lead to inaccurate representation of the measured intelligence or incorrect interpretation of some other type of performance.

EXAMPLE 8. Robert Rosenthal and his colleagues have studied this expectation effect. In one study, students selected *at random* were mentioned to the teacher as potential "intellectual bloomers." The teacher thus expected that those students would show increased IQ scores at the end of the school year. When intelligence tests were administered at the end of the year, some of these selected students had indeed shown significant gains in measured intelligence as compared to the other (control) students. Rosenthal suggested that the teacher's expectations may have contributed to this increase.

IQ and Occupation

The general findings regarding the relationship between IQ and occupations indicate that persons with higher measured intelligence tend to be found in what are judged to be the higher status or more prestigious jobs. A second aspect of this relationship is that measured intelligence is a fairly good predictor of how well a person will train for a job, but not as good a predictor of how well the person will actually perform on the job after training.

EXAMPLE 9. Research studies in industry have shown that the correlation between measured intelligence and job performance is sometimes very low (below $+0.15$). Some of the jobs for which this type of finding was obtained include pottery decorators, welders, meat-packing workers, and electronic-parts assemblers. In fact, for jobs involving one simple assembly task, IQ and job performance showed a negative correlation.

IQ and Race

As mentioned previously, the closer the genetic relationship of individuals, the greater the similarity of their measured intelligence. One related finding is that IQ scores obtained for black populations have been slightly lower than those obtained for comparable (at least as far as geographical location is concerned) white populations.

This finding has led to a major controversy. One interpretation suggests that the poorer performance of blacks can be attributed to heredity, while a second interpretation is that blacks have had inferior environmental opportunities that have slowed intellectual development. Arguments have been advanced supporting both viewpoints, but the consensus seems to support the environmental explanation of the differences in scores.

IQ and Creativity

Correlations relating IQ to creativity have generally been quite low, indicating little or no relationship between the two variables. It has been suggested that any correlation that does exist may result from variables such as the motivation of the subject.

20.6 CREATIVITY

A *creative act* is one which is novel or original, purposeful, useful or worthwhile, and represents a unique solution to a problem.

Convergent versus Divergent Thinking

Convergent thinking will lead to problem-solving responses that are correct, but considered routine or common. *Divergent thinking* leads to attempts to use exceptional or novel responses to solve problems. Divergent thinking often leads to responses which are viewed as creative acts.

The Creative Person

While measured intelligence does not seem to be an important aspect of creativity, there are several characteristics that seem to differentiate creative people from noncreative people. In general, the creative person is quite flexible in thinking patterns, interested in complex ideas, and shows a fairly complex personality pattern. Additionally, the creative person tends to be aesthetically sensitive, is interested in the unusual or novel, and shows a relatively open personality.

Measurement of Creativity

Several attempts have been made to develop measures of creativity. All have in common the aim of evaluating the unique or novel solutions to problems that might reveal the characteristic of creativity. Among such tests are the following:

Unusual uses tests: present an object and determine how many unusual uses the subject can generate for it

Remote association test: present several stimulus words and determine if the subject can "find" the associate that is common to all

Anagram tests: present a stimulus word and determine how many and what smaller words can be created using the letters of the stimulus word

Drawing completion tests: present a partial stimulus and ask the subject to finish the drawing

EXAMPLE 10. In a drawing completion test, the administrator might present a stimulus such as Fig. 20-2 (a) to the subject and ask the subject to "complete" the drawing in any way he or she wanted to. Response (b) might indicate a lack of creativity, while response (c) would be considered creative.

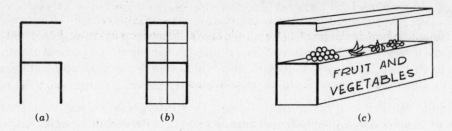

(a)   (b)   (c)

Fig. 20-2

Solved Problems

20.1   What was the original purpose of intelligence tests?

The original, and perhaps still the best, use of intelligence tests was to predict how well students could profit from being in school. In the early 1900s, Alfred Binet was asked by the Paris school system to develop such a test. By 1916, Lewis Terman of Stanford University had revised Binet's quite successful test to suit children in the United States. This latter test came to be known as the Stanford-Binet test and, in revised form, is still used today.

20.2   A psychometrist who is administering a Stanford-Binet intelligence test finds that the child is able to pass all of the tests at age four, some at age levels five, six, seven, and eight, but none at age nine. The total number of tests the child passed in the ages five to nine is 10. What is the basal age, the ceiling age, and the mental age for the child?

Basal age is the level at which all tests are passed; in this case, age four. Ceiling age is the level where no tests are passed; here it is age nine. Mental age is determined by calculating the months' credit accumulated by the child. Each test is worth two months' credit, thus the child's mental age is equal to $4 \times 12 = 48$ (credit for the basal age years) plus $10 \times 2 = 20$ (credit for the tests passed) or a total of 68 months' credit, for a mental age of 5 years and 8 months.

20.3   Are psychologists able to test the intelligence of infants?

A number of infant intelligence tests have been developed. They seem quite useful for detecting *extremes* of mental ability, but they do not correlate very well with later tests of intelligence. Generally speaking, a child must be more than two years old before any dependable measurement of intelligence can occur. (The Stanford-Binet test, for example, is available in a version that can be used to test two-year-olds.)

20.4   What would be the value of the IQ for the child in Problem 20.2 if that child's chronological age was 4 years 3 months?

The child's IQ can be calculated by dividing the mental age (MA) by the chronological age (CA) and multiplying by 100. In this case the mental age is 68 months and the chronological age is 51 months. By dividing the CA into the MA and multiplying by 100, we get the child's IQ, which is approximately 133.

20.5   The intelligence quotient given in Problem 20.4 is called a *ratio IQ*. Why would such a calculation not be considered appropriate for adults? How then would an adult's IQ be calculated?

The difficulty with the ratio IQ is that once a person has reached adult status, there is no way to show a continuing growth of MA to correspond to the ever-increasing of CA. If a ratio IQ were used as a measure for adults, they would receive lower and lower IQ values with increasing age.

Wechsler developed the deviation IQ to solve this problem. The raw scores of intelligence tests are statistically transformed and distributed on a normal probability curve. This curve has a mean of 100 and a standard deviation of 15 for all age levels. Wechsler's deviation IQ is now the accepted method for measuring intelligence.

20.6   Using the Wechsler values for IQ, what levels are considered to represent the exceptional subjects tested?

The Wechsler tests use a standard deviation of 15. (In the Stanford-Binet test, the value is 16.) IQ values which are two standard deviations or more above or below the mean of 100 are considered exceptional. Thus, in the Wechsler tests subjects with IQs of 130 or more and subjects with IQs of 70 or less are labeled exceptional.

20.7   In terms of intelligence, how are the mentally retarded defined and classified? Are the mentally retarded capable of learning?

Subjects whose intelligence scores are at or below the -2 standard deviation point on a normal probability distribution are arbitrarily defined as mentally retarded. Subjects who score IQ values of 70 or below on the Wechsler tests are thus retarded. Those subjects with IQ values of 50 to 70 are called *mildly retarded* or *educable*. Those whose IQs range from 35 to 50 are called *moderately retarded* or *trainable*. Those whose IQs range from 20 to 35 are called *severely retarded*, and any score under 20 represents *profound retardation*.

The mildly retarded are often able to function at an adolescent level, but require supervision. Moderately retarded function at a mental age of about four to seven years. The severely retarded can at best develop minimal personal skills, such as those necessary for hygiene or feeding. The profoundly retarded are unable to learn anything but the simplest responses, and require constant custodial care. (Some of the reasons for mental retardation are discussed in Chapter 21.)

20.8   The mentally retarded can be classified in four subgroups. Are there comparable subgroups for the exceptionally intelligent?

Some investigators have attempted to establish subgroups or categories (such as "genius") for the exceptionally intelligent, but the choice of IQ cutoff points has been arbitrary and not tied to observable behaviors. The little research that has been done has shown that persons with extraordinarily high IQs (perhaps 180 or better) may be more likely to have some social difficulties, particularly as children, but no special label has been used to classify such people or others in this very high range.

20.9   Some people believe that the exceptionally bright are often "weird" and that they often have trouble adjusting to life. Is this belief accurate?

The research evidence available indicates that, in general, people with IQ values of 130 or above are better adjusted than average. (In addition, they tend to be somewhat healthier, to have more hobbies, and to benefit in general from their intelligence.) The difficulty for people with very high IQs seems to be a lack of understanding on the part of parents, teachers, and classmates.

20.10   What are the advantages and disadvantages of group tests of intelligence and individual tests of intelligence?

Group tests are especially useful when the investigator needs to collect data about a large number of people rapidly. Group tests are relatively rapid, less expensive to administer, and require less skill of administration. However, they are generally considered less sensitive than individual tests, perhaps because it is more difficult to maintain a subject's motivation to respond.

Individual tests have the opposite characteristics. They are considered more sensitive than group tests and do allow a closer check on the subject's cooperation and motivation. However, individual tests are more expensive and require a skilled administrator.

20.11   Can intelligence be defined concisely?

No. Trying to define intelligence is very difficult. A simple solution, but one that is not very helpful, is to define intelligence operationally—to say that intelligence is what intelligence tests measure. A better but less clear solution would be to define intelligence as the relatively enduring mental characteristics a person can put to use in solving various types of problems. Still another way to view intelligence is to separate intelligence into (1) inherited potential and (2) demonstrated levels of understanding and performance. Obviously, the variety of these definitions suggests that no one choice is adequate.

20.12   Intelligence can be defined as a *set* of characteristics helpful in problem-solving. What statistical technique can be used to identify these characteristics?

The technique is the statistical procedure called *factor analysis*. Subjects are presented with a number of different problem-solving tasks, which are later analyzed to determine which ones are correlated to each other because they require the same type of responding. Each of these characteristics is then given a label that indicates how they seem to be linked together.

20.13   The best-known multiple-factor interpretation of intelligence was developed by L.L. Thurstone. In one of Thurstone's tests, a subject might be given the following incomplete couplet: To keep from feeling any pain,/The boy made sure to stay _____.

The subject would have 30 seconds to produce as many rhyming solutions as possible. Which of Thurstone's factors would most likely be tested by such an exercise? What other kinds of factors of intelligence did Thurstone propose?

The two factors most likely to be tested here are verbal comprehension (especially the size of vocabulary) and word fluency (the ability to think of words quickly). Other factors proposed by Thurstone were numerical facility, reasoning ability, perceptual speed, rote memory, and the ability to handle spatial relationships.

20.14   Would solving the rhyming exercise in Problem 20.13 require fluid or crystallized intelligence?

Solving novel problems seems to require the use of fluid intelligence, and coming up with a rhyme could be considered such a problem. Crystallized intelligence is used when one is applying what already has been learned. Crystallized intelligence is more likely to be habitual, while fluid intelligence is more apt to be flexible.

20.15   Suppose Catherine is nine years old. According to Piaget's proposal, what stages of cognitive or intellectual development has she passed through? Where is she now? What is yet to come?

According to Piaget's description of cognitive growth, Catherine has passed through the sensori-motor and pre-operational stages and should be in the concrete operational stage. She will have the formal operational stage to complete, beginning at about age eleven. Catherine has already learned about sensations and perceptions, language, conceptualization, and some logic, and she is able to develop coordinated series of ideas. However, she has yet to develop an understanding of abstract logic and generalizations. (Reivew Section 4.5 for a more thorough discussion of cognitive development.)

20.16   Does the tested intelligence of adults either increase or decrease as they get older?

There is no simple answer to this question. Research studies have shown that some subjects will show increases in tested intelligence well into adulthood, perhaps until age 50, for example. The measured intelligence of others may stay the same, and still others may show selective declines. (For example, problem-solving skills may drop off while vocabulary skills remain the same or improve.) In some people, measured intelligence in all areas declines with age. The pattern shown may be a function of the activity in which the subject engages, such as continued familiarity with examination situations or employment that is very stimulating. Therefore, it is difficult to predict what pattern any one person might show.

20.17 What effects do culturally accepted sex roles seem to have upon performance on intelligence tests?

If an analysis of overall intelligence quotients is made, sex roles appear to have no significant effect upon the obtained scores: males and females show virtually the same overall scores. However, if analyses are made for performance on the subtests that make up the overall tests, general trends related to sex roles emerge. In general, females do better than males on vocabulary skills, manual dexterity tasks, and perceptual detail tests. Males generally score better than females on mechanical, spatial, and numerical tasks. Whether these differences are inherited or a function of learning is as yet an unanswered question, but culturally accepted sex roles may play an important part. Additionally, there is evidence to indicate that males are "pushed" more than females by cultural influences to achieve. This, in turn, may lead to greater attempts by males to try to improve abilities and may possibly affect the intelligence scores obtained over a period of time.

20.18 Intelligence tests were first developed in an attempt to predict how much students would profit from instruction in school. How well have the tests satisfied this purpose? What difficulties have been found in trying to make such predictions?

If one is discussing predictions for a group of students, intelligence test scores are quite good predictors of academic success. Summaries of research have shown correlation values in the range of $+0.30$ to $+0.75$. However, it must be recognized that prediction for any one individual may be inaccurate. Factors other than intelligence, such as family or social situations, motivation, or self-confidence may affect academic success. Additionally, the responses of others, as indicated by the research summarized by Rosenthal, may affect academic pursuits also. Previously established expectations may create an atmosphere of success or failure that will continue to persist throughout an academic career.

20.19 Have intelligence tests been used effectively for selecting occupations for people?

Research reports have shown that there are reasonably high correlations between measured intelligence and training for a job. In other words, intelligence test scores are fairly useful as predictors of how well a person will *learn* how to do a job. However, they are not so useful as predictors of how well the person will actually perform on the job.

Correlational studies have shown that, in general, people with higher tested intelligence will have more prestigious (high-status) jobs. But it is not clear whether the brighter people choose such jobs or the jobs require brighter people. (Such a question of cause and effect is not easily resolved.) It appears that measured intelligence may be a fairly good predictor of success in job training, but that caution should be exercised in relying too much on such measurements in making occupational choices.

20.20 What are the important characteristics of creativity?

The research on this issue may be subject to some question, but the characteristics that show up for creative people include a preference for complexity and the less ordinary, independence, openness, aesthetic sensitivity, and emotional and social sensitivity.

20.21 What is a creative act? What are some of the ways in which creativity is tested?

The creative act is considered to be purposeful and productive, and makes use of unusual solutions to problems. That is, a creative act is both original and somehow useful or worthwhile.

Tests of creativity may measure how many unusual uses someone may be able to generate for some object or how well a person can determine the remote associations that exist among several quite divergent stimuli. Drawing-completion tests and anagram tasks are also sometimes used to measure creativity.

20.22 Tests such as those mentioned in the solution to Problem 20.21 often focus on the difference between convergent thinking and divergent thinking. What is the difference?

Convergent patterns of thought are revealed by responses that are considered correct, but conventional or unoriginal. Divergent thinking is characterized by the subject's ability to produce a variety of responses, many of which are unique or original. Divergent thinking is considered to be representative of creativity.

Key Terms

Basal age.   The highest year level at which a subject passes all the subtests of an intelligence test.

Ceiling age.   The year level at which a subject fails to pass any subtests of an intelligence test.

Convergent thinking.   Routine or common problem-solving.

Creativity.   Original, purposeful, worthwhile, and unique approaches to problem-solving and other activities.

Crystallized intelligence.   Intelligence used in the application of already-learned materials; usually considered to be rigid or unchanging.

Deviation IQ.   The value of intelligence established by using normal probability distributions of scores obtained for various age levels.

Divergent thinking.   Unique or novel problem-solving.

Exceptional subjects.   Those subjects whose scores are more than 2 standard deviations from the mean of an intelligence test.

Fluid intelligence.   Intelligence that can adjust to new situations; usually considered as flexible or adaptive thinking.

Gifted subjects.   Those subjects whose scores are above the +2 standard deviation point on a normal probability distribution of intelligence scores.

Intelligence.   Those enduring characteristics that allow an individual to solve problems.

Intelligence quotient (IQ).   The ratio obtained by dividing mental age by chronological age and then multiplying by 100.

Mental age.   A measurement of a person's performance on an intelligence test; the basis for measurement is the chronological age at which people typically pass tests.

Mental retardation.   Arbitrarily established as a characteristic of a person who scores below the −2 standard deviation point on a normal probability distribution of intelligence scores.

Chapter 21

Abnormal Personality Patterns

In psychology, one of the most difficult areas to define accurately has been that of abnormal personality patterns. While it is recognized that the word *abnormal* means away from the norm, the difficulties have arisen because it is difficult to determine what norm or norms to use.

21.1 DEFINITION OF ABNORMAL PERSONALITY PATTERNS

Abnormal personality patterns are evidenced by behaviors that produce significant and often persistent discomfort or upset for a person or for others in that person's society. Thus, the personal and social setting will, to a great extent, determine whether or not a pattern of behavior is considered abnormal.

EXAMPLE 1. A famous television star has a reputation for being insulting. His remarks are often rude and outrageous. However, he makes these remarks in the context of his "act" or performance, and as a result no significant societal upset occurs. If the same kinds of remarks were made in a different social context, such as in a business meeting or a classroom, a totally different interpretation might be made, and the pattern could easily be judged as abnormal.

Other terms used to describe abnormal personality patterns have included *mental illness* and *emotional disturbance*. Some psychologists prefer to avoid such terms because they may imply characteristics that are not present in an abnormal response.

Properties of Abnormal Personality Patterns

Some actions that are temporarily upsetting for either a person or the person's society may not be interpreted as abnormal. Because such interpretations are relatively subjective, both the *quantity* and *quality* of the behavior should be considered in judging whether or not the behavior is abnormal. In other words, both the frequency and intensity of the behavior in question should be considered.

EXAMPLE 2. Practically everyone experiences anxiety at one time or another. Anxiety can be considered a normal part of anyone's personality. However, if the frequency and intensity of the anxiety seriously affect a person's actions, it will be considered abnormal. For example, temporary anxiety about making a public speech would be considered normal, while constant anxiety about life in general would be considered abnormal.

Predisposing and Precipitating Factors

The onset of abnormal personality patterns seems to be the result of an interaction between a person's background and the person's current environment. The background factors, which include hereditary patterns and childhood experiences (with parents, peers, and others) are called *predisposing factors*. The stimuli that finally initiate the abnormal pattern are called *precipitating factors*. In a few instances, as in the case of brain damage, it may be impossible to distinguish between predisposing and precipitating factors.

EXAMPLE 3. A person's childhood experiences could predispose him or her to show an abnormal personality pattern in later life. Parents who showed an inordinate amount of concern for cleanliness in their children, for example, could predispose their children to abnormal anxieties about dirt and disorder. Such a predisposition, once it was well established as part of the child's personality, could create great anxieties later in life.

Other Factors for Judging Abnormality

Psychologists have tried to identify characteristics that help distinguish normal from abnormal behaviors. Some of those characteristics include whether or not the person shows voluntary control of the behavior, the productivity of the behavior, the judgment, attention, and planning that go into the behavior, and the frequency of the behavior. Any or all of these factors may be considered in characterizing a behavior as normal or abnormal.

EXAMPLE 4. Many people, by virtue of the nature of their jobs, must formulate and operate according to rather rigid plans of behavior. For example, an airline pilot must go through an exhaustive routine of instrument checks before setting an airplane in motion. Such a routine must be time-consuming and very exacting, but no one would question its importance or interpret it as a sign of an abnormal personality pattern.

If, however, the pilot went through an equally detailed series of checks each time he drove his car, his behavior might very well be considered abnormal. The extremely careful routine appropriate to the former situation would not be appropriate to the latter.

Difficulty with Determining Abnormality

Two major difficulties seem most apparent in deciding whether or not a pattern of behavior should be called abnormal. One of these has been mentioned earlier in this chapter, that of determining how the behavior compares to the personal or societal norms. The second is that, for any number of reasons, a person may choose to pretend to have (or not have) abnormal responses. Research evidence has shown that it is often possible for a person to "fool" a psychologist and be characterized as abnormal or "mask" abnormality and appear normal.

21.2 EXPLANATIONS OF ABNORMAL BEHAVIOR

Attempts to understand why people behave abnormally have led to several different models of abnormality.

The Psychodynamic Model

Originating with the work of Freud, the *psychodynamic model* places emphasis on internal or intrapersonal sources of abnormal behavior. Conflicts residing in the unconscious are thought to cause abnormal patterns of responding.

The Biomedical Model

Biomedical models emphasize the influence of bodily functions upon personality. Disease, genetic inheritance, or the condition of the person's nervous system may be seen as the sources of abnormal behavior. Therapies based on a biomedical model of personality may make use of drugs or surgery. One of the problems with biomedical models is that a great demand is placed upon psychiatrists, who are expected to give medical treatment for problems that may not really have medical solutions. Another problem is that patients who consider themselves sick may not accept responsibility for their actions, thus making treatment more difficult.

The Social Learning Model

The *social learning model* proposes that abnormal personality patterns are the result of learning. The abnormal responses are acquired because of observation, imitation, and reinforcement. Therapies based on this model may make use of the principles of instrumental conditioning, classical conditioning, and modeling.

The Existential Model

The major thrust of the *existential model* is an emphasis upon present experience, rather than past experience or history of learning. A basic principle of the model is that a person must take responsibility for behavior, which cannot be attributed to past experience or illness.

Combining Models

Some abnormal personality patterns may be best explained by reference to more than one of the above models, and most psychologists have come to recognize that each model makes an important contribution to the understanding of abnormal personality patterns. As a result, acceptance of the several models has been quite widespread, and the use of combinations of two or more models is not uncommon.

21.3   NEUROSIS

A number of abnormal personality patterns have been categorized as *neurotic*. A neurosis is usually characterized by a high level of anxiety, the cause of which is not easily identified. Usually, a neurotic person is able to continue living in normal day-to-day circumstances, but may have considerable problems with the specific area of behavior that generates the anxiety.

Anxiety Neurosis

A person may repress the cause of anxiety but continue to experience the anxiety at a mild or moderate level (with occasional short periods of intense anxiety). Such a personality pattern is evidence of what is called an *anxiety neurosis*.

Phobias

Phobias are intense, compelling fears of a specific situation or object. The fears are usually much more intense than the circumstances warrant. Phobias have been explained as the result of classical conditioning or as the result of displacement, in which fear of one thing is actually a symbolic fear of something else.

EXAMPLE 5.   Claustrophobia, or the fear of being in enclosed spaces, is a fairly common phobia. The desire to avoid severe overcrowding—or the danger of being trapped or of suffocating in a small space—can be considered reasonable. A person with severe claustrophobia, however, may go to unreasonable lengths to avoid being in an enclosed space. Thus, someone who walked up fifteen flights of stairs to avoid having to use an elevator would be showing an abnormal behavior.

Obsessions and Compulsions

Some people find themselves thinking thoughts or performing actions in a repeated and disturbing fashion. Such thoughts (called *obsessions*) or actions (called *compulsions*) may be unwanted by the individual, but she or he may not be able to prevent them. Often, the neurotic individual experiences both obsessions and compulsions, and is referred to as an *obsessive-compulsive type*.

EXAMPLE 6.   Having no rational reason to believe so, a person may come to have a recurring thought that he or she has contracted a fatal disease. Such an individual may try to get rid of this very upsetting and unwanted obsession, but find this is impossible.

Dissociative Reactions

In some cases people may attempt to behave in ways that will dissociate them completely from anxiety-producing stimuli. Such behaviors are called *dissociative reactions*. Examples include *amnesia*, or a loss of memory, and multiple personality, in which a person takes on seemingly different personalities in an attempt to cope with anxiety-producing situations.

Conversion Reactions

The anxiety resulting from a stressful situation may be transformed into a physical symptom. In such a case, the resulting neurotic pattern is called a *conversion reaction*. Conversion reactions show no evidence of actual organic disturbance and, somewhat paradoxically, persons displaying such reactions may show little anxiety.

EXAMPLE 7. Confronted with a situation where seeing some event might be tremendously anxiety-producing, a person may become "blind," although there is no physiological explanation. This "blindness" keeps the person from experiencing the unwanted situation and thus "protects" the person.

Experimental Neurosis

As mentioned in Chapter 11, Pavlov's laboratory research indicated that forcing the dogs to make difficult differentiations sometimes seemed to lead to what was called *experimental neurosis*. Apparently, the stress associated with very demanding decision-making processes led to a behavioral pattern that was comparable to what has been called neurosis. The dogs reacted normally in other respects, but when they were confronted with the laboratory task, they showed marked deterioration of behavioral control.

21.4 PSYCHOSOMATIC DISORDERS

Psychosomatic disorders (also called *psychophysiological disorders*) are physical problems involving actual tissue damage or malfunctioning which are precipitated by psychological causes. These may include problems such as nausea, high blood pressure, ulcers, headaches, and the like.

21.5 PSYCHOSIS

Psychosis is characterized primarily by a person's apparent loss of contact with reality. The psychotic person often seems unable to distinguish reality from fantasy and may experience *delusions*, or false beliefs, and *hallucinations*, or false sensory experiences. Psychotics often require special care or confinement.

Organic versus Functional Psychoses

Organic psychoses are thought to be caused by some fairly clear physical problem, usually involving the brain. *Functional psychoses* have no apparent physical cause, and are thought to be the result of experience. (*Note*: It is important to consider, however, that the distinction between these two types of psychoses is not always clear-cut: the same type of brain injury in two people may result in psychosis in one person and not the other, just as an experience blamed for one person's psychosis may leave another person unharmed.)

Organic psychoses may be caused by physical problems such as untreated syphilis, excessive use of alcohol, brain damage, encephalitis, or senility. Functional psychoses may have almost any experiential cause. (It is assumed that psychological rather than physiological events bring about functional psychoses.)

Schizophrenia

The most commonly diagnosed type of psychosis is *schizophrenia*, characterized by noticeable loss of contact with reality, delusions, hallucinations, and a tendency toward very unresponsive emotional behavior. Several subcategories of schizophrenia have been distinguished.

Simple schizophrenia. *Simple schizophrenia* is typified by a steady withdrawal from reality leading to a pronounced state of apathy. The simple schizophrenic seldom has delusions or hallucinations.

Hebephrenic schizophrenia. The most frequently observed patterns of behavior of the *hebephrenic schizophrenic* are wild and silly responses, often accompanied by complete disregard for social convention. Hallucinations and delusions are also common.

Catatonic schizophrenia. *Catatonic schizophrenia* is characterized by extreme passivity or by extreme activity. The most widely recognized symptoms of catatonic schizophrenia are total muscle rigidity and a single body position that is held for very long periods of time.

EXAMPLE 8. A catatonic schizophrenic who suffers from a delusion that the food being served is poisoned, may hold his jaw tightly shut, clench his hands behind his back, and turn his head to the side so that he cannot be fed. Any attempts to modify this body position will be resisted strenuously.

Paranoid schizophrenia. The *paranoid schizophrenic* usually shows pronounced delusions of grandeur and persecution, accompanied by disconnected thought patterns. The delusions are frequently linked with hallucinations.

Paranoia

Another basic type of psychosis is known as *paranoia*, in which an individual has delusions of persecution and grandeur as a major personality characteristic. (Paranoia differs from paranoid schizophrenia in that the paranoid generally functions quite normally except when having delusions, showing well-connected thought patterns much of the time.) The paranoid's ability to interpret events to fit his or her belief in persecution makes it difficult for reality to be separated from fantasy.

EXAMPLE 9. A design consultant who developed a package for a product was extremely disappointed when it was rejected by the interested company. Soon after, the consultant became very suspicious and began to believe that a conspiracy within the company was the reason for the rejection. This belief grew even stronger after several other companies rejected the proposal, and finally the consultant believed that the public in general had conspired in not recognizing a "great" design. Eventually, the consultant called the sheriff's office to report this major conspiracy. As a result, he was diagnosed as a paranoid and confined.

Affective Psychoses

Affective psychoses are typified by extremes of mood—great elation or deep depression. A person consistently showing elated, hyperactive states is called *manic*, while a person who shows minimal activity and despondency is called *depressive*. A person who alternates between these two states is called *manic-depressive*. This last personality pattern often occurs in a regular cycle. People who try to commit suicide are characteristically in a depressive state. (Twice as many women attempt suicide as men, but men are three times more likely to "succeed" in their attempts.)

Infantile Autism

One abnormal personality pattern that is sometime classified as a separate type of psychosis is *infantile autism*, which is shown by children under the age of ten. The most predominant characteristics of this type of psychosis are poor communication, strenuous attempts to maintain everything just as it is, and no desire for personal contacts. The autistic child often appears to be bright, but does not operate well within a normal environment. This pattern of behavior is not at all well understood and, as a result, treatment techniques have been difficult to develop.

Comparison of Neurosis and Psychosis

Several factors distinguish neurosis and psychosis. In general, the neurotic has difficulties in only limited areas of thought or behavior, while the psychotic's abnormalities are more widespread. Neurotics are more often responsive to treatment than psychotics and, once cured, are more likely to remain cured.

21.6 PERSONALITY DISORDERS

Personality disorders exist when a person fails to act in accordance with societal standards. Quite frequently, the individual with a personality disorder does not believe help is needed. One difficulty with the treatment of personality disorders is that the public very often considers them only as problems of law, rather than as problems with a psychological basis.

Antisocial Behaviors

Antisocial behaviors (also called *psychopathic* or *sociopathic* behaviors) have two major characteristics: a failure to act according to the standards of society *and* the absence of anxiety about such behaviors. People showing such responses know the societal standards, but simply refuse to accept them and act as if special sets of rules apply to themselves.

EXAMPLE 10. "Con artists," or "confidence artists," provide good examples of antisocial behaviors in action. While understanding that society says it is incorrect to illegally manipulate situations for personal gain, the con artists do so anyway and often feel no guilt about acting in this manner. Although many of their manipulations may not work, their occasional successes create a partial reinforcement situation, thus making their behavior very resistant to extinction. When caught, these people are usually tried, convicted, and sentenced to prison rather than given treatment for their psychological problems.

Addictions

Another class of personality disorders is *addiction*, the dependence upon a drug or chemical that comes with repeated use. Addictions are subdivided into *physiological addictions*, meaning that withdrawal of the substance will lead to physical illness, and *psychological addictions*, when withdrawal of the substance results in pronounced anxiety or psychological discomfort. In our society, some of the most frequently abused substances are alcohol, caffeine, tobacco, prescription drugs, heroin, and cocaine.

EXAMPLE 11. Prescription drugs such as barbiturates (which depress the functioning of the central nervous system) or amphetamines (which act as stimulants) can be obtained quite easily, and they are widely abused. Barbiturates can be both physiologically and psychologically addicting, while amphetamines apparently are not physically addicting. Both drugs, however, may create pronounced psychological dependence. Students have been known to use these drugs as a way of "escaping" the frustration and stress of the academic setting.

Sexual Deviations

What constitutes *sexual deviance* is dependent upon the standards of a society. Any number of sexual behaviors—including premarital intercourse, extramarital intercourse, homosexuality, prostitution, incest, transsexualism, exhibitionism, voyeurism, pedophilia, transvestism, and fetishism—have been considered deviant.

EXAMPLE 12. It is interesting to note that many people will enjoy a night club or television show featuring a female impersonator and yet condemn transvestism (dressing in clothing appropriate to the opposite sex) as a deviant behavior. Obviously, what they accept as a form of entertainment they will not accept as a way for someone to live.

21.7 MENTAL RETARDATION

Mental retardation is designated as subnormal intellectual performance, generally as measured by some standardized test of intelligence. The origins of mental retardation may be either prenatal or postnatal, but the result is always impairment of learning.

Using obtained IQ values, psychologists have generally agreed on four subcategories of mental retardation. (Refer to Chapter 20, Problem 20.7.)

Causes of Retardation

Three different potential causes of retardation have been proposed. It should be recognized that these may operate individually or together, depending upon the particular circumstances.

Lack of environmental stimulation. One proposed cause of mental retardation is simply a lack of sufficient environmental stimulation during a child's early years. Learning experiences are limited, resulting in a reduced IQ value.

Inheritance or genetic upset. The possibility that some biochemical disorder may be inherited or that some noninherited chromosomal abnormality exists is the second proposed cause of retardation. These occur at the time of conception.

Physiological or medical causes. Some upset of development not related to conception, occurring either pre- or postnatally, may bring about mental retardation. Poor nutrition, the mothers' prenatal diseases and birth injuries are examples.

EXAMPLE 13. Mongolism is an example of a chromosomally caused mental retardation. The child is conceived with forty-seven rather than the normal forty-six chromosomes, and the result is mental retardation and somewhat unusual physical features. Cretinism results from a prenatal lack of iodine in the system. By adding iodine to the salt used in the parent's diet, this problem can be avoided. These two forms of mental retardation differ in that one is determined at the moment of conception, while the other results from a nutrition condition. The latter condition may be correctable, while the first is not.

21.8 RELATIONSHIP OF ABNORMAL PATTERNS TO OTHER FACTORS

Attempts to establish some understanding of the relationships of abnormal patterns to other factors have been quite difficult because of the problems inherent in trying to label the abnormal behavior. Despite this, research results have tended to support the following findings.

Sex

Research relating gender to various types of disorders has shown that, in general, females are more likely to be treated for neurotic or psychotic patterns of behavior, while males are more likely to show addictions, sexual deviations, or brain syndromes.

Age

Careful study has shown that the peak for neuroses and personality disorders comes in adolescence. Psychoses and alcoholism peak during middle age, while brain syndromes reach a maximum in old age.

Marital Status

Abnormal personality patterns occur with the greatest frequency for divorced or separated persons. Single persons are found to be next highest, followed by widowed persons, with married people showing the lowest frequency.

Social Class

A summary of a number of studies has shown that the lower the designated social class, the higher the rate of serious abnormal personality patterns. This may be because the stress of being in the lower social classes leads to abnormal behavior or because patterns of abnormal behavior lead the person to become part of a lower social class. Furthermore, behaviors tolerated in an upper class may be considered abnormal in a lower class.

Ethnic Group

Little or no difference has been found when comparing different ethnic groups for incidence of abnormal personality pattern. There is no established evidence to indicate that membership in a particular ethnic or racial group leads to a higher rate of abnormality than membership in any other group. However, the specific symptoms of abnormal behaviors may vary considerably from one ethnic group to another.

Solved Problems

21.1   What is abnormal behavior? Is it always a reason for concern?

When someone shows behavior noticeably different from the average, it is called abnormal (away from the norm). Such behavior may be of concern when it creates either personal discomfort or difficulties for others in the person's society. Often, both the quantity and quality of the person's behavior must be evaluated before a decision is made regarding whether or not some attempts should be made to modify or correct the abnormal pattern.

21.2   What kind of abnormal behavior pattern might not be a cause for seeking help or change?

Some of an individual's behavior patterns could be abnormal but not upsetting to either the individual or society at large. For example, suppose a man who jogged every day always stopped in the middle of his running sessions to do push-ups, sit-ups, and stretching exercises at the side of the road. Such behavior might be considered pretty far away from the norm, but it wouldn't necessarily signify that the man needed help. However, if that same man insisted upon doing his exercises in the middle of an intersection, disrupting traffic and endangering himself, then the abnormal pattern would need some modification.

21.3   How do psychologists decide whether or not a person's personality pattern is abnormal enough to require treatment? What are some of the basic causes of abnormal personality patterns that a psychologist might look for?

A psychologist's decision about a subject's personality pattern would be based on a number of different factors, including the subject's ability to show good judgment, the kinds of activities the subject pursues, the subject's ability to plan and control his own behavior, and even the subject's attention span. If any one of these or some combination of these creates personal discomfort or problems with society, the subject could be labeled as abnormal and treatment may be recommended.

In examining a subject with a possibly abnormal personality pattern, a psychologist might look for predisposing and precipitating factors that caused the pattern. It is very possible that something in the subject's background combined with a particular recent event to set off the abnormal pattern.

21.4   Give examples of predisposing factors from a person's past experience that might lead to an abnormal personality pattern.

Predispositions generally refer to any hereditary tendency or past experience that plays a significant role in the subsequent development of an individual's personality. Two experiential factors psychologists have studied are *double-bind situations* and *self-fulfilling prophecies*. Double-bind situations exist when someone is presented with two conflicting messages, such as verbally expressed affection along with physical rejection. Such an ambiguous circumstance may predispose the person to take on maladaptive patterns of responding. A self-fulfilling prophecy is often the result of repeatedly expressed expectations for behavior. A person who is constantly expected to act abnormally may accept abnormality as the normal mode of behavior.

21.5   Is it always correct to say that a person with an abnormal personality pattern is "sick"?

No. Some abnormal personality patterns result from physiological problems, but many do not have any physical causes. The term *mental illness* seems to imply that the person is sick, but it is probably not a good term to use because it may confuse the issue.

Some other terms, such as *emotional disturbance* and *behavioral disorder*, are also not very descriptive either; for example, emotions are not always involved in abnormal personality patterns, nor are disturbances as such always apparent.

21.6   Could a normal person convincingly "fake" the symptoms of an abnormal personality pattern, or are diagnosis techniques foolproof?

If the results of a study conducted by D. Rosenhan and his associates are accepted as evidence, it seems that a normal person could successfully "fake" the symptoms. Rosenhan's study points out one of the serious difficulties with evaluation or diagnosis of behavioral patterns: It may quite possible for a person without an abnormal personality to act as if she or he had one, just as it would be possible for people with abnormal personality patterns to "act normal" and thus avoid diagnosis and subsequent treatment.

21.7   Name the four basic types of theories that have been proposed to try to account for abnormal personality patterns, and give the basic position of each.

The four theories or models that have been most widely accepted are as follows: (1) the psychodynamic model, which arose from Freud's conception that there could be conflicts between different parts of a person's personality; (2) the biomedical model, which stresses the influence of body functioning upon behavior; (3) the social learning model, which emphasizes the possibility of abnormal behaviors being learned through observation, modeling, and reinforcement; (4) the existential model, which stresses a person's responsibility for his or her own behavior and downplays the influence of past experience.

21.8   What are the general characteristics of a neurotic pattern of behavior?

The overriding characteristic of neurosis is the evidence of anxiety. Often the cause of the anxiety is not readily recognized. The neurotic usually can continue to function in everyday life, but may have pronounced difficulties in some limited area of behavior. (For example, a neurotic may have an intense fear of failing at work).

21.9   Claude experiences an almost continuous vague fear or apprehension, which is occasionally interrupted by short periods of intense anxiety. When questioned about why he feels this way, Claude is unable to give a reason. Nevertheless, he continues to experience the anxiety even though he is able to function reasonably well in his day-to-day activities. What label is given to the pattern of behavior shown by Claude? What differentiates this from normal behavior?

Claude's behavior illustrates anxiety neurosis. The characteristics are distinguished from normal behavior in that the source of anxiety apparently has been repressed and yet serves as the cause for continual anxiety. Normal anxiety is temporary and can be attributed to a cause; for example, worry about a forthcoming exam will usually dissipate after the event. Anxiety neurosis is more likely to continue over prolonged periods of time, until the cause is recognized or coping behaviors are learned.

21.10 Phobias have been described as intense, compelling fears. Consider a phobia such as a fear of darkness. How could classical conditioning serve as an explanation of the development of such a phobia? How could the phenomenon of displacement also be used to account for the phobia?

If it can be assumed that darkness is originally a neutral stimulus that is then paired with a fear-producing stimulus (for example, a sudden, loud, unidentifiable noise), this coupling may be looked at as a CS–UCS combination, and the CR would be fear produced by darkness (the CS).

Displacement might occur when a child has an intense dislike of a parent, but is afraid of expressing it because that would be socially unacceptable. The fear may then be displaced to a more acceptable stimulus—in this case, darkness. This becomes a symbolic expression of the fear of the parent, perhaps because the child links the parent with the darkness associated with being put to bed.

21.11 Over a period of time, Ramona has developed a pattern "requiring" her to take a fresh tissue every fifteen minutes, blow her nose, and then discard the tissue immediately. When asked about this, she explains that it prevents any possible infections from starting. Would Ramona's behavior be classified as obsessive or compulsive? What distinguishes the two?

Ramona's behavior represents a compulsion, an act that intrudes repetitively on her behavior. It is called a compulsion because it is an overt act. (An *obsession* refers to a thought that intrudes repeatedly on a person's consciousness.) The possibility that Ramona has obsessive thoughts accompanying her compulsive actions is quite high. Often, persons are identified as obsessive-compulsive types because of the close correspondence of their continually repeated thoughts and actions. (*Note*: Ramona may realize that her behavior is unreasonable, yet feel compelled to carry out the repetitive ritual anyway.)

21.12 In March, a teacher prepares his income tax return. He looks for every loophole, manufactures a few business deductions that really did not exist, and fails to report a small amount of income that came to him as a cash payment. When he is done, he has a return that calls for a small refund and is proud of his accomplishment. Several weeks later, the same teacher fails one of his students for cheating. He believes he has done the correct thing and publicly states that he hopes this will serve as an example for that student and all the others as well.

This teacher's behavior is closest to which of the types of neurosis? What is the difference between this teacher's behavior and neurotic behavior? What are examples of neurotic forms of this behavior?

The teacher has assumed the two different roles—"crafty" taxpayer and "righteous" instructor—and managed to keep these separate, thus showing mild dissociation. The difference between this dissociative behavior and that of a neurotic is in degree. Normal dissociation involves a separation of roles, but neurotic dissociative reactions are often bizarre or incapacitating.

The two most common examples of neurotic dissociative reactions are amnesia and multiple personality. Each serves as a means of escaping from an anxiety-producing situation and may have been developed through learning over a period of time.

21.13 A woman was admitted to a hospital with paralysis of the legs. Careful examination indicated there was no physiological cause for the paralysis, so other variables were investigated. It was found that the woman was working to put her husband through college. The day before the onset of her paralysis, her husband had left to "go home" to his parents, leaving her to continue working and to take care of their one-year-old child.

The woman's reaction is called a *conversion reaction*. What is this? How does it differ from an actual illness? How does it differ from a psychosomatic disorder?

A conversion reaction is a physical reaction that allows the person to escape from an anxiety-producing situation. It differs from a physical illness in that there is no apparent precipitating physiological or biological cause. (In this case, for example, there was no damage to the spinal column or leg. Yet, the physical symptoms are truly present.)

Conversion reactions are usually thought to differ from psychosomatic disorders in that psychosomatic disorders are generally accompanied by actual physiological damage to some body organ or malfunctioning in an organ system; this is not usually true of conversion reactions.

21.14   What behavioral patterns are characteristic of psychosis? How do these differ from neurotic patterns?

The psychotic is out of touch with reality, confusing reality and fantasy. Psychotics often experience delusions (false beliefs that persist in the face of evidence to the contrary) or hallucinations (sensory experiences in the absence of stimuli that normally cause them). The psychotic is often so disturbed that he or she is unable to function within normal society and requires special care or hospitalization.

In general, the psychotic is more out of touch with reality than the neurotic, less likely to be cured than the neurotic, less likely to stay cured than the neurotic, and more likely to be feared or rejected by society because of the bizarre or irrational behaviors often shown.

21.15   Name the two basic categories of psychosis, distinguish between them, and give examples of each.

There are basically two types of psychoses, organic psychoses and functional psychoses. Organic psychoses are caused by some physical problem, while the functional psychoses do not appear to have any physiological cause. Senile psychosis is one example of an organic psychosis. It has been fairly well established that the symptoms of senility result from a deterioration of the flow of blood to the brain.

Another example of organic psychosis occurs when syphilis is not treated. This may eventually lead to deterioration of the nervous system and psychotic patterns of behavior. Alcohol may also be ingested in quantities great enough to poison the system and cause such reactions. Brain damage, encephalitis, or even vitamin deficiencies may also lead to psychotic behaviors.

Functional psychoses are thought to develop as a result of experience rather than as a result of a physiological change. For example, a person whose childhood was filled with emotional traumas might very well grow up to be psychotic. (It must be remembered, however, that some biologists and psychologists believe that all psychotics were physiologically predisposed to psychosis to begin with.)

21.16   A patient is quite out of touch with reality and displays childish behaviors such as giggling and crying at inappropriate moments. What type of schizophrenia is this patient showing? How does this type of schizophrenia differ from other types?

This patient's childish behaviors are typical of hebephrenic schizophrenia. This differs from simple schizophrenia, in which the patient shows delusions or hallucinations and does not appear to be as out of touch with reality as the hebephrenic schizophrenic is. The catatonic schizophrenic usually will be either extremely agreeable or totally uncooperative, but additionally often shows total muscle rigidity, which is not common in the other types of schizophrenia. Paranoid schizophrenics may show disjointed delusions of grandeur and persecution, often accompanied by hallucinations.

21.17   How is a distinction made between paranoid schizophrenics and paranoids?

The paranoid schizophrenic often shows disconnected thought patterns and often has hallucinations accompanying the delusions of grandeur and persecution. A psychotic labeled simply as paranoid will also show the delusions of grandeur and persecution, but will seldom have the accompanying hallucinations and usually shows no obvious disorder of thinking except for the delusions.

21.18   Research evidence has shown that most attempted suicides are people who are seriously depressed; in fact, psychotic depression has been called the only "fatal" abnormal personality pattern. Depression is considered to be representative of what type of psychosis? What other behavior patterns also fit into this category?

Depression is considered one of the affective psychoses, which are characterized by extremes of mood. The affective psychoses also include manic patterns of behavior. Some individuals will show only depressive reactions, others only manic patterns, while still others will fluctuate between the two extremes. This latter group frequently shows a cyclical pattern of change, for example, two months of extreme depression followed by two months of elation.

21.19   At age 8, Matthew appeared to be physically healthy, quite bright, and well coordinated. Yet his communication skills were poor and he resisted both physical and social contact, even from his parents and others close to him. Instead, Matthew seemed to find great pleasure in mechanical objects and tried very hard to maintain his environment just as it was. These behavior patterns are most likely to be diagnosed as what type of psychosis? Has there been much success in treating this type of behavior?

Matthew's condition would probably be labeled as infantile autism. His behaviors are characteristic of this quite puzzling psychosis, which, as yet, has no definite or identifiable cause. As a result, treatment for infantile autism has proved difficult. Behavior modification techniques (see Chapter 22) seem to work in some cases, but much is still be be learned about this type of psychosis.

21.20   One area in which psychology and psychiatry have had conflict with social standards is the topic of personality disorders. Why is this so?

Personality disorders are seen as failures to behave according to the demands of society. Psychologists tend to view these patterns as abnormal and requiring therapeutic treatment, while society is more likely to see them solely as legal problems, requiring no more than decisions from the courts and, in some cases, incarceration.

21.21   A number of years ago, a young man was convicted of first-degree murder. He had been hitchhiking, and a family stopped to give him a ride. When he asked for a cigarette and found that none of them smoked, he killed them all. The man was asked if he knew that killing was considered wrong. He said that he did know this, but persisted in explaining his actions by saying no one in the family had any cigarettes. This pattern of behavior is representative of what kind of abnormal personality pattern?

Several labels have been used to describe this type of behavior; *psychopathic behavior*, *sociopathic behavior*, and *antisocial reactions* are three of these. No matter which label is used, this type of personality disorder is characterized by a persistent failure to act according to the rules of society. It seems that psychopaths believe that special sets of rules apply only to themselves, and they seldom have any anxiety about such a feeling.

21.22   What is the most significant factor in determination of sexual deviation?

Sexual deviations are judged on the basis of the beliefs of a particular group of people. What is considered sexually deviant by one group may be socially approved by another. Some of the sexual behaviors that have been considered deviant by at least some groups of people are exhibitionism, voyeurism, fetishism, transvestism, transsexualism, homosexuality, incest, pedophilia, prostitution, premarital intercourse, and extramarital intercourse.

21.23 Many drugs and chemicals are capable of altering behavior, and many of these may lead to addiction. What does it mean to say a person is addicted? Are there different kinds of addiction? What substances are frequently abused in our society?

A person who is addicted is virtually compelled to continue taking some substance. In other words, the person has developed a dependence upon the drug or chemical. Such dependence may be physiological, meaning that discontinued use would lead to physical illness, or psychological, meaning that discontinued use might lead to anxiety or other psychological discomfort. In the United States, the substances most frequently abused are alcohol, caffeine, nicotine, prescription drugs, heroin, and cocaine.

21.24 Tested at an IQ value of 65, Douglas was placed in a class for exceptional children. He was designated as mentally retarded, but expected to profit from training. How would Douglas be labeled within the categories of mental retardation? What are the other levels frequently designated?

Douglas would be called mildly retarded. Generally, this designation is used for people with IQ values between 70 and 50. The expectation is that they are educable if special teaching techniques are used.

The other levels of mental retardation are based upon IQ scores and how much the person can be expected to benefit from training. Those who are moderately retarded (IQs of 50–35) can be trained to function at a level comparable to a normal child in the age range of four to seven years. The severely retarded (IQs of 35–20) may learn basic personal skills. The profoundly retarded (IQs of 20–0) will require constant custodial care and are not expected to profit from training.

21.25 What are the causes of retardation?

Three possible causes of retardation have been proposed. One is simply lack of environmental stimulation during the child's early years. A second is inheritence, or genetic upsets; for example, the child may inherit some biochemical disorder or may be retarded because of some noninherited chromosomal abnormality. The third possibility is that medical or physiological conditions may bring about retardation; perhaps the most common instance of this is poor childhood nutrition, although illnesses suffered by the mother during pregnancy would also be included in this category.

21.26 A persistent question about abnormal personality patterns has been whether or not certain groups of people are more likely to show such patterns when compared with others. Variables that have been studied include age, sex, marital status, ethnic group, and social class. Is it possible to point to any one of these variables and say there is a well-established relationship between it and abnormality? What kinds of results have been obtained?

Several of these variables show fairly strong correlations with abnormal personality patterns, although this may not necessarily indicate that causal relationships exist. For example, alcoholism seems to peak during middle age, while brain syndromes are more likely for the elderly.

Other relationships include higher incidences of neurosis and psychosis in females, while males show higher rates of alcoholism, addictions, and sexual deviation. Separated and divorced people show a higher rate of abnormal patterns than do married people. People in lower social classes show a higher rate of psychosis than do people from higher social classes. Very little difference in rate of abnormal personality patterns has been found when comparing various ethnic groups, although some cross-cultural studies have shown fairly substantial differences in abnormal behavior patterns, as in the ratio of depression to schizophrenia in the population.

Key Terms

Abnormal personality patterns.	Behaviors that produce significant personal discomfort or create problems for others in a person's society.

Addiction.	Dependency on a drug or chemical.

Affective psychoses.	Psychotic behavior characterized by extremes of mood (manic and depressive).

Antisocial behavior.	Behavior characterized by a failure to act according to societal standards *and* the absence of anxiety about such behavior; also called *psychopathic* or *sociopathic behavior*.

Anxiety neurosis.	When a person continues to experience anxiety at a moderate level, with occasional intense periods, but does not recognize the cause of the anxiety.

Biomedical model.	An explanation of abnormal personality patterns emphasizing the influence of body functions.

Catatonia.	A pattern of schizophrenic behavior characterized by extremes of cooperation and activity; the best-known example being total withdrawal accompanied by complete muscle rigidity.

Compulsion.	An unwanted but not preventable pattern of action that recurs often.

Conversion reaction.	When anxiety is transformed into a physical reaction.

Cretinism.	A physiologically caused form of mental retardation resulting from a prenatal lack of iodine.

Delusion.	A false belief.

Depressive.	Despondent, low-activity patterns of behavior.

Dissociative reaction.	Banishing completely an anxiety-producing thought or action.

Existential model.	An explanation of abnormal personality patterns that stresses the influence of present events rather than past experiences.

Functional psychoses.	Psychotic reactions provoked by psychological or experiential influences.

Hallucination.	A false sensory experience.

Hebephrenia.	Psychotic behavior showing wild or silly responses, often accompanied by hallucinations and delusions.

Infantile autism.	Psychotic patterns of behavior shown by children under age ten; poor communication, no desire for personal contact, and a desire for status quo are characteristic symptoms.

Manic.	Elated, hyperactive patterns of behavior.

Mental retardation.	A designation for exceptional subjects whose IQ scores are below the -2 standard deviations from the mean of a normal probability distribution of intelligence test scores.

Mongolism.	A chromosomally caused form of mental retardation in which the child is conceived with forty-seven chromosomes rather than with the normal forty-six.

Neurosis.	A category of abnormal personality patterns characterized by a high level of anxiety in one particular area but the ability to continue functioning in daily activities.

Obsession.	An unwanted but not preventable thought pattern that recurs often.

Organic psychoses.	Psychotic reactions provoked by physical disorders.

Paranoia.	An abnormal personality pattern characterized by feelings of persecution and grandeur.

Personality disorders.	A classification of abnormal personality patterns characterized by the person's inability to act in accordance with societal standards.

Phobia.   An intense, compelling fear of some situation or object; the fear is more intense than the circumstance appears to warrant.

Precipitating factors.   Stimuli that actually initiate behavioral patterns.

Predispositions.   The background characteristics of a person that serve to influence personality patterns.

Psychodynamic model.   As proposed by Freud, an explanation of abnormal personality patterns based upon the concept of unconscious conflicts.

Psychosis.   An abnormal personality pattern characterized by loss of contact with reality.

Psychosomatic disorder.   Actual physiological disorders (damage or malfunctioning) brought about by psychological causes.

Schizophrenia.   The most common of psychotic reactions, often characterized by pronounced loss of contact with reality, delusions, hallucinations.

Self-fulfilling prophecy.   A theory proposing that a person will act in accordance with expectations that have been expressed about anticipated behaviors.

Sexual deviation.   Any sexual behavior judged as deviant according to a particular society's standards.

Social learning model.   An explanation of abnormal personality patterns based primarily upon learning principles.

Chapter 22

Therapies

Psychologists have been interested not only in the identification or diagnosis of abnormal personality patterns, but also in trying to develop techniques to treat these problem behaviors. This chapter discusses some of the therapies that have been developed.

22.1 GENERAL OVERVIEW OF THERAPY

The overall purpose of therapies is to try to help individuals overcome problems such as those described in Chapter 21. Individuals may receive help from a number of different types of therapists.

Percentage of the Population Showing Abnormal Personality Patterns

While varying estimates have been made regarding the percentage of the American population showing abnormal personality patterns at sometime in their lives, a fairly well agreed-upon minimum ratio is one in ten. (This is based on hospitalization rates and clinical records.) Further subdivisions by category of abnormal personality pattern has resulted in the following estimates: about half of these people show neurotic patterns of behavior. Of the others, 30 percent show some kind of addiction, 15 percent are categorized as having other personality disorders, and 5 percent are labeled psychotic. If these estimates are accurate, it means that at any given time, 5 percent of the overall population is neurotic, 3 percent is addicted, 1½ percent shows other personality disorders, and ½ percent is psychotic.

Types of Therapists

There are a number of different types of therapists. Probably the best known are psychiatrists and clinical psychologists. Psychiatrists are medical doctors who have had specialized training following medical school. Clinical psychologsts usually obtain a Ph.D. along with specialized training in therapy techniques.

Other types of therapists include psychoanalysts (usually psychiatrists with specialized training in Freudian therapeutic techniques), psychiatric nurses, psychiatric social workers, and some paraprofessional personnel. (Paraprofessionals are often volunteers with limited training who may work for organizations such as crisis intervention centers.)

EXAMPLE 1. Ready access to some supportive personnel may be crucial in helping a person overcome a crisis. In recent years, many different kinds of agencies and organizations that specialize in providing initial support have been established. These include crisis or suicide prevention centers, drug or alcohol rehabilitation centers often called halfway houses, call-in services for runaways, and the like. Frequently, the paraprofessional personnel in these organizations are minimally trained but capable of helping the person overcome the momentary problem and then guiding the person to a more thoroughly trained person for additional help.

Trends in Treatments

Therapies for abnormal personality patterns have generally not become so rigidly standardized that the people administering them are unwilling to change techniques as new developments occur. As a result, the therapeutic techniques to be discussed in this chapter may find differing interpretations and uses as therapists adjust to changing trends in treatment.

Several trends are noticeable. Greater community involvement in dealing with abnormal personality patterns has produced the development of community psychology as a field, the increase in agencies and organizations that specialize in support for people with behavioral problems, a decrease in the hospitalization rate for people with abnormal patterns, and the extension of community values into the hospital setting in the form of milieu therapy. Additionally, greater knowledge and better techniques in physiology and biology have produced increased genetic counseling, with which parents can better know the probabilities of whether a baby may be born abnormal.

EXAMPLE 2. The probability of some forms of mental retardation such as Down's syndrome (Mongolism) can be identified while the mother carries the fetus. During pregnancy, it is possible to consult with the parents, explain the chromosomal upset and the effect it could have upon the child, and the courses of action available. In some cases, this may lead to a choice of therapeutic abortion. In other cases, the parents may decide to carry the child, but they will certainly be better prepared for the behavior to be expected than if the information had not been made available.

22.2   MEDICAL THERAPIES

Physical procedures used to treat abnormal personality problems are called *medical therapies*, or *somatic therapies*. Two of these, electroconvulsive shock therapy and chemotherapy, are used fairly frequently. A third, psychosurgery, was once used much more extensively.

Electroconvulsive Shock Therapy

Electroconvulsive shock therapy (ECST) involves tightly strapping the patient to a table, placing electodes on either side of the head, and then passing a brief, high-intensity electric current through the brain. This causes immediate unconsciousness, followed by repetitive convulsions.

ECST seems to overstimulate the brain, but is followed by no memory of the events leading up to and including the actual administration of the shock. Upon regaining consciousness, the patient will remain in a docile or passive state for several days. Because of this, ECST has sometimes been used simply as a way of making patients more manageable, although a more appropriate and quite successful application has been its use in helping depressive patients obtain relief.

EXAMPLE 3. While ECST is not used with great frequency, certain types of behavioral symptoms may prompt therapists to choose this technique. Probably the most common case would in the case of a psychotic depressive who is contemplating suicide; in such a case, there is an immediate need for a behavioral change if the patient's death is to be prevented. The likelihood of using ECST is increased when other types of therapy have been tried unsuccessfully.

Chemotherapy

The most prevalent of medical therapies today is *chemotherapy*, the use of drugs to change brain functioning and, as a result, modify abnormal personality patterns. Two advantages of chemotherapy are set forth by its proponents: (1) there is no tissue destruction as in psychosurgery; and (2) the patient allegedly can be made more open to therapeutic influence.

EXAMPLE 4. Patients with affective psychotic reactions are often treated with chemotherapy. Manic patients may be administered some form of tranquilizer to reduce their agitation, while depressive patients may be given antidepressants such as imiprimine. In such cases, it is hoped that the behavioral pattern resulting will be closer to the norm and make the patient more amenable to other forms of treatment.

Several cautions are appropriate at this point: While chemotherapy may relieve symptoms of abnormal personality patterns, this relief may last only as long as the chemotherapy continues.

Once the therapy is stopped, the symptoms may return. Additionally, the patient may become psychologically dependent upon the drugs. In many cases, it may be important to see to it that other forms of therapy accompany chemotherapy if an eventual cure is to be expected.

Psychosurgery

Psychosurgery refers to any technique that involves surgical destruction of brain tissue. Such surgery is performed with the hope of modifying severely abnormal behavior patterns. Probably the best known of these techniques is a *lobotomy*, where the neural tissues connecting the prefrontal lobes to the rest of the brain are severed. This technique proved only partially successful in reducing abnormal behavioral patterns and sometimes caused the patient to become confused and unresponsive. In some cases, it has even resulted in seizures or death, and has thus fallen from favor as a therapeutic technique.

22.3 PSYCHOTHERAPY

Psychotherapies are nonmedical techniques used to try to help a client or patient overcome a problem or problems. There are several different types of psychotherapy, but the concept of psychotherapy can probably be viewed as originating from the work of Sigmund Freud. His procedures formed the basis of psychoanalysis, perhaps the best-known of the psychotherapies.

Psychoanalysis

The bases of *psychoanalysis* were developed by Freud, who belived it was the therapist's responsibility to help and guide the client, providing direction during the therapy sessions. Several aspects of the client's responding during the sessions were considered most important.

Developing out of what Freud and his partner Breuer called the "talking cure," a major aspect of psychoanalysis is the process of *free association*. Free association means the client is expected to say whatever comes to mind, regardless of the distastefulness or apparent irrelevance of the statement.

As the therapy progresses, the client often demonstrates what Freud called *transference*, the development of an emotional relationship with the therapist. Freud believed this relationship represented a reenactment of the association the person had with a parent while a child.

When the client develops trust in the therapist, it becomes possible to explore more and more of the conflicts that have created the problem. The therapist directs the sessions to try to encourage the person to recognize and evaluate these conflicts. However, as the crucial causes of the problem come to be expressed, clients often exhibit *resistance*; that is, they are often unwilling to discuss the topic. If the resistance can be overcome, the therapy may be successful.

Freud felt one way of generating ideas and exploring desires within the therapy setting was *dream analysis*. To Freud the dreams represented thoughts and wishes the client held but was unable to express consciously. Often, even the content of the dream did not express the message directly, but through symbolic representation. (*Note*: Symbolism in dreams has created some problems of interpretation because more than one possible explanation often can be suggested.)

EXAMPLE 5. The client may start a therapy session by relating the content of a recent dream. The therapist may pursue this in different manners, perhaps exploring the meaning of the dream or possibly using the dream material as the initial step in a free association series of thoughts. The therapist needs to recognize the possibility that the dream's content may be symbolic and not something that can be taken at face value.

Client-centered Therapy

Another approach to psychotherapy is called *client-centered therapy*, where the therapist is less directive than in psychoanalytic therapy. Progress depends more upon the client verbalizing and working through his or her problems. This type of therapy has been called nondirective because the therapist often plays a minimal role in "steering" the client through the expression and resolution of conflicts. Client-centered therapy seems to work best with patients who are highly verbal.

Gestalt Therapy

Gestalt therapy, as its name implies, is based on the idea that the personality must be treated as an organized whole. The Gestalt therapist encourages a client to make use of inner resources to gain more control and become more active and responsible for his or her own actions. The client's aim is thus to overcome behaviors such as passivity, irresponsibility, and poor self-concept. Gestalt therapy often involves various kinds of exercises to help the client accomplish these goals.

Play Therapy

Play therapy, which is used most often with children, involves creating a permissive atmosphere in which the child can play with toys, dolls, puppets, art supplies, or other kinds of equipment. One aim of such therapy is to give the therapist an opportunity to observe behaviors that might not be expressed under ordinary circumstances by the child. The permissiveness of the therapy setting is thus supposed to "encourage" the child to express, both verbally and nonverbally, attitudes that might otherwise remain unexpressed.

"Pop" Therapies

A number of therapies that are only loosely based upon the psychoanalytic tradition have emerged in recent years. These have come to be called "*pop*" (for *popular*) therapies. They include *primal therapy, Rolfing* (structural integration), and *growth therapies*.

Primal therapy concentrates on releasing pain which has been "frozen" in the person since childhood. This release may take many forms, although the best known is the *primal scream.*

Structural integration, or Rolfing (named for its founder, Ida Rolf), is a body therapy. Based on the belief that the mind and the body are indistinguishable, Rolfing focuses on adjusting the body posture and musculature so that the "correct balance" of the body can be attained; the lack of balance in the body, supposedly brought on by emotional stress, can thus be eliminated.

Growth therapies are attempts to help individuals achieve maximum self-actualization. All of these approaches have attracted considerable interest, but it should be recognized they may be unable to provide support for all of their therapeutic claims.

EXAMPLE 6. A Rolf practioner may use her or his fingers, closed or open hands, and elbows to exert force on the client's body. The intent is to reposition the body—restoring grace, balance, and economy—and is thus supposed to reinstate mental balance. Rolfing (in a 10-hour session) supposedly accomplishes this latter result by creating the conditions for a massive emotional discharge, which releases memories of past painful experiences. However, evidence to support the claims of Rolfing has been hard to establish.

22.4 GROUP THERAPIES

In a group therapy, more than one client is involved in the therapy setting at the same time. The belief supporting such a therapy technique is that the group provides a social setting where resolution of problems first developed in a social setting may be achieved.

Groups may be made up of several patients from different backgrounds, or they may, in some cases, be members of one family. Some groups, called *encounter groups*, consist of people who do not necessarily show abnormal personality patterns, but who have chosen to meet together to attempt to increase awareness and achieve self-actualization.

22.5 BEHAVIOR MODIFICATION

Based upon the principles developed in the study of learning, *behavior modification* techniques try to deal directly with the symptoms of abnormal personality patterns. Several different approaches have been developed.

Instrumental Conditioning Techniques

Changing the behavior patterns by using instrumental conditioning techniques concentrates on reinforcing responses that are appropriate and lead to desirable goals and attempting to extinguish maladaptive responses. It is necessary to have a very consistent reinforcement pattern, because even an occasional reinforcement for the maladaptive response may make it very resistant to extinction. (This is because of the partial reinforcement effect; see Chapter 12.)

One application of instrumental conditioning in behavior modification is called a *token economy*. Used mostly in hospitals or other institutional settings, the patients are able to earn tokens (poker chips, tickets, etc.) which, when accumulated, can be traded in for privileges or rewards. The tokens are awarded for adaptive responses and withheld when maladaptive patterns are shown.

EXAMPLE 7.   The sophistication of a token economy may advance with the increasing abilities shown by the patient. At first, tokens (and eventually rewards) may be given for behaviors as simple as maintaining personal cleanliness, caring for one's possessions, or showing good manners toward others in the setting. As these are achieved, they will continue to be reinforced, but additional responses may be added to the behavior repertoire. For example, rewards may be given for the acquisition of job skills. Eventually, it is hoped the patient will be able to return to normal functioning.

Classical Conditioning Techniques

Classical conditioning is also used in behavior modification. A correctional experience (serving as an unconditioned stimulus) may be paired with a conditioned stimulus that appears to provoke maladaptive responses. The UCS experiences may be pleasant or unpleasant (positive or aversive), depending upon the type of behavior modification being attempted.

Systematic desensitization relies upon the use of relaxation (a positive experience) being paired with various forms of the anxiety-producing situation. This step-by-step procedure or hierarchy of stimuli is designed so that each CS used comes closer to the one that is most anxiety-provoking. The therapist's task is to monitor each experience, providing effective relaxation cues and maintaining a moderate pace through the hierarchy.

EXAMPLE 8.   If a patient has an intense, compelling fear of the dark, systematic desensitization may be used to help overcome these symptoms. At first, the patient may be asked to read stories about or descriptions of dark places. While this occurs, the patient is reassured and helped to experience relaxation. Successive steps following this might include observing a movie about people going into caves, then actually seeing someone else in a dark room, and finally entering a dark room. Each step would pair relaxation (the new UCS) with images or experiences of the dark (the CS), until the person was able to confront the dark without experiencing intense anxiety.

A different version of confronting the anxiety-provoking stimulus occurs in *implosion therapy*. The patient is asked to imagine the very worst possible version of the anxiety-provoking stimulus and to experience all the attendant anxiety. However, this is done in a totally reassuring environment, and the patient is made to see that the imagined anxiety cannot hurt.

Aversive therapy is a behavior modification technique used on patients showing self-destructive behaviors. The therapist pairs painful or unpleasant stimuli as unconditioned stimuli in the situations that induce the maladaptive behavior. The patient learns that responding in a self-destructive manner will lead to aversive stimuli, and the frequency of such responses decreases.

Modeling Techniques

The basic principles of modeling can also be used in behavior modification. By observing someone who is coping successfully with the anxiety-producing situation the patient can discover and perhaps imitate responses that will be adaptive in the situation.

EXAMPLE 9.   Consider again the description of desensitization described in Example 8. Some of the latter steps in that process would incorporate modeling techniques. Both the movie and the actual observation of another person would serve not only as conditioned stimuli to be paired with relaxation, but also as models of appropriate or adaptive responses. (*Note:* It is not uncommon for several behavior modification techniques to be combined.)

Biofeedback Techniques

Biofeedback uses monitoring devices to provide information to a person about physiological events that would otherwise be difficult or impossible to recognize. *Biofeedback therapy* uses the information provided to help the person learn to control bodily processes, and thus overcome or avoid some problem. Biofeedback therapy may be very helpful in situations involving conversion reactions or psychosomatic disorders.

EXAMPLE 10. Therapists using biofeedback procedures have claimed that appropriate monitoring and learned physiological control can help alleviate many potential physiological problems. One example of this is the treatment of "tension headaches." Chronic sufferers are able to observe feedback from neck and shoulder muscles, learn how to relax these muscles, and thus reduce the tension that appears to contribute to headaches.

Assertiveness Training

Some persons come to a therapist because they recognize they are timid or withdrawn and they wish to change that pattern of responding. While such behavior often would not be called abnormal, the people see it as a problem to be overcome. *Assertiveness training*, which frequently uses instrumental conditioning, classical conditioning, and modeling in combination, helps the patients learn how to express emotions and beliefs in a more forthright manner.

22.6 THERAPY EFFECTIVENESS

The effectiveness of therapy techniques has been debated vigorously. There are basically three difficulties in establishing estimates of the effectiveness of therapy techniques: (1) The data collection techniques in therapy are especially subject to biases, including what is recorded in the case history and what criteria are used for interpreting that information. (2) Additionally, some people simply recover from abnormal personality patterns without any therapy. (This is called *remission*.) (3) Comparable to the phenomenon in medicine, there is sometimes a *placebo effect* in therapy situations. (This occurs when the patient approaches the therapy situation with such energy and determination that virtually any style of therapy would effect a cure.)

EXAMPLE 11. Consider the biofeedback therapy described in Example 10. It is possible that the patient may be developing the headaches for any number of reasons. However, the fact that the patient simply believes in biofeedback may be enough to relieve the problem. (Correspondingly, if the belief is that the technique will not work, it is much less likely to be successful.)

Solved Problems

22.1 What percentage of the adult population in the United States can be expected to show abnormal personality patterns? What percentages have been assigned to subgroups within this category?

The percentage varies depending upon which agency or group of people you might ask. But, based on hospital and clinic records, the generally accepted estimate is that 10 percent of the adult population will show some sort of abnormal personality pattern at any given time. Of this group, the greatest number are neurotics—perhaps half of all those showing abnormal patterns. Of the rest, the estimates are that about 30 percent are addicted in some fashion, 15 percent show other personality disorders, and 5 percent are psychotic.

22.2 What professionals besides medical doctors are involved in the treatment of individuals with abnormal personality patterns?

Psychiatrists and some psychoanalysts are medical doctors. Some of the other professionals involved in treatment are clinical psychologists, who have Ph.D.s. Other people who help treat individuals with abnormal personality patterns are psychiatric social workers, psychiatric nurses and paraprofessional personnel. People in this last group are often volunteers, many of whom need only limited training for the jobs they do.

22.3 What are some of the recent trends in the treatment of individuals with abnormal personality patterns, and can these trends be expected to continue in the future?

It is difficult to predict future developments very accurately because we never know what might be learned or discovered and provide a major breakthrough. However, there are some recent trends that have been identified.

One is that the rate of hospitalization or custodial care for people with many forms of abnormal personality patterns is dropping. Part of this is the result of better therapeutic techniques and part the result of a more tolerant or understanding attitude in the population in general. However, because of the overall growth of the population, the absolute number of patients hospitalized for the treatment of abnormal personality patterns has increased.

Other noticeable trends include greater community involvement, with community psychology and crisis intervention programs becoming more and more common. Furthermore, there has been an increase in the number of "halfway houses" to ease the transition for patients who have been hospitalized or imprisoned and are returning to the society at large. Milieu therapy, or the attempt to bring many of society's functions and demands into the custodial or hospital setting, is another recent development. Finally, there has been a trend toward increased genetic counseling, which allows estimates of the probability a baby will be born abnormal. This information may sometimes lead to a choice of therapeutic abortion.

22.4 In a popular movie about a mental hospital, several of the patients were "treated" with electroconvulsive shock therapy (ECST). In one instance, the ECST was used to keep the patient in a docile attitude, although the ECST did not appear to be the appropriate therapeutic treatment for the circumstances. Is this a common occurrence? What example can you give of an appropriate use of ECST?

Opinions vary as to the extent to which ECST has been used to "create" docile patients. However, there is evidence that this serious abuse of treatment has sometimes occurred. A more appropriate use of ECST is made when the patient is diagnosed as a psychotic depressive. ECST seems to bring rapid and effective relief from depression, making the patients more amenable to other therapeutic treatment and in some cases relieving suicidal tendencies.

22.5   Psychosurgery is another form of medical therapy. How commonly is it used? What are the potential benefits and difficulties with psychosurgery? What other type of therapy is often substituted for psychosurgery?

Psychosurgery has been used less and less with succeeding years. The potential uses of psychosurgery remain valuable in certain instances (for example, when a tumor creates hallucinations because of unusual stimulation of the visual cortex). However, the practice of performing prefrontal lobotomies to try to treat certain psychotic patterns has proved inconsistent and possibly dangerous, occasionally leading to seizures or death. With increased research, the use of drugs has taken the place of psychosurgery in many cases.

22.6   The affective psychoses were described in the previous chapter. Two states of this psychosis, the manic and the depressive, were discussed. If the patient is in either one of these states, chemotherapy may be used. What is chemotherapy? What might be done for a manic patient? From what kind of treatment might a depressive patient benefit?

Chemotherapy is the use of drugs to alter brain processes and therefore influence abnormal personality patterns. Tranquilizers may be given to the overenergetic (manic) patients to calm them and make them more cooperative. Depressive patients may be given antidepressants to relieve anxieties and alleviate the depressive state. A distinct advantage of this kind of therapy is that no tissue damage results. In psychosurgery, on the other hand, there is damage to the brain tissue, which cannot regenerate.

22.7   Chemotherapy does not cause tissue damage, but it may create a different type of problem for the patient. What is this problem? What *should* be done in conjunction with chemotherapy?

There seem to be two problems related to the same source. Because chemotherapy often produces noticeable and rapid changes in behavior, the patient may develop a dependence upon the drug as a means of alleviating the problem, rather than developing alternate patterns of responding. In a similar vein, the persons in charge of the patients may come to rely upon and be satisfied with chemotherapy, not making an effort to help the patient develop alternate behavior patterns. In instances such as these, chemotherapy should be combined with psychotherapy, phasing out chemotherapy as more and more adequate behaviors are developed.

22.8   Is psychotherapy intended only for those with seriously abnormal personality problems? What is the purpose of psychotherapy?

The aims of psychotherapy vary with each and every case. It is probably safe to say that all psychotherapy has as its overall aim helping the patient overcome a particular problem or problems. But the types of problems treated vary considerably. For example, abnormal personal frustrations, motivational conflicts, abnormal personality patterns, or current living situations may all be dealt with in the course of psychotherapy. Clearly, one does not *need* to have a seriously abnormal personality pattern to encounter these problems.

22.9   Is there more than one kind of psychotherapy?

There are many different kinds of psychotherapy, including psychoanalytic, client-centered, Gestalt, existential, group, play, and what are called "pop" therapies. It probably is reasonable to think that all of these therapies should give some credit to Freud because the psychotherapeutic movement started from his work. However, many other people have made major contributions to the development of the different techniques. Freud's influence is seen directly in psychoanalytic therapy, and psychoanalysts are trained in what are called Freudian techniques. (See Section 1.5 for a review of the differences between psychiatrists, psychoanalysts, and clinical psychologists.)

22.10   What is free association, and what role does it play in the therapeutic situation?

Free association is a technique in which the patient in psychoanalysis lets each thought lead to the next without restriction. The purpose of free association is to get the patient to consider all the different factors that might be creating problems. Speaking what comes to mind, without forethought, is supposed to facilitate the release of information from the unconscious. It is hoped that the person will express even those things that seem objectionable or irrelevant, and thus reveal fears or conflicts that cannot be reached through ordinary rational discourse.

22.11   Some patients in psychoanalysis have found themselves unwilling or unable to make use of free association. What is this phenomenon called, and what are some possible explanations for it?

This unwillingness is one aspect of what Freud called *resistance*. Presumably, the patient is in analysis or therapy because of painful conflicts that persist in the unconscious, and it stands to reason that the patient may resist exposing such conflicts, even through free association. In addition, the patient may have an inability to remember certain anxiety-laden events, or show resistance at an unconscious rather than a conscious level. Much of a psychoanalyst's work may involve helping the patient overcome these resistances, recognize the sources of anxiety, and learn to cope with them.

22.12   When asked about how therapy is going, patients have been known to say, "I just love my therapist!" Some people don't recognize that this may actually be true and an important part of the therapy situation. What is this called? Why might this be important in therapy situations?

The situation described may represent *transference*, or the transfer of attitudes about one person to another. Quite frequently, such transference is the reenactment of a child-parent relationship, with the therapist substituting for the parent. In this problem, the situation illustrates positive transference, which often helps the patient overcome resistance. A patient who shows an aggressive or hostile attitude toward the therapist may be experiencing negative transference. Even this may help the therapist and patient understand what the difficulties are.

22.13   Therapists have been known to interpret dreams as evidence of wish fulfillment. What does this mean?

Freud believed that thoughts which were too anxiety-provoking or threatening to be expressed directly, even in dreams, may be disguised and symbolically represented in dreams. If these symbols can be correctly interpreted, they reveal particular urges that the person would like to fulfill. Thus, the concept of wish fulfillment represents what the person is able to accomplish symbolically in dreams, but not in actual behavior.

22.14   After several therapy sessions, Arthur is perplexed. He expected the therapist to take an active and guiding role, but instead has found he does most of the talking himself. The therapist listens and gives relatively little direction. Finally, Arthur "gets up his nerve" and asks the therapist why there isn't more guidance. Using the different descriptions of psychotherapy given in the text, pick the one that best seems to fit this circumstance and then describe the answer the therapist might give to Arthur.

This situation seems to be an instance of nondirective therapy. The client's role in this is to actively explore various possibilities that might help explain the problems being experienced. The therapist attempts to create a permissive atmosphere, and usually keeps interpretations and advice to a minimum.

In this case, the therapist might tell Arthur that nondirective therapy is being used because Arthur is doing so well without a lot of direction. With a client like Arthur, who is quite verbal and can express feelings freely, there is not always a need for a therapist to take a guiding, active role.

22.15   Children may have behavioral problems but be unable to express them in words. What type of therapy have psychologists developed in order to treat children?

Play therapy has been developed for use with children. Placed in a permissive atmosphere, the child may be given the opportunity to play with dolls, toys, puppets, drawing equipment, modeling materials, and other supplies.

Two outcomes of play therapy are considered important. First, the play may serve as a release of tensions and anxieties that otherwise might not be expressed. Additionally, the play behavior may reveal attitudes the child cannot express verbally. Both results may help the child overcome the problem at hand.

22.16   Imagine a client writhing on the floor, muttering, yelling, twisting and turning, and all the while being urged by the therapist to "get it all out." What kind of therapy is this client probably engaging in? What purpose is it trying to serve? How do many psychologists view this and other comparable therapies?

The situation described probably represents primal therapy. The client is urged to reexperience the painful events of childhood that have been repressed. According to therapists conducting this type of therapy, the release of pain is found in these expressive behaviors, and the client will experience relief following such sessions. Perhaps the most characteristic of these release behaviors has come to be called the primal scream.

Many psychologists view primal therapy and several other techniques such as structural integration (Rolfing) and therapies at "growth centers" as poorly established "pop" psychologies. This may be because such therapies lack a tradition and have so far failed to substantiate their claims. Whatever the reason, increased interest in psychology has made many of these therapies quite popular.

22.17   A fairly well-known book about psychotherapy deals with the experiences of a therapist attempting to help three patients, each of whom believes he is Jesus Christ. The therapist arranges to have all three meet and interact, with the hope that this might help the men eliminate their delusion. What is the name given to such a therapeutic approach? What does such an approach try to accomplish? Are there other varieties of this approach?

Bringing several patients together in a therapeutic setting is called group therapy. The purpose of group therapy is the same as that of any other therapy: to help each client overcome a particular problem or problems. The rationale of group therapy is that if problems develop in a social setting, they may also be resolved in a social setting.

Other types of group therapies are family therapy and encounter groups. Family therapies are used in situations where an outsider (the therapist) can be of some help in resolving family conflicts. Encounter groups try to help people expand awareness and achieve self-actualization rather than overcome abnormal personality patterns.

(*Note*: Not everyone benefits from group therapy. One survey showed that while 1 out of 3 participants seemed to gain from the situation, perhaps 1 in every 10 became more distressed or maladjusted.)

22.18   Diane's parents are very upset because Diane, age six, has developed a persistent hacking cough that will not go away. Her parents have taken her to several medical doctors, but no physical cause for the cough can be found. Finally, on the recommendation of one of the medical doctors, they take Diane to a psychologist. After careful observation, the psychologist determines that the parents (and many other people) are very attentive any time Diane begins a coughing spell. The psychologist suggests the parents institute almost exactly the reverse sequence of attentiveness; that is, they should be very attentive when Diane is not coughing, but ignore the coughing attacks. This suggestion represents what kind of therapy technique? What principles are involved? What success may be expected?

The psychologist's suggestions for Diane's parents are an example of behavior modification. This particular circumstance involves operant (or instrumental) conditioning, with reinforcement (attention) for the appropriate "not-coughing" behavior and extinction (no attention) for coughing. The success of such a technique often depends upon the consistency with which it is maintained. Even an occasional period of attention to the coughing may result in the persistance of such responding because of the partial reinforcement effect. (Remember, partial reinforcement may lead to great resistance to extinction; see Section 12.4)

22.19 The director of a home for teen-age girls with behavioral problems decides to institute a "ticket" system. The girls are instructed that responses which are positive (that is, appropriate to the social setting) will be rewarded with "tickets" that may be used for various items such as clothing, special foods, attendance at the movies, and use of the telephone. Girls who make negative responses will not receive tickets or even have tickets taken away. A list of appropriate and inappropriate responses, along with their ticket values, is posted and discussed. In this case, the director is using behavior modification procedures. Describe the principles in effect in this situation.

The plan the director has created is called a *token economy*. The girls' responses are rewarded (or punished) by the use of secondary reinforcers, the tickets. They will be likely to learn very quickly that reinforcements and punishments are contingent upon certain types of behaviors, and thus will learn which responses to make and which to avoid.

22.20 Brent is disturbed by a very compelling fear of cats, so he decides to consult a psychologist. The psychologist sets out an eight-step procedure for Brent, starting with reading some stories about cats and eventually ending with Brent actually handling a cat. Brent is told that he should relax at each successive stage, and when anxiety does arise, the therapist helps him calm down. The procedure involves only several short sessions over a period of several weeks, but Brent's fear of cats finally is eliminated. What is the name of this technique? Explain the principles of this technique as they apply to Brent's situation.

Brent has been guided through a procedure of systematic desensitization. The basis of such a procedure is that relaxation and anxiety are incompatible. Therefore, if Brent can remain relaxed at each successive stage of exposure to cats, he will not experience anxiety. Basically, this is a counter-conditioning procedure, pairing relaxation with the stimuli while extinguishing the anxiety that had previously existed.

22.21 Suppose the psychologist Brent visited believed in the use of implosion therapy rather than systematic desensitization. How would the procedure employed differ from the one described in Problem 22.20?

Implosion therapy involves having the client imagine the worst possible situation and experiencing the strongest anxiety produced by the feared stimulus, but this is done so that reinforcement of the conditioned response to anxiety is absent. The psychologist would ask Brent to imagine cats climbing on him, scratching, screeching, and jumping about. Rehearsing such thoughts in a totally nonthreatening situation would force Brent to learn that his imagined fears could not hurt him. This "flooding" of anxiety and subsequent recognition that it does not hurt him should help Brent overcome his fears.

22.22 By age six, Nathan was showing more and more self-destructive responding. For example, he would knock his head against a wall several hundred times each day. Tranquilizers and anticonvulsant drugs had proved ineffective. In an attempt to reduce and eventually eliminate this behavior, a therapist strapped to Nathan's body a small device that could deliver an electric shock. (The device could be activated by a remote-control transmitter.) Nathan's behavior was monitored constantly, and each time he hit himself, a shock was administered. What type of therapy was Nathan given? Explain the principles that apply to Nathan's case.

  This procedure is called aversion therapy. The principle is simple—something unpleasant is associated with the undesirable response. The result hoped for is that the stimulus situation (whatever it may be) that provokes the undesirable response will instead come to be aversive and no longer generate the abnormal response pattern.

22.23 Consider again Brent's fear of cats (Problem 22.20.) Suppose the therapist decided to use a modeling procedure in the treatment Brent received. How might this be done? Why?

  Modeling involves having the client observe someone who is coping successfully with what for the client is an anxiety-producing situation. Brent would be given the opportunity to observe a model handling a cat and petting and playing with it with no fear. The belief is that the patient can learn simply by watching the behavior of others. Brent should be more able to cope with cats by having seen what kinds of successful responses toward cats can be made.

22.24 Jean uses easily-applied "temperature strips" to detect changes in her body temperature. She has found that she is able to control her reactions and overcome her previous problem of having cold feet. This is a practical application of what therapy technique? What category of abnormal personality patterns may be treated using this technique?

  Jean's ability to control her temperature reactions by observing the information provided by the "temperature strips" represents a biofeedback technique. The strips furnish indications of slight bodily changes that could not be easily recognized directly.

  As more sophisticated monitoring devices become available, it is hoped that biofeedback techniques will help people deal with many more psychosomatic disorders. For example, a person might learn to identify and control the flow of acid in the stomach and thus avoid ulcers.

22.25 Raymond has always felt somewhat unsure of himself. One day, after he picked up some cleaning, he found that the cleaners missed a big stain. However, he found he was unable to make himself complain. Raymond decides to get some help in learning to be firmer in his dealings with others. What kind of help does Raymond probably get? What principles are involved?

  Raymond probably receives training in being more assertive. Using principles from modeling and classical and instrumental conditioning, assertiveness training helps a person learn new skills that allow a more open expression of thought and action. Assertiveness may be important in many different circumstances, including business dealings such as Raymond's, expressions of sadness or joy, or rejection of unwanted personality patterns.

22.26 Why is it often difficult to determine the effectiveness of various therapies?

  The effectiveness of therapies is debated for several reasons. First, the accuracy of data collected is suspect because much of it comes from case histories, which may contain biases and are probably judged against varying criteria. Second, there is a possibility that some people show spontaneous remission (that is, they recover, but not because of the therapy). Finally, there is evidence that a "placebo effect" may exist for certain therapies. In such cases, it is probably the enthusiasm or determination of the client, rather than the therapy itself, which effects the cure.

Key Terms

Assertiveness training.   Teaching someone to express emotions and beliefs in an "open" or forthright way.

Aversive therapy.   A technique that pairs unpleasant (aversive) stimuli with inappropriate responding.

Behavior modification.   Procedures that change behaviors by using instrumental conditioning, classical conditioning, and modeling techniques.

Biofeedback.   The use of monitoring equipment to inform a person about physiological responses that might otherwise remain unobservable.

Chemotherapy.   A medical therapy involving the use of drugs to try to treat abnormal personality patterns.

Client-centered therapy.   A therapy technique that emphasizes the restructuring of the self to be consistent with past experience; also called nondirective therapy.

Clinical psychology.   A branch of psychology concerned with the theory and practice of helping someone overcome behavioral or personality problems.

Community psychology.   A branch of psychology based on the premise that a better community attitude can help prevent abnormal personality patterns.

Dream analysis.   In psychoanalysis, the procedure of interpreting the meaning of dreams reported by the patient.

Electroconvulsive shock therapy (ECST).   A medical therapy involving the passing of an electric current through the patient's brain; this produces unconsciousness, followed by a series of convulsions.

Encounter group.   A therapy in which normal people meet together to try to increase interpersonal skills and self-awareness.

Family therapy.   A group therapy involving members of the same family.

Free association.   A psychoanalytic technique in which the client says whatever comes to mind, letting each thought lead to the next.

Genetic counseling.   Counseling in which potential parents are advised of the likelihood that their children will be normal; based on chromosomal studies of one or both parents.

Gestalt therapy.   A therapy technique that emphasizes the patient's responsibilities for behavior; based upon perception of the total personality.

Group therapy.   Any therapy in which more than one patient is present in the therapy setting at the same time.

Growth therapies.   "Pop" therapies aimed at helping an individual achieve maximum self-actualization.

Implosion therapy.   A technique involving pairing of the worst possible anxiety-producing stimuli with a nonthreatening setting.

Medical therapies.   Therapies that involve the use of physical procedures to try to treat abnormal personality problems.

Milieu therapy.   A type of therapy that tries to incorporate the social standards of a culture or community into the hospital or treatment setting.

Paraprofessional.   The designation of a person with relatively little training who works (often as a volunteer) to help individuals confront personal problems.

Placebo effect.   When a technique for therapy works only because the patient believes it will.

Play therapy.   A therapy technique used mostly with children; the expression of personality patterns are made by the children in unrestricted play situations.

Primal therapy.   A "pop" therapy technique emphasizing the release of "frozen" pain, often through the primal scream.

Psychiatry.   A specialty of medicine that is concerned with the diagnosis and treatment of abnormal personality patterns.

Psychoanalysis.   The theory and form of therapy proposed by Freud; emphasizes personality conflicts and unconscious motivations.

Psychoanalyst.   A person (usually a psychiatrist) trained to use the therapeutic techniques developed by Freud.

Psychosurgery.   A medical therapy involving the surgical destruction of brain tissue.

Psychotherapy.   Use of psychological methods to try to treat abnormal personality patterns.

Resistance.   In psychoanalysis, the phenomenon in which the patient does not wish to discuss a particular topic.

Rolfing.   A "pop" therapy that suggests that adjustment of body posture and musculature will release emotional stress; named for its founder, Ida Rolf.

Somatic therapies.   See *medical therapies*.

Spontaneous remission.   Recovery from abnormal personality patterns without any therapy.

Structural integration.   See *Rolfing*.

Systematic desensitization.   A step-by-step classical conditioning in which an anxiety-producing stimulus (CS) is paired with relaxation (UCS).

Token economy.   A behavior modification technique in which secondary reinforcers (tokens) can later be traded in for rewards.

Transference.   In psychoanalysis, the phenomenon in which the patient develops a strong emotional attachment (reminiscent of an earlier emotional attachment) to the therapist.

Chapter 23

Social Psychology

Psychology primarily concerns itself with the study of individual behavior, but the influence of group membership on an individual cannot be ignored. *Social psychology* is the study of the individual's behavior as it is influenced by membership in a group.

23.1 RELATIONSHIP OF THE INDIVIDUAL TO THE GROUP

It should be recognized that almost every person's behavior is influenced by membership in groups almost all of the time. Some of these groups are *formal*, with designated titles and rules. Other groups are *informal*; they are organized casually and have unwritten (and perhaps very flexible) rules. The groups may also be *present* (that is, the other members are actually physically in the person's environment) or *absent* (meaning the other people are not physically present, but association with them remains an important influence on the person's behavior).

EXAMPLE 1. Adam, who is a Mormon, attends a gathering where he is offered a cup of coffee. He refuses politely. In doing so, Adam is influenced by the beliefs he holds as part of his formal membership in a particular church. The influence of his group membership is important even though other group members are not present at the moment.

Socialization

As an individual grows up within a given culture, the family, school, peers, and the community at large furnish many influences that help establish the values and norms by which the individual lives. This rather general process, called *socialization*, seems to result from both modeling and the reinforcement of what are considered appropriate behaviors.

Cultural Relativity

The process of socialization establishes values and norms that affect daily life. However, it must be recognized that the values and norms may be appropriate only for the particular culture or subculture involved. The principle of *cultural relativity* proposes that behavior must be judged according to the cultural setting in which it occurs.

EXAMPLE 2. One difference between American and certain European cultural values can be seen in the ways in which men greet one another. American men most often greet each other with a handshake (which may be of several different varieties). In some European countries, men kiss each other on both cheeks when they meet after a long separation. What is considered appropriate and ordinary in one culture might be considered out of the ordinary in another.

Social Facilitation and Social Interference

The presence of others may influence performance on a task. If the presence of others seems to improve performance, *social facilitation* has taken place. *Social interference* occurs when the presence of others seems to impair performance. Quite frequently, social facilitation will occur when the person is performing a task that has been well learned, while social interference may be more likely when the person is performing a task that has not been learned well.

EXAMPLE 3. The amount of experience that a person has had in teaching is often reflected by the style with which a lecture is delivered. The "rookie" teacher may have difficulties with pronunciation, remembering sequence of topics, or answering questions asked by the class. The "veteran" teacher, on the other hand, may actually relax in front of the class and in fact be more personable and confident in teaching situations than in nonteaching situations. The new teacher's difficulties illustrate social interference, while the experienced teacher's abilities illustrate social facilitation.

23.2 SOCIAL ROLES

It is necessary to understand status to be able to understand social roles. *Status* refers to the position held or the function served by a person at some given time. *Role* is the expected range of behavior of a person holding a particular status. (*Note*: The word *status* has a second meaning, implying prestige or standing. The two meanings of status are not necessarily the same, although an individual's position may give him or her prestige.)

Expectancy

Because a role is defined by a certain range of behaviors, the person holding a role can be expected to act in a certain way. In some cases, this is exactly what happens; the person acts in accordance with the role he or she has accepted. Research on social roles has shown that they may influence behavior significantly. A person in a given role may have expectations based on that role, and these expectations may cause certain kinds of behaviors. When a behavior is the result of such an expectation, it is called a *self-fulfilling prophecy*.

EXAMPLE 4. Imagine two groups of high school students who are given a lengthy word problem in algebra. One group is told that the solution to the problem will be time-consuming but easy because it involves only a rudimentary knowledge of mathematics. (This description of the problem is accurate.) The other group is told the problem is a real "brain-teaser," and is often given to graduate students in mathematics. Such descriptions could create a self-fulfilling prophecy: the students in the second group could probably be expected to perform less well on the problem because of the expectations created by the false description.

Role Conflict

No person holds only a single role. The multiple roles one has may not always call for compatible behaviors. When two or more roles are in conflict, so that fulfilling the expectations of one role means being unable to satisfy the expectations of the other, an *inter-role conflict* exists.

EXAMPLE 5. Many organizations sponsor physical-fitness runs. The stated objective is to get as many participants as possible, and frequently some sort of nominal award is given to every person who completes the course. However, at some of these runs, participants can be seen taking shortcuts to try to finish ahead of some of the other runners. Apparently, the role of a participant who is in the race for its stated purpose— physical fitness—is important to some people. But the role of competitor (with a strong need to "win") seems to be more important to others, and thus leads to cheating on the part of some people.

On some occasions, a single role may call for more than one possible behavior, and these behaviors may be in conflict. This situation is called an *intra-role conflict*.

EXAMPLE 6. Supervisors in factories often experience intra-role conflicts. One aspect of the supervisor's job is to guide the workers and try to help them experience some job satisfaction. Another aspect, however, is to keep production at a level that satisfies management. These two purposes are not always in agreement, so the supervisor must choose which goal to pursue in any given situation, and in the long run find the proper "balance" between satisfying management and satisfying the workers.

Conformity

Some behaviors are established by group opinion. A person who behaves according to the expectations of a group shows *conformity*. A person who recognizes the expectations of a group but acts in an opposite fashion shows *noncomformity*. A person whose behavior is not influenced one way or the other by social expectations shows *independence*.

EXAMPLE 7. Group opinion exerts a powerful effect upon styles of dress. Some of the fashions presented by designers will "catch on" if many people conform to the style of the moment; other designs will be rejected by the public and become financial disasters for the designers and clothing manufacturers. In the fashion industry, financial success thus depends to a large degree on how many people will conform to a new style or "look."

Obedience. One aspect of conformity that has been investigated experimentally is *obedience*. The surprising results of the studies indicate that subjects who believe they have little or no choice about responding (even if they are told they have a choice) are likely to obey. It seems that if subjects can attribute responsibility for their actions to some other person who is judged superior or in authority, they will do as they are told, even if their actions may be potentially harmful to someone else.

Stereotypes. Stereotyping is another aspect of conformity that has been widely investigated. *Stereotypes* are overgeneralizations that suggest that all members of a particular group can be expected to behave in an identical fashion. Thus, a person who thinks in stereotypes may expect all members of a particular group to conform in certain behaviors. (Stereotypes are discussed fully in Chapter 24.)

23.3 PAYOFFS AND COSTS OF ROLES

The role a person fulfills may lead to either payoffs or costs. A *payoff* means the role has led to a positive event or a reinforcement, while the *cost* of a role means the result has been aversive or negative in nature. A commonly observed result of noncomformity is discrimination; that is, a person who fails to conform to the standards of group opinion may suffer rejection and unfair treatment.

23.4 COMPETITION AND COOPERATION

One topic in social psychology that has received a great deal of attention is the comparison of competitive and cooperative behaviors. Whether a person is competitive or cooperative may be a function of the expectations of the group to which the person belongs.

The basic nature of *competition* is the attempt to get the best of a situation—that is, to do better than someone else. *Cooperation* means working with or assisting someone else in the hope of achieving a mutual goal.

Some researchers have claimed that competitiveness is a characteristic of all people. Other researchers have found that a cooperative group is generally more successful than a competitive group in achieving good performance on a task. Within a group, however, there must be successful communication if cooperation is to result in benefits.

23.5 GROUP DYNAMICS

The social interactions that occur within groups have been summarized under the heading of *group dynamics*. Research on group dynamics has focused on variables such as the effect of the size of group upon behavior and decision-making processes.

Group Size

A gathering of two or more people is called a *group*. The size of a group appears to affect the type of social interactions that will develop within it.

Dyads. A group consisting of only two people is called a *dyad*. Social interactions within a dyad are generally cooperative and positive. A spontaneously created dyad promotes *social exchange*, a reciprocity of give-and-take. Each person seems to experience superiority in some ways and inferiority in others.

EXAMPLE 8. The relationship between an editor and a writer illustrates the principles of social exchange. The writer generates ideas, creating a manuscript. The editor reads and comments on the manuscript, suggesting additions, deletions, and perhaps changes in wording. Each is dependent upon the other: the writer requires the guidance and assistance of the editor, while the editor of necessity must have the raw materials produced by the writer. Each must recognize the superiority of the other in certain aspects of the publishing process.

Triads. A group of three people is called a *triad*. Research has shown that triads are frequently unstable and promote internal competition. A frequent occurrence is that the triad disintegrates into a dyad and one outsider, and the outsider is usually dissatisfied with this outcome.

EXAMPLE 9. Perhaps the most famous example of triad relationships is the "eternal traingle," consisting of either two women and one man, or two men and one woman. There is an inherent instability in such a situation, and the potential for a great deal of competition. Such a triad often dissolves into a stable dyad and an outsider, who will most likely be dissatisfied.

Groups of more than three. Study of groups of more than three members has shown that as group size increases, there is an increase in competition within the group. Groups of four or five are thus often found to yield greater satisfaction than larger groups.

Leadership

Attempts to identify the common characteristics that are most important for leadership within a group have generally proved fruitless. Both the purpose of the group and its composition seem to affect the choice of leader. One interesting point is that if a person who is designated by title as a leader refuses to lead, the group may rebel against that person and choose a new leader.

Group Decisions—The Risky Shift

The social interaction produced by a group's discussion of a problem sometimes leads to a phenomenon known as the *risky shift*: the group, acting as a whole, may take risks greater than those that any single member, acting alone, would dare to take.

The term *risky shift* developed only because most researchers have studied movement toward greater risks. It is also interesting to note that individual decisions may to some extent follow group decisions, even if the individual was not present when the group made its decision.

The shift need not always be toward greater risk, however. Research into this phenomenon indicates that the shift is made in the direction of the strongest arguments. This *role of arguments* means that a group's decisions could be more conservative than the decisions of some of its members, depending on the number and strength of the arguments in favor of various courses of action.

Group Decisions—"Groupthink"

Research studies of group decision-making processes have revealed an interesting phenomenon described as "*groupthink*." The members of a group may create an atmosphere in their meetings that takes hold and dominates the thoughts or opinions of all the members. Characteristically, the members of such a group believe the group's opinions are invulnerable to outside criticism, and the apparent unanimity of the members' opinions may be enough to convince them of their inherent rightness, in spite of evidence to the contrary. Evidence opposing their viewpoint may be ignored, and dissenters may be urged to change viewpoints to conform with that of the group.

EXAMPLE 10. During the early part of World War II, the "groupthink" phenomenon could be observed in the behaviors of some Americans of German descent. People who were otherwise firm in their admiration for democracy and justice would meet to extol the virtues of the changes taking place in Germany. They would also try to encourage other German-Americans to accept these beliefs, and became upset with those who did not. As more information regarding the conduct of the war became available, these people simply could not believe the reports. It was not until later in the war, when the evidence was overwhelming, that they were persuaded to change their thinking about the Nazi regime.

Crowding

One aspect of group behavior that has been studied extensively is the effect of *crowding*. In laboratory experiments, rats have been allowed to breed until their environment becomes extremely overcrowded. Such conditions led to many pathological behaviors, including unusual sexual behaviors, high levels of hostility, and even cannibalism. An overcrowded environment like the one that the rats were in has been described as a *behavioral sink*, where the unusual responses occur even when normally adequate amounts of food, water, and shelter are provided.

EXAMPLE 11. A research study investigating a similar phenomenon showed that people in high-density population areas (big cities) are not likely to trust a stranger who comes to the door and asks to use the telephone; people in rural areas are much more likely to be trusting in such a situation. It is unclear how much population density (rather than other variables such as crime rate) explains this finding.

Personal Space

Another variable to be considered is summarized by the term *personal space*. This is the physical distance that surrounds a person, who is likely to think of it as his or her "own." Two important factors seem to be important in determining what constitutes adequate personal space. One of these is the standard accepted by a particular culture. The other is the intimacy of the given situation; in general, the distance defining personal space decreases as the intimacy of a relationship increases.

EXAMPLE 12. Consider the story of two diplomats at a formal reception. One came from a very "proper" country, where personal space was measured in feet. The second came from a much more "intimate" country, where courtesy called for leaning toward your companion and even making physical contact. When these two met at the reception, they began a conversation. Each time the second diplomat came closer to the first, the first would move back slightly. In this way, the two managed to move almost forty feet across the reception hall before their conversation was ended.

Prosocial Behavior

Prosocial behavior exists when one person or a group of people come to the aid of another person or group. Helpful behavior seems to be more likely if only a single person is asked for help or recognizes someone else's need for aid. Groups are less likely to offer aid or agree to help someone in need. The significant factor appears to be the "spreading" of responsibility: one person alone cannot reasonably expect others to come to the aid of someone in need; people in groups, on the other hand, can always rationalize their lack of involvement by assuming that someone else will give the necessary aid.

EXAMPLE 13. The incident that provoked the initial research investigations into this area was the killing of a young woman in New York City. More than thirty people admitted having witnessed some or all of the incident, yet not one went to the woman's aid or even called the police. When interviewed later, they stated they felt "someone else" could or would take the responsibility. Research studies under controlled conditions have confirmed that this type of behavior is common in many groups.

Solved Problems

23.1 Nearing the end of a poorly attended psychology seminar, the instructor stops the discussion and tells her class she would like them to take part in an experiment. At the next class meeting, she will begin her lecture with the sentence, "Today we will be discussing social psychology." At this point, the teacher wants the students present to laugh, cheer, whistle, and generally carry on, while at the same time observing those students who were absent the previous day.

In the next day's class meeting, this is exactly what the instructor does. What kind of reaction do you think the previous day's absentees show? What phenomenon is the instructor trying to illustrate?

When the class starts cheering, yesterday's absentees at first show surprise, then join in the cheering, although somewhat halfheartedly and with some feelings of embarrassment and confusion. The instructor has arranged this situation to show the influence of group response upon an individual's behavior. In this case, the absentees from the previous day show some signs of *conforming* by joining in and participating in the applause, even though they have no understanding of why they are cheering.

23.2 Americans point to things by extending the arm, clenching all but the index finger into a fist, and then indicating a direction with that finger. In other societies, pointing may be accomplished quite differently. For example, one group "points" by twisting lips, chin, and nose in the direction to be indicated. What principle of social psychology is illustrated by the differences between these two kinds of "pointing" behavior?

Cultural norms determine behaviors such as pointing (among hundreds of other behaviors) through the process of socialization. Family, school, peer groups, and the community may both provide models and reinforce those patterns of responding that are "appropriate" to the given culture or subculture. Behavior must therefore be interpreted according to the norms that have been developed and maintained (often through many generations) in a culture. In other words, in observing and interpreting any behavior, the principle of cultural relativity must be considered.

23.3 A track coach is concerned because one of the high jumpers on his team has shown an unusual pattern of behavior. In practice, the jumper is quite capable of clearing 6½ feet. But when a meet is held, his best jumps are almost always lower. It seems that the athlete's performance is impaired by the presence of other jumpers and spectators. What principle of social psychology explains the fact that as the size of the meet and the number of spectators increase, the athlete's performance deteriorates?

The athlete's jumping seems to be affected by the number of people watching. Indeed, in this case, there appears to be a strong correlation between the size of the crowd and the quality of performance. The athlete is thus showing the effect of social interference, which occurs when the mere presence of others makes performance more difficult (and poorer) than it might otherwise be. (The presence of others may in some cases help performance rather than hinder it; this phenomenon is called *social facilitation*.)

(Note: This athlete's performance is somewhat unusual. The presence of others usually facilitates a well-learned behavior; it is usually recently learned behaviors that suffer most from the effects of social interference.)

23.4 A number of years ago, a well-known sociologist wrote a book devoted to the topic of status-seeking. The book focused, to a great extent, on the concept of status as prestige. In social psychology, what other meanings does the word *status* have?

The sociologist used the word *status* as a synonym for prestige, implying a set of values or norms by which a person (or the person's position) is judged important or significant. Descriptive terms such as *high status* or *low status* are thus used to label individuals or positions according to their "standing." In social psychology, the word *status* also has a more "neutral" meaning, referring to the position or function someone has within a community or organization. Thus, status does not necessarily imply prestige.

23.5   Called at home one evening, Vernon's parents are asked to come to the police station to get their fourteen-year-old son, who has been arrested for drinking alcoholic beverages. When they get there, their first question is, "Why did you do it?" Based on your knowledge of the concept of expectancy, what answer do you think Vernon might give?

Vernon's response would mirror his role as teen-ager and he might say, "Well, all the gang does it; it's just what's expected!" Such a response would illustrate the fact that people will often act according to what is expected of them if they have a particular status. In this case, Vernon's status (position) as a teen-ager apparently promotes attempts at drinking alcoholic beverages.

23.6   Linda, an architect, is busily developing the plans for an elaborate presentation she is to give to a client. The presentation is an important one because Linda's firm will receive thousands of dollars in fees if the client accepts it. Several people compliment Linda on her first major assignment, and a few remark on how anxious she must be about it. Linda, who at first was not anxious, finds she is beginning to get nervous. What principle of social psychology explains, at least in part, Linda's anxiety?

Other people, by commenting on the importance of the project and the anxiety usually experienced by those in the same situation, may be creating an expectation of anxiety in Linda. This expectation, in turn, may produce anxious behavior on her part. Such a phenomenon, in which an expectation seems to lead to an anticipated behavior, is called a *self-fulfilling prophecy.*

23.7   Linda's role as architect is not always an easy one. Several of the merchants and representatives of city government have spoken to her about the project, an addition to a downtown mall. One group has stressed that the addition *must* be visually appealing and blend in with the existing structure. Others have emphasized that the addition must be built at the lowest possible cost, since it will be paid for in part by taxpayers' dollars.

These potentially contradictory demands point out a type of problem which may arise when one assumes a particular role. What is such a problem called? How would Linda resolve this problem?

As an architect, Linda is facing an intra-role conflict. She is being asked to satisfy demands for both style and economy, and these demands may very well be in conflict. Most likely, Linda would resolve this conflict by satisfying whichever was the stronger of the two motives (in this case, probably the budget limitation) and then try to incorporate as much of the other as possible.

23.8   Suppose you were told that Linda was experiencing an inter-role conflict. How does this differ from an intra-role conflict? Can you give an example of what an inter-role conflict might be like for Linda?

Almost every person has more than one role, and these roles are often in conflict. For Linda, the conflict may be between her role as architect and her role as daughter. If she had promised to spend the Thanksgiving holiday with her parents and now finds she is expected to work straight through the holiday to produce some revised drawings, she is confronted with a conflict. This differs from an intra-role conflict in that more than one role is involved in creating the conflict. The resolution, however, probably would be the same: the strongest motive would be satisfied first, and the other would be made to fit in, if possible.

23.9 For years, the residents of Belknap Homes have had an unwritten policy of keeping all the backyards open so that children and pets might play wherever they wished. However, when the Brune family moved in, they immediately began constructing a fence around their property. Although several of the neighbors told the Brunes about the neighborhood "rule," they continued with the construction. The Brunes' behavior. illustrates what pattern of responding? Is this type of behavior fairly common?

The building of the fence in spite of the neighborhood pattern illustrates noncomformity. The Brunes recognized the social expectations operating in the environment but chose to act in an opposite fashion. Nonconformity is not as common as conformity, the tendency to go along with group opinion. (An additional category, independence, exists when a person simply ignores or does not recognize the social norms and acts without the influence of such standards.)

23.10 If the Brunes persist in showing nonconformist patterns of behavior, what pattern of response is likely to be shown by their neighbors?

The Brunes are likely to become outcasts in the neighborhood, and may be subject to unfair discrimination or sanctions from their neighbors. (The neighbors may also continue to try to persuade the Brunes to change their behavior.)

23.11 Wanting very much to be initiated into a high-school "secret society," Rosalie has begun to go through a "pledge" period. One day, after walking to school with her friend Edna, Rosalie is taken aside by some of the members of the group and told not to hang around with Edna anymore. When Rosalie protests that Edna is her friend, the other girls say, "You let us worry about that. If you want to be one of us, you'll stop seeing Edna."

Rosalie complies with the demands and stops seeing Edna. Rosalie's compliance is somewhat comparable to compliance behaviors that have been researched by psychologists interested in the responses subjects will make to the demands of superiors or authorities. What are the general findings of these studies?

Rosalie's compliance is similar to the obedience shown by subjects in laboratory experiments. When the person is given what seems to be almost no choice, and especially if responsibility for that choice appears to be that of a superior or authority, the level of conformity is quite high.

In the most famous study of obedience, researchers predicted that most subjects would not obey or conform when they were asked to do something that seemed harmful to another person. Surprisingly, the number of subjects who showed conformity and obedience under such circumstances was much higher than expected. (Over 60 percent were willing to obey and conform in participating in an experiment that they believed harmed other people.)

23.12 Once she is a member of the group, Rosalie asks why the members do not like Edna. The response she receives is that people of Edna's ethnic group are "sneaky." Such a response illustrates what principle of social psychology?

The response represents a stereotype—an overgeneralization in which a person believes that all members of a group behave in the same way or share some significant characteristic. Grossly inaccurate stereotypes are relatively rigid and resistant to change, partly because of group support and partly because of the occasional confirmation of the mistaken belief. In other words, the partial reinforcement effect tends to strengthen stereotypes and make them very difficult to overcome. (See Chapter 24 for a more thorough discussion of stereotypes.)

23.13 Many psychologists claim that evidence indicates people always will compete and hope to "get the best of a situation." Explain how the typical pattern of automobile buying in American society often illustrates the competitive nature of the buyer and seller, who negotiate an acceptable price.

The frequently observed pattern in the purchase of an automobile involves the dealer establishing a price much higher than he expects to be able to get. The customer then makes a counteroffer that is much below what he expects to pay. Each continues to adjust his offer until they settle upon some price in the middle.

The negotiations seem to satisfy some need to compete, while the eventual selling price satisfies both seller and buyer, because each feels he has obtained the better deal.

23.14 Baseball is a game that involves competition between teams, yet there is frequently a feeling of competition among the individuals on one team, who may compete with each other over batting averages, fielding percentages, pitching performances, and the like. One baseball rule takes into account the cooperation required of a player who bunts, and thus reduces his chances of getting on base and improving his batting average. A bunt is called a *sacrifice*, and is not counted as a time at bat, if it is made with the aim of advancing a teammate one base. Thus, the bunter is not penalized for making a sacrifice in which he is called out.

Judging from the research on cooperation and competition, this rule is probably a reasonable compromise. What is the typical finding regarding the success of a group that operates cooperatively, as opposed to one that has internal competition?

The general finding is that a group that acts cooperatively will be more efficient or successful than one that has internal competition. Yet competition appears to be a common pattern displayed by individuals. Thus, the sacrifice bunt rule provides a reasonable alternative for the player, allowing a teammate to advance one base (which helps the team) but not penalizing the bunter by affecting personal statistics.

23.15 Trying to increase the production of her very successful small firm, Lydia has hired ten additional personnel and tried to organize one large work group of fifteen workers. She finds that instead of increased production, there is increased absenteeism, greater turnover of personnel, and more job dissatisfaction than before. Had she studied research on the size of groups, how many people would Lydia have placed in each work group in order to maximize production? Why?

Lydia probably would have been better off if she had organized three work groups of about five people each. Job satisfaction appears to be highest when the workers are grouped in small numbers. (As the number gets greater than five, there seems to be an increase in competition within the group, and each member's sense of "personal" responsibility seems to decrease.)

23.16 Lydia tries switching to five work groups of three (triads), but soon finds there are a number of workers who remain dissatisfied. What may have happened this time?

Research has shown that triads are almost always unstable, breaking down into a dyad (two people) and an outsider. It is possible this has happened with the work groups Lydia organized, leaving the outsider as a dissatisfied member of the group. Interactions in dyads usually are positive and cooperative, while in triads, competition and instability can be expected.

23.17 The motorist who stops at a filling station to ask directions from the attendant creates a social exchange by doing so. Explain how a "social balance" may be established in this situation.

Social exchanges appear to involve reciprocal rewards. In this case, the motorist, who might appear superior because he apparently is not at work, must adopt an inferior role and recognize the superior knowledge of the attendant. The attendant recognizes that he is working and being used, but the position of superiority accorded him because he is the one with the knowledge allows him to participate in the exchange. Thus, both persons receive reciprocal rewards, and a balance of social interaction is achieved.

23.18　Investigations of leadership qualities have been quite inconclusive. Why? What may happen when a person designated as leader refuses to lead?

　　　Studies of leadership have been inconclusive because the characteristics required of the leader appear to vary considerably depending upon the purposes of the group and the nature of its membership. When a designated leader refuses to lead, reactions from the members of the group may vary, depending upon the members' orientation toward authority. In some cases, group annoyance at the lack of leadership may lead to rebellion by the group, and perhaps to the installation of a new leader.

23.19　A group is gathered to discuss a potential business venture. After the discussion, it occurs to several members that they are embarking on a hazardous and possibly even ruinous course. What principles seem to explain such decision-making, in which the group as a whole is willing to take risks that none of the members would take alone?

　　　The group's decision reflects what has been called the *risky-shift phenomenon*. The best explanation of such behaviors seems to be the role of the arguments presented during the group's discussion. If the arguments favor a liberal or risky decision, the group decision will tend to be risky. On the other hand, if a conservative decision seems to be favored in the discussion, the group's decision will tend to be conservative. Either way, however, the decision of the group will tend to be more extreme than the decision that would be expected from the individual members acting separately, without the effect of group discussion.

23.20　Based on their knowledge of the principles of the risky-shift phenomenon and what has been called "groupthink," political scientists have expressed fears that national planning agencies or councils may create potentially dangerous situations while acting in good conscience. Explain why this conclusion may be a very reasonable one.

　　　The risky-shift phenomenon predicts that a group decision will tend to be more risky than the decision which would be reached by the individuals if they had not had a group discussion about the topic. Furthermore, study of "groupthink" situations has shown that the members often view the group as invulnerable, and correct and unanimous in its decisions. As a result, evidence contrary to the decision made can be ignored, and unfair pressure might be placed upon those who dissented.

　　　When they consider the combination of these two phenomena, political scientists predict that national planning agencies or councils might make potentially dangerous decisions, even while believing the decision is both reasonable and appropriate.

23.21　Suppose you were one of only three passengers on a large bus. When the bus stopped to pick up one more passenger, that person got on, paid the fare, and then proceeded to sit down right beside you—in fact, somewhat against you. How would you feel? What principle would explain your reaction?

　　　You would probably feel uncomfortable. People in our society tend to maintain what has been called *personal space*, unless either conditions make this impossible or one decides to be intimate. If the new passenger was a close friend, or if the bus had been very crowded, this behavior would not have provoked the same kind of uncomfortable reaction.

23.22　For a class project, two students organized a "lost book" experiment. Using a coffee room in the student center as their area for investigation, one would stay in the background and record reactions, while the other approached a table where either one person or a group of people were seated.

　　　The student approaching the table would say, "Excuse me, I think I left a book under here earlier," and then begin to try to look for the supposedly lost book. The observer would then determine whether or not the searcher received any cooperation or help.

What results would you expect the students to obtain? What explanation might be given for such results?

It is likely that the searcher would get some help or cooperation from one person sitting alone; from a group of people, the searcher would be less likely to get help. This fairly frequently obtained result appears to be a function of the diffusion, or "spreading," of responsibility—one person alone is likely to help because there is no one else there to offer aid. In a group of people, on the other hand, each person might expect someone else to offer aid.

Key Terms

Behavioral sink. When overcrowded conditions lead to pathological responding, despite environmental conditions that are otherwise normal.

Competition. Trying to get the best in a situation.

Conformity. When a person responds in accordance with a group's expectations or opinions.

Cooperation. Working with or assisting someone else in an attempt to reach a mutually satisfying goal.

Dyad. A group of two people.

Formal group. A gathering of people in which formal titles, rules, and other designations are significant.

Group dynamics. The general term describing social interactions within groups.

"Groupthink". An atmosphere found in the discussions of some groups; an air of invulnerability and unanimity of decision in group discussion.

Independence. When a person's responses are not influenced one way or another by social expectations or opinions.

Informal group. A casual gathering of people in which there are no formal rules or titles; however, unwritten guidelines may exist for the members of this group.

Inter-role conflict. When an individual is confronted with expectations based upon two (or more) different roles that cannot be fulfilled simultaneously.

Intra-role conflict. When an individual is confronted with two or more expectations that arise from only one role but that cannot be fulfilled simultaneously.

Nonconformity. When a person responds in a manner opposite to a group's opinions or expectations.

Personal space. The physical distance surrounding a person; often considered by the person as his or her "own."

Prosocial behavior. Helping behavior.

Risky shift. A group decision that is more venturesome than what could have been predicted from the responses of any one individual in the group.

Role. The expected range of responding that accompanies a particular status.

Role of arguments. The effect of discussion upon a group decision; generally the decision follows the strongest arguments.

Self-fulfilling prophecy. When an expectation appears to lead to or cause the anticipated behavior.

Socialization.   The gèneral process of learning and establishing values and norms within a cultural setting.

Social exchange.   The interaction of two people, usually involving some feelings of superiority and inferiority on the part of each.

Social facilitation.   When the presence of others appears to help performance of a particular response.

Social interference.   When the presence of others appears to hinder performance of a particular response.

Social psychology.   The branch of psychology concerned with the effect of group membership upon an individual's behavior.

Status.   A person's position or function.

Stereotype.   A relatively rigid, overgeneralized interpretation of some aspect of reality, especially persons or groups.

Triad.   A group of three people.

Chapter 24

Attitude Formation

A major aspect of social psychology is the study of *attitudes*, which are learned evaluative reactions to objects, events, and other stimuli. This chapter considers the development of attitudes, the ways to change attitudes, and the topic of prejudice.

24.1 COMPONENTS OF ATTITUDES

To say that an attitude is a learned, evaluative reaction to a stimulus only partially explains the concept. Attitudes have different components, which combine to create the overall reaction a person may have to a stimulus.

Affective Component

One aspect of attitudes is the *affective component*, the feeling or emotional reaction the individual has toward the stimulus. Affective reactions may be positive or negative.

Cognitive Component

The *cognitive component* of an attitude refers to the beliefs the individual holds about the stimulus object. These beliefs are essentially the acceptance of some conclusion about the stimulus.

Conative Component

The behavioral tendencies toward the stimulus are called the *conative component*. This aspect describes the actions, either favorable or unfavorable, which the person may take toward the stimulus.

EXAMPLE 1. The stimulus in question need not be a tangible or visible one such as a person, group of people, or institution; it may be an abstract stimulus such as the idea of education. It is very possible a person could develop a positive feeling toward education (affective component) based on the belief that everyone can benefit from education (cognitive component); such a person might very well make a contribution to a local educational institution (conative component). This example pictures a favorable reaction to or attitude about education. It should be recognized, however, that others may hold exactly opposite attitudes, involving a negative feeling, no belief in the benefits of education, and actions that would work against an educational institution. Both types of attitudes would be learned, evaluative reactions to the stimulus.

Complexity of Attitudes

Attitudes are often categorized according to their level of complexity. A set opinion that can be identified in something like "yes–no" or "good–bad" terms is called a *simple attitude*. Attitudes that involve several reactions are called *multiple* or *complex attitudes*.

EXAMPLE 2. A person who reacts to a particular comedian by always feeling amused, thinking the comedian is funny, and laughing at any of the comedian's routines shows a simple ("always good") attitude. Someone who reacts to the comedian by saying that his impersonations are good but his pantomime routines are not funny demonstrates a more complex attitude involving a mixture of feelings, beliefs, and reactions.

Theories of Attitudes

Many aspects of attitudes have been studied extensively. Two that seem to apply quite generally to many different attitude situations are discussed here.

Exposure to the stimulus. A number of studies of attitudes have shown that repeated exposure of the person to a given stimulus will usually lead to a more favorable reaction to that stimulus.

Cognitive dissonance theory. It is possible that exposure to a particular stimulus may occur under more than one set of conditions. If the conditions differ significantly, the person may learn conflicting attitudes toward the same stimulus, resulting in what has been called *cognitive dissonance*. Just as with other conflict situations, a person will try to reduce the cognitive dissonance, often by changing one of the two beliefs to bring it more "in line" with the other.

EXAMPLE 3. Suppose Norma has had a great desire to attend a rock music concert in a city about ninety miles from her home. She has worked extra hours to save enough money to be able to afford the ticket, transportation, and time off from her job. Finally, the night of the show arrives. However, the featured group is late, plays poorly, and uses a bad sound system. Furthermore, the weather is rotten. Norma is now quite disappointed.

The next day, when she is asked if the show was worth all the effort she put in to go see it, Norma answers by saying that the show really was pretty bad, but she really hadn't made such a special effort to be able to see it. Her "playing-down" of her extra labors may be viewed as an attempt to reduce cognitive dissonance. Admitting that the show was poor means that it wasn't worth much effort. Therefore, Norma reinterprets her previous behaviors to fit better with the result.

Measurement of Attitudes

Two means of measuring attitudes are used more often than other techniques. *Public opinion polls* usually ask one or only a few questions on any given topic. They are given to a sample of people taken from the population. The questions are worded to try to avoid eliciting a biased response, and answers are usually of the simple "yes–no" or "agree–disagree–no opinion" type.

The other frequently used measurement technique is the *attitude scale*. Subjects are presented pretested statements and asked to indicate agreement or disagreement (or sometimes the degree of agreement) to each of the stimuli.

EXAMPLE 4. Attitudes toward various professions may be determined by using an attitude scale, which often makes use of comparison statements like the following: "A doctor has more prestige than a lawyer," or, "A nurse has less prestige than a secretary." A tally of the agreements and disagreements with these statements would allow the investigator to create a hierarchy of prestige for the professions compared.

24.2 DEVELOPMENT OF ATTITUDES

Certain sources of influence and reinforcement are very important in the development of attitudes. Some of the most important of these will be discussed here.

Parental Influence

For young children, parents are by far the most important source of attitudes. The parents' own attitudes and the reinforcements they give to the child for reacting in certain ways are extremely influential on the child. In general, as the child grows older, this influence becomes less and less important.

Peer Influence

The single greatest replacement of parental influence (as the child grows older) comes from the peers. This begins at a fairly early age (perhaps four to six years) and grows more important as the child grows older.

Influence of Education

Another important source of information and reinforcement comes from education. In general, the more years of formal education a person has, the more liberal the person's attitudes seem to become.

Influence of Mass Media

The mass media may help form attitudes; for example, a number of television shows may present crucial information regarding political concerns. It is not likely, however, that the information presented by mass media, in and of itself, creates attitudes. Rather, it provides support for attitudes that have already been stimulated by one of the other major sources of influence.

Critical Period for Attitude Development

At least one proposal has suggested that the decisive time for establishing most attitudes occurs between the ages of twelve and thirty. After age thirty, the attitudes are said to be *crystallized*, and are unlikely to change.

EXAMPLE 5. In the 1960s, one singing group introduced not only a somewhat different style of popular music, but also a different fashion for men's hair styles. Perhaps no one aspect of behavior demonstrated the difference in attitudes between children and parents than the acceptance of these new, longer hair styles. The adults (at first) were simply unable to accept what they considered to be a radical change; their attitudes were crystallized. Young people and children, on the other hand, had a greater flexibility of attitudes. They changed styles quite quickly. (*Note*: It will be interesting to determine what flexibility or lack of it will be found in the 1980s and 1990s for those who so rapidly accepted the changes of the 1960s.)

24.3 INTERPERSONAL ATTRACTION

It is possible to consider interpersonal attraction from either a "like" or "dislike" position, but this section will concentrate on why one person is attracted to (or likes) another. (Dislikes will be considered in Section 24.4, which discusses prejudice; changes of attitude from one viewpoint to another will be covered in Section 24.5.)

Primacy and Recency Effects

A person who is forming an impression about someone or something shows evidence of the *primacy effect* if information presented first is more likely to be influential than information presented later. (This effect may not be observed if the observer is specifically instructed to pay attention to the later materials or to ignore the earlier information.) The *recency effect* is shown when later-presented materials are more influential than those presented earlier.

EXAMPLE 6. The primacy effect explains the importance of first impressions. A shy child who finds it difficult to respond in class during the first few days of the school year may be labeled by the teacher as "dull." Although there may be later evidence that contradicts this evaluation, the teacher is likely to retain the initial attitude. (*Note*: Because of a self-fulfilling prophecy, the child may realize that the teacher's expectation is that he or she will be dull; the child may thus begin to respond according to that expectation.)

Proximity

Proximity, the real or perceived distance between one person and another, has been found to be a very important determinant of interpersonal attraction. In general, the greater the real or perceived distance between two people (or groups), the less likely it is that interpersonal attraction will develop.

EXAMPLE 7. Shopping preferences are often established on the basis of proximity. You are likely to prefer a grocery store half a mile from your home over one that is five miles away. (This assumes that no other compelling variables, such as price or the selection of goods, comes into play.)

Similarity

Repeated research studies investigating the correlation of characteristics shared by friends, married partners, and other people with positive interpersonal attractions have shown these correlations to be fairly high. That is, people with similar characteristics are often attracted to each other. This holds for sociological characteristics (such as socioeconomic status, education, or the like) and for physical characteristics (such as height, hair color, or skin color).

Complementarity

Complementarity occurs when two people have dissimilar characteristics that blend nicely and form the basis for interpersonal attraction. (For example, a dominant person and a submissive person might get along well together because they fulfill each other's needs.) It should be recognized that both must agree that the dissimilarity is a good foundation for a relationship.

EXAMPLE 8: "Traditional" sex roles would illustrate the principle of complementarity. A marriage in which the partners agree that the male should be dominant and aggressive and the female should be submissive and passive could be very successful.

Attractiveness

Another factor that helps determine interpersonal attraction is *attractiveness*. People who are judged to be physically attractive may often be better liked than those who are rated as unattractive. Such a judgment of attractiveness may influence other people to perceive additional positive qualities in the attractive person. (This is called the *halo effect*.)

EXAMPLE 9. The attractiveness of a person may lead others to expect a certain kind of behavior from that person. Thus, if a man is very handsome, people may expect him to be charming also, and they may perceive such charm regardless of whether or not it actually is one of the man's characteristics.

Anxiety and Attraction

Investigations on the effect of anxiety on interpersonal attraction has shown that as anxiety levels increase, the need for affiliation with others also increases. The explanation of this phenomenon has been summarized by the concept of *social comparison*: a person who is anxious about something will tend to seek out others in order to compare reactions and possibly find some resolution for the anxiety.

The Principle of Least Interest

The behavior of a pair of people is sometimes the result of the level of attraction each holds for the other. One of the effects of such attraction has been labeled the *principle of least interest*; that is, the person who has the lesser involvement in the relationship is able to establish the conditions of the relationship, while the person having the greater interest agrees to the other person's conditions in order to maintain the relationship.

24.4 PREJUDICE

A *prejudice* is a learned reaction that is overgeneralized and unjustified. Although a prejudice may be thought of as a favorable or positive reaction, most research has centered around unfavorable or negative attitudes. Thus, this section will treat prejudices as unfavorable biases.

EXAMPLE 10. The statement, "All Chinese are sneaky," is an example of a prejudice. By including *all* Chinese, the reaction is overgeneralized. By ignoring evidence to the contrary, the statement is unjustified. A statement such as, "Some people are sneaky," would not be considered prejudiced because it is both limited and justified by evidence.

Developing and Maintaining a Prejudice

Prejudices are developed and maintained in the same way as other learned responses. It is interesting to note that modeling (see Chapter 13) appears to be the most important source of learning a prejudice. In other words, a prejudice is likely to be learned from someone who is prejudiced rather than from actual contact with the stimulus against which the prejudice is held.

Once developed, prejudices are supported by occasional reinforcements—thus demonstrating the partial reinforcement effect. Occasional or infrequent support for the prejudice will thus be enough to make it very resistant to extinction.

Stereotypes

The term *stereotype* is frequently used to describe the prejudiced reactions shown by an individual. A stereotype can be defined as an oversimplified and relatively rigid conception of a person or group of people.

Purposes of Prejudices

Holding a prejudice may serve several different purposes. Expressing a prejudice may help a person achieve some goal, satisfy some need, protect his or her self-image (comparable to a defense mechanism), or simply serve as a kind of knowledge, providing an explanation for a particular event. It also is possible that some combination of the above may be operating.

One term that often appears in connection with the concept of prejudice as a defense mechanism is *scapegoating*, which is the displacement of aggression toward an "available" person or minority group.

24.5 CHANGING ATTITUDES

Trying to change attitudes has been called *persuasion*. The important variables that either facilitate or hinder attitude changes have been studied extensively.

Source of the Message

One of the most important factors in trying to change a person's attitudes is the source of the message or persuasion. Three factors have been found to be most significant: how *believable* the source appears to be, how *attractive* the source is judged, and how much *power* or *prestige* the source seems to have. Maximizing these three factors should lead to a high probability of accomplishing attitude change.

EXAMPLE 11. In the early 1960s, President John F. Kennedy combined the three factors of being believable, attractive, and in a position of power very well. He did this so well, in fact, that many of his followers accepted his statements without criticism. Later historical evaluations have shown that some of his judgments may not have been as good as they seemed at the time, when Kennedy's personality made them completely acceptable to large numbers of people.

The Message

Phrasing the message itself may be crucial in determining whether or not it will be accepted and bring about a change in attitude. Because the message must provide the *suggestion* to be accepted, hopefully without criticism, it must avoid creating a feeling of doubt. For example, the use of biased or domineering terms in a message will make it especially liable to criticism.

Other important aspects of the message include: the *order of presentation* of information (the primacy and recency effects influence messages, too); whether one or both sides of an argument are presented; and how closely the message corresponds to the receiver's current attitudes. *One-sided messages* appear to work best when the receiver is either neutral or already somewhat in favor of the message being presented, while *two-sided messages* are more effective when the receiver currently holds the opposite point of view.

The Receiver

The characteristics of the receiver also influence the possibilities of attitude change. Among these are how much the receiver can be persuaded, how the message affects the needs of the receiver, how selective the receiver is about perceiving information in the message, and how much resistance to the message the receiver may have developed.

One reason resistance may develop is because of what has been called the *inoculation effect*. Suppose the receiver is first exposed to mild arguments against his or her position. In such a case, the receiver not only is able to learn to cope with such arguments, but also builds up a resistance to stronger arguments that may follow. Thus the term *inoculation*; the person seems to become "immunized" against the stronger arguments that may follow.

A second possible explanation for resistance to an attitude-changing message is called the *anchorage effect*. Generally, this refers to the development of strong beliefs that are supported by, or anchored to, the rules or principles of some organization.

EXAMPLE 12. Religious affiliation may provide strong anchorage against attitude change. For example, some religious groups hold beliefs that do not allow the drinking of coffee or cola drinks, while other groups will not eat pork products. People who believe in and practice one of these religions would be very resistant to persuasion that suggested they consume one of the restricted products.

Intergroup Contact

It might appear that increasing amounts of intergroup contact should increase the similarity of attitudes held by two groups. This is not always the case, however. Several factors appear to affect the outcome of intergroup contact.

In general, greater similarity of attitudes will develop if the members of the two groups have similar status, characteristics that support change (such as a lack of prejudice), or possibly some sort of dependency upon each other. However, if the intergroup contact supports already held beliefs, the differing attitudes of the groups will become even more solidified.

24.6 SOCIAL MOVEMENTS

Social movements are attempts to cause *social change*, or a significant alteration in the existing social structure and accompanying changes in attitudes and behaviors. Attempts to resist social change are called *countermovements*.

Examples of social movements in the United States are the civil rights movement, the feminist movement, and the antiwar movement prompted by the Vietnamese conflict. All of these showed similar patterns of development, including an unevenness of progress, strong recruiting efforts, and the development of formal organizations that carried out public appeals designed to influence behavior and change attitudes.

Solved Problems

24.1   What are the three basic components of an attitude?

One aspect of attitudes is the affective, or feeling, component. The second is called the cognitive component, which refers to the beliefs a person develops. The third is the conative, or action, component, referring to the tendency to act in accordance with the feelings or beliefs that have developed. Thus, when we talk about attitudes, we are talking about feelings, opinions, and actions keyed off by some sort of stimulus.

24.2   Attitudes are often categorized according to their complexity. What does this mean?

Attitudes are reactions that can vary tremendously in complexity. Some reactions are simple "yes–no" or "like–dislike" reactions to a stimulus. Others are complex combinations of feelings, beliefs, and actions. Sometimes the components of a single attitude may be in conflict. For example, a person with heart trouble may believe that drinking beer is wrong, or at least inadvisable. Yet this person may like beer very much, and occasionally drink a glass of it with dinner. (This attitude could be classified as a complex one, and yet it is not nearly as complex as some of the attitudes most people have.)

24.3   Where do our attitudes come from? How are they developed? How are conflicts in an attitude, like the conflicts described in Problem 24.2, resolved?

Attitudes are learned, and in the same way that other responses are learned. Quite often, the development of attitudes depends upon the frequency of exposure one has to a particular stimulus. In general, the more often one is exposed to some stimulus, the more likely a favorable reaction to it can be expected. It is possible, however, to feel two different ways (or to have a complex attitude) about one stimulus. This is sometimes described by the term *cognitive dissonance*. Usually, a person who recognizes such a conflict in herself or himself will try to reduce the discrepancy. This is done by changing the attitudes to get a better "fit." For example, the person who drinks beer in spite of his heart ailment might think, "I'm really not that ill," or "An *occasional* beer can't hurt."

24.4   A member of the school board claims that the board has evidence indicating that a majority of the people in the community have reacted favorably to the suggested new borders for the school district. How did the board probably gather this information? What other techniques are used to measure attitudes?

The board probably used a public opinion poll to determine reactions to the proposed change in borderlines. If their questions were worded to avoid creating a bias, and if their sample was truly representative of the community at large, the results might be fairly used to describe the community's attitudes.

The other major technique for measuring attitudes is to use some sort of attitude scale. The respondent may be asked to agree or disagree with a series of statements that have been scaled, or valued, by the designer of the survey. Respondents can then indicate their degree of agreement by reacting to some scale of values ranging from one extreme to the other.

24.5   How important are parents in influencing the development of a child's attitudes?

Research has shown that children are more likely to hold attitudes similar to those of their parents than they are to hold attitudes that are different. Studies investigating religious, political, and occupational attitudes have supported this conclusion. However, it is difficult to say whether or not parental influence is the strongest in helping determine the attitudes of children. As children grow older, the importance of parental beliefs seems to decline, while influence of peer attitudes, education, and information from the mass media all seem to increase.

24.6   How is it that peer influence, education, and the mass media affect the child's but not the parent's attitude development?

Peer influence, education, and the mass media all seem to provide more influence as a child grows older. This influence may or may not be incorporated into beliefs that differ from those of the parents. The attitudes of the parents are less likely to change for several reasons. Their peer influence will remain the same, and their education is likely to cease or slow down considerably. They may also not select the same information from the mass media as do the children. Additionally, or perhaps because of these reasons, older adults (past age thirty) seem to *crystallize* most of their attitudes and maintain them throughout the rest of their lives. (One researcher has called the period from ages twelve to thirty the *critical period* for attitude development.)

24.7   On Saturday night, Joanne has her first date with Dennis. At the beginning of the evening, Dennis is charming and seems to be very mannerly and polite. Later, however, his manners seem to "slip," as he belches and becomes very argumentative. Sunday morning, Joanne reflects on the previous evening. Is she more likely to remember Dennis as charming or rude?

If Joanne's attitude formation follows the typical pattern shown by a majority of subjects in research studies, the primacy effect should be strongest, and she will remember Dennis as quite charming. This primacy effect means that Joanne is most likely to be affected by the first information received and will probably have her later judgments "colored" by these initial impressions.

24.8   Joanne's older sister talks to her about her date, and after hearing about how Dennis acted, tries to convince Joanne that Dennis may not be as great as he seems. Then, as it happens, both Joanne and her sister go to the same party the next Friday night. Again, Dennis is very pleasant at the start of the evening. About midway through the evening, Joanne's sister reminds her not to make any snap judgments, but to wait and see how Dennis acts later. As the evening continues, Dennis again loses his "polish" and is quite uncivil. Is Joanne's judgment of Dennis likely to be as favorable the next morning as it was after her first date? Why?

In all likelihood, Joanne's evaluation of Dennis will be less positive than it was previously. The interruption by her sister, midway through the party, separated or divided Joanne's attention and gave greater significance to the later-received information. This is called the *recency effect*; that is, the later information has greater impact than that received first.

24.9   Joanne's mother has tried to encourage her to date Tom, a young man who lives in the next community. Joanne was more interested in Dennis, who lived nearby. A very simple but very important principle seems to explain Joanne's preference for Dennis. What is it?

Joanne's choice of Dennis rather than Tom may reflect the principle of proximity, or nearness. In general, people are more attracted to those who live near them as opposed to those who live at a greater distance. This principle holds for both actual distance and "perceived" distance, perhaps because the proximity allows greater familiarity, which in turn leads to attraction.

24.10   Two old-fashioned sayings are, "Birds of a feather flock together," and "Opposites attract." Both may sound sensible, but they are contradictory.

Which one is correct? Or are they both correct? What principles explain each of these sayings?

Both of these sayings may be correct. Interpersonal attraction may be a result of similarity of interests ("Birds") or of complementarity ("Opposites"). The latter principle is like the story of Jack Spratt, who would eat no fat, and his wife, who would eat no lean. They matched perfectly because what one didn't like, the other did.

24.11 Attractiveness has been recognized as an important variable affecting interpersonal attraction. Describe at least two ways in which attractiveness may influence interpersonal attraction.

Physical attractiveness itself appears to be important in determining interpersonal attraction. In general, better looking people are liked more than less attractive people (according to whatever standards of attractiveness are current in a culture or subculture).

There is also the possibility that physical attractiveness may create what has been called a *halo effect*; that is, people may perceive in an attractive person characteristics that they normally associate with physical attractiveness, even if such a judgment is not warranted.

Additionally, attractiveness may be affected by preconceived notions the observer holds. This in effect is an example of a self-fulfilling prophecy; the observer may expect the person to be attractive, and thus perceive the person as attractive, even in spite of evidence to the contrary.

24.12 Mary hears on the radio that a tornado may strike the community where her college is located. She has a choice of staying alone in her dormitory room to listen to the radio or going to the lounge to join others listening to radio reports. Which is she most likely to do?

According to studies investigating the relationship of anxiety to affiliation, Mary would be more likely to go to the lounge than stay in her room. In general, when confronted with anxiety-provoking situations, people are more likely to choose to be with others rather than stay alone. The explanation of such a choice seems to be the concept of social comparison. When uncertain about something, being with others allows one person to compare this reaction with that of others and perhaps reach some resolution.

24.13 Suppose the "star" of a social group in high school seems to be able to order another member of the group around. The "star" thus seems to reflect the principle of least interest. What does this mean?

The "star" has a lesser involvement in the relationship than the other member, who seems to be more interested and dependent upon the relationship for social standing. The fear of losing the association may make the more involved person likely to agree to the terms established by the less involved person.

24.14 Consider the statement, "All whites hate all blacks." It represents an example of prejudice. Explain why.

The key characteristics of a prejudice are that the belief is overgeneralized and unjustified. The attitude is applied indiscriminately to all members of a particular group, despite evidence that contradicts the generalization. Most often, beliefs such as the one expressed here are learned by coming in contact with others who hold the belief, rather than contact with the object of prejudice itself.

24.15 Suppose a white person approached a black who held the prejudice expressed in Problem 24.14. If the white said, "I don't hate you, so why do you believe such a thing?" What kind of response might be expected? What learning principle explains why such beliefs may be very difficult to change?

A phrase such as, "Well, you're the exception to the rule," or, "You're only saying so," might be used. Once a prejudice is established, it may be quite difficult to change because of the partial reinforcement effect, which states that responses followed by occasional reinforcement are very resistant to extinction. A belief like the one expressed in the previous problem is likely to be supported by occasional examples, and thus will be very resistant to extinction.

24.16 One word is often used to describe these overgeneralizations of prejudice. What is it? What kinds of purposes are served by holding such attitudes?

  The prejudiced overgeneralizations are called *stereotypes*. People who stereotype others often do so to satisfy their own needs, perhaps for status or superiority, or perhaps to express hostility. Sometimes stereotypes are used as a defense mechanism to protect self-image; for example, they may displace aggression to a convenient target. Or sometimes prejudices expressed as stereotypes may help the individual achieve some goal; that is, they may serve a purely utilitarian function such as gaining approval from some social group.

24.17 For years, advertising firms have used famous people to promote products. To be most effective in persuading the public to buy a product (that is, to change the public's attitude), what characteristics should the famous person have?

  Three characteristics appear to be most important if an attitude change is to be achieved. The person providing the message should be credible (believable), attractive, and in a position of power or prestige. For example, if the product to be sold is a baseball glove, the person picked might be a handsome major league player who projects an image of honesty.

24.18 What are some of the ways in which a message sender (such as a writer or speaker) can increase the persuasiveness of his or her message?

  The composition and organization of the message appear to be very important in determining its persuasiveness. While the exact factors may vary, depending on the content, elements such as the order of presentation, the use of "loaded" words, the correspondence of the content to the beliefs already held by the receivers, and the one-sidedness of the message may all be important.

24.19 Talking with her son before he leaves for college, a mother is careful to stress the importance of the values her son has been taught. She tells him how she hopes he will continue to hold firm to his family's and religion's beliefs. When the son gets to college, he finds that a number of people try to persuade him to change his ideas, but he does not. What effect has his mother's talk had upon his behavior? What is the term psychologists use to describe this? What other aspects of the "receiver's" characteristics appear to be important when considering attitude change?

  The mother's talk probably has helped the son solidify his beliefs and become less likely to be persuaded than he might have been otherwise. This is called the *anchorage effect*; that is, the son anchors his beliefs to those of his family and religion.

  The son's tendency to hold on to these beliefs may also be influenced by other factors. His needs or goals may be served by his beliefs, and he may restrict the amount of information he allows himself to receive. (He may thus avoid those who persuade him to change his belief.) Furthermore, the son may have been exposed to mild arguments against his beliefs in the past, and will thus be able to resist later, stronger arguments against his beliefs. This is called the *inoculation effect*. (The mild arguments seem to "immunize" the son against the stronger arguments.)

24.20 The civil rights and antiwar movements gained great support during the 1960s. Perhaps the most important movement of the 1970s was the feminist movement. Explain how this campaign for women is like other social movements.

  The aim of the feminist movement can be summarized as equality with men in all areas of behavior. As is typical of almost all social movements, progress toward this goal has been uneven, and is still unattained. The movement has recruited people both directly affected by the changes and those sympathetic to the cause, and has resulted in the development of formal organizations (such as NOW, the National Organization for Women) which try to achieve the desired changes through advertising, demonstrations, and other appeals to the public. Furthermore, *countermovements* have arisen in an attempt to stop, or at least slow down, the movement toward social change; this, too, is typical of what happens when social movements arise.

Key Terms

Affective component.   The emotional (or feeling) aspect of an attitude.

Anchorage effect.   Resistance to attitude change because of particularly strong beliefs or group support.

Attitude.   A learned evaluative response to a social stimulus.

Attitude scale.   Pretested attitude statements to which the subject indicates his or her degree of agreement.

Cognitive component.   The part of an attitude revealing the beliefs the person has about a stimulus.

Cognitive dissonance.   When a person holds conflicting attitudes toward the same stimulus.

Complementarity.   When people with dissimilar characteristics are attracted to each other, and thus fulfill each other's needs.

Conative component.   The part of an attitude revealed by the actions a person takes in response to a stimulus.

Countermovement.   An attempt to resist social change.

Halo effect.   When expectations regarding behavior are affected by the attractiveness of the person.

Inoculation effect.   When first exposure to mild arguments creates a set for a person so that later, stronger arguments can be resisted.

Prejudice.   An overgeneralized and inappropriate learned reaction to a social stimulus; often used without differentiation.

Primacy effect.   When first-presented information is remembered best or is considered most significant.

Principle of least interest.   In a dyadic relationship, when the person with the least involvement establishes the conditions, and the other accepts these in order to maintain the relationship.

Public opinion poll.   When a sample from a population is asked a few questions regarding attitudes toward a particular topic.

Recency effect.   When the most recently presented information is remembered best or is considered most significant.

Scapegoating.   Displacement of aggression from the precipitating cause to some available person or minority group.

Social change.   A significant alteration of social structure.

Social comparison.   In situations of uncertainty, seeking others to determine the similarity or difference of reactions.

Social movement.   An attempt to cause social change.

Stereotype.   A relatively rigid, overgeneralized interpretation of some aspect of reality, especially persons or groups.

Examination III

For each of the first twenty-five questions, circle the best answer. (The correct answers appear on page 321.)

1. Relying on feelings as well as test results obtained would illustrate _____ .

    (a) test batteries
    (b) statistical judgment
    (c) intuitive judgment
    (d) none of the above

2. The comparison standards established by testing a group are sometimes called _____ .

    (a) reliability
    (b) norms
    (c) cross-sectional standards
    (d) speed tests

3. The potential for acquiring a skill defines _____ .

    (a) ability
    (b) personality
    (c) validity
    (d) criterion

4. Consider the following distribution of scores: 8, 5, 6, 4, 4, 7, 8. Which measures of central tendency have the same value?

    (a) mean and mode
    (b) mean and median
    (c) median and mode
    (d) mean, median, and mode

5. Bruno scored 82 on an exam with a mean of 72 and a standard deviation of 10. Alfredo scored 38 on a test that had a mean of 32 and a standard deviation of 4. Given these scores and standard deviations, which of the following statements is true?

    (a) Bruno did relatively better than Alfredo.
    (b) Bruno and Alfredo did about the same.
    (c) Bruno did relatively poorer than Alfredo.
    (d) There is not enough information to judge Bruno versus Alfredo.

6. Which of the following is the correlation with the highest predictive value?

    (a) −0.70
    (b) +0.32
    (c) +1.14
    (d) +0.65

7.   A bar graph with many scores bunched at one end of the distribution would be described as _____ .

    (a) a skewed frequency polygon
    (b) a symmetrical histogram
    (c) a symmetrical frequency polygon
    (d) a skewed histogram

8.   For Freud, control of behavior according to societal standards rests in _____ .

    (a) the id
    (b) the ego
    (c) the superego
    (d) the libido

9.   According to body-type theory, 6′6″, 145-pound Ralph can be expected to be _____ .

    (a) visceratonic
    (b) somatotonic
    (c) endomorphic
    (d) cerebrotonic

10.   Value and respect for *all* of a person's behavior would be classified by Rogers as _____.

    (a) unconditional positive regard
    (b) negative regard
    (c) conditional positive regard
    (d) self-actualization

11.   A most creative person would probably show which of the following characteristics?

    (a) fluid intelligence, convergent thinking
    (b) crystallized intelligence, convergent thinking
    (c) fluid intelligence, divergent thinking
    (d) crystallized intelligence, convergent thinking

12.   The label "exceptional child" would include _____ .

    (a) mentally retarded children
    (b) gifted children
    (c) children in the +1 to −1 standard deviation range on an intelligence test
    (d) a and b

13.   Determine the ratio IQ for a child who is eight years old and scores at the ten-year mental age level.

    (a) 80
    (b) 100
    (c) 125
    (d) 133

14.   Suppose a brain tumor causes a person to hallucinate; psychologists might describe this behavior as _____ .

    (a) compulsive neurosis
    (b) functional psychosis
    (c) mental retardation
    (d) organic psychosis

15.   Jeanette is convinced that the difficulties she is having with her job are the result of a conspiracy organized by her secretary, one of the custodians, and two of the people in the next office. Assuming the conspiracy does not really exist, Jeanette's behavior could be described as _____ .

     (a) paranoid
     (b) sociopathic
     (c) phobic
     (d) autistic

16.   Which of the following would probably be most likely to classify abnormal behaviors as an "illness"?

     (a) psychodynamic theorist
     (b) biomedical theorist
     (c) social learning theorist
     (d) existential theorist

17.   Which of the following is a somatic therapy?

     (a) Gestalt therapy
     (b) client-centered therapy
     (c) behavior modification therapy
     (d) none of the above

18.   A return to "normalcy" without the help of therapy is called _____ .

     (a) regression
     (b) repression
     (c) remission
     (d) resistance

19.   Token economies are based upon _____ .

     (a) modeling
     (b) operant conditioning
     (c) classical conditioning
     (d) biofeedback

20.   If the presence of others seems to make the professional actress perform better than in rehearsals, _____ has probably been illustrated.

     (a) social facilitation
     (b) socialization
     (c) social interference
     (d) social exchange

21.   Warren wears crew-neck sweaters and khaki pants simply because he likes them. Warren's choice of clothes represents _____ .

     (a) nonconformity
     (b) conformity
     (c) independence
     (d) obedience to group opinion

22.   Severe overcrowding has led to a condition that has been described as a _____ .

    (a) behavioral sink
    (b) "groupthink"
    (c) risky shift
    (d) triadic difficulty

23.   Suppose a couple gets along because one or the other often says things like, "I'll do the dishes if you'll change the bed." Their behavior might be said to illustrate _____ .

    (a) complementarity
    (b) primary effect
    (c) scapegoating
    (d) anchorage

24.   Social movements attempt to _____ .

    (a) maintain existing attitudes
    (b) create social change
    (c) develop the principle of least interest
    (d) support current prejudices

25.   The most effective attitude changers probably would be _____ .

    (a) unbelievable—absolutely "wild"
    (b) relatively weak—"one of the group"
    (c) quite attractive—pleasing to look at
    (d) a combination of all three of these characteristics

26.   How is a criterion orientation used in evaluating test results?

Criterion orientation means the results are judged against some absolute standard. This standard is established without reference to the performance of a particular age level or other group.

27.   Compare speed and power tests. Which is typically used in educational or psychological testing situations?

Speed tests are tests in which time limits have a significant effect upon each subject's performance. Power tests have time limits, but they are not so restrictive as to have a significant effect on the performance of most subjects. Typically, educational and psychological tests are speed tests, with rather restrictive time limits.

28.   What purposes are served by trying to design culture-free or culture-fair tests?

Both culture-free and culture-fair tests are designed to try to eliminate unfair biases that may result from being raised in one setting as opposed to another. For example, test items that favored specifically rural or urban knowledge would be avoided or balanced in an attempt to create an equitable test for all.

29.   What are the values for the measures of central tendency in a distribution with the following scores: 6, 10, 4, 4, 8, 11, 8, 7, 5?

There are three measures of central tendency. The value for the mean of this distribution would be equal to 7 (63/9 = 7). The median would be 7 (the middle score). The modes would be 4 and 8 (the most frequently occurring scores).

30. What are the pictorial representations of data often used in reporting results of experiments?

Three pictorial representations are used most often. Two typically have the independent variable plotted on the *x*-axis and the dependent variable plotted on the *y*-axis and are called frequency polygons (line graphs) and histograms (bar graphs). The third shows the relationship (correlation) of two variables and is called a scattergram.

31. In a normal probability distribution with a mean of 64 and a standard deviation of 6, what percentage of the population falls between scores of 58 and 76?

There will be 81½ percent of the population between scores of 58 and 76 (The score of 58 is one standard deviation below the mean, while 76 is two standard deviations above the mean.)

32. Explain why defense mechanisms may be either normal or abnormal.

According to Freud, defense mechanisms protect the ego. In many cases, a person who is coping well within society must defend his or her ego. In some cases, however, the person is not able to cope with the demands of the environment, yet hopes to protect the personality structure. In such situations, abnormal adoptions of defense mechanisms may be tried.

33. As a child grows older, what happens to peer influence on personality development?

In general, as a child grows older, the influence of peers increases, while that of parents decreases. (These two sources are seen as the most important in personality development.)

34. According to Rogers, there are two kinds of positive regard. What are they and how do they differ?

Rogers described unconditional positive regard and conditional positive regard. The former means that *all* actions of a person are accepted or valued, while the latter means that responses to at least some of the person's behaviors are not accepted or rejected. Rogers believes unconditional positive regard is necessary if a person is to fully realize all potentials.

35. Ratio IQs have been replaced by deviation IQs as the most commonly used form of IQ. Why?

Ratio IQs did not take into account the fact that after a certain number of years, a person's mental age is likely to stabilize (while chronological age continues to increase). Thus, if ratio IQs were used, practically all adults would have ever-decreasing IQs.

36. Measured intelligence correlates more highly with school success than any other variable. However, these correlations are relatively low. What are some explanations for this?

Motivation, social status, financial considerations, the expectations of others, previous successes or failures, and many other factors besides intelligence may affect school success. Thus, the predictions made on the basis of measured intelligence alone will often not be terribly accurate.

37. Brought to a clinic by his wife, Henry appears to be very excited, even boisterous, yet his wife says that he frequently becomes very morose and reluctant to communicate. What type of abnormal personality pattern does Henry show?

Henry is probably a manic-depressive. This affective psychosis is characterized by extreme swings of mood, often in a cyclical pattern. Manic-depressive patterns are usually considered functional psychoses rather than organic ones, although some recent research indicates there may be physiological patterns that reflect the behavioral cycles observed.

38. Why is it that several people may have the predisposing factors for abnormal personality patterns, yet some will show the patterns and others will not?

It is likely the determining factor is whether or not some precipitating factor "keys off" the abnormal personality pattern. In other words, the particular environment may prompt such a reaction in some situations but not in others.

39. Why are certain sexual behaviors, psychosomatic disorders, and forms of mental retardation considered abnormal?

Many behaviors are classified as abnormal simply because they are judged to be significantly away from the accepted societal norm. Just which behaviors are considered abnormal depends upon what standards a particular society accepts.

40 What is the difference between encounter groups and group therapy?

Basically, the difference is in the type of client served. Encounter groups are organized for normal people who hope to use the circumstances to increase self-awareness and self-actualization. Group therapies are usually used for treating people with abnormal personality patterns.

41. One aspect of the "women's movement" has been the development of assertiveness training sessions. Why?

In the past, the prevailing attitude in our society was that women should not "stand up" for their rights. Recent changes in attitudes, brought about in part by the women's movement, has meant that many women believe it is correct for them to be assertive. In many cases, however, women believe they must learn assertive behaviors. Thus, assertiveness training sessions for women have been instituted.

42. Any social role may lead to both "payoffs" and "costs." Explain why.

Every social role carries with it both advantages and disadvantages. For example, a medical doctor may have a good deal of prestige and be well paid, but she or he must often work long hours and has to attend school for many years. It seems that society establishes these costs and payoffs, and that anyone who takes on a social role must be willing, to some extent, to accept them.

43. Randy is attempting to learn a new movement in his gymnastics routine. By chance, several people are observing his practice. What effect might this have on his performance?

It is likely that social interference will occur; that is, the presence of the others will hinder Randy's performance of the recently learned task. (In the case of a well-learned task, the presence of others often helps the performance, resulting in what is known as social facilitation.)

44. If a person performs one task exceptionally well, others may expect him or her to perform other tasks with great skill also. Why? Why is it true that such a result may actually occur?

The expectation that someone who is good at one task is good at all tasks is called the *halo effect*—just as a "good boy" is always seen as "good," regardless of the circumstances. This may actually happen because the person responds according to those expectations, an example of the self-fulfilling prophecy.

45.   At a party, Collette is asked to try cocaine. She chooses not to, and those trying to convince her to try it soon leave her alone. Later in the evening, however, a much more vigorous argument is made, but Collette again says no. What is one explanation of what might have happened here?

The sequence of events may have created an inoculation effect. The early, mild argument and the ability to resist it may have helped "immunize" Collette against the later, more persuasive argument.

Answers to Problems 1–25

1. (c)	6. (a)	11. (c)	16. (b)	21. (c)
2. (b)	7. (d)	12. (d)	17. (d)	22. (a)
3. (a)	8. (b)	13. (c)	18. (c)	23. (a)
4. (b)	9. (d)	14. (d)	19. (b)	24. (b)
5. (c)	10. (a)	15. (a)	20. (a)	25. (c)

Final Examination

For each of the first fifty questions, circle the best answer. (The correct answers appear on page 334.)

1. Although both use many of the same techniques, one major difference between a psychologist and a psychiatrist is that _____ .

    (a) a psychologist studies Freudian techniques exclusively
    (b) a psychiatrist studies only Freudian techniques
    (c) a psychiatrist is medically trained
    (d) a psychologist may be a psychoanalyst, while a psychiatrist cannot

2. Credit for the start of the science of psychology in _____ is given to _____ .

    (a) 1879, Wundt
    (b) 1885, Freud
    (c) 1858, Fechner
    (d) 1913, Watson

3. An experimenter who tests the proposition that the results obtained from the experimental groups will not differ significantly from those obtained from the control group is testing _____ .

    (a) a molar variable
    (b) a directional hypothesis
    (c) the null hypothesis
    (d) the naturalistic observation

4. One reason for using naturalistic observation as a technique for gathering information is _____ .

    (a) the high level of control possible
    (b) the accuracy of clinical records
    (c) the possibility of avoiding "forced" responses
    (d) none of the above

5. When genes that were previously linked become unlinked or linked with a different set of characteristics, _____ has occurred.

    (a) a mutation
    (b) crossing-over
    (c) zygote
    (d) eugenics

6.   Ann and her brother Fred are twins. Their hereditary pattern must be such that _____ .

      (a) they developed from the splitting of a single zygote
      (b) they resulted from two separate conceptions
      (c) they would both show the recessive characteristics of their parents
      (d) they would have the same color eyes

7.   Until the baby-to-be has become attached (linked) to the mother's system, it is described as _____ .

      (a) a fetus
      (b) an embryo
      (c) an infant
      (d) a chromosome

8.   The need to collect information about a developmental question in a short period of time would probably be reflected by the use of _____ .

      (a) a developmental scale
      (b) a longitudinal study
      (c) a deprivation study
      (d) a cross-sectional study

9.   In general, the sympathetic system _____ .

      (a) acts as a unit in active situations
      (b) acts only in part in active situations
      (c) operates only in quiet situations
      (d) operates only after electrical stimulation of the brain

10.   A signal may be transmitted from one nerve cell to the next when _____ .

      (a) the absolute refractory phase is occurring
      (b) the cerebral cortex is in a state of resting potential
      (c) the transmitter substance passes across a synapse
      (d) all of the above may be correct

11.   An absolute threshold is defined as _____ .

      (a) a just noticeable difference (j.n.d.)
      (b) the level at which correct detection of a stimulus occurs 50 percent of the time
      (c) the level at which correct detection of a stimulus occurs 100 percent of the time
      (d) the difference threshold of the stimulus

12.   The "chemical senses" include _____ .

      (a) taste
      (b) kinesthesis
      (c) vestibulation
      (d) a and c

13.   One binocular cue that affects perception is _____ .

      (a) subliminal perception
      (b) stimulus intensity
      (c) perceptual constancy
      (d) retinal disparity

14. Many "fortune-tellers" claim to be able to predict their clients' futures. If, indeed, they could do this they would have what is called _____ .

    (a) telepathy
    (b) precognition
    (c) clairvoyance
    (d) psychokinesis

15. It is likely that the most widely used of all the psychoactive drugs is _____ .

    (a) alcohol
    (b) marijuana
    (c) LSD
    (d) heroin

16. The attempt to focus on a single sound or object is likely to be part of _____ .

    (a) opening-up meditation
    (b) circadian rhythm
    (c) REM sleep
    (d) concentrative meditation

17. Which of the following statements is *not* correct?

    (a) Very low levels of motivation usually lead to poor performance of a task.
    (b) Homeostasis is the body's tendency to maintain an internal "balance."
    (c) Deprivation is often used as a measure of level of motivation.
    (d) Very high levels of motivation usually lead to outstanding performance of a task.

18. If Ruth is thirsty, but will satisfy this thirst only with a cola drink, she has demonstrated _____ .

    (a) cognitive dissonance
    (b) goal specificity
    (c) functional autonomy
    (d) sensory adaptation

19. To identify the emotion being expressed, it is probably most important to know _____ .

    (a) the provoking stimulus
    (b) the respondent's social background
    (c) the physiological indicants
    (d) the respondent's personal reports

20. The concept that emotions resulted from perceived bodily changes was the key to _____ .

    (a) the James-Lange theory
    (b) the Cannon-Bard theory
    (c) the activation-arousal theory
    (d) attribution theories

21. While walking on the sidewalk, three-year-old Charles is surprised by the loud blast of an automobile horn. He slips, falls, bumps his knee, and cries from the pain. Later, he is out again and hears another auto horn, and he begins to cry. In this example, the CS is _____ .

    (a) the bump on the knee
    (b) the crying to the pain
    (c) the crying to the sound of the horn
    (d) the sound of the horn

22. That evening, Charles is watching television and, by chance, the show features a "chase" scene with much honking of automobile horns. Charles starts to whimper. His reaction represents _____ .

    (a) primary stimulus generalization
    (b) secondary stimulus generalization
    (c) response generalization
    (d) differentiation

23. Many soldiers returning from war found that their language was not appropriate for "proper" society. Most were able to extinguish the incorrect responses. However, once in a while, when a particularly provocative situation occurred, the soldiers might revert to their wartime language. Such a response would illustrate _____ .

    (a) stimulus generalization
    (b) response generalization
    (c) spontaneous recovery
    (d) stimulus contiguity

24. Which of the following would lead to the poorest operant conditioning?

    (a) feedback as a reinforcer
    (b) conditioned reinforcers
    (c) delay of reinforcement
    (d) response as reinforcement

25. A practical application of instrumental conditioning is _____ .

    (a) modeling
    (b) programmed learning
    (c) desensitization
    (d) higher-order conditioning

26. Following directions would be classified as _____ .

    (a) verbal modeling
    (b) vicarious learning
    (c) live modeling
    (d) pure imitation

27. Showing a client that a response would be appropriate in a situation where the client is unwilling to use that response is representative of _____ .

    (a) inhibition procedure
    (b) disinhibition procedure
    (c) effect of status
    (d) symbolic learning

28.   Lowell needs to go shopping for many items, but he tries to memorize them rather than write a list. Later, he finds he can recall only the first items he memorized. This illustrates _____ .

   (a) long-term retention
   (b) free recall
   (c) paired-associate learning
   (d) the primacy effect

29.   The most easily recalled words in a list would have _____ .

   (a) high pronouncability and low imagery
   (b) low pronouncability and low imagery
   (c) low pronouncability and high imagery
   (d) high pronouncability and high imagery

30.   Suppose the word *murder* is introduced in a long list of fruits and vegetables. The resultant high level of recall of that word in its place in the list would illustrate _____ .

   (a) the reminiscence effect
   (b) short-term memory
   (c) the von Restorff effect
   (d) the TOT phenomenon

31.   Jerry learned to play tennis. One winter, he learned to play badminton. When he started to play tennis again the following spring, Jerry found that much of the badminton learning interfered with his tennis game. This is an example of _____ .

   (a) negative transfer
   (b) positive transfer
   (c) proactive inhibition
   (d) retroactive inhibition

32.   Aimless thoughts are sometimes representative of _____ .

   (a) directed thinking
   (b) simulation
   (c) autistic thinking
   (d) psycholinguistics

33.   The basic sound or inflection components of a language are called _____ .

   (a) syllables
   (b) phonemes
   (c) morphemes
   (d) words

34.   Prediction of future performance is the intent of _____ .

   (a) achievement tests
   (b) aptitude tests
   (c) group tests only
   (d) culture-biased tests

35. Results of psychological testing should be released on demand to _____ .

     (a) only the individual tested and those the individual names
     (b) the individual, close relatives, and school personnel
     (c) any competent psychologist, relatives, or close friends
     (d) any one with a need for the information

36. The percentage of the population falling between +1 and −1 standard deviations on a normal probability distribution is _____ .

     (a) 16
     (b) 34
     (c) 68
     (d) 95

37. Which of the following is *not* a measure of central tendency?

     (a) correlation
     (b) mode
     (c) median
     (d) All are measures of central tendency.

38. The resolution of crises at each stage of personality development was part of the theory of _____ .

     (a) Jung
     (b) Freud
     (c) Adler
     (d) Erikson

39. According to Freud's theory, if Abner tends to be sloppy and disorderly it may be because he is fixated at _____ .

     (a) the oral stage
     (b) the anal stage
     (c) the phallic stage
     (d) the latent stage

40. The highest age at which the child can pass all items on that level of the Stanford-Binet Intelligence test is called_____ .

     (a) the basal age
     (b) the mental age
     (c) the ceiling age
     (d) the chronological age

41. Suppose a child were able to use logical concepts as long as they were tied to observable things. According to Piaget, the child would probably be how old?

     (a) less than two years
     (b) two to seven years
     (c) seven to eleven years
     (d) eleven years or older

42. Which of the following probably would *not* be used to try to measure creativity?

    (a) remote association test
    (b) anagram test
    (c) thematic apperception test
    (d) drawing completion test

43. A persistent need to wash one's hands at least once every half hour probably represents _____ .

    (a) a dissociative reaction
    (b) an obsessive reaction
    (c) a hysterical reaction
    (d) a compulsive reaction

44. An individual who understands society's rules but chooses to ignore them and act according to personal wishes is described as _____ .

    (a) psychosomatic
    (b) psychopathic
    (c) retarded
    (d) autistic

45. Using drugs to treat an abnormal behavior pattern is classified as _____ .

    (a) psychosurgery
    (b) ECST
    (c) psychotherapy
    (d) chemotherapy

46. The placebo effect would be best illustrated by _____ .

    (a) the use of ECST to overcome psychotic depression
    (b) overcoming resistance in a psychotherapeutic setting
    (c) a patient's recovery based on the belief that the therapist *must* know all the answers
    (d) the use of genetic counseling regarding the possibilities of birth defects

47. Two conflicting expectations that arise out of a single role would be called _____ .

    (a) social interference
    (b) an intra-role conflict
    (c) dyads
    (d) an inter-role conflict

48. Suppose four teenagers get together and decide to try smoking marijuana. Alone, no one of them would have done this, but as a group they would. This illustrates _____ .

    (a) the quadratic effect
    (b) the risky shift phenomenon
    (c) a stereotype
    (d) the socialization effect

49. Jack is willing to take long hikes with Jill even though he hates them. His behavior probably illustrates _____ .

    (a) social comparision
    (b) prejudice
    (c) complementarity
    (d) the principle of least interest

50. If you believe in the saying, "First impressions count," you agree with the principle of _____ .

    (a) the primacy effect
    (b) the halo effect
    (c) least interest
    (d) the recency effect

51. What are the general trends found in the development of psychology as a science today?

Several trends appear most prominent. Psychology has expanded into many new areas in business, the community, and research. In general, psychologists tend to study fairly specific topics rather than large or general areas. Additionally, there seems to be growing cooperation among the different specialties of psychology, which helps lead to a better understanding of behavior.

52. Although Freud is often mentioned as the most important person contributing to the development of psychology, he is not given credit for starting psychology. Why?

Freud is not given credit for starting psychology because he did not claim to be a psychologist. He was a medical doctor and developed a specialty in psychiatry. Wundt is credited with starting psychology because he claimed to be a psychologist and started the first psychology laboratory.

53. Why is it necessary to write a research report in a form that would allow the study to be repeated exactly?

It is possible the results obtained in any one study might have occurred by chance. If it is not possible to repeat the study, there is no way for other experimenters to check and confirm or revise the findings. Replicability is thus a cornerstone of the experimental method.

54. How do human germ cells (eggs and sperm) differ from body cells?

Germ cells are the only body cells that may unite to create a zygote. Moreover, they have only half the number of chromosomes body cells have. (When the egg and sperm unite, the 23 chromosomes of each germ cell pair to create the 46-chromosome complement in the zygote.)

55. Suppose a bird's fixed-action pattern (FAP) for nesting involved pulling up grass to use as a building material. If the bird tried the response on artificial turf in a laboratory environment, what would most likely happen to the response?

The bird will probably adjust and no longer show the FAP. This phenomenon, called habituation, occurs when the FAP is made to an inappropriate stimulus. (*Note*: this is comparable to the extinction of a learned response.)

56. How does the growth rate of a child's head compare with the growth rate of the rest of his or her body?

One trend of physical development is called the cephalo-caudal trend. This means the head area grows before the other portions of the body. (In the human developmental sequence, this is necessary in part because of the rapid growth of the brain.)

57. Why do children in different cultures learn different languages?

Children in different cultures learn different languages simply because of the models they have. Evidence indicates that all normal children may have the capacity to learn any spoken language, and indeed may produce the sounds of all different languages early in life. However, a combination of modeling and reward for appropriate responses helps to form the selected languages for the children.

58. There are two aspects to the refractory phase. What are they called, and how do they differ?

The refractory phase is divided into the absolute refractory phase and the relative refractory phase. During the absolute refractory phase, no stimulus, no matter how strong, can cause the neuron to conduct a signal. In the relative refractory phase, a stronger-than-normal stimulus can generate a signal. Once the refractory phase is completed, a normal signal will fire the neuron.

59. Why is the autonomic nervous system sometimes described as "antagonistic"?

The autonomic nervous system is composed of the sympathetic and parasympathetic systems. In general, these work in opposite (or antagonistic) manners, with the sympathetic system stimulating or supporting action and energy expenditure and the parasympathetic system involved with energy conservation and body recuperation.

60. Why is a description of the "basic five" senses misleading?

A description of the basic five senses is misleading because it is incomplete. Evidence indicates that there are at least seven basic senses, with kinesthesis and balance added to the traditional five. In addition, there is much evidence to indicate there are distinct subcategories of most, if not all, of these seven.

61. Many researchers have tested people for their sensitivity to touch. Most people can tell when there are two points slightly touching their lips or the mouth region. However, when the same stimulus is applied to their backs, people show much less sensitivity. Why?

Touch receptors are not equally distributed on the body. The number of receptors and the amount of brain area devoted to touch reception around the mouth area are considerably greater than those associated with the back. This means that the region around the mouth will have greater touch sensitivity than the back will.

62. In general, what are the factors that influence attention for perception?

The two major factors that influence attention in perceptual processes are the properties of the stimulus and the properties of the perceiver. The former are usually called *external cues*, and the latter are called *internal cues*. There is evidence that the external and internal cues often interact.

63. What is the principle of biofeedback?

Biofeedback involves the use of mechanical equipment to provide information regarding body processes that are otherwise not readily observable. By having such information available, a person may be able to learn to control the physiological process associated with a response.

64. What are the characteristics of a person *least* likely to be hypnotized?

It is most difficult to hypnotize someone who is unwilling to be hypnotized, relatively rigid in thinking patterns, and does not trust the hypnotist. People most likely to be hypnotized would show the opposite characteristics.

65. Why is human sexual behavior not considered a survival motive?

Sexual behavior is necessary for the survival of the species, but not for the survival of any one individual. The other survival motives must be satisfied or an individual will die. However, the individual can remain celibate throughout life without significantly influencing his or her chances for survival.

66. Learned motives seem predominant in our society. Why?

The reason learned motives appear to be predominant in our society is that survival motives are, in general, easily satisfied. If for some reason survival motives become difficult to satisfy, they would certainly become predominant.

67. What are some of the physiological indicants of emotional arousal?

Physiological indicators of emotion include changes in heart rate, respiration rate, blood pressure, GSR, glandular secretions, and other bodily processes. These are sometimes more revealing than the expression of emotion through language or gesture.

68. Some illnesses seem to be brought on by psychological causes. What are these illnesses called?

Such illnesses are called psychosomatic disorders. There is a good deal of research that indicates that some actual physical problems result from psychological causes rather than any organic malfunctioning. For example, an ulcer may be caused by excessive acidity that is prompted by stress rather than by a malfunctioning gland.

69. In the early stages of a classical conditioning procedure, the subject sometimes responds by turning toward the CS as well as reacting to the UCS. What is the reaction to the CS called? What usually happens to it?

The reaction to the CS is called an orienting response. Usually, as the subject becomes accustomed to the conditioning procedure, the orienting response drops out. (This is comparable to habituation.)

70. Suppose the CS in a classical conditioning procedure is a very strong or dominant stimulus while the UCS is relatively weak. If the procedure is supposed to involve forward conditioning with such stimuli, what may happen instead?

The relative dominance of the two stimuli may produce a backward conditioning situation; that is, the strength of the supposed CS may be sufficient to make it effectively serve as a UCS, and a CR may develop to what was supposed to be the UCS.

71. Behavior modification is often used as a therapeutic technique for autistic children. What is behavior modification? Why might it be particularly useful in the treatment of autistic children?

Behavior modification involves the use of instrumental conditioning principles to change responding patterns: appropriate responses are reinforced, and inappropriate responses are extinguished or sometimes punished. Such treatment is sometimes very effective for autistic children because such children are reinforced for communicating, and they therefore become more amenable to other therapeutic treatments.

72. Explain what is meant by an advanced, or complex, schedule of reinforcement.

An advanced schedule of reinforcement requires the subject to respond according to more than one contingency condition in order to be reinforced.

73. Unable to cope with the anxiety produced by the thought of giving a public speech to several hundred people, Greg seeks some help. It is suggested he observe a successful public speaker as a model, then try to use similar behaviors. If this modeling works, what term describes this success?

This modeling creates disinhibition—that is, a reduction of anxiety by copying the actions of a successful model. If, on the other hand, the respected model showed difficulty or anxiety, this might promote greater inhibition.

74. Why is knowledge of results (KR) often considered to be reinforcing?

Knowledge of results provides information about the success of responding. Assuming the response has "worked," KR would be judged as reinforcing. This, in turn, would strengthen or maintain the response, making it more likely the same response would be used in the next similar situation.

75. What is the concept of learning without awareness? Why is it controversial?

Learning without awareness means that a response may become part of the person's behavioral repertoire without that person making a conscious effort to learn. The controversy surrounding such a concept involves the difficulties with defining just what is awareness, the problems with measuring this after it has been defined, and the lag between the occurrence of the learning and the attempt to measure awareness.

76. Why might different measures of retention reveal considerably different values?

The three most commonly used measures of retention—recognition, recall, and relearning—do not measure exactly the same things. In addition, because of the possibilities for chance responses, the values which can be obtained vary. (For example, only relearning could yield a negative value.) Thus, when a report of retention is given, the measure used should also be specified.

77. What is comparable about the psychological terms forgetting, habit, and ego?

These three terms (and many other psychological terms) refer to qualities that cannot be measured or observed directly. They are useful explanatory or summary concepts, but they must be used carefully. Terms such as these are often called *intervening variables*, meaning they cannot be observed directly but are "tied to" observable or measurable variables.

78. Given an opportunity to suggest different uses for a chair, Patrick finds he can only think of a chair as something one sits on. What term describes Patrick's limited responding?

Patrick's "block" is a form of set called functional fixedness. Functional fixedness means the respondent can only think of an object in terms related to its usual or normal function and is unable to break that set and generate other ideas.

79. Arrange the terms *clause, phoneme, syllable*, and *sentence* into a hierarchy and explain the order you choose.

The hierarchy for these terms would be (1) phoneme, (2) syllable, (3) clause, and (4) sentence. A phoneme is a sound or stress component of a spoken language. Syllables are composed of one or more phonemes. Words are composed of one or more syllables, and are used to form clauses. A sentence may be composed of one or more clauses.

80. What are the differences between projective and situational tests?

Projective tests present a pictorial or written stimulus and ask the subject to respond. The responses are interpreted in an attempt to assess personality. Situational tests are comparable in that they attempt to assess personality, but differ in that the subject is placed in a predetermined situation and actual responses are observed, rather than reactions to a picture or description of the situation.

81. What is a regression procedure? How commonly are these used?

A regression procedure involves making predictions about future behaviors on the basis of past correlations that have been calculated. Knowing the value of a correlation and the values of one comparable variable, predictions about the values of a second comparable variable can be made.

82. What emphasis did Freud place upon the stages of development of personality?

Freud felt the first three stages of personality development (oral, anal, and phallic) were more important than the latter stages (latent and genital) in the formation of the personality. Fixation at these early stages could carry over and affect adult expression of personality. Freud placed emphasis on the sexual and aggressive aspects of development during these stages.

83. Suppose Patricia finds she can never have a baby of her own. What might she do that would be an example of direct compensation? What would be an example of indirect compensation?

Direct compensation probably would take the form of adoption. Unable to have her own child, but still wanting a child, Patricia could satisfy her desire by adopting one. Indirect compensation might take the form of the avid pursuit of a career. Patricia's feeling might be expressed as, "Well, if I can't be a mother, I'll be a really top executive."

84. Why are tests of infants' intelligence not considered too helpful?

Tests of infants' intelligence are not considered too helpful because they do not correlate highly with later measures of intelligence. They are useful for identifying some extreme cases, but do not give reasonable distinctions among most infants.

85. What is a phobia? Why are phobias considered neurotic rather than psychotic?

A phobia is an intense, compelling fear of some stimulus. Phobias are considered neurotic rather than psychotic because the anxiety is usually limited to one area of behavior, while behavior in the remainder of the person's life is relatively normal.

86. Distinguish between physiological and psychological addictions.

A physiological addiction refers to a dependence upon some substance, such that if that substance were removed abruptly, a physical illness would result. Psychological addiction means that the dependence is such that if the substance were removed, pronounced anxiety or psychological discomfort would result. In some cases, addictions may be a combination of both.

87. Psychotic depression has been called the only "fatal" mental illness because so many people in this condition commit suicide. What relatively rapid therapy seems to relieve this condition?

Psychotic depressives are often given electroconvulsive shock therapy (ECST). This procedure seems to alleviate the depression and make the people more receptive to other therapies.

88. Statistically, what is the most frequently found type of abnormal personality pattern? Of the major designations, which occurs least frequently?

Neurosis comprises about 50 percent of the identified instances of abnormal personality. Psychosis is least frequently found, occurring in about 5 percent of the cases. Other abnormal personality patterns, such as addictions, fall in the middle range.

89. In a situation that requires assisting someone else, when is a person most likely to help?

In assistance situations, a person is most likely to volunteer help when he or she is alone. When a person in need is confronted by a group of people, their responsibility appears to become diffused, and helping behavior becomes less likely.

90.   What are the three major components of an attitude?

Attitudes have affective (feeling) components, cognitive (belief) components, and conative (action) components. These interact to comprise the overall attitude.

Answers to Problems 1–50

1. (c)	11. (b)	21. (d)	31. (d)	41. (c)
2. (a)	12. (a)	22. (a)	32. (c)	42. (c)
3. (c)	13. (d)	23. (c)	33. (b)	43. (d)
4. (c)	14. (b)	24. (c)	34. (b)	44. (b)
5. (b)	15. (a)	25. (b)	35. (a)	45. (d)
6. (b)	16. (d)	26. (a)	36. (c)	46. (c)
7. (b)	17. (d)	27. (b)	37. (a)	47. (b)
8. (d)	18. (b)	28. (d)	38. (d)	48. (b)
9. (a)	19. (a)	29. (d)	39. (b)	49. (d)
10. (c)	20. (a)	30. (c)	40. (a)	50. (a)

Index

Abnormal personality patterns, 2, 3, 12, 263–277
  relationship to other factors, 269–270, 275
Abscissa, 17, 22, 25
Achievement:
  need for, 108–109, 114
  tests, 213, 218, 221
Acquisition, 163–176
Action potential, 51–52, 57, 62
Activation-arousal theory, 110–111, 115
Addictions, 268, 275, 276, 278
Adler, A., 241–242, 247, 250
Adolescence, 38, 43, 48
Adrenal gland, 56, 61
Affiliation, need for, 109
All-or-none principle, 51, 57, 62
Amnesia, 265, 272
Anal stage, 240, 246, 250
Anchorage effect, 309, 313, 314
Anger, 119, 123–124, 126
Anthropomorphism, 118, 123, 126
Antisocial behaviors, 268, 274, 276
Anxiety neurosis, 265, 271, 276
Aptitude tests, 213, 218, 221
Assertiveness training, 283, 289, 290
Associationism, 4, 10, 13
Asymptote, 129, 132, 136, 165, 171, 175
Attachment, 42, 47, 48
Attitude scales, 305, 310, 314
Attitudes, 304–314
  complexity of, 304, 310
  components of, 304–305, 310
  crystallized, 306
  development of, 305–306, 310
  measurement of, 305
  theories of, 305
Attribution theory of emotion, 121, 125, 126
Audition (see Hearing)
Auditory localization, 68, 73, 75
Autism, infantile (see Infantile autism)
Aversive stimulus, 143, 148–149, 150
Aversive therapy, 282, 289, 290
Avoidance behavior, 143, 148–149, 150
Axon, 50–52, 56–58, 62

Balance, 69, 74
Basal age, 252, 258, 262
Behavior disorders (see Abnormal personality patterns)

Behavior modification, 149, 281–283, 287–288, 290 (See also Behavior therapy)
Behavior therapy, 144, 150 (See also Behavior modification)
Behavioral genetics, 30, 35
Behavioral sink, 296, 302
Behaviorism, 4, 10, 13
Binet, A., 211, 252, 258
Biofeedback, 89, 93–94, 97, 283, 289, 290
Biomedical model, 264, 271, 276
Birth defects, 29
Blind spot, 67, 71, 75
Brain structure, 53–55
Breuer, J., 280

Cannon-Bard theory of emotion, 121, 125, 126
Case histories, clinical (see Clinical case histories)
Catatonia, 267, 273, 276
Ceiling age, 252, 258, 262
Central core, 53, 58–59
Central fissures, 54
Central nervous system, 52–55, 58–60, 62
Central tendency, 225, 232, 236
Cephalo-caudal trend, 38, 44, 48
Cerebellum, 53, 59
Cerebrotonia, 243, 248, 250
Cerebrum, 53–55, 58–59, 62
Chemotherapy, 279–280, 285, 290
Chromosomes, 28, 32–34, 35
Circadian rhythms, 89–90, 94, 97
Clairvoyance, 80, 86, 87
Class interval, 224, 236
Classical conditioning, 127–137
Client-centered therapy, 280–281, 286, 290
Clinical case histories, 19, 24, 25
Closure, 77, 83, 87
Cochlea, 67, 72, 75
Cognitive dissonance, 305, 310, 314
Cognitive theory of emotion, 121
Collective unconscious, 241, 247, 250
Colorblindness, 67, 72
Color vision, 67
Compensation, 241, 247, 250
  direct, 241, 247
  indirect, 241, 247
Competition, 294–295, 299–300, 302
Complementarity, 307, 311, 314
Compulsions, 265, 272, 276

Concepts, 191–192, 197, 203
  conjunctive, 192, 198, 203
  disjunctive, 192, 203
  hierarchy, 192, 203
  relational, 192, 198, 204
Concrete operational stage, 41, 47, 48
Conditional positive regard (see Positive regard, conditional)
Conditioned response, 128, 132, 136
Conditioned stimulus, 128, 132, 137
Cones, 66–67, 71–72, 75
Confabulation, 183, 189
Conflict, 109–110, 114, 115, 156, 161
  approach-approach, 109, 114, 115
  approach-avoidance, 110, 114, 115
  avoidance-avoidance, 110, 114, 115
  multiple approach-avoidance, 110, 114, 116
  (See also Inter-role conflict; Intra-role conflict)
Conformity, 42, 48, 293–294, 297, 299, 302
Conscience, 239, 245, 250
Conscious, 1–2, 13
Consciousness, 88–97
Conservation, 47
Consummatory response, 145
Contact comfort, 108, 113, 115
Contingency, 229, 236
Control group, 16–17, 21, 25
Conversion reactions, 266, 272–273, 276
Cooperation, 294–295, 300, 302
Corpus callosum, 54–55, 60, 62, 91
Correlation, 228–229, 235, 236
  rank difference, 228
Cortex, 54, 59–60, 62
Cortical lobes, 54, 62–63
  frontal, 54, 62
  occipital, 54, 62
  parietal, 54, 62
  temporal, 54, 63
Counter-conditioning, 133
Countermovements, social, 309, 313, 314
Creativity, 194, 201, 203, 257–258, 261–262
  measurement of, 257
Cretinism, 269, 276
Criterion, 212, 217, 221
Critical period, 39–40, 45, 48
Crossing-over, 29, 33, 35
Cross-sectional investigations, 39, 44, 49, 215, 219, 221
Crowding, 296
Cultural relativity, 292, 297
Cumulative record, 139–140, 146, 150

Darwin, C., 26, 31
Delusions, 266, 276
ndrite, 50–52, 56–57, 62
  yribonucleic acid, 28, 32, 33
  dency, 109
  nt variable, 17, 21–22, 25

Depolarization, 51–52, 58, 62
Depressive behavior, 267, 274, 276, 279
Deprivation, 40, 45, 49
Detachment, 42, 47, 49
Detection theory, 65–66, 70, 75
Development:
  cognitive, 40–41, 46–47
  moral, 42–43, 48
  motor (see Development, physical)
  physical, 40, 46
  social, 41–43, 46–48
Developmental scales, 39, 45, 49
Deviation IQ, 253, 259, 262
Differentiation, 130, 134–135, 137, 143, 147, 148
Discriminability, 168, 173–174, 175
Discrimination (see Differentiation)
Discriminative stimulus, 142, 150
Disinhibition, 156, 161, 162
Displacement, 28, 241, 246, 250, 272
Displacement activity, 27–28, 32, 35
Dissociative reactions, 265, 272, 276
Distribution of practice, 166, 172
DNA (see Deoxyribonucleic acid)
Dominance, need for, 109
Double-bind situation, 270
Double-blind control, 24, 25
Down's syndrome, 33
Dream analysis, 280, 290
Dreams, 90, 93, 95
Drive, 106, 112, 115
Drugs:
  abuse of, 91, 96–97
  hallucinogenic, 92, 97
  narcotic, 92, 97
  psychedelic (see Drugs, hallucinogenic)
  psychoactive, 91–92, 96, 97

Early childhood, 37–38, 43, 49
Ebbinghaus, H., 180
ECST (see Electroconvulsive shock therapy)
Ectomorphy, 243, 248, 250
Ego, 239, 250
Ego defense mechanisms, 240–241, 246–247, 250
Electra complex, 240
Electrical brain stimulation (ESB), 55, 60
Electroconvulsive shock therapy, 279, 284, 290
Electroencephalogram (EEG), 88, 97
Embryo, 37, 43
Emotion, 117–126
  expression of, 119–120, 124
  indicators of, 118
  as motivation, 117, 122
  theories of, 121
Emotional disturbance (see Abnormal personality patterns)
Encounter groups, 281, 287, 290
Endocrine glands, 55–56, 61, 62
Endomorphy, 243, 248, 250

Enrichment, 40, 45–46, 49
Environment, influence on behavior, 1
Erikson, E., 242, 248
Escape behavior, 143, 148–149, 150
Ethology, 26–28, 31, 35
Eugenics, 30, 35
Evolution, 26–28, 30–32, 35
  adaptation, 26, 35
  selection, 26, 36
  variability, 26
Exceptional subjects, 253, 259, 262
Existential model, 265, 271, 276
Exocrine glands, 55, 61, 62
Experimental group, 16–17, 21, 25
Experimental method, 15–16, 25
Experimental neurosis, 130, 137, 266
Experimenter bias, 18–19, 23–24
Extinction, 128–129, 133, 137, 140, 146
Extraneous variables, 17, 22, 25
Extrasensory perception (ESP), 80, 86, 87

Factor analysis, 242, 248, 250, 254, 260
Family, influence on personality, 243
FAPs (see Fixed-action patterns)
Fear, 118–119, 124, 126
Feature extraction, 163–164, 170, 175
Feedback, 143–144, 148, 150, 165, 172 (see also
  Knowledge of results)
Fetus, 37, 43
Figure-ground relationship, 76, 81, 87
Fixation, 240, 250
Fixed-action patterns, 27, 28, 31, 32, 36
Flavor, 68, 73, 75
Forgetting, 177–190
  curve of, 180, 186, 189
  theories of, 181–183
Formal operational stage, 41, 47, 49
Fovea, 66, 71, 75
Free association, 280, 286, 290
Free recall, 167, 173, 175
Frequency distribution, 224, 230, 236
Frequency polygon, 224, 231, 236
Freud, S., 5, 10, 110, 182, 187, 239–241, 245–247,
  250–251, 264, 271, 280, 285–286
Functional autonomy, 106, 112, 113, 115
Functional fixedness, 194, 200, 204
Functionalism, 4, 10, 13

Generalization:
  response (see Response generalization)
  stimulus (see Stimulus generalization)
Genes, 28–29, 32–34, 36
  dominant, 29, 33–34, 35
  recessive, 29, 33–34, 36
Genetic counseling, 29, 34, 279, 284, 290
Genetics, 26, 28–30, 32–36
Genotype, 34
Germ cells, 28, 32, 36

Gestalt psychology, 5, 10, 13
Gestalt therapy, 281, 290
Gifted subjects, 253, 262
Goal specificity, 106, 111, 116
Graded potential, 51, 62
Group dynamics, 294–296, 302
Group therapies, 281, 287, 290
"Groupthink," 295, 301, 302
Growth therapies, 281, 290
Guilford, J., 254
Gustation (see Taste)

Habit, 193, 200
Habituation, 28, 32, 36
Hallucinations, 80, 86, 87, 266, 276
Halo effect, 307, 314
Hearing, 67–68, 72–73
Hebephrenia, 267, 273, 276
Helping (see Prosocial behavior)
Helplessness, learned (see Learned helplessness)
Heredity, influence on behavior, 1, 8, 13 (see also
  Evolution; Genetics)
Higher-order conditioning, 130, 135–136, 137
Histogram, 224–225, 231, 236
Homeostasis, 107, 112, 116
Hormones, 55–56, 61, 62
Humanistic theory, 110, 114
Hypnosis, 90–91, 95, 97
Hypothalamus, 53, 56, 59
Hypothesis:
  directional, 16, 20–21, 25
  null, 16, 20–21, 25

Id, 239, 245, 250
Identification learning (see Modeling)
Illusions, 79–80, 86, 87
Imagery, 168, 174, 175, 192, 199, 204
Implosion therapy, 282, 288, 290
Imprinting, 45
Independence, 293, 299, 302
Independent variable, 17, 21–22, 25
Infancy, 37, 43, 49
Infantile autism, 267, 274
Inferiority complex, 242, 250
Inferiority, real vs. imagined, 247
Influence, 154, 159, 162
Information-processing, 177, 184
Inhibition, 156, 161, 162
Inner speech, 192, 199, 204
Inoculation effect, 309, 313, 314
Insight, 194, 201, 204
Instinct, 27, 32, 36, 106, 112, 116
Instrumental conditioning, 138–151
Instrumental response, 138, 145, 150
Intelligence, 252–262
  composition of, 254–255
  crystallized, 255, 260, 262
  fluid, 255, 260, 262

Intelligence (Cont'd.)
  quotient, 252–253, 258, 262
  relationship to other factors, 255–257, 260–261
  tests for infants, 254, 258
Interpersonal attraction, 306
Interposition, 78, 84, 87
Inter-role conflict, 293, 298, 302
Inter-stimulus interval, 128, 132–133, 137
  backward, 128, 132–133, 136
  delayed, 128, 132–133, 137
  simultaneous, 128, 132–133, 137
  trace, 128, 132–133, 137
Interviews, 213
Intra-role conflict, 293, 298, 302
Introspection, 4, 13
Introversion-extroversion, 242, 250
IQ (see Intelligence quotient)
Isolation effect (see von Restorff effect)

James-Lange theory of emotion, 121, 125, 126
Jung, C., 241–242, 247, 250–251
Just noticeable difference (j.n.d.), 65, 70

Kinesthesis, 69, 74, 75
Knowledge of results, 165, 172, 175 (See also
  Feedback)

Language:
  for animals, 196–197, 203
  deep structure, 196, 202, 203
  development, 195–197, 201–203
  expressive, 195, 202, 204
  receptive, 195, 204
  spoken, 195, 201–202
  surface structure, 196, 202, 204
  written, 195, 201–202
Latency stage, 240, 251
Later childhood, 38, 43, 49
Lateral fissure, 54
Law of effect, 138, 145, 150
Learned helplessness, 120–121, 126
Learning:
  curves, 164, 170–171, 175
  definition of, 127
  by imitation (see Modeling)
  incremental, 165, 170–171
  and maturation, 127
  one-trial, 165, 170–171
  part (see Part learning)
  verbal (see Verbal learning)
  whole (see Whole learning)
  without awareness, 169, 174
Learning-performance distinction, 127, 131
 earning sets (see Learning to learn)
   rning to learn, 169, 174, 175
    interest, principle of, 307, 312, 314
     239, 245, 251
      tion, 120, 126

Limbic system, 53, 58–59
Lobotomy, 280, 285
Locke, J., 2
Longitudinal investigations, 39, 44, 49, 215, 219, 221
Long-term storage, 178, 185, 189

Manic behavior, 267, 274, 276
Maslow, A., 110, 114
Massed practice, 166
Maturation, 43, 49
Mean, 225, 232, 236
Meaningfulness, 167–168, 175
Measurement, psychological, 211–222
Median, 225, 232, 236
Mediation, 191
Medical model, 3
Meditation:
  concentrative, 89, 94, 97
  opening-up, 89, 94, 97
Medulla, 53, 59
Meiosis, 32
Memory, 177 (See also Forgetting; Retention)
Memory trace, 181–182
Mental age (MA), 252, 258, 262
Mental illness (see Abnormal personality
  patterns)
Mental retardation, 253, 259, 262, 268–269, 275, 276
Mesomorphy, 243, 248, 251
Milieu therapy, 279, 284, 290
Mitosis, 37, 49
Mode, 225, 232, 236
Model:
  position, 154
  role, 154, 158
  status of, 154, 159, 161, 162
Modeling, 124, 152–162
  verbal, 153, 159–160
Mongolism, 33, 269, 276, 279
Moral development (see Development, moral)
Morphemes, 196, 202, 204
Motivation, 105–116
  assessment of, 105, 111
  cycle, 105, 111, 115
  theories of, 110–111
Motives:
  combination, 107–108
  learned, 108–109, 113, 116
  social (see Motives, learned)
  survival (see Motives, unlearned)
  unlearned, 107, 112–113, 116
Mutation, 28, 33, 36
Myelin, 50, 57, 62

Naturalistic observation, 19, 24, 25
Needs, 106, 112, 116
  hierarchy of, 110, 114–115, 116

Negative reinforcement, 138, 143, 148, 150
Nerve, 50, 62
Neuron, 50, 52, 56–57, 62
Neurosis, 265–266, 267, 271–273, 276, 278
Noncomformity, 293–294, 299, 302
Nondirective therapy (see Client-centered
    therapy)
Normal probability distribution, 227–228,
    233–234, 236
Norms, 212, 217, 221

Obedience, 294, 299
Object permanence, 47
Objectivity, 15, 25, 212, 217–218
Observation, naturalistic (see Naturalistic
    observation)
Observational learning (see Modeling)
Obsessions, 265, 272, 276
Oedipal complex, 240, 251
Olfaction (see Smell)
Operant conditioning (see Instrumental
    conditioning)
Operant conditioning chamber, 139, 150
Oral stage, 240, 246, 251
Ordinate, 17, 22, 25
Orienting response, 128, 132, 137
Overlearning, 165, 171, 175

Paired-associate learning, 167–168, 173, 175
Paradoxical sleep (see REM sleep)
Paranoia, 267, 273, 276
Parasympathetic system, 55, 60–61, 62
Parsimony, 118, 123, 126
Part learning, 166, 172
Partial reinforcement, 129, 134, 137, 146
Partial reinforcement effect (PRE), 129, 134, 137,
    140–142, 146
Pavlov, I., 128–130, 132, 266
Pavlovian conditioning (see Classical
    conditioning)
Peers, influence of, 42, 48, 49, 243, 249
Percentile, 212, 236
Perception, 76–87 (See also Extrasensory
    perception; Subliminal perception)
Perceptual constancy, 78, 83–84, 87
Peripheral nervous system, 52, 55, 58, 60, 62
    autonomic, 55, 58, 60–62
    somatic, 55, 58, 63
Personal space, 296, 301, 302
Personal unconscious, 241, 247, 251
Personality, 238–251
    body-type theory, 243, 250
    humanistic theories of, 243–244
    learning theories of, 243, 248–249
    motivational theories, 239–242
    self theory, 243–244, 251
    tests, 213, 218–219, 221
    trait theories, 242, 248, 251

Personality (Cont'd.)
    type theories, 242–243, 248, 251
Personality disorders, 268, 276, 278
Perspective, 78, 84, 87
Persuasion, 308–309
Phallic stage, 240, 246, 251
Phantom-limb phenomenon, 74
Phenotype, 34
Phenylketonuria, 29
Phobias, 5, 123, 126, 131, 136, 265, 272, 276
Phonemes, 195–196, 202, 204
Phrenology, 3, 9
Physiognomy, 3
Piaget, J., 40–41, 47, 255, 260
Pituitary gland, 56, 61
PKU (see Phenylketonuria)
Placebo effect, 21, 25, 283, 289, 290
Plateau, 165, 171, 175
Plato, 2
Play therapy, 281, 287, 290
Pleasure, 119, 124, 126
Pleasure principle, 239, 245, 251
Population, 18, 25
Positive regard:
    conditional, 244, 249, 251
    unconditional, 244, 249, 251
Positive reinforcement, 138, 143, 148, 151
Postnatal development, stages of, 37–38, 43
Power, 154, 159, 162
Precipitating factors, 263, 270, 277
Precognition, 80, 86, 87
Predisposing factors, 263, 270, 277
Prejudice, 307–308, 312, 314
Premoral stage, 42, 48
Prenatal development, stages of, 37, 43
    embryonic, 37, 43, 49
    fetal, 37, 43, 49
    germinal, 37, 43, 49
Pre-operational stage, 41, 47, 49
Preparedness, 164, 170, 175
Prepubertal growth spurt, 38
Primacy effect, 166, 172, 175, 306, 311, 314
Primal therapy, 281, 287, 290
Principle of least interest (see Least interest,
    principle of)
Proactive inhibition (PI), 182–183, 188, 189
Problem solving, 192–195, 199–201
Programmed learning, 144, 149, 151
    branching, 144, 149, 150
    linear, 144, 149, 150
Progressive-part learning, 166, 172 (See also Part
    learning)
Projection, 241, 246, 251
Projective tests, 213, 218, 221
Pronounceability, 168, 175
Prosocial behavior, 296, 301–302
Proximity, 306
Proximo-distal trend, 38, 44, 49

Psychiatry, 3, 11, 13
Psychoanalysis, 5, 10, 13, 280, 291
Psychoanalysts, 11, 13
Psychoanalytic theory, 110, 115
Psychodynamic model, 264, 271, 277
Psychokinesis, 80, 86, 87
Psycholinguistics, 195, 204
Psychological tests, 19–20, 24
Psychology:
  clinical, 3, 6, 10, 11, 13
  community, 7, 12, 13
  comparative, 3, 6, 11, 13
  consumer, 7, 12
  counseling, 6, 10, 13
  developmental, 7, 13, 37–49
  educational, 6–7, 12
  engineering, 7, 12, 13
  experimental, 6, 13
  industrial, 7, 12, 13
  physiological, 6, 11, 13, 50–63
  school, 6–7, 12, 13
  social, 7, 12, 13, 292–303
  systems of, 4–5
Psychopathic behavior (see Antisocial behaviors)
Psychopharmacology, 92, 96, 97
Psychosexual stages, 239–240, 245–246, 251
Psychosis, 266–267, 273–274, 277, 278
  affective, 267, 274, 276
  functional, 266, 273, 276
  organic, 266, 273, 276
Psychosomatic disorders, 120, 125, 126, 266, 272–273, 277
Psychosurgery, 280, 285, 291
Psychotherapy, 280–281, 285–287, 291
Puberty, 38, 43, 49
Public opinion polls, 305, 310, 314
Punishment, 143, 146, 148–149, 151

Range, 226, 232, 237
Rationalization, 241, 246, 251
Readiness, 39–40, 45, 49
Reality principle, 239, 245, 251
Reasoning, 193, 199, 204
Recall, 178–179, 185, 189
Recency effect, 166, 172, 175, 306, 311, 314
Receptor, 64, 70, 75
Recognition, 178, 189
Redirection, 28, 32, 36
Refractory period:
  absolute, 52, 58
  relative, 52, 58
Refractory phase, 52, 58, 62
ression, 241, 247, 251
ession, statistical, 229, 235–236, 237
cement:
oned, 148 (See also Secondary
orcement)

Reinforcement: (Cont'd.)
  contingency of, 138, 145, 150 (See also Contingency)
  delay of, 144, 149, 150
  negative (see Negative reinforcement)
  noncontingent, 138, 145, 150
  positive (see Positive reinforcement)
  schedules (see Schedules of reinforcement)
  secondary (see Secondary reinforcement)
Relearning, 179, 185, 189
Release from PI, 188
Releaser stimulus, 27, 32
Reliability, 211, 217, 222
REM sleep, 90, 94–95, 97
Reminiscence, 180, 186, 190
Remission, 283, 289, 291
Repression, 182, 187, 190, 240–241, 247, 251
Resistance, 280, 286, 291
Respondent conditioning (see Classical conditioning)
Response generalization, 130, 135, 137
Resting potential, 51, 57, 63
Retention, 177–190
  measures of, 178–180
  qualitative measurement, 179–180
Retention interval, 177
Reticular activating system, 53, 59, 63
Retina, 66–67, 71, 75
Retinal disparity, 78, 85, 87
Retrieval, 177
Retroactive inhibition (RI), 182–183, 188, 189, 190
Retrospective studies, 39, 45, 49
Risky shift, 295, 301, 302
Rods, 66–67, 71, 75
Rogers, C., 243–244, 249, 251
Role, 293, 302
Role of arguments, 294, 302
Rolf, I., 281
Rolfing, 281, 287, 291
Rorschach test, 213, 222
Rosenhan, D., 271
Rosenthal, R., 256

Sampling:
  accidental, 18, 23
  matched, 18, 23, 25
  random, 18, 23, 25
  stratified, 18, 23, 25
Savings score, 179, 185, 189, 190
Scapegoating, 308, 314
Scattergram, 228, 235, 237
Schedules of reinforcement, 141–142, 151
  compound, 142, 147, 150
  concurrent, 142, 150
  conjunctive, 142
  drh, 147
  fixed interval (FI), 141–142, 147
  fixed ratio (FR), 141–142, 146

Schedules of reinforcement (Cont'd.)
  interlocking, 147
  multiple, 142, 150
  variable interval (VI), 141–142, 147
  variable ratio (VR), 141–142, 146–147
Schizophrenia, 266–267, 273, 277
Secondary appraisal, 121, 125, 126
Secondary reinforcement, 131, 136, 137
Selective breeding, 30, 35
Self-accepted values (see Values, self-accepted)
Self-arousal, 155, 160, 162
Self-fulfilling prophecy, 270, 277, 293, 298, 302, 306
Self-reinforcement, 155–156, 162
Sensation (see Sensory processes)
Sensori-motor stage, 41, 47, 49
Sensory adaptation, 65, 71, 75
Sensory deprivation, 80, 86, 87
Sensory gating, 163, 170, 176
Sensory overload, 80, 86, 87
Sensory processes, 64–75
Sensory storage, 177–178, 184, 190
Serial learning, 167, 173, 176
Set, 79, 85, 87, 193–194, 200, 204
Sex, as a motive, 107–108, 113
Sex roles, 42, 48
Sexual deviations, 268, 274, 277
Shaping, 140, 146, 149, 151
Short-term storage, 178, 184, 190
Sign, 195, 201, 204
Sign stimulus (see Releaser stimulus)
Simulation, 177, 194–195, 199, 201, 204
Single-blind control, 24, 25
Situational tests, 214, 219, 222
Skew, 225, 231, 237
Skin senses, 68–69, 73–74
Skinner, B., 138, 145
Skinner box (see Operant conditioning chamber)
Skinnerian conditioning (see Instrumental conditioning)
Sleep, 89–90, 93
  rhythms, 90, 94
Smell, 68, 73
Social change, 309, 314
Social comparison, 307, 312, 314
Social development (see Development, social)
Social exchange, 295, 300, 303
Social facilitation, 292–293, 297, 303
Social interference, 292–293, 297, 303
Social learning (see Modeling)
Social learning model, 264, 271, 277
Social learning theory, 110, 115, 153, 157
Social movements, 309, 313, 314
Socialization, 156, 292, 303
Sociopathic behavior (see Antisocial behaviors)
Somatotonia, 243, 248, 251
Species-specific behavior, 27, 31, 32
Split-brain research, 55, 60, 63, 91, 96

Spontaneous recovery, 129, 133, 137
Spontaneous remission (see Remission)
Spreading depression, 54
Standard deviation, 226-227, 233, 237
Standardization, 212, 217, 222
Stanford-Binet Intelligence Test, 252–253, 258–259
State-dependent learning, 167, 173, 176
Statistics, 223–237
  descriptive, 223, 230, 236
  formulas, 223–224
  inferential, 223, 230, 236
  symbols, 223, 230
Status, 293, 297–298, 303
Stereotype, 212, 217, 294, 299, 303, 308, 313, 314
Stimulus generalization, 129–130, 134–136, 137, 142, 148
  primary, 129–130, 134, 137
  secondary, 129–130, 134, 136, 137
Stimulus properties:
  apparent movement, 78, 83, 87
  continuity, 77, 82
  contrast, 77, 82
  grouping, 77, 82–83
  intensity, 77, 82
  shadow, 78, 84–85
Structural integration (see Rolfing)
Structuralism, 4, 10, 14
Subjectivity, 25
Subliminal perception, 80, 86, 87
Superego, 239, 245, 251
Superstitious behavior, 138, 151
Syllables, 195–196, 202, 204
Symbol, 191, 195, 197, 201, 204
Symbolism, 280, 286
Sympathetic system, 55, 60–61, 63
Synapse, 51, 56–57, 63
Systematic desensitization, 282, 288, 291

Tachistoscope, 177, 190
Taste, 68, 73
Telepathy, 80, 86, 87
Temporal conditioning, 128, 133, 137
Terman, L., 252, 258
Test batteries, 214, 219, 222
Testing, psychological, 211–222
Tests:
  abuses of, 216, 220–221
  culture-fair, 215, 220, 221
  culture-free, 215, 220, 221
  individual vs. group, 214–215, 219–220, 254, 259
  psychological (see Psychological tests)
  speed vs. power, 215, 219
  uses of, 215–216
Texture gradient, 78, 84, 87
Thalamus, 53, 59
Thematic Apperception Test, 109, 213, 222

Therapies, 278–291
    effectiveness of, 283
    medical, 279, 280, 284–285, 290
    somatic (see Therapies, medical)
Thinking, 191–192, 197–199
    autistic, 191–192, 197, 199, 203
    convergent, 194, 201, 203, 257, 262
    directed, 191–192, 197, 203
    divergent, 194, 201, 204, 257, 262
    generative, 193, 199, 204
Thorndike, E., 138, 145, 150
Threshold:
    absolute, 64–65, 70, 75
    difference, 65, 70, 75
Thurstone, L., 254, 260
Thyroid gland, 56, 61
Tip-of-the-tongue phenomenon, 183, 189, 190
Titchener, E., 4
Token economy, 282, 288, 291
Touch (see Skin senses)
Transduction, 65, 70, 75
Transfer of training, 168–169, 174, 176
Transference, 280, 286, 291
Transmitter substance, 50, 51, 56–57, 63
Twins, 30, 34, 36
Typology, 3

Unconditional positive regard (see Positive
    regard, unconditional)

Unconditioned response, 128, 132, 137
Unconditioned stimulus, 128, 132, 137
Unconscious, 1–2, 5, 14
    collective (see Collective unconscious)
    motives, 182, 187, 190
    personal (see Personal unconscious)

Vacuum activity, 27, 32, 36
Validity, 211, 217, 222
Values, self-accepted, 42, 48
Variability, measures of, 226–227, 232–233, 237
Verbal learning, 167–168
Vestibular sense, 75 (See also Balance)
Vicarious learning, 152–153, 157–158, 160, 162
Visceratonia, 243, 248, 251
Vision, 66–67, 71–72
von Restorff effect, 180–181, 186, 190

Warm-up, 166, 176
Watson, J., 4
Wechsler, D., 253, 259
Whole learning, 166, 172
Wundt, W., 2, 9, 10

Zygote, 28, 33, 36